A detailed history of
THE STANIER
CLASS FIVE 4-6-0s

Volume 1 – Nos.5000-5471

John Jennison

THE RAILWAY CORRESPONDENCE AND TRAVEL SOCIETY
2013

© RCTS 2013

www.rcts.org.uk

ISBN 978 0 901115 98 0

Published by The Railway Correspondence and Travel Society,
16 Welby Close, Maidenhead SL6 3PY, United Kingdom.

Printed by The Amadeus Press, Cleckheaton BD19 4TQ.
Typesetting and page layout by David Bird, RCTS.
Cover design by David Kelso, RCTS.

FRONT COVER CAPTION

Newly repainted in LMS 1936 livery, Armstrong Whitworth-built 5131 was photographed in colour at Crewe North in August 1938. It had just completed a Heavy General repair at Crewe Works during which its crosshead vacuum pump was removed and it received the boiler previously fitted to 5049, which had been rebuilt with a dome and 21-element superheater. 5131 was allocated to the former LNWR shed at Monument Lane, Birmingham in March 1936 and was to be transferred to Crewe South in October 1938.

L. Hanson / Colour-Rail

FOREWORD

If one class of locomotives typifies the London Midland and Scottish Railway it is the Stanier Class 5 4-6-0, known to many enthusiasts as 'Black Fives', which formed the backbone of the company's massive pre-war investment programme. Although in its first decade the LMS lagged behind its competitors in the provision of modern mixed traffic engines, that position would change within five years of William Stanier's appointment as Chief Mechanical Engineer in 1932, as almost 500 Class 5s were built.

Although they were introduced in quantity virtually straight from the drawing board and were an immediate success in terms of their operational impact across the whole length of the LMS system, two serious weaknesses soon began to emerge. The first of these, the provision of insufficient superheating, was common to all of Stanier's early designs and was rectified within a short time, after less than a hundred of the class were in service. The second, which was the development of serious cracks in the mainframes, took much longer to deal with and it was not until the early 1950s that an effective solution was applied to all the engines affected.

One of the most difficult issues faced in producing a book on a class which ran to a total of 842 engines was the sheer impossibility of packing everything into a single book while including the depth of material needed to properly deal with the subject. Therefore I took the decision to split the work into two books which, when taken together, will form a cohesive whole. It was logical to draw the dividing line so that this first volume deals with the 472 Class 5s built before the second world war. The development of the design under George Ivatt and the 370 engines that were introduced between 1943 and 1951 are covered in detail in the second volume which also covers the post-war and British Railways operation of the class as a whole.

Therefore Volume 1 describes the background and development of the pre-war engines, and for completeness and ease of understanding, takes this group to final withdrawal in 1968 as far as the individual details of allocations, modifications, boilers and tenders are concerned. Their operations up to the outbreak of war are described in detail but once building of the class started again in 1943 it becomes increasingly difficult to separate the earlier and later engines.

In writing this volume I have drawn on and would like to acknowledge the work of three gentlemen who are sadly no longer with us, Ron Simpson, John Wright and Arthur Cook. Some years ago, Ron had started work on a Class 5 book in the *Locomotives of the LMS Series* and the chapters on 'Names' and 'Allocation and duties' are taken from his research and draft manuscript. John Wright and I corresponded for several years on the subject of Class 5 variations, and in particular changes in boilers, and his input is included in the chapter dealing with 'Repairs and maintenance'. I have made use of Arthur Cook's two books in this series, **LMS Locomotive Design and Construction**, for the chapter on 'Modifications in service', and **Raising Steam on the LMS** in the chapter on 'Boilers'.

The photographs I have selected are, wherever possible, those which have not previously been published, though a number which have been used elsewhere have had to be chosen to illustrate specific points on variants and liveries. There is a deliberate bias towards pre-1948 pictures because the British Railways period will be covered in the second volume. I would like to express thanks to Brian Stephenson for allowing me to use a number of photographs from Rail Archive Stephenson, Rail-online for several photographs from their collection and also to the many photographers within the pages of the book. Where no photograph credit is given, the photographer is unknown.

Finally I would like to record my thanks to Gordon Davies, David Bird, David Kelso, Rodney Lissenden and the other members of the RCTS Publications Committee for their help and encouragement.

John Jennison

CONTENTS

THE AUTHOR

John Jennison comes from a railway background, his grandfather and several uncles worked in the works at Crewe and his father was a driver at Crewe North. Unsurprisingly, Class 5s were an everyday run of the mill sight and merited little attention. It was only many years after the end of steam that John started to look in more detail at the class when as one of the owners of the 4mm scale kit manufacturers, Brassmasters, he carried out detailed research in preparation for the production of a highly detailed kit for the Class 5. This led to an association with Wild Swan Publications where he became a member of the team responsible for the LMS Locomotive Profiles series. In addition, John has produced a number of books in his own right for Irwell Press, as well as assisting in the research for their 'Book of' series and co-authoring several books for Ian Allan. This is the first book written by John to be published by the RCTS.

LMS CLASS 5 4-6-0s - SUMMARY OF CONSTRUCTION

LONDON MIDLAND & SCOTTISH RAILWAY

Built	1934	1935	1936	1937	1938	1943	1944	1945	1946	1947	Totals
Crewe	-	25	-	-	20	-	35	60	26	25	191
Derby	-	-	-	-	-	20	34	-	-	-	54
Horwich	-	-	-	-	-	-	-	12	33	25	70
Armstrong Whitworth	-	100	74	153	-	-	-	-	-	-	327
Vulcan Foundry	46	54	-	-	-	-	-	-	-	-	100
Totals	46	179	74	153	20	20	69	72	59	50	742

BRITISH RAILWAYS

Built	1948	1949	1950	1951	Totals
Crewe	20	30	-	-	50
Horwich	20	2	26	2	50
Totals	40	32	26	2	100

PARTICULARS OF 4-6-0 CLASS.5. M.T. ENGINES AS BUILT.

ENGINE NUMBERS	NO OF ENGS	CLASS	BOILER					SMOKEBOX		ASHPAN			REMARKS
			BOILER NUMBERS ORIGINALLY FITTED	TYPE OF THROAT PLATE	SUPERHEATER ELEMENTS	TOP FEED POSITION	MANUALLY OPERATED BLOW-OFF COCK	DEFLECTOR PLATE ARRGT	SELF CLEANING	ORDINARY TYPE	HOPPER TYPE	ROCKING GRATE	
45000-45006	7	3B	8817-8823	STRAIGHT	24	2ND BARREL	NO	YES	NO	YES	NO	NO	
45007-45019	13	" "	8824-8836	"	21	"	"	"	"	"	"	"	
45020-45069	50	" "	8637-8686	"	24	"	"	"	"	"	"	"	
45070-45224	155	" "	8905-9059	"	21	"	"	"	"	"	"	"	
45225-45451	227	" "	9345-9571	SLOPING	24	"	"	"	"	"	"	"	
45452-45461	10	" "	10339-10348	"	28	"	"	"	"	"	"	"	
45462-45471	10	" "	10366-10375	"	28	"	"	"	"	"	"	"	
45472-45481	10	" "	11021-11030	"	28	"	"	"	"	"	"	"	
45482-45491	10	" "	11041-11050	"	28	"	"	"	"	"	"	"	WALSCHAERTS VALVE GEAR, PLAIN BEARINGS
45492-45499	8	" "	11323-11330	"	28	"	"	"	"	"	"	"	
44800-44806	7	" "	11331-11337	"	28	"	"	"	"	"	"	"	
44807-44871	65	" "	11886-11940 / 11978-11987	"	28 / 28	" / "	"	"	44825 ONLY	"	"	"	
44872-44966	95	" "	12117-12136 / 12210-12249 / 12293-12312 / 12342-12356	"	28 / 28 / 28 / 28	"	"	44872-44884	44885-44966	44872-44884	44886-44920 44921-4493 / 44932-4494 44942-44966	44885	
44967-44996	30	" "	12440-12469	"	28	"	YES / NO	NO	YES	NO	YES	YES	
44997-44999	3												WALSCHAERTS VALVE GEAR, PLAIN BEARINGS ℄ OF BOILER 8'-9" TO RAIL.
44738-44747	10												CAPROTTI VALVE GEAR, PLAIN BEARINGS ℄ OF BOILER 8'-11" TO RAIL.
44748-44754	7												CAPROTTI VALVE GEAR, ROLLER BEARINGS ℄ OF BOILER 8'-11" TO RAIL.
44755-44757	3	3B	12813-12877	SLOPING	28	1ST BARREL	NO	NO	YES 4" LONGER SMOKEBOX	NO	YES	YES	CAPROTTI VALVE GEAR, ROLLER BEARINGS ELECTRIC LIGHT,℄ OF BOILER 8'-11"TO RAIL, DOUBLE CHIMNEY
44758-44764	7						YES						WALSCHAERTS VALVE GEAR, ROLLER BEARINGS, ℄ OF BOILER 8'-9" TO RAIL.
44765-44766	2												WALSCHAERTS VALVE GEAR, ROLLER BEARINGS, ELECTRIC LIGHT, OF BOILER 8'-9" TO RAIL, DOUBLE CHIMNEY.
44767	1												STEPHENSON VALVE GEAR, ROLLER BEARINGS ELECTRIC LIGHT ℄ OF BOILER 8'-9" TO RAIL, DOUBLE CHIMNEY
44768-44799	32							NO	YES	NO	YES	YES	WALSCHAERTS VALVE GEAR, PLAIN BEARINGS ℄ OF BOILER 8'-9" TO RAIL.
44698-44717	20												
44718-44727	10	3B	12908-12947	SLOPING	28	1ST BARREL	YES / NO	NO	YES 4" LONGER SMOKEBOX	NO	NO	YES	WALSCHAERTS VALVE GEAR, PLAIN BEARINGS,℄ OF BOILER 8'-9"TO RAIL, BOILER№11938-12937 STEEL FIREBOXES
44728-44737	10												
44658-44697	38	3B	13335-13374	SLOPING	28	1ST BARREL	YES / NO	NO	YES 4" LONGER SMOKEBOX	NO	NO	YES	WALSCHAERTS VALVE GEAR, PLAIN BEARINGS, ℄ OF BOILER 8'-9" TO RAIL.
44686 & 44687	2												CAPROTTI VALVE GEAR, ROLLER BEARINGS, ℄ OF BOILER 8'-11"TO RAIL, DOUBLE CHIMNEY

Contrary to the contention of many enthusiasts, not all Class 5s were the same as shown in this table produced by British Railways which summarises the main variants, as built, for the 842 engines in the Class. It will be seen that the pre-war engines, Nos. 45000-45471, were more uniform than their later brethren with many changes made to Stanier's original design between 1943 and 1951.

1 INTRODUCTION

"The ideal locomotive, dreamed of and longed for by the operating departments of large railway systems everywhere, is one that could go anywhere and do anything" - J. H. Follows, LMS Vice President.

1.1 Evolution of the mixed traffic locomotive in Britain

It was not until the beginning of the 20th Century that the first modern mixed traffic locomotives were built in Britain. Until then, locomotives generally had been designed for specific types of traffic, and the requirements for higher speed passenger work were completely different from those for goods train haulage. On many railways, the more prestigious express goods trains were often scheduled to be worked by passenger engines, and goods engines were sometimes pressed into service to haul passenger trains. Some classes did operate regularly on both passenger and goods work, for example the Caledonian's Oban Bogie and Highland's Skye Bogie 4-4-0s, which because of local conditions handled almost all the traffic on the lines from which they derived their names. Designs such as the LNWR 19" Goods, Experiment and Prince of Wales classes, although sometimes referred to as 'mixed traffic' did not conform to the modern interpretation of an engine which could be diagrammed equally for express passenger work as for slow unfitted freight trains.

Before the 1923 grouping of the railways, many of the larger companies had one or more general purpose or mixed traffic classes of locomotive. They were mainly used on the faster freight trains but at busy periods could be used on duplicate services, additional trains operated on summer weekends or on excursion traffic where high speeds were not expected. Driving wheels on these engines were usually less than 6'0" in diameter, so there was little chance of them being able to cope with higher speed passenger work.

Probably the first really successful engines designed as true mixed traffic locomotives were the Great Western Railway Churchward 43xx Moguls introduced in 1911. The 2-6-0 wheel arrangement had originated in America and offered advantages of stability over the 0-6-0 at anything above low speeds, as well as enabling the use of a larger boiler and cylinders on a locomotive without increasing its coupled wheelbase. It was adopted widely in the decade following World War One on many railways including the South Eastern & Chatham, the London & South Western and the Great Northern and further developed after the 1923 grouping by the SR and LNER. The 43xx were a great success on all types of duties, proving themselves capable in passenger service of speeds in excess of 60mph despite the fact that they had only 5' 8" diameter driving wheels.

A year after the GWR Mogul appeared, Nigel Gresley produced his Class H2 two-cylinder 2-6-0s on the Great Northern Railway which were subsequently developed through Class H3 in 1913 to the 1920 three-cylinder Class H4; the latter was reported as reaching speeds in excess of 75mph, again with driving wheels of only 5' 8" diameter. When the LNER was formed, these three classes became K1, K2 and K3 respectively.

Each of the Southern Railway constituents had also modern outside-cylindered mixed traffic designs: the first of these was the 1913 LBSCR Billinton K class 2-6-0 which had 5' 6" driving wheels. In 1914 Urie on the LSWR produced the H15, an outside cylindered 4-6-0 with 6' 0" driving wheels,

The Great Western Railway Churchward 43xx Moguls introduced in 1911 were probably the first really successful British engines designed as true mixed traffic locomotives. 5355 passes under Skewen Arches with the 4pm Swansea to Cardiff train in 1929.

(F. R. Hebron / Rail Archive Stephenson)

Each of the Southern Railway constituents produced modern outside-cylindered mixed traffic designs. LSWR 483, built in 1914 and pictured at Nine Elms shed around 1922, was one of Robert Urie's H15 class, an outside-cylindered 4-6-0 with 6'0" driving wheels.

Rail Archive Stephenson

The London & North Western Railway did not have any true mixed traffic 4-6-0s although the 19" Goods 4-6-0s with 5'3" diameter driving wheels introduced in 1909 were occasionally used on excursion trains. 8865 is pictured on an up coke train near Tebay. The class was the first major victim of the large scale Class 5 building programme with 108 replaced by the 1936 Armstrong Whitworth engines.

Real Photographs

The LMS inherited over 200 Prince of Wales 4-6-0s in 1923 and within less than ten years had produced several different design proposals for a mixed traffic 4-6-0 described variously as a "Modernised Prince of Wales" and "superheated converted Prince of Wales". They were incurring considerable maintenance costs and the final replacement design which became the Class 5 was significantly different from the Prince of Wales. Like the 19" Goods, the class was decimated by the new Class 5s with over 200 withdrawn between 1934 and 1937. One of those taken out of service in 1934 was 5687 *Hotspur* which had been built as LNWR 2300 by the North British Locomotive Co. in December 1915.

Real Photographs

and three years later on the SECR Maunsell introduced the N class 2-6-0 with 5' 6" driving wheels.

The LMS constituents

In contrast to these other railways, the constituent companies of the LMS did not have any modern, true mixed traffic designs. The Midland Railway employed large wheeled inside-cylindered 4-4-0s on passenger work and large numbers of relatively small 0-6-0s on freight; the only type which came near to being a mixed traffic engine was the 4F 0-6-0 which had 5' 3" diameter wheels and although some were used on passenger work on secondary lines and for excursion traffic they were and remained primarily freight engines.

The Caledonian Railway had a handful of Class 60 4-6-0s introduced in 1916 with 6' 1" diameter driving wheels, and this company and the Glasgow & South Western Railway had a few 2-6-0s with 5' 0" driving wheels. On the LNWR the largest class of mixed traffic locomotive was the DX class of 0-6-0, built between 1858 and 1874, many rebuilt as the Special DX class and lasting into LMS days. These were followed by the 18" Goods class 0-6-0s, affectionately known as Cauliflowers. For many years these engines worked the bulk of LNWR excursion traffic and extra passenger trains at holiday periods and were used regularly on local passenger trains. There were also George Whale's 19" Goods 4-6-0s with 5' 3" diameter driving wheels which dated from 1906, although these were essentially goods engines and the Prince of Wales 4-6-0s which were primarily passenger engines.

1.2 Post-grouping developments

Following the 1923 grouping, the LNER built almost two

hundred more Gresley K3 2-6-0s over the next ten years, while on the Southern Railway Maunsell developed the N class into the similar U class 2-6-0 which had 6' 0" driving wheels. In 1924, in response to requests from the GWR Running Department for a 43xx 2-6-0 with a leading bogie instead of a pony truck, one of the Saint class 4-6-0s was fitted with 6' 0" diameter driving wheels in place of its original 6' 8" wheels. The engine was 2925 *Saint Martin*, which was renumbered as 4900 and given also a side window cab similar to that used on the Castle class. During a long period of testing, *Saint Martin* proved very successful and became the prototype of the Hall class. The Swindon authorities were so confident about the design that an initial order for 80 engines was placed, with the first, 4901 *Adderley Hall*, entering traffic in December 1928. The production engines differed from the prototype in having a higher pitched boiler, outside steam pipes and modified frames. In service, the engines proved they could run almost as freely with passenger trains on level sections of line as their Saint class precursors, despite having 8" smaller driving wheels. They were ideal also for working over the steep banks in Devon and Cornwall.

The LMS

At the grouping the LMS had over two thousand 4-6-0s and 4-4-0s, the majority of which were less than twenty years old with many years of remaining useful life. The duties on which generally they were employed were those for which a modern mixed traffic design would be used, and it was not until the mid-1930s that they either would be scrapped or relegated to secondary services.

Table 1.1. LMS 4-6-0 and 4-4-0
Locomotive Stock at 1st January 1923

	4-6-0	4-4-0
LNWR	650	299
MR	-	386
LYR	34	71
CR	65	171
GSWR	19	181
HR	50	80
NSR	-	5
FR	-	20
	818	1,213

One of the priorities for the newly formed Company was to reduce the 393 different locomotive classes it inherited, and after completing outstanding orders from the constituent companies during 1923, large numbers of engines based on Midland Railway designs were built from 1924 to 1929 to eliminate 'existing engines of inferior performance and efficiency'. Within a decade the number of classes was reduced by almost half, down to 230. As the two largest constituent companies, the Midland Railway and LNWR engines bore the brunt of this reduction with around 40% of the inherited stock from each taken out of service during this period.

Table 1.2 New locomotives added to LMS stock 1923-32

STANDARD DESIGNS		1923	1924	1925	1926	1927	1928	1929	1930	1931	1932	Totals
Class 6	4-6-0 Pass.Tender (Royal Scot)					50			20			70
Class 5X	4-6-0 Pass.Tender (Patriot)								(2*)		15	15
Class 4	4-4-0 Pass.Tender (Compound)		40	95	5	50					5	195
Class 2	4-4-0 Pass.Tender						50	19	4	30	35	138
Class 4	2-6-4 Pass.Tank					4	21	50			10	85
Class 3	2-6-2 Pass.Tank								21	39	10	70
Class 2	0-4-4 Pass.Tank										9	9
Class 7	0-8-0 Freight Tender							100	3	32	40	175
Class 5	2-6-0 Freight Tender				13	87	8	22	95	10	10	245
Class 4	0-6-0 Freight Tender			11	161	132	137	89				530
	2-6-6-2 Freight Tank (Garratt)						3		30			33
Class 3	0-6-0 Freight Tank			42	8	128	36	157	36		15	422
Class 2	0-6-0 Freight Tank (Dock)							7	3			10
Class 0	0-4-0 Freight Tank (Saddle)										5	5
TOTAL STANDARD DESIGNS			93	264	278	367	332	230	173	126	139	2,002
EXISTING NON-STANDARD DESIGNS PERPETUATED												
Class 5	4-6-0 Pass.Tender (4-cyl L&YR Class 8)	21	16	4								41
Class 4	4-6-0 Pass.Tender (LNWR Prince of Wales)		1									1
Class 4	4-6-0 Pass.Tender (Caledonian 14630 Class)			2	18							20
Class 3	4-4-2 Pass.Tank (LTSR)	10		5		10			10			35
Class 2	0-4-4 Pass.Tank (Caledonian)			10								10
Class 7	2-8-0 Freight Tender (SDJR)			5								5
Class 3	0-6-2 Freight Tank (North Stafford)	4										4
TOTAL NON-STANDARD DESIGNS PERPETUATED		35	17	26	18	10	0	0	10	0	0	116
NON-STANDARD NEW DESIGNS												
Class 5	4-6-4 Pass.Tank (4-cyl Baltic)		10									10
Class 7	0-8-4 Freight Tank (Shunter)	29	1									30
TOTAL NON-STANDARD NEW DESIGNS		29	11	0	0	0	0	0	0	0	0	40
SENTINEL LOCOMOTIVES								2	4		1	7
GRAND TOTAL		64	121	290	296	377	332	232	187	126	140	2,165

* These two engines were counted as rebuilds and are not represented, therefore, as additions to stock

From its inception, the LMS recognised the need for a new mixed traffic engine of its own and its first CME, George Hughes, started by reviewing the projects in the various constituent drawing offices. He found that the Caledonian Railway had made considerable progress on the design work for a 2-6-0 with 5' 6" driving wheels. It had many features in common with the Caledonian 60 and the Highland River classes of 4-6-0 but its large 21" x 28" horizontal outside cylinders would have ruled out many English lines and an axle weight of 20 tons would further have restricted its use.

Therefore Hughes decided a fresh start was needed; work began at Horwich in January 1924 and after a number of alternatives had been evaluated a final proposal was approved in November, four months after the Locomotive & Electrical Committee had authorised a hundred engines of 2-6-0 type for mixed traffic requirements. The new design had a high running plate, 180lbs boiler pressure, 5' 6" diameter driving wheels and 21" by 26" outside cylinders, sharply inclined to clear the composite LMS loading gauge which was especially restrictive on the Midland Division. The layout of the cylinders and valve gear followed that of the rebuilt Hughes 4-6-0s incorporating long lap valves and wide steam ports. The first of these Horwich Moguls was completed in June 1926 and within four years over two hundred were in service and eventually 245 of them were built, distributed widely across all four Divisions.

Many LNWR 4-4-0s were also taken out of service as part of the economic case for building new Class 5s with almost one hundred withdrawn in 1935 and 1936. A few escaped the cutter's torch including Precursor 5300 *Hydra* which lasted until July 1940. It was built as LNWR 617 in August 1905 and gained its third number, 25300, when the ex-LNWR locomotives were renumbered to make way for new Class 5s.

Real Photographs

The Class 5s became quickly the most common type to be seen in North Wales and worked most of the expresses, except for the Irish Mails. The George the Fifth and Precursor class 4-4-0s were relegated to the local services between Chester and Bangor or Llandudno and had only one or two regular express turns. George the Fifth 4-4-0 5361 *Challenger*, pictured on a North Wales local, was originally LNWR 888 built in July 1911. It was withdrawn in November 1935 without being renumbered in the 20000 series.

Real Photographs

In 1912 on the Great Northern Railway Nigel Gresley produced his Class H2 two-cylinder mixed traffic 2-6-0s with 5' 8" diameter driving wheels. These were developed through Class H3 in 1913 to the 1920 three-cylinder Class H4. When the LNER was formed, these three classes became K1, K2 and K3 respectively and by 1933 almost 200 were in service. Colwick allocated K3 120 passes Greenwood signal box, south of Hadley Wood, with a down goods in 1925. It was built at Darlington at the end of 1924 and was renumbered as 1834 in June 1946, becoming BR 61834.

F. R. Hebron/Rail Archive Stephenson

On the South Eastern & Chatham Railway, Maunsell introduced in 1917 the mixed traffic N class 2-6-0 with 5' 6" driving wheels which he developed after the 1923 Grouping into the similar U class 2-6-0 which had 6' 0" driving wheels. U Class 1633, seen at Willesden shed around 1933, was built at Ashford in March 1931.

T. G. Hepburn/Rail Archive Stephenson

authorisation before final approval by the Board. From 1932 this sub-committee was the Mechanical & Electrical Engineering Committee, which was attended by Stanier. It met on the day before the monthly board meetings. Reports and papers were presented to the committee in support of major expenditure proposals such as locomotive building; normally these were submitted by Stanier, together with the Chief Operating Manager and the Chief Accountant, and they contain useful background on the way in which the locomotive building policy was developed and the pivotal role of the Class 5s.

The 1933 and 1934 Locomotive Renewal Programmes

On 28th July 1932 the LMS Board approved the 1933 Locomotive Renewal Programme which included ten 4-6-0 'Superheated Converted Prince of Wales' at an estimated cost of £56,000 for the engines and £9,000 for the tenders. "Having regard to the heavy Passenger stopping trains now worked by Prince of Wales type engines, these engines are heavy on coal and are falling due for re-boilering. It is suggested that they be replaced by a similar engine of modern design". However, the replacements were not to appear during 1933 because Stanier informed the M&EE meeting on 24th May 1933 that "it would not be possible to complete the design of the ten converted Prince of Wales included in the programme to ensure their being built this year", and so the 1933 programme was amended at the board meeting on the following day with 15 additional three-cylinder Claughtons [Patriots] to be built in place of the ten Prince of Wales.

The ten converted Prince of Wales re-appeared in the Locomotive Renewal Programme 1934 approved by the M&EEC on 28th June 1933 which were justified because "the frames of the present locomotives gave a great deal of trouble, and the cost of maintenance and coal was heavy. The new locomotives would be of 17% increased tractive power, whilst

the cost of maintenance and coal would be about 11% less". The programme also included ten Northern Division 4-6-0 passenger engines at a cost of £56,500, although the ten converted Prince of Wales remained at £65,000. The former were needed because "The present locomotives had reached the end of their theoretical life, and it would not be economical to reboiler them. They were saturated engines, heavy on coal, and not satisfactory in service, and the new locomotives to replace them would reduce maintenance and coal costs by about 6%. The capacity would remain about the same, as the weight was restricted by physical considerations".

The scrap and build policy

Before construction of the 20 new 4-6-0s had commenced, the LMS had started to make fundamental changes to its locomotive building policy. Whereas in the late 1920s and early 1930s the accepted policy had followed similar lines to that of the Midland Railway, where older classes were rebuilt and relatively few new engines constructed or purchased, the LMS management had now moved to the opposite view, that it was preferable to implement a large scale scrap and build policy. At the Board Meeting on 26th October 1933 the Chairman referred to "a memorandum dated October 1933, which had been circulated, giving particulars of the estimated stock of locomotives at 31st December, 1934, compared with the stock at 1st January, 1923, and recommending that 121 locomotives, the boilers of most of which would require renewal shortly but which otherwise would not in the ordinary course be broken up for some years, be replaced by 100 engines, 50 of which would be the Improved Claughton type, and 50 an improved Prince of Wales type. This would result in an 18% saving in coal consumption, a 25% saving in cost of repairs per mile, and the estimated unproductive time during which the new locomotives would not be available for

A pristine Crewe-built 5014 at Perth on 4th May 1935. Its first shed at the end of the previous month was recorded on its Engine History Card as Crewe but this was only a loan from Carlisle Kingmoor and it clearly went to the Northern Division within a few days; it was transferred in July to Inverness.

Fred A. Plant/Caledonian Railway Association

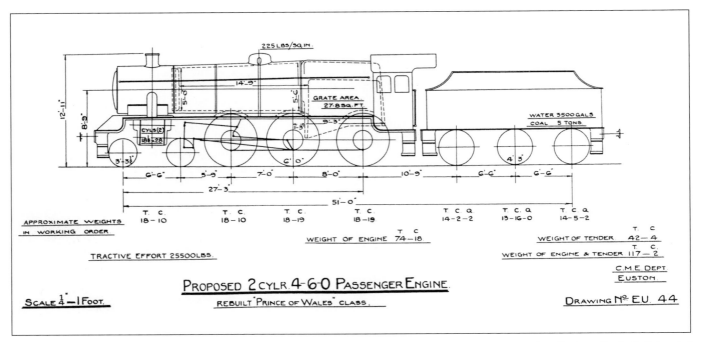

225 LBS/SQ IN.

14'-9"

GRATE AREA
27·8 SQ. FT.

WATER 3500 GALS.
COAL 5 TONS

12'-11"
8'-9"

CYLS (2)
18½ × 28

9'-3"
1'-3"

3'-3½"
6'-0"
4'-3"

6'-6"   5'-9"   7'-0"   8'-0"   10'-9"   6'-6"   6'-6"
27'-3"
51'-0"

APPROXIMATE WEIGHTS
IN WORKING ORDER

T. C.	T. C.	T. C.	T. C.	T C Q	T C Q	T C Q
18—10	18—10	18—19	18—19	14-2-2	13-16-0	14-5-2

T C
WEIGHT OF ENGINE   74—18

T C
WEIGHT OF TENDER   42—4

T. C.
WEIGHT OF ENGINE & TENDER 117—2

TRACTIVE EFFORT 25500 LBS.

C.M.E. DEPT.
EUSTON

PROPOSED 2 CYLR. 4-6-0 PASSENGER ENGINE.
REBUILT "PRINCE OF WALES" CLASS.

SCALE ¼"—1 FOOT.

DRAWING Nº E.U. 44

A number of outline designs were issued on 8th July 1932 over Stanier's signature including Diagram EU 44, described as a "Rebuilt Prince of Wales class". This replaced two earlier alternative proposals for a three-cylinder taper boiler 4-6-0 with 6' 0" driving wheels on a 7' 0" + 8' 0" wheelbase to replace the Prince of Wales class. Both were discarded due to weight considerations and this version with two 18½" x 28" cylinders and a vertical throatplate boiler, was the basis for the final Class 5 proposal.

traffic owing to shop and shed attention would be 20%, compared with 34% for the old units. It was agreed that the locomotive trade be asked to submit alternative tenders for each type in lots of 25 and 50 locomotives". The Chairman also said that "with the increased reliability of the new stock it was considered that a further 221 locomotives, which are at present stored, could be broken up without replacement".

Quotations were invited by the LMS for two-cylinder and three-cylinder 4-6-0 locomotives and tenders, in lots of 25 or 50. Eight different firms tendered for the two-cylinder type, in lots of 25, at prices ranging from £5,625 to £6,900, and four of these also tendered for lots of fifty at prices ranging from £5,485 to £6,795. The same firms tendered for the three-cylinder type at prices ranging from £5,810 to £7,525 for lots of 25, and from £5,710 to £7,400 for lots of fifty.

At the Board Meeting on 23rd November 1933 the Chairman submitted the tenders received from the eight firms, and it was "Resolved that the tender of the Vulcan Foundry Company Limited, Newton-le-Willows, Lancashire, for 50 4-6-0 two-cylinder Mixed Traffic Engines and Tenders, at the price of £5,540 each; and that the tender of the North British Company Limited for 50 4-6-0 Superheated three-cylinder Passenger Engines and Tenders at £5,710 each, be accepted". Although Vulcan's price was £55 higher than that of North British, it was accepted owing to the better deliveries obtainable by dividing the work and the need to address the motive power crisis in Scotland; the additional cost of £2,750 was a price worth paying to accelerate deliveries. If North British had won both orders the delivery would have extended over 54 weeks, but by dividing them, delivery of 37 weeks from Vulcan and 49 weeks from North British could be achieved. The Chairman also explained that the Government had indicated their agreement to regard the expenditure on this programme as a fulfilment of the company's remaining obligation of about £100,000 under the "Remission of Passenger Duty arrangement" on being satisfied the

programme was in fact an addition to the company's normal locomotive renewal programme.

The lightweight 4-6-0 passenger engines for use in Scotland finally were abandoned in April 1934 because civil engineering improvements, particularly on the Oban line, would allow the new mixed traffic design to be widely used on the Northern Division. Stanier and the Chief Operating Manager recommended "that 20 4-6-0 engines and tenders of a new type suitable for mixed traffic work both in England and Scotland be built in the company's workshops in place of the ten improved 4-6-0 Prince of Wales type and the ten 4-6-0 engines and tenders for the Northern Division authorised as part of the Locomotive Renewal Programme for 1934, and that in order to give a wider use of the engine, the tenders be of 4,000 gallons capacity, similar to the 50 engines of this type ordered from the Vulcan Foundry Company". The variation of the programme would not affect the estimated outlay on the engines, but the provision of the larger tenders would "somewhat increase" the original estimated outlay of £121,500. They were to be built in LMS Works and emerged as nos.5000-5019, although the first engine was not delivered until the month following the final engine of the 50 ordered from Vulcan (5020-69).

Before the first of the new engines had been delivered from Vulcan, the 1935 Renewal Programme approved in June 1934 authorised construction of another 55 mixed traffic 4-6-0s and tenders at a cost of £338,250 and a further 30 Class 5X Jubilee 4-6-0s. In July 1934, tenders were obtained from ten firms for both classes and the quotations received again showed considerable variation:

	20	30	50
Class 5	£5,428 to £6,575	£5,395 to £6,575	-
Jubilee	£5,879 to £7,220	£5,843 to £7,180	£5,813 to £7,150

The price for the Class 5s was appreciably lower from one firm, Armstrong Whitworth, than that of the 1933 batch ordered from Vulcan Foundry, albeit the tenders would have

the slightly cheaper welded rather than riveted tanks. As there was a good case for increasing the number of mixed traffic engines and in order to test Armstrong-Whitworth's tender, supplementary enquiries were sent out for 50, 75, 100 and 150 locomotives. The new tenders were received from each of the ten firms in August, the quotations being:

50	75	100	150
£5,365/6,575	£5,353/6,350	£5,343/6,350	£5,335/6,350

The lowest price for each number in both the July and August tenders was from Armstrong Whitworth, whose Scotswood munitions factory on Tyneside had been extensively re-organised and re-equipped after the first world war to provide a capacity of up to 400 locomotives annually. However it struggled to attract locomotive business and between 1931 and 1934 built only 30 steam engines. At the time the LMS was requesting quotations it had just ten locomotives on order for the LNER and had supplied none to the LMS since the company was formed, so it is hardly surprising that its bid was far below the other firms who tendered. The LMS cautiously informed Armstrong Whitworth that, before discussing orders, the company required to be satisfied:

(1) that their tender was not based on an unremunerative cut price,

(2) that no question of extras arose,

(3) that their facilities and inspection arrangements were adequate.

The recent work done by the firm for the LNER settled the second and third points, and an examination of their costs the first one. Prices for 100 were only quoted by four firms, with Beyer Peacock the highest at £6,350. The five lowest tenders were then considered. These were:

	For 50	For 100
Armstrong Whitworth & Co. Ltd.	£5,365	£5,343
R. Stephenson & Co.	£5,600	did not tender
Vulcan Foundry Ltd.	£5,668	£5,608
Hawthorn Leslie & Co.	£5,770	did not tender
North British Locomotive Co.	£5,790	£5,790

Therefore it was decided to order a hundred engines and tenders from Armstrong Whitworth at £5,343 and fifty from the other four firms whose deliveries were:

	20 weeks	30 weeks	50 weeks
R. Stephenson & Co.	41	49	65
Vulcan Foundry Ltd.	22	25	32
Hawthorn Leslie & Co.	56	69	95
North British Locomotive Co.	37	42	36

The LMS wanted the new engines as quickly as possible and therefore offered 25 each to Vulcan Foundry and North British Locomotive at the price of £5,500, or £168 and £290 respectively below their tenders. In the meantime, Beyer Peacock who had tendered at £6,550 (20), £6,525 (30) and £6,400 (50) pressed their claim, but not surprisingly were ruled out on price. North British refused the LMS offer but Vulcan Foundry agreed to supply the full fifty at £5,500. Although this was £40 below the price for their first order, Vulcan would have enjoyed economies arising from already having patterns, tools, dies and blocks thereby reducing their set-up costs for the batch.

The additional order for the Class 5s was approved retrospectively by the Board on 29th November 1934 which accepted the Traffic Committee recommendation for the "Purchase of 100 additional locomotives and displacement of 228 locomotives", for which "Orders for these locomotives had already been placed with the trade" (5125-5224). The 100 additional 4-6-0 mixed traffic locomotives were to displace 108 19" Goods locomotives (in addition to the programme already authorised for 1935) at an approximate net outlay of £511,882 and would produce an estimated net annual saving of £17,386, and withdrawal, without replacement, of 120

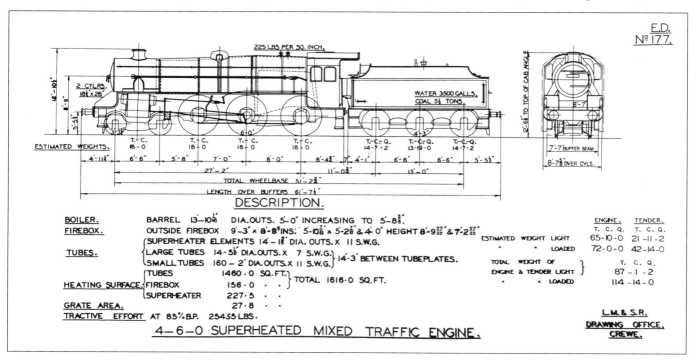

ED 177 was the final design proposal for the Class 5, albeit with a Fowler 3,500 gallon 'Old Standard' tender. Except for the substitution of a new Stanier 4,000 gallon tender, this was the version actually built.

This photograph shows four of the five 1935 Crewe-built Class 5s, 5070-74, under construction in the Erecting Shop at Crewe Works in April 1935. The one at the front is 5070 identified by E393 –1, the first engine in Order E393, chalked on the smokebox rim.

A. W. V. Mace

5097 was built by Vulcan Foundry as evidenced by the oval works plate above the steam pipe and entered traffic on 27th April 1935. It is pictured in front of the erecting shop; the letters VES on the building are, as far as is known, an abbreviation of 'Vulcan Erecting Shop' because the company never used the letters for any of its operations or publicity.

J. A. Peden

2 DESIGN AND SPECIFICATION

A tapered boiler with Belpaire firebox and a working pressure of 225lbs/sq.in. was provided and, to reduce weight, 2% nickel steel plates were used which produced a boiler about 19cwt lighter than an equivalent mild steel one. To outward appearances the boiler had a regular angle of taper from front to rear but this was an illusion created by the lagging plates because, inside, the boiler was parallel in the front ring but the middle ring was sharply tapered from 5' 8" at the rear to 5' 0" at the front. It resembled that on the early two-cylinder 4-6-0s of the GWR, although Swindon later adopted a regular degree of taper on its No.1 standard boiler. The boiler contained 160 firetubes of 2" diameter, pitched in horizontal diamond pattern, and 14 fire tubes containing superheater elements in two rows, each of 5 1/8" outside diameter. This arrangement followed Stanier's Swindon experience using low temperature superheat, but the elements were in bifurcated form and not the triple single-pass small bore type favoured by the GWR. The distance between the tube plates was 14' 3". The tube arrangement resulted in a very satisfactory A/S ratio (the relationship between the cross sectional area of the tubes to their gas swept surface area) but the small size of the front plate restricted the free area to 3.9sq.ft. which was inferior to that of the GWR Halls and rather limited the maximum evaporation.

One of the main improvements, compared with the traditional Derby design, was the cylindrical smokebox resting on a saddle. This prevented smokebox leaks which later became a serious problem with the Royal Scots and Patriots. The smokebox had the same outside diameter as the boiler barrel and it was the outside plating which made the taper appear even. Had the lagging plates followed the contour of the inner boiler ring and had the Derby type smokebox of greater diameter than the barrel been used, the outward appearance of the new 'mixed traffic' engines would have looked very different. The main regulator was incorporated in the superheater header in the smokebox. The blast pipe and front end design followed GWR practice with a blast pipe cap of 5 1/4" diameter.

The firebox design followed Swindon practice in the careful shaping of the inner and outward plates. The firegrate had a steeply sloping front half with a straight tube plate and provided a grate area of 27.8sq.ft., with 3 3/4" water spaces. A steam manifold (with a main shut-off valve) was provided on top of the firebox back plate in the cab on which were arranged the valves for the ejector and steam brake, injectors, train heating, whistle, pressure gauge and sight-feed lubricator to the regulator. The horizontally mounted whistle was the Caledonian type 'hooter'.

The 8' 6" wide cab was spacious, having a high flat floor giving a good driving position. There were two sliding windows on each side with a small hinged window which acted as a draught protector for the enginemen when looking out. There were also hinged windows in the front plate. Tip-up seats were on each side of the cab, the drive was on the left hand side and there was a backward extension to the roof. The firehole had double sliding doors which was a new feature in British practice, the lower part of the door being provided with baffled air inlets which were supposed to give some pre-heat to the air and eliminate glare.

Two pop safety valves 2 1/2" diameter were mounted on the crown of the firebox. A Davies & Metcalfe patent exhaust steam injector was on the right hand (fireman's) side of the firebox and a Gresham & Craven live steam injector was on the left hand side. Other boiler fittings such as the water gauge frames and glass gauge protectors were of the LMS standard pattern.

Two outside cylinders of 18 1/2" diameter by 28" stroke had Walschaert type motion and a valve travel of 6 1/2". Mechanical lubrication, using a LMS standard pattern Silvertown lubricator on the right hand running plate and driven from the top of the right-hand combination lever, was applied to the piston valves and cylinders, piston rod packing and valve spindle bushes, with the oil to each point of delivery being steam atomised. The coupling and connecting rods were of high tensile manganese molybdenum steel, the connecting rods being of fluted section and the coupling rods of rectangular section.

The 6' 0" diameter 19-spoke wheels had triangular section rims, cast steel centres and Gibson tyre retaining rings. Balance weights for the coupled wheels were built up with two steel plates riveted together, the spokes acting as distance pieces, the requisite weight being provided by filling in between the plates with lead.

The cast steel axleboxes for the coupled wheels were fitted with pressed-in brasses with suitable white metal crowns. Oil grooves were provided on both sides of each crown to ensure a thorough distribution of oil to the journal. The coupled axleboxes were so arranged that the oil pads could be examined by sliding out the underkeep while the axlebox was in position. Each axlebox was fitted with a dust shield carried on the inside face of the box. They were mechanically lubricated from a second Silvertown mechanical lubricator on the right hand running plate, each box having an independent oil feed to the crown of the box with the standard back pressure valve and flexible oil pipe connection. The engine and tender bearing springs were made of silico-manganese steel, the plates being of ribbed section with cotter type fixing in the buckle, whilst the spring links were of the screwed, adjustable type.

The four-wheeled leading bogie was of the LMS standard type, the weight being taken through side bolsters, and bogie side check spring gear was provided to ensure smooth riding. It had 3' 3 1/2" diameter wheels and a wheel base of 6' 6".

Mechanical trickle type sanding equipment delivered sand to the front of the leading coupled wheels and to the front and back of the middle coupled wheels. In addition, water de-sanding apparatus was fitted which automatically came into action, so that after the engine had used sand in the fore and reverse direction, the rails were cleaned with hot water to prevent interference with track circuits.

The six-wheel tender had a water capacity of 4,000 gallons and carried nine tons of coal; full details are provided in Chapter 5.

The total wheel base of engine and tender was 53' 2 3/4" and the total length over the buffers was 63' 7 3/4". The leading dimensions were:

Cylinders (2-outside)	18 1/2" x 28"
Driving Wheel Diameter	6' 0"
Bogie Wheel Diameter	3' 3 1/2"
Boiler Pressure	225lbs/sq.in.
Tractive Effort (at 85% Boiler Pressure)	25,455lbs
Heating Surface	
Tubes	1,460sq.ft.
Firebox	156sq.ft.
Total	1,616sq.ft.
Superheater	227.5sq.ft.

Grate Area	27.8sq.ft.
Engine Weight (in working order)	72T 0C
Tender Weight (in working order)	42T 14C
Tender Capacity	4,000 gallons water
	9 tons coal

2.1 Detail differences

The Class 5s were ordered in quantity straight from the drawing board and the first 50 Vulcan Foundry engines in particular exhibited numerous minor detail differences from those built at Crewe and the later contractor-built batches; these are described in the following paragraphs. Some of the changes were inevitable as the new engines settled down into service, but more fundamental were problems with steaming which quickly emerged on both classes of Stanier's new taper boilered 4-6-0s. Although the effect on the Jubilees was more severe, and warranted more urgent action, the solutions developed were also applied to the Class 5s. Significant changes were made to the boilers, and these are covered in detail in the next chapter.

2.2 Frames

In order to keep the weight down and achieve maximum route availability the frames were of lightweight construction, only 1" thick and lightly stayed. Those on 5000-5224 were made from Chromador steel and a similar material, LMS specification 4B, was used for 5225-5451.

By the time construction of the latter were nearing completion, the problems with frame cracking that were to plague the Class 5s were beginning to appear and starting with 5452, built at Crewe in September 1938, several modifications were introduced. The thickness of the frame plates was increased to $1^1/_{16}$", the drag box was strengthened and the arrangement whereby the coupled axle spring links worked under compression was altered because the twisting forces set up tended to loosen the spring plates in the buckles, resulting in shifted spring plates and high usage of spare springs. The

links were now attached under tension to large 'J'-hangers, or 'mutton chop' hangers as they were sometimes called, which were fixed to the bottom edges of the frames. This was a more mechanically stable system and helped to prevent the buckles moving. In order to increase internal friction of the springs so that riding was improved, the ten $5/_8$" thick plates used previously were replaced by sixteen $1/_2$" ones. Axlebox design was also altered slightly and instead of oil being fed through slots subtending 40° either side of the crown, there was a thin white metal lining covering 140° of the brass at the top with the oil feed through rows of small holes at the horizontal centreline.

The frame cracking on all the pre-war engines worsened over time and expensive modification work eventually had to be carried out in the early 1950s to rectify the problems; this is covered in detail in Chapter 4.

2.3 Wheels and running gear

The coupled wheels on the first 70 engines, 5000-69, and Vulcan Foundry 5075-94, had stiffening webs at the rear of the four spokes adjacent to the crankpin. In an attempt to save weight, the coupled wheels had a 3" hollow bore through the axles and the bogie wheels on Vulcan Foundry 5020-69 and the first four built at Crewe, 5000-03; all subsequent engines had a small turning centre. Over the years, wheelsets were swapped during works visits and different wheel combinations resulted.

The straight throatplate engines, 5000-5224, were balanced for $66^2/_3$% of the reciprocating masses, which was within the recommendations of the Bridge Stress Committee produced in 1928 for maximum hammer blow at speeds of up to about 70mph. In service, however, the engines were regularly exceeding this by a substantial margin and must have been causing damage to the track. As a result, the sloping throatplate locomotives 5225-5451 were only balanced to 55% and, on 5452-71, this was further reduced to 50%.

The first Armstrong Whitworth-built engine 5125 illustrates another modification to the Class 5 design: Nos.5000-69 had the Horwich pattern of combination lever which was plain rectangular in section, offset below the spindle guide and forked at the lower end. From 5070 onwards the combination lever was straight and fluted with a slight offset, still forked at the bottom pin, allowing use of the same union link and crosshead arm secured to the crosshead by two bolts. The firebox shoulders have two domed shaped covers as fitted to all except the first three 21-element domeless boilers. The rectangular shaped Armstrong Whitworth works plate is above the steam pipe, although after the first six engines these were repositioned to the front frames.

Further confirmation that official pictures were not always what they seemed as evidenced by 5125 aka 5131. The rectangular shaped Armstrong Whitworth works plate is above the steam pipe which was only the case for 5125-26 so it appears that these are probably the two engines in this view.

2.4 Cylinders and inspection covers

On 5000-69 the cylinder wrappers were completely plain with no access holes or covers for the steam chest drain or its neighbouring oil pipe adapter for the top barrel feed. A small circular cover plate with four-bolt fixing, to provide access to the steam chest drain pipe instead of removing the complete cylinder wrapper, was used on 5070-5224 and the earlier locomotives were soon modified. Two rectangular covers at the top of the wrappers were added from 5225 onwards. In the late 1930s/early 1940s larger covers were fitted and all the locomotives eventually received the later pattern.

2.5 Running plate and cab

The Crewe-built engines and Vulcan Foundry 5045 onwards, were built with a raised step between the frames in front of the smokebox saddle which allowed easier access to the smokebox and top lamp bracket by footplate and shed staff. The first 25 Vulcan Foundry engines, 5020-44, didn't have these steps when built but were fitted with them by the late 1930s. Vulcan and Armstrong Whitworth-built locomotives could also be identified by the two round-head rivets at each end of the buffer beam; those from Crewe had flush rivets. In BR days round-head rivets were generally used on repairs.

5020-69 were built without rain gutters at the edges of the cab roof but as the enginemen tired of water running off the roof below the strips and blowing in through the windows or running down over the their heads when leaning out of the cab, gutters were fitted from early 1937; all the other engines had the ends of the roof plates turned up to form gutters from new.

A minor change to the cab was made on the 1938 engines, 5452-71. Instead of being bent through 90° and bolted directly into the wing plates, the lower ends of the commode handrails at the rear of the cabsides were straight and fitted into pillars at both top and bottom.

5452-71 were built with sandguns which allowed firemen to direct a stream of sand into the boiler tubes to scour them and keep the plates and tubes clean while the engine was running. They were mounted just above the firedoors and were fed with sand from a hopper below the right-hand front cab window. Job No.5303 was issued in December 1942 for the fitting to older engines under NWO 5993, although a few engines were given 'unauthorised' modification from 1938 onwards. The guns proved unreliable in service as the nozzles got burnt, firemen resorting to the simple but equally effective alternative of flinging shovelfuls of sand through the fire hole and over the brick arch towards the tubeplate whilst the engine was working hard, and the guns were removed starting in 1952 to Job No.5663.

2.6 Boiler fittings
Chimney and top feed pipes

The first 50 Vulcan Foundry engines originally had chimneys 12' 10½" above rail whereas those from Crewe and all subsequent contractor-built engines had chimneys which were 2½" shorter. The taller chimneys on 5020-69 were soon replaced, mostly at their first general repair, although a few retained the tall variety into BR days. 5058 had the tall chimney for some years after being fitted with a domed boiler whilst 45345, which did not have the tall chimney when new, received one in the 1949/50 period.

5020-69 originally had the delivery pipes to the top feed clacks outside the boiler clothing under separate prominent covers while on 5000-19 and 5070-74 and all other members

An official view of sloping throatplate Armstrong Whitworth-built Class 5 5241 and, interestingly, not of the first locomotive built. The most important difference from the earlier engines is the domed sloping throatplate boiler with separate top feed, easily distinguishable by the position of the front of the firebox over the centre of the middle driving wheel and the spacing of the washout plugs. It also has a Derby style crosshead arm with three stud fastening and a straight, fluted combination lever with the union link forked at each end. The engine is in 1936 livery with its sans-serif lettering as applied to all of the 227 engines in the batch.

No official pictures were taken of the final 20 pre-war engines built at Crewe but 5452 was only two weeks old when this picture was taken at Crewe North on 25th September 1938. More subtle changes in the design are visible compared with the picture of 5241. There is a bracket for the BTH speed indicator although the equipment had not been delivered when the locomotives were ready for traffic. The crosshead vacuum pump has finally disappeared and the atomiser cover is in a lower position below the handrail so that it was more in the driver's line of sight. Although difficult to see in a monochrome photograph 5452 is in 1938 livery with chrome yellow shaded characters rather than the gold leaf shaded pattern used on 5000-5224.

W. L. Good/Rail Archive Stephenson

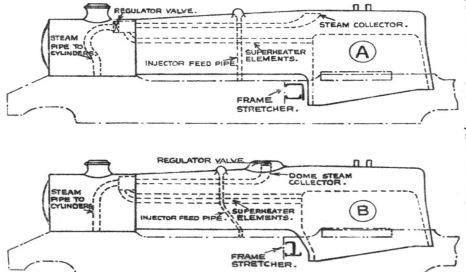

INTERCHANGEABILITY OF BOILERS.

DIAGRAMS ILLUSTRATING THE MAIN FEATURES OF LATER TYPES OF BOILERS WHICH VARY FROM THOSE OF EARLIER TYPES TOGETHER WITH THE ALTERATIONS REQUIRED ON ENGINES WHEN BOILERS OF THE LATER TYPES ARE FITTED.

TENDER ENGINES.

REGULATOR VALVE.
STEAM COLLECTOR.
STEAM PIPE TO CYLINDERS
INJECTOR FEED PIPE
SUPERHEATER ELEMENTS.
Ⓐ
FRAME STRETCHER.

REGULATOR VALVE.
DOME STEAM COLLECTOR.
STEAM PIPE TO CYLINDERS
INJECTOR FEED PIPE
SUPERHEATER ELEMENTS.
Ⓑ
FRAME STRETCHER.

MAIN FEATURES OF BOILERS.

Ⓐ EARLY TYPE.
STRAIGHT THROAT PLATE.
REGULATOR IN SMOKEBOX. NO DOME.

Ⓑ LATER TYPE.
SLOPING THROAT PLATE.
REGULATOR IN DOME.
INCREASED NUMBER OF SUPERHEATER ELEMENTS.

ALTERATIONS TO ENGINES.

BOILER & FIREBOX CLOTHING ALTERED.
INJECTOR FEED PIPES ALTERED.
STEAM PIPE TO CYLINDERS ALTERED.
FRAME STRETCHER IN FRONT OF FIREBOX ALTERED.
MISCELLANEOUS PIPEWORK IN SMOKEBOX ALTERED.

An LMS diagram explaining the relatively minor alterations needed to allow sloping throatplate boilers to be fitted to engines built with vertical throatplate boilers.

5089 on 29th September 1938 at Litton near Millers Dale with the 12.25pm Manchester Central-London St. Pancras. It was given newly rebuilt domed 24–element boiler No.8684 during a Heavy General overhaul between 21st October and 19th November 1937, but reverted to a domeless 21–element boiler at its next Heavy repair in late 1939, receiving boiler No.8926 which had been built with 5146.

E. R. Morten

TABLE 3.5 CONVERSIONS TO SLOPING FROM STRAIGHT THROATPLATE BOILERS

Engine	Sloping throatplate with top feed on 2nd ring	1st ring	Reconverted to straight throatplate
5002	12.37 – W		
45007	01.60 – W		
45008	01.60 – W		
45011		01.49 – 10.54	10.54 – W
5020	03.37 – W		
5022	11.36 – 10.58		10.58 – W
5023	02.37 – 03.53		03.53 – W
5026	02.37 – 01.59		01.59 – W
5027	12.36 – W		
5040	11.36 – W		
45045	11.54 – W		
5047	12.36 – 09.55		09.55 – W
45049	07.54 – 08.59		08.59 – W
5054	01.37 – W		
5057	12.37 – W		
5058	11.37 – W		
5059	07.45 – W		
45066	06.60 – W		
45082	04.62 – W	12.56 – 04.62	
45087	09.55 – 12.60	12.60 – W	
5097	03.37 – W		
5108	06.45 – W		
45109	05.48 – W		
5142	12.37 – W		
45151	03.51 – 03.57	03.57 – W	
45163	05.61 – W		
45169	07.51 – 07.55		07.55 – W
45177	01.53 – 03.57	03.57 – 11.61	
45197	05.60 – 03.64		03.64 – W
45214	06.61 – W		

W = withdrawal

45151 at Balornock on 6th October 1951 has a sloping throatplate boiler fitted in March 1951 and subsequently replaced with a forward top feed type in March 1957. The Motherwell Class 5 has low positioned large 10" cab numbers and a part-welded tender.

TABLE 3.6 SLOPING THROATPLATE LOCOMOTIVES FITTED WITH FORWARD TOP FEED BOILERS

No.	Forward top feed From	To	Reverted to central top feed
45258	06.48	10.52	10.52-W
45312	03.64	W	
45319	10.57	W	
45320	04.52	01.61	01.61-W
45334	10.53	W	
45355	06.59	W	
45356	12.60	W	
45357	01.53*	?	
45358	09.53	12.57	12.57-W
45361	01.59	W	
45364	12.61	W	
45367	12.54	04.58	04.58-W
45384	12.59	01.62	01.62-W
45389	02.53	03.58	03.58-W
45396	03.55	08.60	Not known
45423	01.63	W	
45453	12.59	W	
45455	05.57	12.61	12.61-W
45456	04.52	03.61	03.61-W
45457	09.60	W	
45458	02.59	W	
45460	03.63	W	
45462	11.54	W	
45463	12.52*	?	
45465	06.51	08.59	08.59-W
45468	01.58	W	
45469	11.62	W	
45470	10.51	01.59	01.59 - W

W = withdrawal   * = assumed

5047 ex-works at its home shed, Crewe North, with new sloping throatplate boiler No.9734 and repainted in 1936 livery following a Heavy General repair between 28th November 1936 and 13th January 1937. This was its first boiler change and it still has its original tall chimney but has lost the prominent top feed pipes.
Real Photographs

TABLE 3.7 CONVERSIONS TO STRAIGHT FROM SLOPING THROATPLATE BOILER	
No.	Date
45433	May 1955 until withdrawal
45443	June 1955 until at least February 1960 and probably until withdrawn
45461	April 1955 until withdrawal

were a straight throatplate boiler available but no spare sloping throatplate examples, locomotives were reconverted. In all, eight reverted to straight throatplate boilers, seven in the 1950s and one as late as 1964, see Table 3.5.

The final forward top feed variant of sloping throatplate boiler was inter-changeable with the earlier type and several of the first 225 engines received them in later years. The first was Scottish Region 45011 in 1949 when it went to Crewe for a frame change, although it reverted to a straight throatplate boiler in 1954. In 1956 45082 was converted with one of these boilers and was followed between 1957 and 1960 by 45087, 45151 and 45177, all of which already had sloping throatplate boilers; 45082 later received the earlier central top feed sloping throatplate type in 1962. At least 28 engines built with central top feed sloping throatplate boilers carried the later forward top feed pattern after the war. Ten of these reverted to the original type with the remainder keeping the forward top feed boilers until withdrawn, see Table 3.6.

Three Scottish Region engines built with sloping throatplate boilers were fitted with straight throatplate boilers in mid-1955. This seems to have happened because St. Rollox, with its smaller spares pool than Crewe, ran short of sloping throatplate spares. In 1955 several of its straight throatplate boilers needed extensive firebox repairs, which delayed their return to the spares pool and so later pattern boilers were fitted to any engines that could receive them, resulting a few years later in the reverse situation with a shortage of sloping throatplate boilers and a relative glut of the vertical throatplate type. Since 45225 onwards could accept straight throatplate boilers with only minor modification, 45433, 45443 and 45461 received the older type which they retained until withdrawal, see Table 3.7.

45011 at Balornock on 14th March 1953 has the final type of Class 5 sloping throatplate boiler with the top feed on the first barrel ring. This was a new spare boiler fitted at Crewe in January 1949 which it kept until October 1954 when it reverted to a vertical throatplate type. Although built at Crewe, 45011 has rectangular Armstrong Whitworth worksplates following the exchange of frames with 45280, a common practice at Crewe Works from 1943 onwards. 45011 also has large 10" cab numbers but surprisingly at such a late date the tender has no insignia.

www.Rail-online.co.uk

TABLE 3.8 RECORD OF BOILERS FITTED TO INDIVIDUAL LOCOMOTIVES

Engine no.	Boiler no.	Type	Fitted	Engine no.	Boiler no.	Type	Fitted	Engine no.	Boiler no.	Type	Fitted
5000	8817	VT-14	23.02.35	5010	8827	VT-21	28.02.42	5020	9402	ST-24	19.09.55
	9036	VT-21	15.03.39		8807	DVT-24	03.09.46		9363	ST-24	21.07.60
	8957	VT-21	16.01.43		8915	VT-21	01.04.50	5021	8638	VT-14	11.08.34
	8683	DVT-24	02.06.44		8828	VT-21	11.02.55		8682	DVT-24	11.06.37
	8685	DVT-24	22.01.49		8994	VT-21	06.06.59		8680	DVT-24	29.05.40
	8919	VT-21	24.04.53	5011	8828	VT-21	03.04.35		9056	VT-21	30.05.44
	9030	VT-21	21.09.57		8830	VT-21	05.07.39		9034	VT-21	11.03.48
5001	8818	VT-14	23.02.35		8658	DVT-24	23.12.42		9042	VT-21	27.09.50
	9020	VT-21	24.02.38		8936	VT-21	20.11.43		9055	VT-21	25.05.55
	8921	VT-21	08.08.41		12876	ST-FTF	03.01.49		8922	VT-21	20.07.61
	8987	VT-21	22.08.44	5012	8829	VT-21	02.04.35	5022	8639	VT-14	08.08.34
	9029	VT-21	01.08.47		9049	VT-21	29.06.39		9733	ST-24	15.10.36
	9034	VT-21	07.11.50		9012	VT-21	23.02.43		9354	ST-24	30.12.39
	9050	VT-21	19.10.55		8969	VT-21	31.08.46		9459	ST-24	12.07.41
	9008	VT-21	14.09.61		8956	VT-21	13.01.51		12467	ST-28	07.07.48
5002	8819	VT-14	27.02.35		8826	VT-21	25.12.54		9351	ST-24	19.03.53
	10132	ST-24	10.12.37		8977	VT-21	14.05.60		8975	VT-21	25.10.58
	9452	ST-24	07.06.41	5013	8830	VT-21	04.04.35	5023	8640	VT-14	08.08.34
	9369	ST-24	23.06.44		8937	VT-21	23.06.39		9738	ST-24	02.02.37
	9355	ST-24	29.07.49		8672	DVT-24	12.08.41		10137	ST-24	31.12.37
	9735	ST-24	12.11.53		8922	VT-21	26.11.45		9534	ST-24	14.05.41
	9443	ST-24	20.12.58		8951	VT-21	25.03.50		9430	ST-24	04.09.43
5003	8820	VT-14	05.03.35		8923	VT-21	23.04.55		10138	ST-24	26.01.48
	8965	VT-21	16.01.39		9044	VT-21	11.07.59		8933	VT-21	07.03.53
	8972	VT-21	20.06.42		8909	VT-21	27.11.63		8945	VT-21	05.06.58
	8661	DVT-24	22.11.45	5014	8831	VT-21	15.04.35	5024	8641	VT-14	05.08.34
	8643	DVT-24	04.05.50		8944	VT-21	24.04.39		8663	DVT-24	07.02.38
	9038	VT-21	05.08.55		8936	VT-21	10.10.40		8977	VT-21	05.06.41
	8997	VT-21	11.10.60		9049	VT-21	22.06.43		9051	VT-21	26.07.45
5004	8821	VT-14	12.03.35		9054	VT-21	12.10.46		9030	VT-21	29.06.50
	8923	VT-21	20.09.39		9010	VT-21	14.06.49		8935	VT-21	17.11.51
	8921	VT-21	28.10.44		8665	DVT-24	19.01.54		9032	VT-21	06.04.57
	9008	VT-21	17.05.48		8974	VT-21	13.06.57		8662	VT-14	?
	8673	DVT-24	07.06.52	5015	8832	VT-21	16.04.35	5025	8642	VT-14	02.08.34
	9026	VT-21	16.05.57		8941	VT-21	11.11.39		8658	DVT-24	21.09.37
	8639	DVT-24	23.03.63		9057	VT-21	12.06.42		9047	VT-21	24.10.42
5005	8822	VT-14	12.03.35		9012	VT-21	07.11.46		8947	VT-21	09.08.46
	8915	VT-21	06.12.37		9051	VT-21	09.10.50		8931	VT-21	09.02.50
	8676	DVT-24	11.10.40		9023	VT-21	11.10.52		9027	VT-21	29.01.55
	8995	VT-21	07.11.45		8980	VT-21	03.05.57		8830	VT-21	22.01.60
	9054	VT-21	29.10.49		8822	DVT-24	17.04.63		9013	VT-21	21.05.66
	8670	DVT-24	17.05.57	5016	8833	VT-21	15.05.35	5026	8643	VT-14	01.09.34
5006	8823	VT-14	15.03.35		8939	VT-21	01.11.39		9739	ST-24	11.02.37
	8639	DVT-24	05.03.37		8940	VT-21	29.08.41		9548	ST-24	17.07.41
	8927	VT-21	10.07.40		9014	VT-21	17.02.45		9550	ST-24	25.09.44
	8828	VT-21	01.09.43		8828	VT-21	10.03.50		9479	ST-24	16.01.52
	9028	VT-21	08.11.45	5017	8834	VT-21	16.05.35		11896	ST-28	29.03.56
	8829	VT-21	05.04.50		8935	VT-21	02.06.39		8650	DVT-24	03.01.59
	8998	VT-21	16.09.54		9003	VT-21	20.12.41	5027	8644	VT-14	01.09.34
	8941	VT-21	28.10.57		8919	VT-21	26.08.43		9736	ST-24	03.12.36
5007	8824	VT-21	19.03.35		8989	VT-21	12.10.48		9483	ST-24	03.08.40
	8827	VT-21	24.03.39		8918	VT-21	26.04.52		9491	ST-24	21.04.45
	8933	VT-21	13.09.41		9002	VT-21	08.09.56		9356	ST-24	05.06.50
	8826	VT-21	17.12.43		9041	VT-21	13.03.59		10142	ST-24	16.03.54
	8684	DVT-24	26.11.49	5018	8835	VT-21	17.05.35		10132	ST-24	01.01.58
	8648	DVT-24	12.02.55		8828	VT-21	27.07.39		11894	ST-28	05.06.63
	12130	ST-28	30.01.60		8915	VT-21	28.07.43	5028	8645	VT-14	08.09.34
5008	8825	VT-21	25.03.35		9004	VT-21	25.02.48		8981	VT-21	24.03.38
	9046	VT-21	10.05.39		8937	VT-21	26.12.53		8966	VT-21	19.12.41
	9011	VT-21	30.05.42		8924	VT-21	01.11.58		9030	VT-21	29.12.45
	8991	VT-21	02.08.45	5019	8836	VT-21	21.05.35		8922	VT-21	08.05.50
	8982	VT-21	05.11.49		8637	DVT-24	23.09.39		8672	DVT-24	14.10.54
	8946	VT-21	20.11.54		8912	VT-21	31.07.43		8983	VT-21	02.09.60
	12912	ST-FTF	16.01.60		8911	VT-21	12.05.48	5029	8646	VT-14	08.09.34
5009	8826	VT-21	22.03.35		9032	VT-21	08.11.52		8916	VT-21	04.04.38
	8832	VT-21	11.01.40		8966	VT-21	23.11.56		9004	VT-21	03.08.40
	8976	VT-21	09.10.43	5020	8637	VT-14	02.08.34		9048	VT-21	27.02.43
	8938	VT-21	29.12.46		9740	ST-24	22.03.37		8952	VT-21	12.07.47
5010	8827	VT-21	27.03.35		9396	ST-24	15.09.39	5030	8647	VT-14	08.09.34
	8936	VT-21	15.02.39		9742	ST-24	29.03.41		8673	DVT-24	11.01.38
	8953	VT-21	05.07.40		9526	ST-24	13.10.45		8640	DVT-24	26.12.42
					10140	ST-24	07.12.50		8829	VT-21	15.09.45

Engine no.	Boiler no.	Type	Fitted
5030	8961	VT-21	16.12.49
	8664	DVT-24	10.10.53
	8944	VT-21	17.05.58
5031	8648	VT-14	08.09.34
	8676	DVT-24	19.07.37
	8682	DVT-24	06.08.40
	8925	VT-21	29.07.44
	8955	VT-21	25.11.48
	8912	VT-21	19.03.54
	8679	DVT-24	01.04.58
	8828	VT-21	?
5032	8649	VT-14	15.09.34
	8967	VT-21	21.06.38
	8638	DVT-24	04.09.41
	8640	DVT-24	10.11.45
	8930	VT-21	17.08.49
	9015	VT-21	15.02.54
	8925	VT-21	01.05.59
5033	8650	VT-14	15.09.34
	8972	VT-21	28.03.38
	8670	DVT-24	16.05.42
	8644	DVT-24	25.01.47
	8968	VT-21	27.09.52
	9028	VT-21	24.03.56
	9056	VT-21	23.09.60
5034	8651	VT-14	15.09.34
	8978	VT-21	29.04.38
	8663	DVT-24	18.09.41
	8986	VT-21	11.11.44
	8650	DVT-24	24.04.48
	8971	VT-21	25.07.53
	8678	DVT-24	27.11.58
5035	8652	VT-14	22.09.34
	8962	VT-21	10.05.38
	8980	VT-21	04.10.41
	8942	VT-21	21.08.46
	9038	VT-21	22.08.51
	9029	VT-21	24.12.54
	9040	VT-21	25.08.60
5036	8653	VT-14	22.09.34
	8917	VT-21	14.03.38
	8991	VT-21	01.08.40
	8656	DVT-24	04.04.45
	8999	VT-21	06.12.47
	8656	DVT-24	27.12.52
	9009	VT-21	19.01.57
5037	8654	VT-14	22.09.34
	8648	DVT-24	09.10.37
	9010	VT-21	01.08.42
	8959	VT-21	28.10.46
	9035	VT-21	04.04.52
	8821	DVT-24	20.09.57
5038	8655	VT-14	29.09.34
	8668	DVT-24	08.09.37
	9034	VT-21	23.11.39
	8983	VT-21	08.09.44
	9039	VT-21	06.12.48
	8925	VT-21	26.01.54
	9017	VT-21	20.02.58
5039	8656	VT-14	06.10.34
	8645	DVT-24	17.04.38
	8646	DVT-24	26.09.42
	8647	DVT-24	29.06.46
	8639	DVT-24	29.01.51
	8948	VT-21	13.10.56
	8836	VT-21	15.04.61
5040	8657	VT-14	06.10.34
	9735	ST-24	25.11.36
	9443	ST-24	30.03.40
	9549	ST-24	02.01.43
	9507	ST-24	05.04.46
	10346	ST-28	29.11.49
	9381	ST-24	22.10.54
	12230	ST-28	09.09.60
5041	8658	VT-14	06.10.34
	8671	DVT-24	16.04.37
	8987	VT-21	03.02.40
	8823	DVT-24	27.05.44
	8906	VT-21	03.06.47
	8823	DVT-24	15.09.51
	8955	VT-21	01.10.54
	8971	VT-21	19.11.59
	8949	VT-21	15.06.65
5042	8659	VT-14	06.10.34
	8647	DVT-24	17.02.38
	8823	DVT-24	25.04.40
	9018	VT-21	11.04.44
	8660	DVT-24	31.03.49
	8993	VT-21	12.08.53
	8981	VT-21	02.03.57
5043	8660	VT-14	13.10.34
	8640	DVT-24	15.12.37
	8949	VT-21	24.10.42
	8951	VT-21	19.07.45
	8964	VT-21	23.09.49
	9036	VT-21	24.09.55
	9007	VT-21	?
5044	8661	VT-14	13.10.34
	8643	DVT-24	20.05.37
	9001	VT-21	18.01.40
	9019	VT-21	30.10.43
	8675	DVT-24	08.09.47
	8992	VT-21	09.12.50
	9019	VT-21	31.12.55
	9042	VT-21	25.02.61
5045	8662	VT-14	13.10.34
	9025	VT-21	24.05.38
	8927	VT-21	16.10.43
	8921	VT-21	09.09.48
	8681	DVT-24	18.03.53
	9471	ST-24	08.11.54
	9474	ST-24	12.12.59
5046	8663	VT-14	20.10.34
	8654	DVT-24	04.01.38
	8653	DVT-24	28.02.41
	8930	VT-21	29.08.45
	8683	DVT-24	20.04.49
	8676	DVT-24	22.05.53
	8665	DVT-24	03.08.57
	9036	VT-21	23.08.62
5047	8664	VT-14	20.10.34
	9734	ST-24	31.12.36
	9485	ST-24	07.08.40
	9489	ST-24	02.11.45
	11321	ST-28	07.10.50
5048	8665	VT-14	20.10.34
	8911	VT-21	22.09.38
	8679	DVT-24	08.02.44
	9035	VT-21	19.02.48
	8906	VT-21	19.01.52
	8655	DVT-24	20.07.56
	8823	DVT-24	20.01.61
5049	8666	VT-14	27.10.34
	9022	VT-21	07.06.38
	8645	DVT-24	29.05.43
	8976	VT-21	14.02.47
	8653	DVT-24	21.04.51
	12442	ST-28	16.07.54
	8820	DVT-24	07.08.59
5050	8667	VT-14	03.11.34
	9027	VT-21	17.05.37
	8983	VT-21	21.08.40
	9023	VT-21	14.03.41
	9053	VT-21	08.05.43
	8680	DVT-24	13.12.47
	8637	DVT-24	02.02.52
	9047	VT-21	16.12.55
	9027	VT-21	?
5051	8668	VT-14	10.11.34
5051	8657	DVT-24	17.03.37
	8925	VT-21	21.11.39
	8964	VT-21	26.04.44
	8993	VT-21	31.05.49
	8921	VT-21	17.04.53
	8911	VT-21	04.07.58
5052	8669	VT-14	17.11.34
	9043	VT-21	07.06.38
	8981	VT-21	31.01.42
	8639	DVT-24	06.10.45
	8654	DVT-24	05.10.50
	8985	VT-21	05.04.56
5053	8670	VT-14	17.11.34
	9019	VT-21	28.03.38
	8929	VT-21	26.07.43
	8965	VT-21	09.04.47
5054	8671	VT-14	17.11.34
	9737	ST-24	27.01.37
	9457	ST-24	15.04.40
	9536	ST-24	04.04.46
	9570	ST-24	18.10.50
	11940	ST-28	15.12.53
	12134	ST-28	12.04.57
	9536	ST-24	21.09.61
5055	8672	VT-14	24.11.34
	8667	DVT-24	04.11.37
	8917	VT-21	10.01.41
	8954	VT-21	21.11.45
	8996	VT-21	12.01.49
	8905	VT-21	16.01.54
	8660	DVT-24	01.02.58
	8964	VT-21	07.03.63
5056	8673	VT-14	24.11.34
	8642	DVT-24	10.11.37
	8999	VT-21	04.06.40
	9059	VT-21	19.02.44
	8926	VT-21	20.10.48
	9012	VT-21	06.07.53
	8833	VT-21	20.03.57
	8980	VT-21	?
5057	8674	VT-14	01.12.34
	10129	ST-24	08.12.37
	9735	ST-24	04.06.40
	9395	ST-24	04.11.44
	11917	ST-28	17.11.48
	9353	ST-24	17.08.53
	9454	ST-24	30.05.58
5058	8675	VT-14	01.12.34
	9742	ST-24	16.11.37
	9486	ST-24	04.02.41
	9349	ST-24	18.07.45
	9416	ST-24	27.09.50
	9379	ST-24	27.05.55
	9465	ST-24	11.03.60
5059	8676	VT-14	08.12.34
	8644	DVT-24	01.04.37
	8930	VT-21	20.12.41
	9356	ST-24	14.07.45
	9486	ST-24	06.04.50
	11336	ST-28	04.06.54
	11918	ST-28	09.05.58
	11909	ST-28	14.11.63
5060	8677	VT-14	15.12.34
	9053	VT-21	16.09.38
	8906	VT-21	19.02.43
	8913	VT-21	08.03.47
	8677	DVT-24	18.09.52
	8639	DVT-24	17.11.56
5061	8678	VT-14	15.12.34
	8918	VT-21	05.12.38
	9036	VT-21	15.03.43
	8643	DVT-24	28.04.48
	9020	VT-21	14.02.50
	8973	VT-21	23.12.54
	8943	VT-21	16.10.59

Engine no.	Boiler no.	Type	Fitted	Engine no.	Boiler no.	Type	Fitted	Engine no.	Boiler no.	Type	Fitted
5062	8679	VT-14	15.12.34	**5067**	8982	VT-21	12.06.39	**5072**	9058	VT-21	27.05.35
	9058	VT-21	10.10.38		8651	DVT-24	04.12.42		8908	VT-21	19.08.38
	8833	VT-21	31.01.42		9037	VT-21	28.12.46		8830	VT-21	06.02.43
	8928	VT-21	12.04.46		8981	VT-21	30.05.51		8821	DVT-24	10.03.45
	8646	DVT-24	13.10.50		8651	DVT-24	10.01.57		8678	DVT-24	28.06.49
	9034	VT-21	17.04.56		8927	VT-21	11.05.63		8986	VT-21	05.05.53
	8918	VT-21	01.03.63	**5068**	8685	VT-14	12.01.35		9031	VT-21	05.09.57
5063	8680	VT-14	22.12.34		8823	DVT-24	03.05.37		8644	VT-14	?
	8664	DVT-24	25.08.39		9040	VT-21	28.03.40	**5073**	9057	VT-21	05.06.35
	8836	VT-21	30.06.44		8637	DVT-24	23.11.43		8966	VT-21	04.04.38
	8640	DVT-24	20.01.50		9002	VT-21	28.08.47		8971	VT-21	23.08.41
	8663	DVT-24	26.05.55		8679	DVT-24	01.01.52		9016	VT-21	12.10.44
	8825	VT-21	18.09.59		8827	VT-21	07.11.57		8834	VT-21	21.08.48
5064	8681	VT-14	22.12.34	**5069**	8686	VT-14	19.01.35		8926	VT-21	28.10.53
	9050	VT-21	01.06.38		9056	VT-21	04.01.39		8910	VT-21	23.09.58
	9015	VT-21	23.03.43		8911	VT-21	27.03.44	**5074**	9059	VT-21	12.06.35
	8673	DVT-24	25.03.48		8679	DVT-24	07.04.48		8980	VT-21	16.09.38
	8827	VT-21	23.02.52		8908	VT-21	08.08.51		8641	DVT-24	14.08.41
	8680	DVT-24	26.06.57		8823	DVT-24	10.02.55		9045	VT-21	04.08.45
5065	8682	VT-14	29.12.34		9047	VT-21	01.11.60		8821	DVT-24	12.10.49
	8664	DVT-24	15.03.37	**5070**	9055	VT-21	23.05.35		9033	VT-21	05.11.52
	8907	VT-21	12.04.39		9059	VT-21	28.11.38		8972	VT-21	17.09.56
	9021	VT-21	31.05.41		8832	VT-21	11.12.43		8921	VT-21	25.04.59
	9027	VT-21	28.02.45		8925	VT-21	02.03.49	**5075**	9005	VT-21	23.02.35
	8973	VT-21	23.06.49		8825	VT-21	10.08.53		8924	VT-21	09.06.38
	8943	VT-21	03.03.54		8644	DVT-24	18.09.58		8914	VT-21	24.12.42
	8905	VT-21	21.10.58		8660	VT-14	?		8957	VT-21	19.09.47
5066	8683	VT-14	05.01.35	**5071**	9056	VT-21	23.05.35		8959	VT-21	15.05.52
	8826	VT-21	21.02.40		8996	VT-21	03.11.38		9033	VT-21	20.12.56
	9022	VT-21	13.10.43		8926	VT-21	21.07.43		9037	VT-21	?
	9049	VT-21	11.01.47		8986	VT-21	05.08.48	**5076**	9006	VT-21	02.03.35
	9046	VT-21	20.10.51		8941	VT-21	28.02.53		9007	VT-21	10.01.39
	8684	DVT-24	14.10.55		8918	VT-21	30.04.57		9042	VT-21	09.11.43
	11982	ST-28	04.06.60		8906	VT-21	?		8970	VT-21	02.05.47
5067	8684	VT-14	05.01.35						8670	DVT-24	14.05.52
	8685	DVT-24	30.06.37						8677	DVT-24	02.02.57
									9058	VT-21	?

45047, ex-works at St. Rollox, when it reverted from the sloping throatplate boiler type it had since 1936 to a vertical throatplate during a General overhaul from 1st August to 24th September 1955. It has a welded tender having been paired with all three patterns of tender in previous years. 45047 had moved from the Central to the Northern Division in 1941 and was allocated to Perth at the time of the photograph.

Russell Leitch

Engine no.	Boiler no.	Type	Fitted	Engine no.	Boiler no.	Type	Fitted	Engine no.	Boiler no.	Type	Fitted
5077	9007	VT-21	02.03.35	5088	8669	DVT-24	09.10.47	5098	8945	VT-21	01.11.47
	8914	VT-21	04.11.38		8928	VT-21	22.02.51		9053	VT-21	10.01.53
	8825	VT-21	14.11.42		8642	DVT-24	10.06.55		8824	VT-21	05.10.57
	8943	VT-21	06.03.48		8995	VT-21	27.02.59	5099	9029	VT-21	26.04.35
	9041	VT-21	21.11.53	5089	9019	VT-21	06.04.35		8651	DVT-24	26.10.38
	9059	VT-21	13.11.58		8684	DVT-24	03.11.37		9008	VT-21	22.08.42
5078	9008	VT-21	02.03.35		8926	VT-21	04.10.39		9013	VT-21	08.03.48
	8649	DVT-24	25.08.38		8665	DVT-24	10.06.43		8923	VT-21	07.06.50
	8669	DVT-24	19.06.43		9041	VT-21	13.10.48		8991	VT-21	29.10.54
	9017	VT-21	26.08.47		8685	DVT-24	29.07.53		8648	DVT-24	09.04.60
	8671	DVT-24	09.04.49		8676	DVT-24	19.11.57	5100	9030	VT-21	01.05.35
	8650	DVT-24	19.12.53	5090	9020	VT-21	06.04.35		9026	VT-21	26.04.38
	8912	VT-21	03.10.58		8822	DVT-24	17.01.38		9000	VT-21	07.09.40
5079	9009	VT-21	09.03.35		8656	DVT-24	01.03.41		8982	VT-21	05.01.45
	8662	DVT-24	17.06.38		8659	DVT-24	15.12.44		8936	VT-21	02.07.49
	8990	VT-21	22.04.41		8924	VT-21	02.07.48		8984	VT-21	24.04.54
	8949	VT-21	15.09.45	5091	9021	VT-21	06.04.35		8658	DVT-24	10.02.58
	8642	DVT-24	16.02.50		8675	DVT-24	17.01.38	5101	9030	VT-21	03.05.35
	8641	DVT-24	07.05.55		8660	DVT-24	24.09.40		9029	VT-21	23.12.38
5080	9010	VT-21	09.03.35		8998	VT-21	15.11.44		8943	VT-21	31.07.42
	8975	VT-21	20.07.38		8968	VT-21	03.05.49		8649	DVT-24	05.02.48
	9027	VT-21	22.02.41		8948	VT-21	21.06.52		8989	VT-21	04.07.52
	8971	VT-21	27.01.45		8939	VT-21	26.07.56		9023	VT-21	18.01.58
	8947	VT-21	08.06.50		9045	VT-21	30.08.62		8925	VT-21	09.01.65
	8960	VT-21	20.08.55	5092	9022	VT-21	13.04.35	5102	9032	VT-21	10.05.35
	8655	DVT-24	26.06.61		8653	DVT-24	03.05.38		8979	VT-21	29.11.38
5081	9011	VT-21	16.03.35		8683	DVT-24	21.09.40		8834	VT-21	12.12.42
	9024	VT-21	04.10.38		8671	DVT-24	09.05.44		8825	VT-21	03.05.48
	8931	VT-21	15.03.41		8927	VT-21	28.12.48		8644	DVT-24	24.01.53
	8984	VT-21	17.09.49		9036	VT-21	01.02.52		9035	VT-21	25.06.58
	8820	DVT-24	31.10.53		8908	VT-21	01.07.55	5103	9033	VT-21	09.05.35
	8957	VT-21	21.02.59		9006	VT-21	06.01.62		8820	DVT-24	20.04.39
5082	9012	VT-21	16.03.35	5093	9023	VT-21	13.04.35		9040	VT-21	03.01.44
	8954	VT-21	02.06.39		8655	DVT-24	29.11.37		8663	DVT-24	11.02.49
	8973	VT-21	24.04.42		8922	VT-21	10.02.38		8983	VT-21	23.03.55
	8820	DVT-24	05.02.44		8675	DVT-24	15.02.41		8949	VT-21	14.05.60
	8988	VT-21	07.02.48		8968	VT-21	16.02.44	5104	9034	VT-21	11.05.35
	9001	VT-21	02.04.52		8983	VT-21	25.01.49		8989	VT-21	29.06.39
	14327	ST-FTF	28.12.56		8995	VT-21	01.02.50		8649	DVT-24	30.10.43
5083	9013	VT-21	23.03.35		9056	VT-21	27.01.54		8948	VT-21	13.12.47
	8952	VT-21	01.12.39		8955	VT-21	10.06.60		9031	VT-21	26.03.52
	9014	VT-21	16.05.42	5094	9024	VT-21	13.04.35		8970	VT-21	23.03.57
	8944	VT-21	06.10.44		8638	DVT-24	05.11.37		8985	VT-21	?
5083	8820	DVT-24	20.03.48		9038	VT-21	25.07.41	5105	9035	VT-21	15.05.35
	8945	VT-21	20.06.53		8830	VT-21	31.05.45		8919	VT-21	13.02.39
	8659	DVT-24	18.04.58		9018	VT-21	02.07.49		9035	VT-21	14.07.43
5084	9014	VT-21	23.03.35		8927	VT-21	02.12.52		8908	VT-21	18.12.47
	8956	VT-21	26.04.39		8909	VT-21	28.07.56		9006	VT-21	14.06.51
	8953	VT-21	25.05.42	5095	9025	VT-21	13.04.35		8931	VT-21	26.02.55
	8956	VT-21	15.06.46		8646	DVT-24	11.05.38		9055	VT-21	01.11.61
	8648	DVT-24	12.08.50		9046	VT-21	26.08.42	5106	9036	VT-21	16.05.35
5085	9015	VT-21	23.03.35		8672	DVT-24	03.04.46		9042	VT-21	03.01.39
	8938	VT-21	14.09.39		8910	VT-21	23.03.50		8681	DVT-24	02.10.43
	8956	VT-21	14.07.42		8967	VT-21	23.10.52		8835	VT-21	15.01.48
	8676	DVT-24	07.03.46		8963	VT-21	29.06.56		8651	DVT-24	13.06.52
	8826	VT-21	22.04.50	5096	9023	VT-21	20.04.35		8913	VT-21	16.11.56
	9022	VT-21	02.10.54		9057	VT-21	14.04.38		8661	DVT-24	20.03.61
	8937	VT-21	20.04.59		8947	VT-21	21.02.42	5107	9037	VT-21	18.05.35
5086	9016	VT-21	23.03.35		8984	VT-21	18.04.46		8655	DVT-24	14.03.38
	8951	VT-21	15.05.39		8919	VT-21	10.05.49		9039	VT-21	11.10.43
	8964	VT-21	15.11.41		8832	VT-21	21.11.52		9020	VT-21	05.05.45
	8989	VT-21	02.02.44		8927	VT-21	29.09.56		9025	VT-21	27.10.49
	8658	DVT-24	21.06.48	5097	9027	VT-21	27.04.35		8669	DVT-24	26.01.56
	8946	VT-21	06.11.52		9741	ST-24	08.03.37		8954	VT-21	04.07.61
	9044	VT-21	07.05.54		9514	ST-24	08.11.40	5108	9039	VT-21	22.05.35
	8961	VT-21	13.02.59		9492	ST-24	07.08.43		9051	VT-21	24.08.38
5087	9017	VT-21	30.03.35		9379	ST-24	24.01.47		8655	DVT-24	15.11.41
	9028	VT-21	15.02.39		9517	ST-24	04.01.52		9517	ST-24	20.06.45
	8666	DVT-24	30.07.42		11922	ST-28	14.03.55		9452	ST-24	08.06.50
	8638	DVT-24	06.04.46		9397	ST-24	26.03.59		9417	ST-24	01.09.54
	9011	VT-21	17.03.51	5098	9028	VT-21	25.04.35		9479	ST-24	17.05.56
	10372	ST-28	02.09.55		8679	DVT-24	12.12.38		9422	ST-24	06.12.58
	13348	ST-FTF	10.12.60		9003	VT-21	02.10.43				
5088	9018	VT-21	30.03.35								
	8920	VT-21	30.01.39								
	8948	VT-21	16.03.43								

Engine no.	Boiler no.	Type	Fitted	Engine no.	Boiler no.	Type	Fitted	Engine no.	Boiler no.	Type	Fitted
5356	9390	ST-24	31.01.47	5370	9490	ST-24	14.06.37	5381	10344	ST-28	20.03.43
	9736	ST-24	07.07.51		9431	ST-24	26.01.40		9470	ST-24	02.03.45
	12447	ST-28	24.11.55		10129	ST-24	26.09.44		9461	ST-24	18.03.47
	13347	ST-FTF	03.12.60		9418	ST-24	31.10.49		11027	ST-28	20.04.51
5357	9477	ST-24	10.05.37		12134	ST-28	16.10.53		9461	ST-24	15.10.55
	9739	ST-24	20.12.41		11983	ST-28	20.02.57		9445	ST-24	17.08.62
	9510	ST-24	10.05.44	5371	9491	ST-24	14.06.37	5382	9502	ST-24	20.07.37
	11022	ST-28	16.04.48		9463	ST-24	03.06.40		9438	ST-24	25.04.40
5358	9478	ST-24	14.05.37		9423	ST-24	22.06.44		9441	ST-24	18.03.44
	9361	ST-24	29.11.41		11932	ST-28	29.11.48		9534	ST-24	01.04.49
	9436	ST-24	11.11.44		9563	ST-24	31.01.53		9551	ST-24	14.09.51
	9482	ST-24	25.06.49		9418	ST-24	21.12.57		9738	ST-24	09.05.56
	13049	ST-FTF	25.09.53	5372	9492	ST-24	21.06.37		9545	ST-24	19.04.60
	9477	ST-24	28.12.57		9349	ST-24	21.03.40	5383	9503	ST-24	20.07.37
5359	9479	ST-24	15.05.37		9567	ST-24	01.07.42		9460	ST-24	29.07.40
	9597	ST-24	25.03.42		9742	ST-24	12.12.45		9432	ST-24	15.01.44
	10342	ST-28	25.10.46		9569	ST-24	30.08.50		9518	ST-24	03.04.47
5360	9480	ST-24	17.05.37		9559	ST-24	13.06.55		12357	ST-28	24.10.51
	10139	ST-24	29.06.42		9534	ST-24	28.08.59		11986	ST-28	06.11.54
	9554	ST-24	03.05.46	5373	9493	ST-24	21.06.37		9440	ST-24	12.09.58
	11024	ST-28	24.04.48		9378	ST-24	09.02.40		12134	ST-28	25.01.62
5361	9481	ST-24	24.05.37		10346	ST-28	13.04.43	5384	9504	ST-24	20.07.37
	9440	ST-24	28.01.42		9496	ST-24	29.04.44		9492	ST-24	15.06.40
	9453	ST-24	10.03.45		9561	ST-24	11.09.48		10367	ST-28	17.04.43
	11030	ST-28	18.12.48		11901	ST-28	23.07.53		9558	ST-24	26.09.45
	9429	ST-24	06.03.54		10143	ST-24	29.05.58		9352	ST-24	23.04.49
	12935	ST-FTF	29.01.59	5374	9494	ST-24	21.06.37		9553	ST-24	05.06.54
5362	9482	ST-24	24.05.37		9733	ST-24	18.01.40		12862	ST-FTF	19.12.59
	10370	ST-28	30.06.42		9534	ST-24	17.12.43	5385	9505	ST-24	21.07.37
	10139	ST-24	18.06.46		11898	ST-28	09.03.48		9441	ST-24	06.06.40
5363	9483	ST-24	31.05.37		12547	ST-28	13.11.52		9545	ST-24	20.11.43
	9504	ST-24	13.07.40		9488	ST-24	23.05.58		9533	ST-24	15.12.45
	9477	ST-24	13.07.48	5375	9495	ST-24	24.06.37		9378	ST-24	31.12.47
	11024	ST-28	22.11.52		9500	ST-24	22.04.40		9548	ST-24	13.03.52
	12463	ST-28	29.11.57		9448	ST-24	04.11.44		9437	ST-24	11.04.56
	10128	ST-24	13.02.63		9372	ST-24	25.04.46		12306	ST-28	17.03.62
5364	9484	ST-24	31.05.37		12234	ST-28	01.08.50	5386	9506	ST-24	21.07.37
	9412	ST-24	07.09.40		10129	ST-24	01.10.55		9560	ST-24	25.09.40
	10370	ST-28	19.06.43		9387	ST-24	04.05.62		9467	ST-24	16.11.40
	10373	ST-28	15.08.47	5376	9496	ST-24	24.06.37		9486	ST-24	12.09.45
	12343	ST-28	23.06.51		9449	ST-24	09.04.40		9367	ST-24	28.02.50
	12344	ST-28	04.05.56		10343	ST-28	08.05.43		11889	ST-28	20.08.55
	14326	ST-FTF	09.12.61		9469	ST-24	16.06.45		9376	ST-24	28.08.57
5365	9485	ST-24	31.05.37		9422	ST-24	01.05.50	5387	9507	ST-24	28.07.37
	9466	ST-24	13.07.40		9562	ST-24	20.08.53		9367	ST-24	17.06.41
	10371	ST-28	25.12.43		12213	ST-28	13.09.56		9552	ST-24	28.11.44
	9482	ST-24	04.06.47		9447	ST-24	10.08.62		9423	ST-24	26.01.49
	11029	ST-28	08.04.49	5377	9497	ST-24	24.06.37		9454	ST-24	06.03.53
5366	9486	ST-24	07.06.37		9386	ST-24	09.02.40		9563	ST-24	14.03.58
	9553	ST-24	28.12.40		9361	ST-24	14.02.45	5388	9508	ST-24	28.07.37
	9391	ST-24	17.11.45		9456	ST-24	15.03.49		9502	ST-24	01.06.40
	12219	ST-28	28.01.50		9511	ST-24	14.04.54		9537	ST-24	22.02.46
	12240	ST-28	22.05.54		9425	ST-24	23.05.59		9469	ST-24	20.06.50
	9409	ST-24	11.05.58	5378	9498	ST-24	02.07.37		9393	ST-24	03.05.56
5367	9487	ST-24	07.06.37		9421	ST-24	27.08.40		12298	ST-28	14.11.61
	9508	ST-24	06.07.40		10344	ST-28	12.04.45	5389	9509	ST-24	28.07.37
	9435	ST-24	06.01.45		9384	ST-24	15.08.49		9737	ST-24	15.03.41
	11925	ST-28	17.06.49		12133	ST-28	25.10.54		10339	ST-28	13.04.44
	12876	ST-FTF	04.12.54		?	?	04.05.60		9430	ST-24	13.04.48
	12307	ST-28	10.05.58	5379	9499	ST-24	02.07.37		?	?	28.02.53
5368	9488	ST-24	07.06.37		9428	ST-24	05.06.40		?	?	07.03.58
	9493	ST-24	21.03.40		9399	ST-24	21.08.43	5390	9510	ST-24	02.08.37
	9514	ST-24	23.09.43		9387	ST-24	25.10.47		9539	ST-24	18.12.40
	9528	ST-24	10.06.47		9506	ST-24	31.01.52		10346	ST-28	01.09.44
	9380	ST-24	08.09.51		9448	ST-24	19.10.56		11919	ST-28	05.10.49
	10348	ST-28	08.07.54		9455	ST-24	28.11.62		9476	ST-24	21.12.53
	11986	ST-28	10.10.58	5380	9500	ST-24	12.07.37		9438	ST-24	30.01.59
	9539	ST-24	11.02.61		9407	ST-24	09.03.40	5391	9511	ST-24	02.08.37
	9522	ST-24	13.02.64		9740	ST-24	06.10.43		9527	ST-24	02.08.40
5369	9489	ST-24	14.06.37		9367	ST-24	06.01.45		9424	ST-24	20.05.44
	9503	ST-24	10.09.40		9413	ST-24	12.12.49		11918	ST-28	24.05.49
	9410	ST-24	13.05.44		9414	ST-24	16.08.55		11933	ST-28	25.06.54
	9738	ST-24	24.03.48		12296	ST-28	21.06.60		11936	ST-28	04.04.61
	12213	ST-28	19.03.52	5381	9501	ST-24	12.07.37	5392	9512	ST-24	02.08.37
	9354	ST-24	04.08.56		9458	ST-24	19.07.40		9525	ST-24	22.07.40
	9546	ST-24	11.10.63								

Engine no.	Boiler no.	Type	Fitted	Engine no.	Boiler no.	Type	Fitted	Engine no.	Boiler no.	Type	Fitted
5392	9440	ST-24	12.07.45	**5404**	9524	ST-24	27.08.37	**5415**	9470	ST-24	16.06.47
	11933	ST-28	19.09.49		9444	ST-24	10.08.40		9538	ST-24	23.02.51
	9371	ST-24	18.05.54		9465	ST-24	29.04.44		9367	ST-24	28.01.56
	9504	ST-24	11.01.58		9395	ST-24	30.12.48		9384	ST-24	22.06.61
	9347	ST-24	15.10.64		11932	ST-28	13.03.53	**5416**	9536	ST-24	28.09.37
5393	9513	ST-24	09.08.37		9741	ST-24	26.06.58		9475	ST-24	20.06.42
	9387	ST-24	18.05.40	**5405**	9525	ST-24	03.09.37		9547	ST-24	27.09.47
	9458	ST-24	23.07.43		9437	ST-24	12.06.40		9528	ST-24	21.11.51
	9475	ST-24	18.12.47		9362	ST-24	12.08.43		9427	ST-24	13.10.55
	9550	ST-24	23.08.52		9424	ST-24	09.06.49		9507	ST-24	21.04.61
	9403	ST-24	17.10.57		9376	ST-24	13.10.53	**5417**	9537	ST-24	04.10.37
	10366	ST-28	16.01.63		9515	ST-24	23.04.57		9569	ST-24	14.03.42
5394	9514	ST-24	09.08.37		10345	ST-28	29.05.63		9354	ST-24	02.08.46
	9511	ST-24	14.09.40	**5406**	9526	ST-24	03.09.37		9541	ST-24	02.03.51
	9355	ST-24	22.04.44		9566	ST-24	27.01.41		12357	ST-28	11.03.55
	11921	ST-28	09.06.49		9366	ST-24	21.02.44		9542	ST-24	13.05.61
	9540	ST-24	21.02.53		9399	ST-24	19.12.47	**5418**	9538	ST-24	04.10.37
	11326	ST-28	09.11.57		9366	ST-24	22.08.52		9358	ST-24	26.07.41
	9401	ST-24	29.09.62		10343	ST-28	01.12.56		9396	ST-24	24.10.45
5395	9515	ST-24	10.08.37		12550	ST-28	15.01.64		9467	ST-24	22.03.51
	9498	ST-24	11.10.40	**5407**	9527	ST-24	03.09.37		9380	ST-24	04.11.54
	9446	ST-24	01.07.44		9435	ST-24	22.06.40		10142	ST-24	01.03.58
	9351	ST-24	26.06.48		9522	ST-24	25.11.44	**5419**	9539	ST-24	04.10.37
	10141	ST-24	28.02.53		9501	ST-24	09.03.48		9456	ST-24	03.09.40
	9356	ST-24	11.06.58		9355	ST-24	02.01.54		9376	ST-24	02.06.45
	9570	ST-24	?		9478	ST-24	17.06.59		9462	ST-24	01.11.49
5396	9516	ST-24	16.08.37		?	?	02.09.65		9422	ST-24	18.12.53
	9561	ST-24	30.12.40	**5408**	9528	ST-24	13.09.37		10347	ST-28	30.10.58
	10143	ST-24	27.01.45		9360	ST-24	09.04.42	**5420**	9540	ST-24	11.10.37
	9405	ST-24	16.03.50		9398	ST-24	16.11.44		10345	ST-28	16.07.42
	?	?	18.03.55		11909	ST-28	02.05.49		9560	ST-24	25.07.46
	?	?	13.08.60		11903	ST-28	27.02.53		12210	ST-28	02.06.51
5397	9517	ST-24	16.08.37		9533	ST-24	13.08.57		9551	ST-24	25.05.56
	9436	ST-24	22.02.40		10141	ST-24	17.04.64		9509	ST-24	28.08.59
	10141	ST-24	05.08.44	**5409**	9529	ST-24	13.09.37		?	?	11.05.65
	9515	ST-24	01.09.49		10132	ST-24	31.07.41	**5421**	9541	ST-24	11.10.37
	9408	ST-24	26.04.52		9375	ST-24	30.05.46		9563	ST-24	26.04.41
	9536	ST-24	09.12.55		9483	ST-24	04.11.49		9570	ST-24	29.09.45
	11889	ST-28	05.06.61		9410	ST-24	03.03.53		9549	ST-24	09.09.50
5398	9518	ST-24	16.08.37		9433	ST-24	31.10.57		9472	ST-24	23.04.55
	10347	ST-28	23.04.42		9375	ST-24	10.04.63		9368	ST-24	13.04.60
	9549	ST-24	20.07.46	**5410**	9530	ST-24	13.09.37		9742	ST-24	19.02.66
	9535	ST-24	26.06.50		9455	ST-24	27.05.41	**5422**	9542	ST-24	11.10.37
	9397	ST-24	13.11.53		9504	ST-24	19.10.46		9532	ST-24	31.01.41
	10130	ST-24	22.11.58		9359	ST-24	17.03.50		9740	ST-24	16.03.45
5399	9519	ST-24	20.08.37		12306	ST-28	06.08.55		9411	ST-24	10.06.48
	9528	ST-24	03.07.42		9452	ST-24	03.08.61		9484	ST-24	20.12.50
	10127	ST-24	20.02.47	**5411**	9531	ST-24	20.09.37		9349	ST-24	02.02.55
	9457	ST-24	04.03.52		9351	ST-24	22.08.40		9367	ST-24	16.09.61
	10140	ST-24	12.11.55		9416	ST-24	16.03.44	**5423**	9543	ST-24	18.10.37
	9484	ST-24	13.09.61		9733	ST-24	08.04.48		9489	ST-24	30.11.40
5400	9520	ST-24	20.08.37		9399	ST-24	13.11.52		9734	ST-24	03.02.45
	9484	ST-24	30.11.40		9740	ST-24	09.06.56		12121	ST-28	13.08.49
	9480	ST-24	16.05.46		11327	ST-28	03.08.63		?	?	18.01.63
	9441	ST-24	08.10.49	**5412**	9532	ST-24	20.09.37	**5424**	9544	ST-24	18.10.37
	9420	ST-24	27.03.54		9512	ST-24	18.12.40		9560	ST-24	06.03.41
	11026	ST-28	09.04.59		9508	ST-24	10.02.45		9567	ST-24	13.04.46
5401	9521	ST-24	20.08.37		10344	ST-28	27.09.49		10369	ST-28	20.10.50
	9410	ST-24	27.07.40		9433	ST-24	19.02.53		9544	ST-24	20.12.55
	9406	ST-24	05.04.44		11903	ST-28	09.10.57	**5425**	9545	ST-24	18.10.37
	9516	ST-24	26.07.48		9527	ST-24	18.12.64		9501	ST-24	30.08.40
	9527	ST-24	21.03.53	**5413**	9533	ST-24	20.09.37		9565	ST-24	23.08.41
	9371	ST-24	22.02.58		9462	ST-24	16.05.40		11894	ST-28	17.06.47
5402	9522	ST-24	27.08.37		9463	ST-24	25.10.44		9389	ST-24	19.11.52
	9590	ST-24	04.12.40		9433	ST-24	16.03.49		9436	ST-24	23.04.57
	9345	ST-24	28.08.45		9442	ST-24	25.10.52		?	?	07.08.64
	12297	ST-28	02.05.50		9552	ST-24	09.11.57	**5426**	9546	ST-24	26.10.37
	9558	ST-24	10.03.55	**5414**	9534	ST-24	28.09.37		9439	ST-24	06.11.42
	9385	ST-24	18.11.60		9542	ST-24	29.03.41		9438	ST-24	13.12.47
5403	9523	ST-24	27.08.37		9460	ST-24	09.11.45		12467	ST-28	18.04.53
	9518	ST-24	15.08.42		9396	ST-24	14.05.51		9543	ST-24	04.05.57
	10347	ST-28	11.10.46		11326	ST-28	25.03.54	**5427**	9547	ST-24	26.10.37
	12301	ST-28	14.03.50		11335	ST-28	06.09.57		9559	ST-24	18.04.42
	11888	ST-28	18.05.55	**5415**	9535	ST-24	28.09.37		9346	ST-24	07.05.47
	9564	ST-24	08.06.61		9371	ST-24	02.01.41		9544	ST-24	08.05.52
					9388	ST-24	30.09.43				

Engine no.	Boiler no.	Type	Fitted	Engine no.	Boiler no.	Type	Fitted	Engine no.	Boiler no.	Type	Fitted
5427	9359	ST-24	13.10.55	**5440**	9560	ST-24	23.11.37	**5451**	9398	ST-24	30.12.52
	12123	ST-28	10.11.60		9487	ST-24	15.08.40		9500	ST-24	12.09.56
5428	9548	ST-24	26.10.37		9426	ST-24	16.08.44		11900	ST-28	21.10.60
	9396	ST-24	07.06.41		9522	ST-24	11.08.48	**5452**	10339	ST-28	15.09.38
	10348	ST-28	17.08.45		11334	ST-28	23.05.53		9383	ST-24	05.09.42
	9397	ST-24	23.01.50		11886	ST-28	28.11.57		9553	ST-24	05.10.46
	9350	ST-24	01.10.53		9493	ST-24	24.10.63		11329	ST-28	30.06.49
	9366	ST-24	14.11.58	**5441**	9561	ST-24	30.11.37		9439	ST-24	05.03.54
5429	9549	ST-24	02.11.37		9545	ST-24	09.10.40		11048	ST-28	19.12.58
	11321	ST-28	08.10.42		10133	ST-24	09.10.43	**5453**	10340	ST-28	19.09.38
	9564	ST-24	06.07.46		9529	ST-24	13.06.47		9390	ST-24	25.04.42
	9526	ST-24	24.01.51		9440	ST-24	16.05.53		11321	ST-28	10.10.46
	9445	ST-24	16.06.56		9428	ST-24	26.09.58		9485	ST-24	19.08.50
	11910	ST-28	09.06.62		9737	ST-24	19.03.63		12238	ST-28	19.03.55
5430	9550	ST-24	02.11.37	**5442**	9562	ST-24	30.11.37		12934	ST-FTF	25.12.59
	9524	ST-24	26.09.40		9372	ST-24	15.04.41	**5454**	10341	ST-28	27.09.38
	9525	ST-24	21.09.45		9358	ST-24	20.12.45		9501	ST-24	06.12.41
	9539	ST-24	06.03.50		9735	ST-24	14.04.49		9568	ST-24	01.11.45
	9416	ST-24	04.08.55		11917	ST-28	17.10.53		9524	ST-24	26.02.49
	11923	ST-28	29.04.60		9382	ST-24	15.08.59		9465	ST-24	03.07.54
5431	9551	ST-24	02.11.37	**5443**	9563	ST-24	30.11.37		11979	ST-28	24.09.59
	9529	ST-24	17.12.41		9564	ST-24	27.01.41	**5455**	10342	ST-28	28.09.38
	9548	ST-24	07.03.47		9473	ST-24	20.10.45		9477	ST-24	06.05.42
	9531	ST-24	02.11.51		9459	ST-24	18.02.50		11322	ST-28	15.07.43
	11911	ST-28	28.01.55	**5444**	9564	ST-24	07.12.37		11025	ST-28	21.08.48
	9557	ST-24	25.03.61		9474	ST-24	11.12.40		9435	ST-24	02.04.53
5432	9552	ST-24	09.11.37		9498	ST-24	23.09.44		12922	ST-FTF	30.05.57
	9473	ST-24	10.06.40		11335	ST-28	28.12.48		12343	ST-28	23.12.61
	9459	ST-24	02.02.45		11916	ST-28	13.11.53	**5456**	10343	ST-28	04.10.38
	11327	ST-28	20.08.49		9501	ST-24	05.06.58		9348	ST-24	12.12.42
	9374	ST-24	06.08.53		?	?	30.06.65		9519	ST-24	23.11.46
5433	9553	ST-24	09.11.37	**5445**	9565	ST-24	07.12.37		12863	ST-FTF	01.04.52
	9515	ST-24	30.11.40		9510	ST-24	08.03.41		13245	ST-FTF	12.11.55
	10369	ST-28	05.08.44		9407	ST-24	15.02.44		10372	ST-28	04.03.61
	9491	ST-24	12.08.50		10370	ST-28	16.08.46	**5457**	10344	ST-28	10.10.38
5434	9554	ST-24	09.11.37		12547	ST-28	19.01.48		10374	ST-28	31.10.42
	9526	ST-24	16.08.41		9370	ST-24	05.09.52		9737	ST-24	01.07.44
	9464	ST-24	04.08.45		11905	ST-28	27.12.57		10372	ST-28	26.08.48
	10347	ST-28	08.05.50		9539	ST-24	23.05.64		12443	ST-28	01.03.52
	9363	ST-24	19.06.54	**5446**	9566	ST-24	07.12.37		11330	ST-28	11.11.55
	11919	ST-28	12.03.60		9520	ST-24	13.12.40		12864	ST-FTF	19.09.60
5435	9555	ST-24	16.11.37		9413	ST-24	01.09.44	**5458**	10345	ST-28	11.10.38
	9373	ST-24	01.01.43		9427	ST-24	28.09.49		9350	ST-24	23.05.42
	10366	ST-28	23.05.47		11929	ST-28	18.06.55		9502	ST-24	18.05.46
	9492	ST-24	21.06.52		9487	ST-24	08.04.60		12295	ST-28	29.04.50
	9444	ST-24	08.02.57	**5447**	9567	ST-24	14.12.37		11925	ST-28	19.02.55
	9537	ST-24	28.07.61		9551	ST-24	07.05.42		12937	ST-FTF	28.02.59
5436	9556	ST-24	16.11.37		9385	ST-24	25.06.46	**5459**	10346	ST-28	14.10.38
	9530	ST-24	12.07.41		12298	ST-28	29.03.51		9381	ST-24	11.12.42
	9516	ST-24	26.10.45		9458	ST-24	05.12.56		9556	ST-24	09.03.46
	9409	ST-24	17.05.48		9449	ST-24	20.04.63		9553	ST-24	15.10.49
	9474	ST-24	21.02.53	**5448**	9568	ST-24	14.12.37		11043	ST-28	25.02.54
	9462	ST-24	25.10.57		9495	ST-24	18.05.40		11047	ST-28	27.02.59
	12303	ST-28	02.11.62		9561	ST-24	22.03.45	**5460**	10347	ST-28	18.10.38
5437	9557	ST-24	16.11.37		9382	ST-24	25.10.49		9507	ST-24	06.12.41
	9741	ST-24	10.12.40		9392	ST-24	23.04.54		10367	ST-28	08.11.45
	9515	ST-24	11.11.44		9547	ST-24	29.06.57		11328	ST-28	08.09.49
	9360	ST-24	29.06.49		9402	ST-24	21.09.60		?	?	09.03.63
	11892	ST-28	21.03.53	**5449**	9569	ST-24	14.12.37	**5461**	10348	ST-28	19.10.38
	9474	ST-24	29.11.57		9461	ST-24	05.09.41		9480	ST-24	19.12.42
	9476	ST-24	07.05.59		9407	ST-24	17.09.46		9530	ST-24	14.02.46
	9419	ST-24	07.12.63		9536	ST-24	16.03.51		12451	ST-28	12.08.50
5438	9558	ST-24	23.11.37		9415	ST-24	28.10.55	**5462**	10366	ST-28	31.10.38
	9522	ST-24	14.01.41		9416	ST-24	07.09.60		9519	ST-24	19.09.42
	9487	ST-24	16.09.44	**5450**	9570	ST-24	21.12.37		9485	ST-24	31.08.46
	11983	ST-28	22.12.49		9736	ST-24	17.09.40		12126	ST-28	13.05.50
	9426	ST-24	06.06.53		9541	ST-24	22.11.45		13348	ST-FTF	20.11.54
	12298	ST-28	16.03.57		10343	ST-28	26.01.51		?	?	14.07.60
	9427	ST-24	28.06.61		10366	ST-28	08.09.56	**5463**	10367	ST-28	07.11.38
5439	9559	ST-24	23.11.37		9380	ST-24	25.08.62		9401	ST-24	07.11.42
	10137	ST-24	08.11.41	**5451**	9571	ST-24	21.12.37		9468	ST-24	17.03.45
	9535	ST-24	30.08.46		9562	ST-24	06.06.41		11045	ST-28	21.10.48
	12229	ST-28	03.06.50		9735	ST-24	10.02.45	**5464**	10368	ST-28	08.11.38
	11337	ST-28	15.10.54		9401	ST-24	24.11.48		10339	ST-28	29.12.42
	11325	ST-28	02.04.60								

Engine no.	Boiler no.	Type	Fitted	Engine no.	Boiler no.	Type	Fitted	Engine no.	Boiler no.	Type	Fitted
5464	10373	ST-28	19.02.44	**5466**	10342	ST-28	14.06.52	**5470**	10374	ST-28	12.12.38
	9383	ST-24	03.05.47		12466	ST-28	01.03.57		10340	ST-28	10.09.42
	12465	ST-28	09.02.52	**5467**	10371	ST-28	30.11.38		12308	ST-28	04.05.46
	12445	ST-28	28.09.56		9477	ST-24	27.11.43		12862	ST-FTF	20.10.51
	12310	ST-28	07.05.60		9554	ST-24	03.06.48		12934	ST-FTF	30.10.54
	11914	ST-28	15.12.62	**5468**	10372	ST-28	01.12.38		11913	ST-28	02.01.59
5465	10369	ST-28	21.11.38		9466	ST-24	23.05.49		9482	ST-24	11.01.64
	9523	ST-24	12.12.42		9739	ST-24	05.03.49	**5471**	10375	ST-28	12.12.38
	9481	ST-24	13.12.46		9482	ST-24	09.01.54		10342	ST-28	05.09.42
	12864	ST-FTF	16.06.51		12917	ST-FTF	31.01.58		10340	ST-28	30.08.46
	12862	ST-FTF	08.01.55	**5469**	10373	ST-28	05.12.38		9530	ST-24	16.09.50
	12121	ST-28	14.08.59		9476	ST-24	12.11.43				
5466	10370	ST-28	25.11.38		10374	ST-28	21.04.48				
	9391	ST-24	25.04.42		12222	ST-28	05.05.51				
	10374	ST-28	14.04.45		?	?	18.05.56				
	9365	ST-24	31.01.48		?	?	21.11.62				

45461 from Inverness shed leaves Boat of Garten with an Inverness via Forres train in September 1957. It was the first of three sloping throatplate engines fitted with vertical throatplate boilers in mid–1955 when St. Rollox ran short of the later type. 45461 was modified during a General repair between 12th February and 2nd April, and it retained the older boiler type until withdrawn.

W. J. Verden Anderson/Rail Archive Stephenson

Although attempts to were made to repair the cracks by chipping away vee-shaped grooves along the cracks with a rivet gun and then welding them up, once welded they cracked more quickly than before, usually at the edges of the welds. Eventually after several years of investigation a solution to the frame problem was reached and the older engines were fitted with manganese steel liners, Horwich pattern horn stays and cottered spring links at a cost of around £600 per engine. 45395 is pictured in the 1960s at Crewe Works with the wheels off and the frames and horn guides clearly visible. Note the conduit for the AWS, fitted in May 1959, along the edge of the running plate and the different fixing of the commode handrail at the top and bottom, the reversing rod and the sandboxes. *www.Rail-online.co.uk*

them to all its trains in 1944. Attracted by the potential for a material improvement in wear characteristics Ivatt fitted the liners on both axleboxes and horns to 1946 new-build Class 5s 4922-31 from Crewe and 4953-66 from Horwich. Also, 35 of the earlier engines had their gun metal liners replaced by manganese steel liners as experiment D/LD/1175 under Job 5444 and financial authority NWO 6811 dated 14th March 1946 (closed 23rd July 1951).

The axlebox liners were 11-13% manganese steel plates riveted to mild steel backing plates that were welded to the box and machined before the brass was pressed in, with provision made for wear by providing the axlebox guide with a bolted on sandwich liner and shims that could be inserted between the liners and guides as necessary. The manganese steel quickly hardened in use so that the rate of wear slowed down, producing a dramatic improvement. Clearances and alignment of the boxes with the frames were maintained to within very close limits over much higher mileages than previously, and so this practice was adopted as standard for new construction in 1947 commencing with Lot 187 engines 4997 from Horwich and 4768 from Crewe.

4.3 The final solution

The results of Dr. Johansen's work were published in a paper read jointly with E. S. Cox to the Institution of Locomotive Engineers in 1947 which stated that the investigations on frame cracking had demonstrated the overwhelming importance of a tight connection at the bottom of the horn gap' and that the type of axlebox guides and horn stays used on the Class 5s made this almost impossible to achieve. The service record of the 'Crab' 2-6-0s had shown their frames to be relatively free from cracks and so the types of horn blocks and stays used on these engines were adopted for the Class 5s, beginning in 1946 with 4922-31 from Crewe and 4953-66 from Horwich which had also been fitted with manganese steel liners. One-piece horn blocks and stays were fixed to downward extensions of the frame plates having horizontal bolts. The former were fitted to the leading and driving horn gaps and the latter to all of them, the gaps being opened out and 1¹⁄₈" thick inserts welded in. Link and pin jointed, inverted T-section cross stays were added at the leading and driving horns and the strengthening plates at the driving horn gaps were removed.

At the same time, problems with the screwed spring links on the coupled axles were also dealt with, by the use of flat section links attached under tension to large 'J' or 'mutton chop' hangers fixed to the bottom edges of the frames through which interchangeable flat cotters were inserted. This was a more mechanically stable system than the previous arrangement in which twisting forces tended to loosen the spring plates in the buckles, resulting in shifted spring plates and high usage of spare springs; the revised arrangement helped to prevent the buckles moving as well as reducing to some extent the twisting moments across the horn gaps.

Although the costs per locomotive of over £600 were significant, the Class 5 problems were deemed sufficiently important that the three modifications described above, also termed modernisation on some of the Engine History Cards, were applied to the whole class from February 1951 onwards under Job 5597 to WO/E 1173; this covered the remaining 643 locomotives which had not already been modified. As they underwent general repairs the older engines therefore were fitted with manganese steel liners, Horwich pattern horn stays and cottered spring links. At last, the frame problems were finally cured and the interval between periodic repairs rose from an average of just under 57,000 to over 97,000 miles.

185 of the Engine History Cards for the pre-war engines show the modernisation work, although not until almost three years had elapsed since Job 5597 had been authorised; the first one recorded was completed in March 1954 on 45241 at Crewe and the last one, completed on 30th January 1959, was on 45390 at Horwich. Twenty were carried out at Horwich in 1957/8 and 28 at St. Rollox between 1954 and 1958; the remainder were dealt with at Crewe.

1954	20
1955	18
1956	61
1957	57
1958	27
1959	1
Undated	1
Total	**185**

5093 has just left Watford tunnel with a down express from Euston in 1947 which has a GWR Siphon G at the head. It spent part of the year allocated to 5A Crewe North before going to nearby Crewe South in October where it stayed until 1954. It had a domeless boiler from February 1944, when it was probably repainted in wartime plain black livery with high scroll pattern cab numbers.

F. R. Hebron/Rail Archive Stephenson

5 TENDERS

The tenders built by the LMS between 1924 and 1934 were essentially the Midland Railway 3,500 gallon design, often termed 'Old Standard'. This was not surprising since the majority of the LMS standard locomotives introduced during that period were also of Midland origin. When Stanier's first new designs emerged in late 1933, the 40 5MT 2-6-0s and the first five Jubilees also had these tenders. The reason for the company's choice of what were relatively small tenders compared to those in use on the other railways at the time is explained in a report dated 5th April 1932 from Stanier to the Mechanical & Electrical Engineering Committee.

"In connection with the interchange of engines from one Division to another, it has been found that the smaller capacity tenders in general use on L.&N.W. engines have not sufficient capacity to carry between the troughs on the Midland Division where the spacings are roughly 50 miles against 30 on the Western Division, and it was decided to investigate the whole matter and come to a decision as to the most economical capacity for tenders and spacing of troughs, both for present and future requirements". The report concluded "It will be seen that the cost does not vary much in relation to tender capacity until it becomes necessary to change from six to eight wheels to carry the greater weight of water. The best capacity for any given route depends very much on local conditions, but our experience so far has shown that 3,500 gallons capacity is the best for all general purposes".

It was therefore natural that the first diagram produced for the Class 5s, ED 177, included a 3,500 gallon 'Old Standard' Fowler pattern tender carrying $5\frac{1}{2}$ tons of coal. However, before the first Class 5 was completed a new standard design of tender had been produced.

Firstly, three prototype tenders were built in 1933 (Nos.9000, 9001 and 9002), the intention being to put the first two with the new Princess Royal Pacifics 6200 and 6201, whilst 9002 was to be coupled with the Turbomotive, 6202. However, construction of the latter was not completed until June 1935 and so tender 9002 was paired with 6100 *Royal Scot* in March 1933 for its tour of North America, whilst tenders 9000 and 9001 were duly fitted to the two Pacifics in June and November 1933 respectively.

These three tenders had the 'Old Standard' outline with straight sides but were bigger, having a capacity of 4,000 gallons and nine tons. They were carried on six 51" diameter wheels and were two feet longer than the standard 3,500 gallon tenders, the wheelbase being 15 feet equally divided. All three were built with Timken roller bearings, but 9001 was rebuilt early in 1934 with plain ones.

The Midland pattern level rear coal space on these and the standard 3,500 gallon tenders would not trim very easily, or shake down to the front, causing the fireman to spend a lot of time in the coal space trying to bring it forward. This could be dangerous if coal was still piled up at the sides and rear, and the weight distribution was poor. The design was altered so that as far as possible the coal would be self-trimming and the classic Stanier tender shape with curved top sides emerged.

5.1 Standard 4,000 gallon tenders

By April 1934 Stanier had decided that 3,500 gallons was insufficient for his new standard designs and recommended in his proposal to the M&EE Committee for 20 Class 5 4-6-0 engines and tenders "that in order to give a wider use of the engine, the tenders be of 4,000 gallons' capacity".

The new design had a 15 foot wheelbase, equally divided, and the total length over the buffers was 24' 6¾". The six-spoked wheels were 4' 3" in diameter and had triangular section rims and Gibson fastenings. The sloping coal space floor plate began half-way up the rear coal fender and ended in a 4' long horizontal portion 1' 6" above the platform at the front. Above this was a slightly inclined shovelling plate. The sides of the coal space sloped inwards so that the width of the floor at the front was 5' 6" compared with around 8' 6" at the rear. There was a storage tunnel for the fire irons along the right hand side of the coal space which had a central access door with toolboxes initially provided on the front bulkhead either side of the door, but later this arrangement gave way to a single, enlarged locker on the left hand side. Both the water pick-up and tender hand-brake handles were arranged vertically (i.e., with shaft axis horizontal), bevelled wheels being provided for transferring the motion to their respective gears. The steam brake could be applied simultaneously with the steam brake on the engine to each of the six tender wheels. There were two intermediate buffers, one intermediate drawbar and two safety bars to link the engine and tender and on the rear panel were six footsteps, three on either side, providing access to the water filler.

The tanks of the tenders built with 5001-72 and 5075-5124 were assembled with snap head rivets, the joints being made water-tight with pieces of tarred paper or brown paper and red lead between the plates, but from the first Armstrong Whitworth batch, 5125-5224, onwards a change was made to welded tanks. These were cheaper to build and reduced the weight of the tender by 1ton 2cwt to 26tons 16cwt; subsequent pre-war engines 5225-5471 also had the same type.

However, problems were experienced with leakage from the welded seams of the tanks and a modified design was introduced in November 1945 on Crewe-built Class 5 4912. The internal baffle plates were now riveted to the side, rear and base plates but the remaining seams were welded. In addition to the absence of horizontal lines of rivet heads immediately above the base and at tank top level, these part-welded tenders could be identified by different pattern vents. Instead of the tall mushroom shaped, cylindrical vents on the rear of the tank top, two shorter, rectangular cross-section ones were welded to the rear of the bulkhead.

The three types of 4,000 gallon tender were regularly exchanged between engines because tenders took less time to repair than locomotives and after a works visit an engine would take the next spare available tender, not necessarily the one which it arrived with.

There was a minor detail difference on the tenders of the first 50 Vulcan Foundry engines, 5020-69; these had plain axlebox covers whereas all the others had cruciform ribs cast in. Also, the tank vent pipes on the rear platform behind the coal fender were quite short, reaching only slightly above the level of the tank rear and they were soon extended to the tops of the side plates.

The LMS gave the 4,000 gallon tenders Mark or Type numbers, which unfortunately did not distinguish between the various types and in fact overlapped in at least one area. The original riveted pattern and the final part-welded variant confusingly were both described as Mark 1.

5.2 Rebuilt prototype tenders

The pre-war engines were with three exceptions all built with standard 4,000 gallon tenders, with either riveted or welded

tanks. In 1935 the three 1933 prototype 4,000 gallon tenders were all rebuilt at an authorised cost of £505 as nearly as possible to conform to the new standard. The original flat side sheets were replaced by curved topped sides but they were subtly different from the standard 4,000 gallon tender, with a different rivet pattern on the tank sides and curved cut-out at the top of the side panelling. Tender 9002 was attached to the first Class 5 built at Crewe, 5000, which was ex-works in February 1935, and 9000 and 9001 were coupled to two other new Crewe-built engines, 5073 and 5074, that entered traffic in June 1935. In the immediate post-war period (1947-50) the three tenders were modified by the provision of manganese steel liners to the axleboxes, plus other special measures to overcome corrosion in the boxes.

The subsequent history of these three tenders, from the History Cards, shows that they were attached to the following locomotives on the dates shown:

Tender 9000	Tender 9001	Tender 9002
5073 (05.06.35)	5074 (12.06.35)	5000 (23.02.35)
5312 (28.10.44)	5002 (31.07.45)	5147 (16.02.43)
5144 (30.06.45)	5146 (19.01.46)	5198 (21.06.44)
5298 (21.03.46)	Withdrawn (19.06.65)	Withdrawn (30.09.67)
Spare (30.06.58) 45216 (23.01.59)		
Spare (25.02.61) 45249 (21.07.61)		
Withdrawn (10.12.66)		

5.3 Corridor tender

In 1937 the LMS ordered a special train (with dynamometer car) for use in testing steam locomotives, but wartime conditions interrupted the project and some of the equipment was not completed until 1949. It has been suggested that the tender for use with this train was ordered under X3/285 from Crewe as tender No.9073 although it was completed at Derby under order O-1228. It was painted in full crimson lake livery but numbered 4999, so 9073 in the LMS tender list remained always blank.

This tender had the same frames as the standard 4,000 gallon tenders but its layout and fittings were different and it had a tank capacity of 3,500 gallons. There was a gangway on the left hand side with a centrally placed corridor connection at the rear to give access to the dynamometer car. Below the gangway was a cable duct for electrical monitoring cables and other items linking the locomotive and the test monitoring instruments in the dynamometer car. On the right side was a tunnel for fire irons etc. The bunker was divided into two longitudinal compartments, each of three tons capacity and in one of them was placed carefully graded and weighed bags of coal and in the other equally graded loose coal. The forward bulkhead, bunker and gangway each had a door, all leading into a roofed vestibule.

Most of the service of this tender was post-war, up to around 1955 when the impending dieselisation programme brought steam locomotive testing to an end. The tender then was rebuilt with a new conventional part-welded tank though retaining its distinctive number. It ended its days coupled to

No.9217, the penultimate 4,000 gallon riveted tender built with a Class 5, was paired with Vulcan Foundry 5123 until October 1946 when it was replaced by another riveted example, No.9192.

Engine no.	Tender no.	Type	Fitted	Engine no.	Tender no.	Type	Fitted	Engine no.	Tender no.	Type	Fitted
5138	9031	R	10.02.48	5154	9845	W	29.06.56	5162	9266	W	29.07.35
	10592	PW	27.10.54		10479	W	20.05.60		9556	W	10.03.39
	9277	W	29.09.56		9289	W	16.06.66		9266	W	21.04.39
	10527	W	10.02.58	5155	9259	W	16.07.35		9530	W	05.12.41
	10598	PW	03.07.58		9283	W	11.02.44		9914	W	24.12.41
5139	9243	W	29.05.35		9279	W	09.08.47		9064	R	23.09.49
	10480	W	02.12.58		10547	PW	08.03.48		9277	W	09.01.51
	10483	W	05.09.64		9276	W	26.03.48		10595	PW	?
5140	9244	W	03.06.35		10547	PW	01.04.48	5163	9267	W	29.07.35
	9630	W	30.06.45		9545	W	04.07.49		9298	W	10.08.42
	9203	R	21.03.64		9279	W	16.02.50		9267	W	16.11.42
5141	9245	W	03.06.35		10598	PW	21.02.53		9164	R	27.07.49
5142	9246	W	03.06.35		9015	R	04.10.54		10686	PW	08.01.51
	9320	W	17.03.52		9022	R	20.12.54		9329	R	18.07.51
5143	9247	W	14.06.35		9668	W	20.10.56		9194	R	03.10.51
	9600	W	16.06.43		9269	W	29.11.56		10593	PW	14.08.54
5144	9248	W	14.06.35		10594	PW	?		10601	PW	30.03.56
	9000	Proto	30.06.45	5156	9260	W	16.07.35		10692	PW	16.06.56
	9055	R	09.08.45		9277	W	18.06.36		9823	W	04.07.56
5145	9249	W	14.06.35		9260	W	17.09.48		10582	PW	23.11.57
5146	9250	W	18.06.35		9266	W	07.04.50		10695	PW	01.08.61
	9001	Proto	19.01.46		10508	W	21.12.50	5164	9268	W	29.07.35
5147	9251	W	18.06.35		10674	PW	24.08.51		9262	W	22.05.36
	9002	Proto	16.02.43		9266	W	28.11.52		9708	W	22.05.46
	9504	W	18.04.44		10510	W	15.10.54		9663	W	24.10.47
	10456	W	18.10.55		9832	W	27.04.56		9708	W	29.10.48
	9510	W	23.01.60	5157	9261	W	17.07.35		10556	PW	?
	10702	PW	13.03.63		9269	W	20.03.37		10695	PW	16.11.56
5148	9252	W	18.06.35		9281	W	21.09.44		10690	PW	12.05.61
	9318	W	28.01.43		9545	W	13.04.48		9242	W	16.03.54
	9058	R	?		10547	PW	04.07.49	5165	9269	W	05.08.35
	10518	W	05.09.64		9022	R	19.02.52		9261	W	26.03.37
5149	9253	W	24.06.35		9015	R	20.12.54		9181	R	15.03.38
	9119	R	27.10.45		9287	W	20.01.55		9270	W	06.05.42
5150	9254	W	25.06.35		9679	W	25.08.56		9212	R	26.04.44
	9307	W	18.11.53		9209	R	20.12.62		9250	W	10.01.46
5151	9255	W	25.06.35	5158	9262	W	17.07.35		10688	PW	15.04.53
	9261	W	15.03.38		9268	W	22.05.36		9216	R	22.12.53
	9709	W	18.07.40		9727	W	26.08.41		9594	W	24.12.55
	9261	W	31.07.40		9709	W	31.12.41		10712	PW	23.02.57
	9212	R	23.07.41		9268	W	18.06.42		10510	W	08.05.63
	9719	W	29.04.44		10621	PW	08.10.48	5166	9270	W	05.08.35
	9024	R	02.05.47		9268	W	15.10.48		9181	R	06.05.42
	10675	PW	23.05.51		9023	R	14.11.51		9179	R	08.06.42
	10597	PW	17.12.53		9364	R	23.03.53		9210	R	02.04.46
	9672	W	20.02.57		10685	PW	27.08.54		9712	W	02.07.49
	9069	R	05.06.58		9282	W	18.02.56		10602	PW	28.07.50
5152	9256	W	28.06.35		9117	R	09.11.57		9164	R	15.12.52
	9169	R	27.05.44	5159	9263	W	21.07.35		9268	W	10.03.57
	9273	W	07.01.46		9258	W	16.12.46		10815	PW	?
	9213	R	31.07.47		10686	PW	25.11.51		9836	W	18.11.63
	9209	R	14.09.47		9061	R	09.04.54	5167	9271	W	02.08.35
	10507	W	03.08.51		10582	PW	12.08.55		9211	R	02.04.37
	9502	W	17.06.52		10581	PW	21.11.57		9179	R	01.10.41
	10578	PW	09.07.54	5160	9264	W	21.07.35		9255	W	08.06.42
	9821	W	26.02.57		9245	W	08.02.38		10677	PW	?
5153	9257	W	28.06.35		9240	W	?		10533	W	03.11.53
	9212	R	08.08.39		9553	W	?		9122	R	15.10.54
	9261	W	23.07.41		10503	W	17.12.55		9015	R	02.12.55
	9877	W	12.08.44		9726	W	?		9716	W	20.09.61
	9261	W	04.10.44	5161	9265	W	21.07.35		10684	PW	05.11.63
	9659	W	09.01.45		9280	W	17.10.40	5168	9272	W	17.08.35
	9314	W	25.06.47		9005	R	16.08.42		9062	R	06.12.44
	9214	R	21.03.53		9015	R	20.02.45		9298	W	15.12.44
	9838	W	21.10.55		9185	R	13.01.51		9538	W	29.09.45
	9534	W	03.12.55		10697	PW	?		9837	W	25.02.47
	10676	PW	26.01.57		9097	R	06.03.53		9175	R	07.01.49
5154	9258	W	28.06.35		10502	W	02.12.54		10506	W	21.04.50
	9271	W	25.11.40		9620	W	12.08.55		9176	R	09.02.51
	9116	R	16.01.42		9511	W	04.02.56		9032	R	?
	9727	W	14.10.46		9209	R	14.03.57		10448	W	05.02.55
	9177	R	10.04.47		9679	W	20.12.62		10605	PW	14.04.56
	9835	W	20.01.49		9593	W	09.05.65		9545	W	08.07.57
	9720	W	07.05.52		9531	W	21.10.66		10620	PW	10.11.58
	10683	PW	05.07.52							9545	W	27.02.59
	9215	R	15.11.54									

45198 at Eastfield in 1944 has rebuilt prototype tender No.9002 which had been paired with 5000 from 1935 until it was transferred to 5147 in February 1943 and finally to 5198 in June 1944. When rebuilt, the original flat side sheets were replaced by curved topped sides which were subtly different from the standard 4,000 gallon tender, with a different rivet pattern on the tank sides and deeper curved cut-out at the top of the side panelling.
W. Hamilton

Engine no.	Tender no.	Type	Fitted	Engine no.	Tender no.	Type	Fitted	Engine no.	Tender no.	Type	Fitted
5169	9273	W	13.08.35	**5172**	9283	W	27.08.55	**5176**	9724	W	14.07.50
	9169	R	07.01.46		9777	W	03.08.56		10814	PW	?
	9206	R	18.10.52		9269	W	06.11.56		9277	W	28.01.56
	10582	PW	12.09.53		9365	R	15.11.56		10713	PW	22.09.56
	9722	W	21.07.55		10673	PW	19.11.56		10511	W	03.04.58
	9724	W	19.01.57	**5173**	9277	W	15.08.35		9005	R	08.01.59
	9598	W	11.02.63		9260	W	18.06.36		9665	W	?
5170	9274	W	12.08.35		9723	W	02.09.42		9594	W	12.03.66
	9712	W	06.08.47		9260	W	16.09.42	**5177**	9281	W	06.09.35
	9210	R	05.07.49		9277	W	17.09.48		9269	W	21.09.44
	9064	R	25.02.51		9273	W	18.11.48		9659	W	07.07.47
	9062	R	01.11.52		9059	R	03.07.52		10527	W	15.03.50
	9296	W	21.05.53		10585	PW	27.11.53		9005	R	?
	9287	W	30.10.53		10605	PW	11.01.56		9268	W	12.02.54
	9015	R	14.01.55		10618	PW	14.04.56		9229	W	16.03.57
	9116	R	02.12.55		9636	W	04.10.57		10670	PW	10.05.58
	9595	W	20.12.57	**5174**	9278	W	26.08.35		9679	W	06.06.66
	9120	R	14.04.64		9255	W	03.02.41	**5178**	9282	W	05.09.35
5171	9275	W	15.08.35		9181	R	17.02.50		9122	R	?
	9244	W	29.01.38		9672	W	14.02.53		10671	PW	26.06.54
	9194	R	20.09.44		9538	W	24.09.54		9663	W	01.12.56
	9713	W	?		10812	PW	31.03.56		10586	PW	11.04.58
	9364	R	06.09.54	**5175**	9279	W	26.08.35		10445	W	01.03.62
	10808	PW	08.08.55		9712	W	17.05.44		9261	W	17.04.63
	10525	W	03.09.55		10586	PW	19.07.47		9835	W	11.11.64
	9198	R	08.08.64		10503	W	02.01.50	**5179**	9283	W	04.09.35
5172	9276	W	15.08.35		9216	R	23.01.50		9727	W	07.08.41
	9247	W	11.09.46		10783	R	31.01.53		9283	W	18.08.41
	9277	W	15.12.48		9835	W	20.01.55		9259	W	11.02.44
	9107	R	28.10.49		10718	PW	08.10.55		9314	W	21.07.45
	9277	W	30.10.49		10695	PW	11.06.56		9659	W	25.06.47
	9725	W	19.11.49		10511	W	16.11.56		9269	W	07.07.47
	10579	PW	07.05.51		9283	W	27.03.58		9283	W	09.08.47
	9209	R	15.04.52	**5176**	9280	W	26.08.35		9067	R	11.02.49
	9727	W	07.02.53		9177	R	14.11.38		9242	W	05.09.50
					9727	W	10.04.47		9067	R	01.10.50

Engine no.	Tender no.	Type	Fitted	Engine no.	Tender no.	Type	Fitted	Engine no.	Tender no.	Type	Fitted
5179	10813	PW	23.07.53	5204	9308	W	28.10.35	5235	9471	W	17.08.36
	9317	W	18.11.53	5205	9309	W	28.10.35		9656	W	29.03.46
	9275	W	03.05.58		9239	W	29.01.52		9200	R	05.12.57
5180	9284	W	10.09.35	5206	9310	W	05.11.35		4999	Corr	11.12.59
5181	9285	W	10.09.35		10470	W	?	5236	9472	W	20.08.36
	9487	W	18.04.64	5207	9311	W	05.11.35		9315	W	14.06.45
5182	9286	W	11.09.35	5208	9312	W	05.11.35		9058	R	10.11.45
	9301	W	12.11.55	5209	9313	W	04.11.35		9318	W	?
	10494	W	13.12.60	5210	9314	W	12.11.35		10689	PW	?
5183	9287	W	17.09.35		9233	W	16.06.45	5237	9473	W	20.08.36
	9831	W	06.10.53	5211	9315	W	11.11.35		9071	R	18.04.46
	9190	R	03.11.56		9305	W	28.11.42	5238	9474	W	21.08.36
	9176	R	12.05.61	5212	9316	W	12.11.35		9560	W	31.08.45
	10719	PW	19.05.61	5213	9317	W	18.11.35		10608	PW	16.10.55
5184	9288	W	17.09.35		9601	W	?	5239	9475	W	28.08.36
	9543	W	30.11.45		10684	PW	30.05.53		9136	R	?
	9535	W	17.04.57		10685	PW	17.02.56	5240	9476	W	28.08.36
5185	9289	W	18.09.35		9545	W	10.08.56		9627	W	?
	9254	W	28.03.56		9487	W	11.07.57	5241	9477	W	31.08.36
5186	9290	W	20.09.35		9285	W	11.04.64		9835	W	08.05.46
	9057	R	23.01.46		10510	W	02.12.64		9177	R	04.02.49
5187	9291	W	23.09.35	5214	9318	W	18.11.35		9666	W	14.09.56
	9497	W	17.11.64		9187	R	06.02.43	5242	9478	W	04.09.36
	9676	W	?		9190	R	?	5243	9479	W	04.09.36
5188	9292	W	23.09.35		9823	W	26.02.54	5244	9480	W	04.09.36
	9110	R	07.04.38		9107	R	23.04.55	5245	9481	W	14.09.36
	9137	R	21.06.40		9636	W	03.03.56		10579	PW	?
	9110	R	27.07.40		10618	PW	21.09.57		10808	PW	24.11.53
	9166	R	28.07.44		10510	W	22.11.65		9364	R	08.08.55
	10721	PW	22.02.64	5215	9319	W	19.11.35		9710	W	15.02.57
5189	9293	W	23.09.35		10735	W	18.07.65		9835	W	12.05.58
5190	9294	W	01.10.35	5216	9320	W	25.11.35		9261	W	11.11.64
5191	9295	W	01.10.35		9246	W	17.03.52	5246	9482	W	14.09.36
5192	9296	W	30.09.35		9000	Proto	23.01.59		9536	W	07.12.60
	9069	R	17.05.43		9557	W	15.02.61	5247	9483	W	14.09.36
	9296	W	25.05.43	5217	9321	W	25.11.35	5248	9484	W	21.09.36
	9032	R	20.02.44		10538	PW	08.08.64		9622	W	27.08.55
	9060	R	06.02.45	5218	9322	W	26.11.35	5249	9485	W	18.09.36
	9071	R	06.07.45		9290	W	28.04.49		10446	W	?
	9364	R	18.04.46		10709	PW	06.06.61		9000	Proto	?
	9031	R	28.01.48	5219	9323	W	29.11.35		10683	PW	21.10.63
	9364	R	10.02.48		10555	PW	07.05.48		9197	R	?
	9027	R	07.07.49		10537	PW	25.05.55	5250	9486	W	18.09.36
	9068	R	18.10.56		10588	PW	15.11.56	5251	9487	W	25.09.36
	9715	W	30.11.57	5220	9324	W	29.11.35		9280	W	05.02.43
5193	9297	W	09.10.35		10566	W	?		9247	W	30.09.44
	9613	W	26.04.44		9263	W	02.11.63		9276	W	12.09.46
	9300	W	?	5221	9325	W	29.11.35		10581	PW	23.12.49
5194	9298	W	09.10.35		9290	W	23.01.46		10586	PW	24.04.52
	9267	W	10.08.42		9322	W	28.04.49		10674	PW	06.12.52
	9298	W	16.11.42	5222	9326	W	09.12.35		10677	PW	25.09.53
	9062	R	15.12.44	5223	9327	W	09.12.35		9591	W	06.10.53
	9777	W	20.06.47		9524	W	22.12.56		10681	PW	16.08.54
	9545	W	10.02.50		10799	PW	20.10.62		10674	PW	19.05.55
	9721	W	08.08.56		10787	R	06.11.63		10689	PW	28.01.56
	10509	W	23.04.65	5224	9328	W	10.12.35		9716	W	21.12.57
5195	9299	W	09.10.35	5225	9461	W	27.07.36		9015	R	20.09.61
5196	9300	W	09.10.35		10558	W	12.03.65	5252	9488	W	24.09.36
5197	9301	W	15.10.35		10825	PW	?	5253	9489	W	25.09.36
	9244	W	07.01.49	5226	9462	W	27.07.36		9851	W	18.07.65
	9535	W	15.12.51		10575	W	05.01.60	5254	9490	W	05.10.36
	9543	W	17.04.57	5227	9463	W	28.07.36	5255	9491	W	05.10.36
5198	9302	W	15.10.35		9500	W	08.01.46	5256	9492	W	05.10.36
	9002	Proto	21.06.44	5228	9464	W	31.07.36		9531	W	21.06.39
5199	9303	W	15.10.35		9848	W	13.01.61		9492	W	28.07.39
5200	9304	W	21.10.35	5229	9465	W	31.07.36	5257	9493	W	13.10.36
	10442	W	03.11.42		10724	PW	11.05.61	5258	9494	W	13.10.36
	10636	PW	26.01.67	5230	9466	W	12.08.36		9621	W	14.12.45
5201	9305	W	22.10.35	5231	9467	W	11.08.36	5259	9495	W	13.10.36
	9569	W	01.06.39		9632	W	29.07.52	5260	9496	W	17.10.36
	9164	R	?	5232	9468	W	13.08.36		9589	W	12.09.58
5202	9306	W	21.10.35	5233	9469	W	14.08.36		10557	W	?
	10559	W	13.06.64		9651	W	24.05.66	5261	9497	W	17.10.36
5203	9307	W	28.10.35	5234	9470	W	17.08.36		9291	W	17.11.64
	9254	W	14.11.53		10573	W	13.06.64				
	9289	W	21.03.56								

Engine no.	Tender no.	Type	Fitted
5262	9498	W	21.10.36
5263	9499	W	21.10.36
5264	9500	W	23.10.36
	9256	W	11.05.44
5265	9501	W	23.10.36
	9509	W	08.08.46
5266	9502	W	27.10.36
	10503	W	27.10.51
	9477	W	15.12.55
5267	9503	W	27.10.36
	9578	W	08.02.43
	9531	W	15.01.44
	9280	W	15.02.46
5268	9504	W	30.10.36
	9297	W	26.04.44
5269	9505	W	03.11.36
5270	9506	W	04.11.36
	9191	R	08.10.46
	9204	R	21.11.57
5271	9507	W	04.11.36
	10454	W	?
	10432	W	16.05.64
5272	9508	W	07.11.36
5273	9509	W	10.11.36
	9501	W	08.08.46
5274	9510	W	10.11.36
	10253	R	19.04.55
5275	9511	W	13.11.36
	9474	W	31.08.45
5276	9512	W	14.11.36
	9163	R	23.02.46
5277	9513	W	14.11.36
	9515	W	08.02.43
	9109	R	28.07.44
	10442	W	08.06.59
	9584	W	06.01.62
5278	9514	W	20.11.36
	9649	W	21.10.44
5279	9515	W	24.11.36
	9513	W	08.02.43
	9523	W	?
5280	9516	W	24.11.36
	9011	R	23.12.63
5281	9517	W	27.11.36
	9215	R	12.07.52
	10715	PW	13.11.53
	9198	R	19.03.55
	10525	W	01.11.64
	9657	W	02.12.65
5282	9518	W	27.11.36
	9624	W	25.09.57
	10456	W	23.01.60
5283	9519	W	28.11.36
5284	9520	W	04.12.36
	9085	R	05.09.64
5285	9521	W	08.12.36
	9667	W	12.12.57
5286	9522	W	08.12.36
	10701	PW	01.06.61
5287	9523	W	12.12.36
	9463	W	03.01.46
5288	9524	W	14.12.36
	9619	W	31.05.44
5289	9525	W	15.12.36
5290	9526	W	21.12.36
5291	9527	W	21.12.36
5292	9528	W	21.12.36
	10538	PW	14.07.50
	9321	W	08.08.64
5293	9529	W	23.12.36
	9535	W	07.11.49
	9244	W	15.12.51
5294	9530	W	28.12.36
	9231	W	07.09.38
	9660	W	06.11.55
	9623	W	28.11.60
5295	9531	W	23.12.36
	9492	W	21.06.39
	9531	W	29.07.39
	9578	W	07.01.44
	9652	W	30.01.46
5296	9532	W	28.12.36
	9684	W	05.05.55
5297	9533	W	28.12.36
5298	9534	W	28.12.36
	9000	Proto	21.03.46
	10591	CW	30.06.58
5299	9535	W	04.01.37
	9529	W	07.11.49
	9078	R	06.11.57
5300	9536	W	04.01.37
	9592	W	17.09.52
	9098	R	24.03.57
5301	9537	W	04.01.37
	10432	W	31.12.60
	10454	W	16.05.64
5302	9538	W	04.01.37
	9656	W	23.10.43
	9471	W	28.03.46
5303	9539	W	04.01.37
	9074	R	17.11.62
5304	9540	W	04.01.37
5305	9541	W	15.01.37
5306	9542	W	18.01.37
	9847	W	23.03.48
	9542	W	26.04.48
	9607	W	01.04.55
5307	9543	W	18.01.37
	9494	W	07.12.45
	9840	W	05.09.64
5308	9544	W	25.01.37
5309	9545	W	25.01.37
	9163	R	24.01.45
	9579	W	23.03.46
	9719	W	26.05.47
	9024	R	?
	9209	R	?
	9211	R	19.11.55
	9538	W	14.02.58
5310	9546	W	25.01.37
5311	9547	W	02.02.37
5312	9548	W	02.02.37
	9000	Proto	28.10.44
	9248	W	30.06.45
5313	9549	W	03.02.37
5314	9550	W	08.02.37
	9288	W	26.11.45
	9075	R	19.11.51
5315	9551	W	09.02.37
	9582	W	08.06.44
5316	9552	W	09.02.37
5317	9553	W	15.02.37
	9240	W	08.05.53
5318	9554	W	16.02.37
	10687	PW	10.09.52
	10571	W	22.11.55
	10441	W	?
5319	9555	W	11.02.37
	9040	R	16.11.44
	9058	R	12.12.44
	9663	W	16.11.45
	9708	W	24.10.47
	9663	W	29.10.48
	10816	PW	17.07.52
	9077	R	26.03.66
5320	9556	W	11.02.37
	9266	W	10.03.39
5320	9556	W	21.04.39
	9214	R	08.05.42
	9192	R	26.04.45
	9217	R	17.10.46
	9366	R	20.10.47
	9216	R	03.07.48
	9602	W	24.01.50
	9060	R	11.04.52
	9025	R	29.12.56
	9127	R	07.12.57
	10508	W	21.08.59
5321	9557	W	15.02.37
	9123	R	24.02.61
	9506	W	01.07.66
5322	9558	W	22.02.37
	9208	R	25.09.65
5323	9559	W	23.02.37
5324	9560	W	23.02.37
	9618	W	07.09.45
5325	9561	W	09.03.37
	9588	W	19.12.47
5326	9562	W	02.03.37
	10829	PW	23.07.54
5327	9563	W	02.03.37
5328	9564	W	09.03.37
	9315	W	07.11.45
	10833	PW	?
	10644	PW	16.06.66
5329	9565	W	10.03.37
	9292	W	13.02.52
	4633	3500	22.02.64
5330	9566	W	10.03.37
	9212	R	10.01.46
	9068	R	22.01.55
	9517	W	26.10.56
	10445	W	28.01.58
	9076	R	28.02.58
5331	9567	W	16.03.37
5332	9568	W	16.03.37
5333	9569	W	16.03.37
	9091	R	31.12.39
5334	9570	W	22.03.37
	9282	W	08.10.53
	10580	PW	24.02.56
	9823	W	22.11.57
5335	9571	W	23.03.37
5336	9572	W	22.03.37
	10282	R	09.02.57
	10448	W	14.12.60
5337	9573	W	30.03.37
	10513	W	19.10.47
5338	9574	W	30.03.37
5339	9575	W	30.03.37
5340	9576	W	05.04.37
5341	9577	W	05.04.37
5342	9578	W	05.04.37
	9503	W	08.02.43
	10473	W	22.02.64
5343	9579	W	12.04.37
	9262	W	02.04.46
5344	9580	W	12.04.37
	9683	W	25.02.54
5345	9581	W	12.04.37
5346	9582	W	20.04.37
	9604	W	14.06.44
	9253	W	19.10.45
5347	9583	W	20.04.37
5348	9584	W	20.04.37
	9105	R	27.12.45
5349	9585	W	26.04.37
5350	9586	W	26.04.37
5351	9587	W	27.04.37
5352	9588	W	05.05.37
	9561	W	19.12.47
5353	9589	W	06.05.37
	9083	R	02.11.56

Engine no.	Tender no.	Type	Fitted	Engine no.	Tender no.	Type	Fitted	Engine no.	Tender no.	Type	Fitted
5354	9590	W	06.05.37	5363	10593	PW	07.12.49	5382	9618	W	20.07.37
5355	9591	W	10.05.37		9162	R	30.05.52		9063	R	14.09.45
	9218	R	13.03.45		10593	PW	10.06.52		10489	W	21.07.51
	9827	W	31.05.47		9179	R	10.08.54		9348	R	18.04.64
	9070	R	16.03.51		10556	PW	07.04.56	5383	9619	W	20.07.37
	9260	W	25.08.51		9117	R	06.12.56		9675	W	05.06.44
	9211	R	23.09.54		10580	PW	29.11.57		10701	PW	16.05.59
	9275	W	10.11.55	5364	9600	W	31.05.37		9522	W	01.06.61
	10619	PW	22.02.57		9247	W	19.06.43	5384	9620	W	20.07.37
	9597	W	04.04.58		9280	W	27.09.44		10697	PW	04.06.54
5356	9592	W	10.05.37		9185	R	22.02.46		10674	PW	06.10.61
	9258	W	12.11.45		10549	PW	29.12.48	5385	9621	W	21.07.37
	9263	W	16.12.46		10812	PW	28.04.54		9584	W	15.12.45
	9005	R	26.03.49		10549	PW	06.05.54		10442	W	06.01.62
	9555	W	22.03.50		9029	R	03.09.55		9304	W	03.11.63
	9720	W	07.07.51		10510	W	04.05.56	5386	9622	W	21.07.37
	9835	W	07.05.52		10808	PW	06.02.58		9484	W	20.08.55
	10809	PW	24.04.54	5365	9601	W	31.05.37	5387	9623	W	28.07.37
	10579	PW	24.11.55		9185	R	28.11.50		9660	W	28.11.60
	9602	W	11.05.57		9215	R	28.12.50		9654	W	27.04.64
	10527	W	13.06.58		9837	W	?	5388	9624	W	28.07.37
	10526	W	12.09.59		9061	R	18.04.53		9518	W	25.09.57
5357	9593	W	10.05.37		9269	W	?	5389	9625	W	28.07.37
	9708	W	24.04.44		9212	R	22.01.55		9107	R	?
	9262	W	18.02.46		9716	W	?		9272	W	28.02.53
	9537	W	02.04.46		9212	R	05.08.55		9077	R	01.04.55
	9029	R	23.02.50		10533	W	06.01.56		9625	W	01.07.55
	10682	PW	?		10585	PW	03.02.56		9029	R	11.05.56
	10527	W	?		9723	W	09.01.57		10445	W	07.03.58
	9076	R	16.04.55		9716	W	09.03.57		10510	W	20.02.59
	9620	W	22.03.58		10533	W	09.01.58		9825	W	25.07.63
	10679	PW	09.10.64		9712	W	27.10.65	5390	9626	W	02.08.37
	9097	R	09.07.66		9593	W	21.10.66		9673	W	28.12.51
5358	9594	W	14.05.37	5366	9602	W	07.06.37		9650	W	20.01.65
	10582	PW	22.08.47		10597	PW	23.01.50	5391	9627	W	02.08.37
	9206	R	18.04.53		9274	W	05.10.50		9057	R	18.02.45
	9116	R	07.12.57		10604	PW	08.10.51		9578	W	26.01.46
	9064	R	09.07.60		9064	R	14.05.54	5392	9628	W	02.08.37
	10594	PW	30.01.62		9061	R	26.11.55		10362	W	08.06.66
5359	9595	W	15.05.37		10556	PW	21.07.61	5393	9629	W	09.08.37
	9874	W	23.08.45	5367	9603	W	07.06.37	5394	9630	W	09.08.37
	9599	W	04.09.45		9665	W	04.06.54		9235	W	14.07.45
	9060	R	13.05.48		9097	R	02.12.54	5395	9631	W	10.08.37
	10504	W	27.08.49		10678	PW	21.01.56	5396	9632	W	16.08.37
	9596	W	?		9829	W	26.11.62		9117	R	24.07.43
5360	9596	W	17.05.37		9554	W	28.06.35		9317	W	09.09.53
	9715	W	23.04.48	5368	9604	W	07.06.37		9198	R	29.09.53
	9663	W	17.07.52		9302	W	20.06.44		9107	R	21.03.55
	9481	W	26.11.54		9045	R	16.01.67		9823	W	23.04.55
	10679	PW	16.05.57	5369	9605	W	14.06.37		9215	R	23.06.56
	9120	R	23.09.60	5370	9606	W	14.06.37		9625	W	01.11.57
	9777	W	06.09.62		9638	W	07.11.62		10510	W	25.07.63
5361	9597	W	24.05.37	5371	9607	W	14.06.37		9285	W	02.12.64
	9265	W	25.12.41		9542	W	01.04.55	5397	9633	W	16.08.37
	9216	R	10.01.47		10699	PW	08.01.65	5398	9634	W	16.08.37
	9366	R	03.07.48	5372	9608	W	21.06.37		10099	W	05.02.55
	9023	R	12.08.48	5373	9609	W	21.06.37		9204	R	12.01.57
	9268	W	09.11.51		9292	W	29.04.44		9191	R	02.11.57
	9005	R	23.02.54		9565	W	13.02.52	5399	9635	W	20.08.37
	10511	W	29.01.59	5374	9610	W	21.06.37		9211	R	19.07.61
	9556	W	30.09.61	5375	9611	W	24.06.37		10630	PW	22.02.64
5362	9598	W	24.05.37		9169	R	25.01.64	5400	9636	W	20.08.37
	9727	W	12.01.43		10665	PW	15.04.66		9710	W	15.03.54
	9116	R	14.10.46	5376	9612	W	24.06.37		10603	PW	03.12.55
	9597	W	01.07.48	5377	9613	W	24.06.37	5401	9637	W	20.08.37
	9179	R	09.12.49		9609	W	27.04.44		9687	W	14.10.42
	10505	W	18.10.51		9113	R	13.03.51		9113	R	21.07.43
	10620	PW	14.03.52		9646	W	09.10.51		9609	W	13.03.51
	9847	W	18.06.52		10663	PW	16.10.64	5402	9638	W	27.08.37
	9725	W	07.01.56	5378	9614	W	02.07.37		9606	W	07.11.62
	9710	W	30.07.64		9309	W	08.03.60		9592	W	15.01.65
5363	9599	W	31.05.37		10668	PW	22.02.64		10608	PW	19.01.65
	9713	W	13.08.45	5379	9615	W	02.07.37	5403	9639	W	27.08.37
	9266	W	16.01.48	5380	9616	W	12.07.37		9111	R	20.06.39
	9211	R	15.07.48	5381	9617	W	12.07.37	5404	9640	W	27.08.37
									10640	PW	11.08.62

75

Engine no.	Tender no.	Type	Fitted	Engine no.	Tender no.	Type	Fitted	Engine no.	Tender no.	Type	Fitted
5405	9641	W	03.09.37	5433	9669	W	09.11.37	5456	9724	W	?
5406	9642	W	03.09.37		10676	PW	07.05.55		9101	R	29.08.53
5407	9643	W	03.09.37		9594	W	25.01.57		10693	PW	09.10.54
5408	9644	W	13.09.37	5434	9670	W	09.11.37		10691	PW	21.09.56
	10489	W	18.04.64	5435	9671	W	16.11.37		9206	R	30.11.57
5409	9645	W	13.09.37		10099	W	08.02.57		10693	PW	08.11.61
5410	9646	W	13.09.37	5436	9843	W	16.11.37	5457	9713	W	10.10.38
	9113	R	09.10.51	5437	9673	W	16.11.37		9668	W	17.09.43
5411	9647	W	20.09.37		9626	W	28.12.51		9198	R	25.08.48
5412	9648	W	20.09.37	5438	9674	W	23.11.37		9059	R	03.12.53
5413	9649	W	20.09.37	5439	9675	W	23.11.37		9101	R	10.11.55
	9548	W	25.10.44		9551	W	06.06.44		10674	PW	16.11.57
	9666	W	26.11.55	5440	9676	W	23.11.37		10697	PW	06.10.61
	9177	R	14.09.56	5441	9677	W	30.11.37		9820	W	22.10.63
5414	9650	W	28.09.37	5442	9678	W	30.11.37	5458	9714	W	11.10.38
5415	9651	W	28.09.37		9662	W	22.03.49		9530	W	24.12.41
	9103	R	18.08.45	5443	9679	W	30.11.37		9164	R	15.10.45
5416	9652	W	28.09.37		9271	W	24.09.43		9718	W	01.03.46
	9687	W	06.02.46		9257	W	09.02.50		9821	W	31.08.53
	10557	W	21.02.61		9838	W	23.04.53		9718	W	15.02.54
	9589	W	20.09.63		9709	W	29.03.54	5459	9715	W	14.10.38
5417	9653	W	04.10.37		9715	W	25.06.55		9708	W	09.08.42
5418	9654	W	04.10.37		10691	PW	30.11.57		9593	W	24.04.44
5419	9655	W	04.10.37	5444	9680	W	07.12.37		10550	PW	12.05.52
	10498	W	03.01.59		9239	W	17.12.43		9593	W	07.10.52
5420	9656	W	11.10.37		9309	W	29.01.52		9257	W	02.04.53
	9538	W	23.10.43		9614	W	08.03.60		9593	W	10.04.53
	9166	R	05.11.43	5445	9681	W	07.12.37		10546	PW	22.02.54
	9110	R	28.07.44		9659	W	12.01.66		10698	PW	19.02.57
5421	9657	W	11.10.37	5446	9682	W	07.12.37		10682	PW	18.10.62
	10612	PW	29.07.63		9637	W	17.01.44	5460	9716	W	18.10.38
5422	9658	W	11.10.37	5447	9683	W	14.12.37		9477	W	22.05.46
5423	9659	W	18.10.37		9580	W	16.02.54		10679	PW	10.12.55
	9261	W	09.01.45	5448	9684	W	14.12.37		9819	W	01.09.56
	9713	W	02.02.45		10501	W	04.12.46		9250	W	04.06.57
	9599	W	13.08.45	5449	9685	W	14.12.37		9481	W	11.06.57
	9874	W	04.09.45		10808	PW	10.08.66		9250	W	18.01.58
	9595	W	25.09.45	5450	9686	W	21.12.37		9116	R	19.10.60
	10505	W	12.03.46		10475	W	16.07.56		9726	W	08.06.62
	9595	W	12.04.46	5451	9687	W	21.12.37	5461	9717	W	19.10.38
	9601	W	30.05.53		9205	R	14.02.39		10595	PW	12.08.50
	9593	W	26.04.58	5452	9708	W	15.09.38		10616	PW	03.03.51
	9819	W	02.05.58		9715	W	09.08.42		10595	PW	?
	9077	R	23.03.65		9719	W	05.04.44		9107	R	?
	10816	PW	26.03.66		9718	W	17.05.44		9272	W	01.04.55
5424	9660	W	18.10.37		9164	R	26.02.46		9723	W	08.03.57
	9231	W	06.11.55		9267	W	27.07.49		9028	R	11.08.58
	9569	W	15.04.66		9175	R	06.10.51		9314	W	10.12.63
5425	9661	W	18.10.37	5453	9709	W	19.09.38	5462	9718	W	31.10.38
	10808	PW	?		9261	W	18.07.40		9242	W	17.05.40
5426	9662	W	26.10.37		9709	W	31.07.40		10591	CW	23.05.47
	9678	W	22.03.49		9727	W	31.12.41		10548	PW	25.05.47
5427	9663	W	26.10.37		9598	W	12.01.43		9242	W	27.05.47
	9078	R	17.11.45		9724	W	11.02.63		9825	W	10.03.49
	9529	W	26.10.57	5454	9710	W	27.09.38		9837	W	02.03.56
5428	9664	W	26.10.37		9163	R	12.06.44		9031	R	15.03.56
5429	9665	W	02.11.37		9875	W	10.10.44		9719	W	02.05.36
	9366	R	28.03.47		9163	R	04.11.44		9673	W	18.07.56
	9217	R	20.10.47		9827	W	01.01.45		10597	PW	20.02.57
5430	9666	W	02.11.37		9264	W	06.04.46	5463	9719	W	07.11.38
	9288	W	23.01.54		9209	R	11.02.46		9715	W	05.04.44
5431	9667	W	02.11.37		9213	R	14.09.47		9725	W	28.10.44
	9521	W	14.12.57	5455	9711	W	28.09.38		9277	W	25.11.49
5432	9668	W	09.11.37		9120	R	07.09.44		9064	R	09.01.51
	9713	W	17.09.43		9826	W	16.01.45		9015	R	?
	9178	R	02.02.45		9198	R	10.09.46		9277	W	15.10.52
	10599	PW	12.08.49		9668	W	21.08.48		9717	W	11.02.56
	9538	W	?		9116	R	09.06.50		10783	R	19.05.56
	9260	W	24.09.54		9107	R	25.08.50		10507	W	31.07.56
	10601	PW	09.06.56		10619	PW	20.09.51		9668	W	24.08.56
	10509	W	18.10.58		10618	PW	30.12.54		9022	R	27.10.56
	9593	W	26.11.64		9714	W	12.04.56	5464	9720	W	08.11.38
	10509	W	29.01.65	5456	9712	W	04.10.38		9032	R	30.11.40
	9721	W	23.04.65		9279	W	14.05.44		9296	W	20.02.44
	10626	PW	20.08.65		10672	PW	04.04.50		10640	PW	04.02.52

Engine no.	Tender no.	Type	Fitted	Engine no.	Tender no.	Type	Fitted	Engine no.	Tender no.	Type	Fitted
5464	10585	PW	21.10.53	**5467**	10813	PW	15.01.54	**5470**	9726	W	12.12.38
	9833	W	14.11.53		9273	W	30.04.55		10813	PW	30.10.53
	9215	R	22.10.54		10509	W	03.03.56		10592	PW	22.12.53
	9266	W	26.10.54		10601	PW	07.11.58		9833	W	28.10.54
	10507	W	01.10.55		10693	PW	?		10684	PW	30.04.61
	9835	W	06.10.55		9206	R	08.11.64		9716	W	05.11.63
	10713	PW	03.05.56		9298	W	26.03.66	**5471**	9727	W	12.12.38
	10592	PW	28.09.56	**5468**	9724	W	01.12.38		9283	W	07.08.41
5465	9721	W	21.11.38		9061	R	10.03.43		9727	W	18.08.41
	10523	W	29.06.50		9879	W	23.03.44		9176	R	19.08.41
	10603	PW	?		9061	R	25.03.44		9268	W	26.08.41
	10619	PW	10.01.55		9216	R	17.01.53		9709	W	18.06.42
	10593	PW	24.03.56		10680	PW	08.01.57		9194	R	17.05.44
	9296	W	02.09.54		10677	PW	21.03.57		9184	R	03.09.44
	10593	PW	12.02.61	**5469**	9725	W	05.12.38		9264	W	27.09.44
5466	9722	W	25.11.38		9715	W	15.11.48		9827	W	06.04.45
	9229	W	09.07.55		9596	W	21.04.48		9218	R	31.05.47
	9275	W	01.03.57		9717	W	15.07.50		10505	W	16.09.50
	9669	W	25.04.58		9596	W	31.07.50		9282	W	?
	10699	PW	05.05.62		10502	W	?		9823	W	03.04.53
	10582	PW	25.01.64		9719	W	10.12.54		9190	R	20.03.54
5467	9723	W	30.11.38		9269	W	18.05.56		10594	PW	23.08.58
	9260	W	02.09.42		9777	W	06.11.56		9064	R	27.01.62
	9723	W	16.09.42		9120	R	06.09.62		9287	W	10.03.64
	9176	R	03.06.48		9595	W	14.04.64		9591	W	06.07.65
	10506	W	07.02.51								

All the Armstrong Whitworth-built engines had welded tenders which saved over a ton in weight compared with the riveted type. 5445 from Shrewsbury shed, which was pictured on 18th April 1938 at Craven Arms, kept tender No.9681 until January 1966.

V. R. Webster/Kidderminster Railway Museum

5068 slogs up the Lickey with eight coaches, assisted by one of Bromsgrove's Jinties. The picture was taken before the engine received its first domed boiler in May 1937 and it still has the raised top feed pipes characteristic of a Vulcan Foundry Class 5. *www.rail-online.co.uk*

5145 pilots Jubilee *Victory* on an up express near Shap summit on 18th May 1948. It was allocated to Bushbury from October 1946 until July 1948, when it moved to Shrewsbury. It received its first domed boiler in March 1944, probably when it was repainted in wartime plain black livery, but reverted to the domeless type in March 1949, at which date it was renumbered as 45145. It is paired with its original welded tender which it kept until withdrawn.
W. B. Wilson/Rail Archive Stephenson

6 LIVERIES, NUMBERPLATES AND BUILDERS' PLATES

6.1 Liveries

With three short-lived exceptions only, the class whilst in revenue service always was painted black, although the insignia and lining-out varied between batches and over the lifetime of the engines.

6.2 5000-5224

When built, the engines carried the standard LMS intermediate passenger black livery lined with a single $^{1}/_{2}$"

wide vermillion line on the running plate, cylinder cladding, cab and tender whilst the boiler and firebox cladding bands carried a $^{1}/_{2}$" wide lining. The buffer beams were vermillion with a 1" black edging. Vulcan Foundry applied the lining around all four edges of the cab side sheet and below the cab windows, whereas on the Crewe and Armstrong Whitworth built engines the lining was carried straight to the cab roof. The serif insignia were gold leaf shaded red to the right and

TABLE 6.1 LIVERIES AND PLATES AS BUILT

Nos.	Built by	Smokebox numberplate	Cab insignia	Tender insignia and spacing	Builders' plates
5000-19	Crewe Works	Scroll	12" serif	14" serif at 60"	Oval on front framing
5020-69	Vulcan Foundry	Scroll	12" serif	14" serif at 40"	Oval on smokebox side
5070-74	Crewe Works	Scroll	12" serif	14" serif at 60"	Oval on front framing
5075-5106	Vulcan Foundry	Scroll	12" serif	14" serif at 40"	Oval on front framing
5107-11				14" serif at 40"	Oval on smokebox side
5112-24				14" serif at 60"	Oval on smokebox side
5125-26	Armstrong Whitworth	Scroll	12" serif	14" serif at 40"	Rectangular on smokebox side
5127-36/7				14" serif at 40"	Rectangular on front framing
5137/8-5224				14" serif at 60"	Rectangular on front framing
5225-5451	Armstrong Whitworth	Sans-serif	10" Sans-serif	14" Sans-serif at 60"	Rectangular on front framing
5452-71	Crewe	Scroll	12" serif	14" serif at 60"	Oval on front framing

lake below; the cab numbers were 12", with the power classification (5P with 5F below) in 3" numerals immediately below the side windows.

The 14" LMS letters on the tender were spaced at 40" on Vulcan Foundry nos.5020-69, 5075-5111 and Armstrong Whitworth engines from 5125 up to 5136 (and possibly 5137); those following had the same standard 60" spacing used on the Crewe-built locomotives.

6.3 LMS 1936 livery

5225-5451 were delivered from Armstrong Whitworth in the new LMS 1936 sans-serif style, lined in vermilion with 14" tender lettering spaced at 60" and 10" cab numbers in gold, shaded vermilion transfers. The power classification was in 2" gold characters, with the 5P immediately below the side screens and the 5F underneath. The change was short-lived and by mid-1937 the LMS had reverted to a serif style, albeit with cheaper yellow rather than gold insignia. A number of the earlier locomotives were however repainted in the 1936 style including 5002, 5005, 5014, 5023, 5025, 5027, 5029, 5031, 5032, 5036, 5038, 5041-5047, 5051, 5055, 5059, 5067, 5091, 5093, 5097, 5113, 5114, 5122, 5124, 5125, 5131, 5154, 5180, 5182, 5187, 5188, 5191 and 5200. Some did not receive the livery until mid-1938 as stocks of transfers were slowly used up.

6.4 Final pre-war livery

When 5452-5471 appeared from Crewe in 1938 they had chrome yellow, shaded vermillion scroll and serif characters similar to those used on 5000-5224. The tender letters were still 14" high but the cab numbers reverted to 12" high. Only a handful of the Armstrong Whitworth engines built with the 1936 livery were repainted before the war and received the

scroll and serif transfers with 12" numerals as applied to 5452-71. These included 5239, 5255, 5281, 5283, 5293, 5298, 5301, 5311 and 5356.

Some locomotives repainted in Scotland received 10" figures and it has been suggested that St. Rollox used gold rather than yellow transfers, still with plain vermilion rather than vermilion and lake shading. It is impossible to determine from photographs which of 5000-5224 were repainted prior to the war, except those given 10" numbers such as 5014, 5015, 5150, 5151, 5152, 5171 and 5194.

6.5 Wartime

During the war, in the interests of economy, the few full repaints of Class 5s were plain black although many engines never were repainted and probably kept traces of their original lining for many years, even though it was invisible under the increasing layers of grime. The stock numbers still were mostly in 12" characters, although from around early 1941 they were repositioned just under the cab windows, in line with the tender lettering. The power classification, if it was used at all, was below the number and abbreviated to 5. 5009, 5014, 5015, 5029, 5031, 5043, 5050, 5051, 5059, 5065, 5114, 5116, 5156, 5159, 5190, 5202, 5217, 5228, 5276, 5306, 5323, 5326, 5339, 5344, 5346, 5349, 5357, 5370, 5373, 5376, 5379, 5383, 5398, 5404, 5411, 5416, 5418, 5446, 5448, 5450, 5466 and 5468 had 12" numbers and were without lining. 5084, 5366, 5389, 5453, 5461 and 5465 had 10" numerals and 5005 was still in unlined black with yellow and vermillion transfers in 1948, although its numbers were in the lower position. After the war, plain black continued for a short time and most re-paints had scroll and serif characters in yellow (plain or red-shaded), usually with the cab numbers in the 'high' position.

Vulcan Foundry-built 5044 in the standard LMS intermediate passenger black livery lined with vermillion has 14" LMS tender letters closely spaced at 40". The cab numbers are 12", with the power classification (5P with 5F below) in 3" numerals immediately below the side windows. On the Vulcan engines, the lining was around all four edges of the cab side sheet and below the cab windows, whereas on the Crewe and Armstrong Whitworth-built engines the lining was carried straight to the cab roof. 5044 has an oval workplate above the top of the steampipe.

6.6 Post-war LMS livery

In 1946 the LMS replaced the wartime austerity with a new livery style using sans-serif characters in pale straw with inset maroon lining. It had 14" letters and two sizes of numbers, and normally appeared on newly built locomotives rather than repainted ones. A few of the early Class 5s, however, received the 1946 characters with unlined black paint, the numbers being placed just below the cab windows in line with the tender letters and the power classification underneath. Engines which received 1946 characters with 10" numerals

included 5015, 5018, 5023, 5051, 5084, 5156, 5159 and 5165. Those with 12" numerals included 5031, 5043, 5050, 5059, 5065, 5075, 5088, 5114, 5116, 5148, 5166, 5176, 5190, 5202, 5209, 5217, 5226, 5243, 5281, 5291, 5293, 5298, 5313, 5314, 5406 and 5426.

6.7 Early British Railways transitional liveries

Between 13th and 28th January 1948, three new Class 5s were painted at Crewe Works in different liveries for comparative purposes so that a decision could be made on a standard livery for the newly nationalised railway. All had the letter 'M' before

The second Vulcan Foundry order as shown by ex-works 5104 had a number of detail differences compared with the first (5020-69). There were domed covers on the firebox shoulders indicating the 21-element superheater boiler, the chimney was lower, the plain combination lever was now fluted, the top feed pipes were recessed and the tender axlebox covers had cruciform strengthening ribs. 5104 still has closely spaced tender lettering, but its workplate is on the frames rather than above the steampipe.
Real Photographs

A further livery change part-way through the second Vulcan Foundry order is shown by brand new 5112 which has the LMS on the tender widely spaced at 60" like the Crewe-built rather than the earlier 40" spacing of 5104. There are no longer stiffening webs on the wheels at the rear of the four spokes adjacent to the crankpin; these were dispensed with from 5095 onwards.   *Real Photographs*

5421 is one of the later Armstrong Whitworth engines in the short-lived 1936 sans-serif livery. All the 227 Class 5s built there in 1936/7 were finished in this livery, the largest number of engines painted in this style. Tender lettering was 14" spaced at 60" and the 10" cab numbers were in gold, shaded vermilion transfers. The power classification was in 2" gold characters, with the 5P immediately below the side screens and the 5F underneath. The rectangular pattern worksplates on the front frames had raised, polished characters and borders and red backgrounds.

National Railway Museum

Only a few Class 5s were repainted in the short-lived 1936 livery. Amongst them was 5180, which was allocated to Derby (17A) from September 1937.

5080 from Farnley Junction, seen in the late-1930s, at Skelton Junction in 1936 livery which was probably applied during a Heavy Scheduled overhaul carried out between 17th March and 16th April 1937. It was allocated to Farnley Junction in March 1935, moved to Low Moor in August 1935, and back to Farnley Junction in November 1936 where it remained until its penultimate posting to Stourton in 1966.

C. M & J. M. Bentley

The first sloping throatplate engine, 45225 pictured at York in 1948, was one of three Class 5s selected for painting in the 'experimental' LNWR style livery, emerging from Horwich at the end of April 1948, renumbered and in the same lined black as 45292 and with BRITISH RAILWAYS on the tender. All three had block style smokebox numbers which were used by St. Rollox Works for some time before moving eventually to the standard Gill Sans type employed by Crewe.

R. K. Blencowe

Initially, the tenders carried BRITISH RAILWAYS in full, but this was replaced by the larger version of the early BR 'lion on a wheel' emblem from around August 1949. It consisted of a lion standing sideways over a wheel on which was a panel incorporating the wording BRITISH RAILWAYS. There were right and left handed versions of this emblem so the lion could face forward no matter on which side of the tender it was placed. St. Rollox began using the new emblem with 45213 in week ending 6th October 1949; the engine received the larger 10" numerals also.

At the end of 1956 the emblem was replaced with crests approved by the College of Arms which were in a circle with the words BRITISH RAILWAYS across the centre, at first with forward facing lions on each side, but after complaints from the College of Arms all lions faced left; most of the class received this new style.

With the onset of electrification from around 1960 'electric overhead' warning flashes, white enamel plates with the symbolic warning sign of forked lightning (in red), were fixed to those parts of the locomotive where footplate crews could come into contact with overhead wires.

From December 1963 all locomotives receiving a full repaint were supposed to be painted in plain unlined black. However this does seem not to have been implemented by every works and engines outshopped from St. Rollox in early 1964 still were being lined out.

Cowlairs and Inverurie continued the practice of painting the shed allocation LNER style on the front buffer beam in full into the 1960s; examples recorded were CARLISLE CANAL, EDGE HILL LIVERPOOL and PERTH SOUTH. But sometimes it was wrong and on 2nd May 1964, 45143 of Shrewsbury (shed code 6D), was ex-works with CHESTER NORTHGATE painted on the buffer beam; this shed was

code 6D until it closed completely on 4th January 1960. The code was subsequently allocated to Shrewsbury from 9th September 1963. From 1st September 1964 certain classes were prohibited from working south of Crewe over electrified lines. These had a broad diagonal yellow line on the cab side. This restriction did not apply to the Class 5s.

6.9 Numberplates

5000-5224 had scroll and serif pattern front numberplates whereas 5225-5451 had plates with sans-serif numbers to match their 1936 block style insignia. The 1938 engines, 5452-71, reverted to the scroll and serif pattern.

The British Railways smokebox door numberplates fitted at Crewe on the engines renumbered and released during April and early May 1948 used the pre-war scroll pattern numbers; those recorded included 45034, 45076, 45102, 45249, 45260, 45261, 45326, 45403, 45411 and 45433 together with 45292 for its appearance at Marylebone. As far as is known all were later replaced by British Railways standard Gill Sans plates. At least two engines, 45410 and 45422, renumbered in June left Crewe Works with LMS 1946 type block number plates; those on 45422 had been replaced with Gill Sans by 1951. St. Rollox used these block style numbers for some time before moving to the standard Gill Sans type which had been used by Crewe from mid-1948 onwards. The three engines, 45217, 45225 and 45229, that were early recipients of the lined BR livery at Horwich in April 1948 also had block numbers as did 45253 when it represented the class in the 1948 Locomotive Exchanges.

6.10 Builders' plates

The styles and position of the makers' plates differed between the various batches. Crewe-built locomotives had oval plates with white characters on a black background fitted to the front framing at both sides. 5020-69 and 5075-5106 from

45150 at Crewe North on 12th May 1952 was fresh from a Light Intermediate repair at Crewe Works. It had been repainted in plain black with the first BR emblem. Initially, the tenders carried BRITISH RAILWAYS in full, but this was replaced by the larger version of the early BR 'lion on a wheel' emblem from around August 1949.

www.Rail-online.co.uk

An official photograph of 45080 shows the standard British Railways mixed traffic livery of black, lined with red, cream and grey which was the only variant carried by all of the class. The lettering and numerals were cream Gill Sans edged with a narrow black band. Locomotives repainted in English works had 8" numbers positioned in line with the tender lettering or emblem whereas in Scotland St. Rollox started using 10" numerals, only changing over to the 8" type in the mid-1950s. The power classification 5 was either immediately above or below the numerals in the same style, although when it changed to become 5MT, usually it appeared above the numbers.

Vulcan Foundry had the same pattern but fitted on both sides of the smokebox directly above the top of the steam pipe and above the ejector pipe, although from 5107 onwards they were moved to the front framing. The first two engines built by Armstrong Whitworth, 5125-26, had rectangular pattern plates with raised, polished characters and borders and red backgrounds positioned on the smokebox in the same place as the earlier Vulcan Foundry locomotives; on the remainder, 5127-5451, the plates were attached to the front framing.

The contractor-built engines had their works numbers on the plates, 4565-4614 for 5020-5069, 4618-4667 for 5075-5124, 1166-1265 for 5125-5224 and 1280-1506 for 5225-5451 respectively; they were omitted from the standard Crewe plates on 5000-5019/5070-5074 although numbers 216-40 were allocated to these engines.

When a spare set of frames was made in 1943 at Crewe to enable a quicker return of the engines to traffic, the makers' plates were not normally transferred to the new frames whereas the stock number went with the rest of the engine. Thus the plates on a particular engine often bore no relation to the plates when the engine was new, giving rise to numerous instances of the 'wrong' manufacturer being displayed on engines. Examples of this occurred in June 1943 when 5226 received the spare frames and its original ones, complete with Armstrong Whitworth works plates, were given to Vulcan Foundry-built 5027. Another example was in November 1950 when Vulcan Foundry 45020, the first Class 5 built, was fitted with the frames from Armstrong Whitworth 45130.

A standard oval maker's plate from Crewe Works.

This Vulcan Foundry maker's plate is from 45110 and includes the works number as well as the year built.

The engines built by Armstrong Whitworth had rectangular maker's plates with raised, polished characters and borders and red backgrounds. This plate is from 45234 and like the Vulcan plate includes the works number.

All the nameplates were cast and fitted at St. Rollox Works and used the same lettering style as on the few Jubilees whose plates had been made there. Because of the absence of splashers, the nameplates were mounted on back-plates over the leading driving wheels as shown on 5154 *Lanarkshire Yeomanry*.
Real Photographs

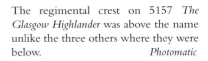

The regimental crest on 5157 *The Glasgow Highlander* was above the name unlike the three others where they were below. *Photomatic*

5158 *Glasgow Yeomanry* had the words "FIELD BRIGADE R.A.T.A." on a curved plate underneath and round the foot of the crest. The radius of its nameplate did not have as its centre the axle of the driving wheel beneath it, as was usual when a locomotive had a splasher, but was noticeably smaller.

5156 *Ayrshire Yeomanry* had the words "EARL OF CARRICK'S OWN" in very small lettering on a separate straight plate under the crest. Both the regimental crest and ancillary plates were attached by studs from the rear.
Real Photographs

7 NAMES

Four of the Class 5s received names, not when originally built, but later during the 1936/37 period. All were based on the Northern Division at the time of naming, 5154 and 5156 at Carlisle Kingmoor, with 5157 and 5158 at St. Rollox. In 1943 the two Carlisle engines were transferred to St. Rollox. The names were as follows:

5154 *Lanarkshire Yeomanry* (named 5th April 1937).

5156 *Ayrshire Yeomanry - Earl Of Carrick's Own* (named 19th September 1936).

5157 *The Glasgow Highlander* (named at Glasgow Central on 6th March 1936).

5158 *Glasgow Yeomanry - Field Brigade R.A.T.A.* (named at Glasgow Central on 22nd May 1936).

All the plates were cast and fitted at St. Rollox Works and used the same lettering style as on the few Jubilees whose plates had been made there. Because of the absence of splashers, the nameplates were mounted on backplates over the leading driving wheels. Regimental crests were fitted to each of them, that for 5157 being above the name and the others below. 5156 had the words "Earl Of Carrick's Own" in very small lettering on a separate straight plate under the crest, and both crest and ancillary plates were attached by studs from the rear. 5158 had the words "Field Brigade R.A.T.A." on a curved plate underneath and round the foot of the crest. The radius of its nameplate did not have as its centre the axle of the driving wheel beneath it, as was usual when a locomotive had a splasher, but was noticeably smaller.

Five drawings for the nameplates and plaques for these engines survived at St. Rollox Works and give some idea of how the final designs evolved.

Drawing G26764 (dated 24th February 1936) - the proposed arrangement of nameplate and plaque depicted the words *The Glasgow Highlander* in a straight line with a blank backing for a plaque above.

Drawing G26769 (dated 5th April 1936) - headed "arrangement of nameplate and plaque for *Glasgow Yeomanry*". This showed a curved plate with two line lettering and backing for a plaque above with a smaller size lettered straight plate beneath:

Top Line   *Queen's Own Royal*
Lower Line   *Glasgow Yeomanry*
Bottom Line   *Field Brigade R.A.T.A.* in small letters

The drawing had details for the steadying bracket also.

Drawing G26769A (undated). There were three drawings on this sheet:

1. Top Right – Same as on Drawing G26769 but the top line was in smaller lettering and was 'stepped'.

2. Top Left – Designated 'Type A'. The site of the plaque now was between the name plate as shown in Top Right but the plaque was fitted in between the name plate and the lower plate (*Field Brigade R.A.T.A.*)

3. Lower Left – Designated 'Type B'. As in Type 'A' but the radius of the stepped name plate had been shortened.

In 1957, two of the four named Class 5s, 45154 and 45156, were transferred from Scotland to Newton Heath and by the early 1960s their nameplates had disappeared. 45154 *Lanarkshire Yeomanry*, seen at Wigan North Western working an RCTS special on 24th September 1966, has had wooden replica plates fitted. The special was organised by the Lancashire and North West Branch and went from Wigan North Western to Aintree and Liverpool Riverside via Leigh and St. Helens, returning via Chorley and Horwich to Wigan Wallgate.

T. J. Edgington

Drawing G26769D (undated)and designated 'Type D'. This was as 'Type B' but 'THE' on the top line of the plate was removed and it specified:

Glasgow Yeomanry in 3 inch letters and

Field Brigade R.A.T.A. in ³/₄ inch letters in a straight line.

Drawing G26805A (undated). This was for *The Ayrshire Yeoman* and showed the words curved with a plaque underneath. Beneath the plaque on a straight plate in smaller letters was *Earl Of Carrick's Own*. It was titled "Proposed nameplate and plaque for the *Ayrshire Yeomanry*", not *Yeoman* as on the drawing.

7.1 Origins

The Lanarkshire Yeomanry was raised in the Upper Ward of Lanarkshire in 1819 and kept in service without a break. They fought at Gallipoli, in Palestine and on the Western Front in the 1914-18 war, after which it was reformed as a cavalry regiment. The Ayrshire Yeomanry was raised circa 1798 and known as the "Carrick Troop". It was re-raised at times after that to serve in the South African War, at Gallipoli and in Palestine in 1914-18. The Glasgow Highlander was the 9th Battalion of the Highland Light Infantry which landed in France in November 1914 and was one of the first Territorial Regiments to go into action in the 1914-18 war. The Glasgow Yeomanry was raised in 1797 in the Glasgow area and re-raised subsequently. It was converted to artillery in 1920 to form a two-battery army brigade. The term Yeoman comes from middle English and means 'a Freeholder under the rank of Gentleman and of respectable standing'.

7.2 The fifth named engine

It seems that a fifth engine also was to be named but there is conflicting evidence about whether actually it ran with nameplates and no photographic evidence at all. The locomotive was 5155 and the name is recorded as *Queens Edinburgh*.

The earliest reference was in two memoranda dated 19th February 1937 dealing with "Naming of Class 5 Engines". At the top of one of them is the name H. G. Ivatt Esq, St. Rollox, but it is not clear if he was the sender or the recipient because it is not signed. It stated "I have been informed that Major Murdoch, Second-in-Command of the Lanarkshire Regiment has been advised by Mr. Ballantyne that Engine No.5155 could be allocated to bear the name "Lanarkshire Yeomanry". This engine has, however, already been allocated to it the name "Queen's Edinburgh" and I have suggested to Mr. Ballantyne that either Engine No.5154 or Engine No.5159 be chosen. On hearing further from him I will write to you again".

The other memo has the name "J. Ballantyne Esq , Glasgow" at the top left hand corner and under the same heading reads: "With reference to the above, as Engine No.5155 has already been allocated the name of "Queen's Edinburgh" I suggest that Engine No.5154 or Engine No.5159 be chosen to bear the name "Lanarkshire Yeomanry".

The name then appeared in a booklet written by the late D. S. M. Barrie published and issued with the authority of the LMS, giving the names of engines 5154, 5156, 5157 and 5158 and also including 5155 *Queen's Edinburgh*. It was titled **Modern Locomotives of the LMS** and bears no date although it must have been after 29th June 1937 because the text mentions the speed record of 114mph made by 6220 *Coronation* when working the trial run of "The Coronation Scot" on that date.

5156 at Carlisle Citadel before removal of its vacuum pump in April 1938. It was built at Armstrong Whitworth in July 1935 and was allocated to Carlisle Kingmoor from January 1936 until February 1943. It was named *Ayrshire Yeomanry* on 19th September 1936.

Real Photographs

5031, at Derby on 24th April 1938, received a rebuilt domed boiler during a Heavy General repair from 22nd June to 29th July 1937 at which it acquired 1936 livery, although it has retained its original tall chimney. The top feed pipes now are recessed and a front footplate step added. 5031 had a BTH speed indicator fitted in February 1938 and lost its crosshead pump in July 1939. *T. G. Hepburn/Rail Archive Stephenson*

Subsequently the order was extended to cover the replacement by BTH gear of the speed indicators of other makes already fitted to certain locomotives including the Hasler equipment on 5278.

The Class 5 used in the 1937 tests was 5264, but as the removal of the gear from 5278 was mentioned in an instruction of March 1938, the gear evidently was not transferred to 5264, or if it was, it was restored to 5278 after the tests.

Work on the fitting of the Midland Division 4-6-0s soon was in hand, and the Works Manager at Derby reported on 19th March 1938 that 25 locomotives had been equipped. The completion date of this part of the programme is not known. By early 1939 various troubles had been encountered with the BTH equipment, involving its return to the manufacturers, and this delayed the progress of the work, which therefore was still in hand at the outbreak of World War Two. On 26th September 1939 an instruction was issued that "in view of the present crisis", no more locomotives should be fitted with speed indicators, and that indicators already fitted should be removed and stored when the locomotives next were in shops. However, there was a 'fair number' of indicators in stock at this time, and therefore the CME changed his mind. A further instruction was issued on 18th December 1939 that the fitting of speed indicators should be resumed, provided that material was available, and that the work would not delay normal repairs, nor interfere with work of greater priority.

The matter still was not settled and on 19th January 1940 another instruction was issued by the CME for the work to be suspended, only to be followed on 13th May 1940 by yet another order for it to be resumed.

At this time the only new locomotives of the classes covered by Job 5043 which had been built since the order was issued were Class 5s from 5452 onward and Pacifics from 6225

onward. These were intended to have speed indicators when built, but although the necessary brackets were fitted, the BTH equipment had not been delivered when the locomotives were ready for traffic, and they went into service without it. Some at least of the Class 5s received the equipment when visiting St. Rollox Works in 1941/2 and, as it was by then too late to charge this work to the original building order, authority was given for the fitting of the speed indicators to 5452-71 to be charged to Job 5043.

On 21st July 1942 the CME wrote to the Works Superintendents saying that BTH would not be able to supply any further complete indicators. "Since no priority can be given for this work", it would not be possible to fit them to any further new locomotives, except for the Pacifics about to be completed at Crewe, which should be fitted with equipment in stock for Job 5043. The fitting of speed indicators to existing locomotives should continue "when it is possible to do so in connection with other demands".

The final stage in the saga was reached when the CME sent a letter to the works on 6th June 1944 which began: "Owing to the difficulty in maintaining the BTH-type Speed Indicators in a satisfactory condition, which is aggravated by the difficulty in obtaining replacement parts from the manufacturers, it has been decided to remove these instruments together with all ancillary equipment from the engines so fitted".

The work was to be done in main workshops and at sheds. The return crank was to be replaced by a standard crank pin nut. No further speed indicating equipment would be manufactured but existing equipment would be stored for possible future use. A supplementary letter on 24th November 1944 extended the instruction to cover the removal of Flaman, Hasler and Stone Deuta indicators from 'several engines' which carried them. The History Cards show 147 Class 5s fitted with the equipment (Appendix 1).

Job 5053, 01.01.38, re-issued 27.01.38. Fitting split cast iron valve spindle guides on standard taper boiler locomotives

The Stanier locomotives built up to 1937 had gunmetal slides for the valve spindle crossheads. Under Job 5053 the design was changed to cast iron guides, split into top and bottom sections. The block on the valve crosshead remained mild steel, case hardened, as before. The Class 5s concerned were 5000-5451. The work was to be carried out as renewals were required, but an amendment was issued on 1st December 1947 saying that it was to be done at the next general repair. The work was to be charged to maintenance. No completion date is known.

Job 5055, 05.01.38. Changing coupled axle springs from 10 plates to 16 plates

The coupled axle springs originally were made with ten $5/8$" thick, ribbed section, silico-manganese steel plates but, to increase internal friction of the springs so that riding was improved, sixteen $1/2$" thick plate springs were substituted when replacements were required to Job 5055 starting in January 1938; 5452-71 had these from new.

Job 5059, 22.03.38. Catches and stops on regulators for fully open position

In order to allow the regulator to be set to the drifting position, rather than being opened too far, Job 5059 was issued in March 1938 for stops to be fitted on the regulator stuffing boxes and catches to regulator handles. The modification was to be carried out as engines passed through the shops for repairs and was applicable to many Stanier classes; it was reported complete on 6th May 1947.

Job 5064, NWO 4939, 06.04.38. Providing steam sanding in lieu of trickle sanding

The earlier Stanier locomotives were fitted with gravity sanding, instead of the steam sanding which had been standard on the LMS. This was one of the GWR practices introduced by Stanier which proved unsuccessful on the LMS, where the sand supplied to locomotives was not always of the quality and dryness required for successful operation of gravity sanders. It is noteworthy that trouble with sanding in high winds on Shap was one of the few difficulties encountered during the trials of GWR Castle 5000 *Launceston Castle* on the LMS in 1926.

Job 5064 covered the conversion of 487 locomotives from hand-operated or steam-operated trickle sanding to steam sanding including 5000-5224, which had been of the former type. At the same time the hot water de-sanding gear was removed. The estimated cost was £15,451, and the work was to be done as locomotives passed shops for repairs. It required more than ten years for the job to be finished, the recorded completion date being 29th October 1948, although the Engine History Card of 45029 had a date of 27th November 1948. It is uncertain when this work actually was carried out on some of the Northern Division engines because their History Cards show it dated as either 19th or 20th May 1945, which appears to have been an accountancy exercise with the modifications actually done some years earlier.

Job 5088, DWO 5149, 18.08.38. Removal of vacuum pump from Standard locomotives

The first LMS Standard locomotives to be built with vacuum pumps for maintaining the train pipe vacuum when running were the Royal Scots; under Fowler a batch of 25 2P 4-4-0s and the Patriot 4-6-0s also were fitted. Stanier came from a railway where vacuum pumps were standard, and 737 of his locomotives built up to 1936 thus were equipped. In service, the pumps proved to be unreliable and costly to maintain and were not used, the crews preferring to use the small ejectors to maintain the vacuum.

On 18th August 1938 Job 5088 was issued with the following instruction: "Certain Standard engines at present are fitted with combined ejectors and vacuum pumps, but it has been found that the combined ejectors function satisfactorily without the pumps. In addition it is thought that the pumps have been a contributory factor in cases of fracturing the left-hand piston rod in the crosshead and the vacuum pumps therefore should be removed from the Standard engines". The locomotives were to be dealt with at any visit to the shops for repairs, and the estimated cost was £27,346. Those concerned included Class 5s 5000-5451. The pumps were removed from most engines during 1938 and 1939 and the last one, 5254, in March 1940. Only eight are dated later and these appear to be a housekeeping exercise with five of them recorded as February 1941 when the Northern Division engines concerned were not in works; the other three all had works visits in 1939 at a time when the pumps were being removed.

Job 5107, 15.11.38. Replacing pump controlled atomising lubrication by cylinder cock controlled atomisers

The first 50 engines from Vulcan Foundry had a valve to control the admission of steam to the atomiser that was opened by oil pressure from the mechanical lubricator when the engine was in motion. There were problems with this arrangement and on subsequent engines the steam supply to the atomiser was controlled by a linkage from the cylinder drain cocks so that when the cocks were open, steam was shut off. In November 1938 Job 5107 was issued to replace the pump controlled atomisers on 5020-69 with cock controlled ones, but was not reported complete until 23rd June 1947.

Job 5141, 25.08.39. Monel metal stays in lieu of copper stays in parts of firebox

After problems were experienced with steel firebox stays some of those at the sides of all except the Type 1 boilers were replaced by copper or monel metal ones during repairs from November 1936 onwards. In March 1937, this was specifically applied to the stays adjacent to the breaking zones of the Type 3B Class 5 boilers and two months later was extended to the top three rows, where monel metal was specified. The alterations were unauthorised until Job 5141 was issued in August 1939.

Job 5145, DWO 5402, 25.05.39. Welding-up intermediate ashpan doors

The instruction for this job read as follows: "Certain classes of engine were originally fitted with intermediate ashpan doors in addition to those fitted at the front and back of the ashpan. It has been found in service that ashes are blown from these intermediate doors on to the trailing axleboxes, resulting in hot boxes, and it has also been demonstrated that the steaming of the engines is entirely satisfactory without the doors. The intermediate doors on existing ashpans of the engines quoted below should therefore be fastened up in the closed position by spot welding at 3" pitch and the operating gear from these doors removed".

The work was to be carried out when locomotives visited shops for repairs and the estimated cost was £4,891. Those involved included 5000-5471. The work was reported as completed on 9th September 1947 at a cost of £3,384.

Job 5168, 24.07.40. Increased side play in wheels

This was one of a series of jobs that covered certain alterations to the running gear of locomotives to give increased side play, thereby enabling the locomotives to traverse curves more readily. Amongst alterations in some or all of the classes were the removal of $1/8$" of metal from the inside faces of the leading and trailing coupled wheels, and increases in the clearance in bogies and pony trucks. The changes did not lead

to any reduction in the minimum radius of curve over which they were permitted; for most of the larger LMS locomotives this was six chains, or 4½ chains 'dead slow'. The alterations for the Class 5s were given Job number 5168. There is no record of the progress of this job.

Job 5207, 02.04.40. Alterations to bogies and pony trucks to compensate for the difference in the wear of tyres

The Stanier locomotives were fitted with bogies and pony trucks in which the weight was transmitted from the locomotive frame through spherical bolsters with sliding pads. If the tyres of the driving wheels wore more rapidly than those of the carrying wheels, the effect would be to increase the load on the pads, thus transferring some weight from the coupled axles to the carrying axles. Greater wear of the carrying wheel tyres would have the opposite effect.

Job 5207 set limits on the differences in tyre diameters which were permissible, and introduced a range of bolster pads of varying thickness to be used at repairs to compensate for differences in tyre diameters. The tyres of the bogie or pony truck wheels must be no more than ¼" thicker or ¾" thinner than the tyres of the coupled wheels. No adjustment was needed if the difference was less than ¾" but when the thickness of the carrying wheel tyres was more than ¼" less than the thickness of the coupled wheel tyres, pads of the appropriate thickness were to be fitted to compensate. There is no further information on this job.

Job 5208, 08.04.40. Fitting drain cocks to Class H exhaust injectors

The instruction read: "During the recent severe cold weather considerable trouble was experienced due to the Class H exhaust injectors freezing up, and with a view to avoiding such

trouble in the future, it has been decided to fit a drain cock in the cap nut below the water strainer". The drain cocks were of a standard pattern produced by Davies & Metcalfe, the makers of the injectors, and were to be bought from that firm at 6/4¼d each. The cocks were to be fitted as the injectors passed through works for repairs.

The price quoted by Davies & Metcalfe evidently produced a quick response from the LMS works, for a further note was circulated on 29th April 1940 saying the manufacture of drain cocks had been concentrated at Derby at a cost of 2/5d each. The other works were to order from Derby unless they were able to manufacture the valves themselves at the same price.

As the winter approached the CME wrote to the works on 13th December 1940 saying that the Superintendent of Motive Power had agreed to the work being carried out at motive power depots as well as in the main workshops. The weather at the beginning of 1940 was the most severe that had been experienced in Britain since the LMS began to fit exhaust steam injectors on a large scale, and the work appeared to be urgent. Nevertheless it was not reported as complete until 19th February 1947 – which happened to be in the middle of the next spell of equally severe weather. The locomotives concerned included all of the pre-war Class 5s.

Job 5256, 01.08.41. Air Raid Precautions - modified catches for cab windows

This instruction read: "It is necessary to provide means of additional ventilation for engine cabs which become overheated when the screens are fitted to prevent firebox glow during blackout hours and it has been decided to modify the front window fastenings so that the windows may be opened about 2", and secured in this position".

5029 at Perth on 20th May 1935 has been equipped with Manson automatic tablet exchange apparatus for working over the single track routes in the Northern Division. The apparatus was fixed at footplate height, the jaws normally being held upright against the side plate. When an exchange was about to be effected, they would be swung downward through 90 degrees to project the required distance from the engine. 5029 was built at Vulcan Foundry in September 1934 and was allocated initially to Perth, moving to Inverness the same month before going south to Crewe in November 1935 when the Northern Division exchanged its two-row superheater engines for later three-row engines. It has all the features unique to the Vulcan Foundry engines: open front footplate, tall chimney, prominent top feed pipes, 'scalloped' steampipe covers and plain axleboxes on the tender.
Fred A. Plant/Caledonian Railway Association

A special window catch had been designed at Derby which suited most of the Standard locomotives fitted with front hinged windows. The locomotives covered by this instruction were 5000-5471. There is no further information on this job.

Job 5303, 29.12.42. Fitting sand guns to standard engines

Although the specification issued for the first sloping throatplate Class 5s included them and other LMS engines were being built with sand guns on the fireboxes, they were not fitted to new construction until 5452-5471 in 1938. The guns allowed firemen to direct a stream of sand into the boiler tubes to scour them while the engine was running. Over the next few years, some of the earlier engines were given 'unauthorised' modification, i.e., without the financial authority of a Works Order, from 1938 onwards before Job 5303 was issued in December 1942 for the fitting of sand guns under NWO 5993. They were justified "Owing to the greater calls at present being made on locomotive boilers due to heavier loads and to the reduction in time spent in depots, advantages could be derived from the use of sand guns, which provide a very effective method of keeping the plates and tubes in very clean condition". The gun was mounted just above the firedoors, fed from a sand hopper below the right-hand front cab window that provided enough sand for five applications and its direction controlled by a wheel on the firebox backplate.

The sand hoppers originally were open-topped but moisture getting in caused blockages so Job 5179 in February 1940 detailed the fitting of cover plates. There also were problems with the connecting pipes from the hoppers being damaged so, in April 1944, under Job 5371 instructions were issued to replace the fixed type with flexible ones that could be removed when not in use. In service, the sand guns were unreliable because the nozzles got burnt and firemen resorted to the simple alternative of flinging shovelfuls of sand through the fire hole and over the brick arch towards the tubeplate whilst the engine was working hard, and therefore the guns were removed starting in 1952 to Job 5663.

Job 5276, 12.12.41. Modified scoop for boiler top feed trays; Job 5539, 09.11.49. Top feed deflector plates in lieu of top feed trays

If not cleaned regularly, the boiler feed trays below the clacks rapidly filled with sludge and the feed water then ran straight on to the superheater flues which caused a build-up of scale, and in December 1941 Job 5276 was issued for modifications to the scoops. However, before it was completed, replacement of the whole arrangement by simple deflector plates was instigated under Job 5539 of November 1949. The plates caused the feed water to flow round the boiler side and reduced scaling of the tubes, but it was not until 1961 that all boilers were modified.

Job 5351, NWO 6319, 16.07.43. New design valve, casing and filter for air relief valve on Standard locomotives

When a locomotive runs with steam shut off, the pistons act as pumps, and tend to draw hot gases (and foreign matter) down the blastpipe. In addition, the temperature during compression may become sufficiently high to interfere with lubrication. In slide valve locomotives the valves fall off their faces, creating a by-pass between the ends of the cylinders, and this makes conditions in the cylinders acceptable. In piston valve locomotives some form of relief valve commonly is provided to admit air to the steam chests if the pressure falls below atmospheric due to the pumping action of the pistons, either in the form of a relief or 'snifting' valve fitted to the saturated side of the superheater header, or an air relief valve fitted directly to some part of the cylinder casting.

Midland superheated locomotives were fitted with the Fowler/Anderson by-pass valve, but nevertheless Derby introduced an air relief valve in 1917 and this was fitted to all Midland and LMS Standard locomotives with piston valves built up to 1935, except the 2P 4-4-0s. This valve was visible on certain designs of locomotive, for example on the framing below the smokebox on the 4F 0-6-0, and attached to the front of the outside steam pipe on the Princess Royal Pacifics. In this design of valve, a vertical poppet valve of gunmetal was housed in a casting which was bolted to a vertical surface on the cylinder or steampipe. Below the valve was a casing with holes, through which air could reach the valve, the holes serving as an air filter. When the valve was in its lower position it was shut. In its upper position it admitted air to the steam chest or steampipe. Under its own weight it remained shut and steam pressure from the steam chest acting above it held it firmly so. With steam off, when the pumping action of the pistons created a sufficient vacuum, air pressure overcame the weight of the piston, which lifted and admitted air. At low locomotive speeds, the pressure in the steam chest varied during each stroke, causing the valve to open and shut intermittently. This produced a characteristic chattering sound, and caused wear on the valve and its seating.

In 1935 a new design of valve was introduced, in which a downward extension of the piston slid in a cylinder formed on the bottom of the valve seating, with two piston rings to seal it. At the bottom of the cylinder was a small air hole. When the valve lifted, the piston created a partial vacuum in this cylinder, and air rushed in through the hole. Likewise when the piston fell, air was trapped below it, and had to escape through the hole. The obstruction to air flow caused by the hole provided a damper or dashpot to slow down the motion of the piston and reduced the chatter. The casing around the lower part of the valve was made of sheet metal, and because of the dashpot, it was deeper than in the earlier design. Experience showed that the sheet metal casing corroded, while the alloy valve gave trouble by breaking.

In 1939 a new and simpler design of valve was introduced, in which the dashpot was eliminated, but the valve was still of alloy and the casing of sheet metal. Still this did not give satisfaction, and in 1940 a new design of valve in steel and a cast iron casing were introduced, and tested successfully on a locomotive. The new parts could be fitted to the existing design of relief valve, with some modification to the valve body and replacement of some other parts in certain variants. Up to this stage there had been no recognised modification for bringing older air relief valves into line with the newer pattern, although some changes in the types of valve had been made at repairs, but in 1943 Job 5351 was issued to cover the fitting of steel valves and cast iron covers as existing valves needed replacement. One effect of the change was to eliminate the dashpot.

The modification applied to 3,000 locomotives including 5000-5471. On 26th August 1953 a note was issued closing LMS financial authority NWO 6319.

Job 5382, DWO 6454, 28.07.45. Standardisation of driver's brake valve

492 of the early Stanier locomotives were fitted with standard Gresham & Craven Dreadnought combination driver's brake valve and ejector steam valve, instead of the normal LMS Midland-type fittings. Job 5382 covered the replacement of the G&C equipment by standard LMS brake valves with separate ejector steam control, as used on the later Stanier locomotives, "in the interests of economy both in initial cost and maintenance".

The work was to be done at general repairs at an estimated cost of £ 11,922. Apparently no work was done on the conversion for three years, for a new job sheet was issued on

22nd September 1948, saying that "firm estimates have now been prepared for carrying out the work", at an estimated cost of £15,789. By 2nd September 1953, 436 locomotives had been dealt with at a cost of £11,782, and the LMS financial authority DWO 6454 then was closed, and Job 5382/1, WO/R3839, was issued to cover the alteration of the 27 locomotives on the LMR still outstanding. A separate instruction was issued to cover the 19 locomotives outstanding on the Scottish Region. The Class 5s concerned in the job were 5000-5224. The final completion date is not recorded.

Job 5391, 03.04.46. Two extra washout plugs at front of taper boilers

Job 5391 to financial authority NWO 6453 was issued in April 1946 for the addition of two washout plugs at the front of the barrel on boilers not already having them, including the type 3Bs on the Class 5s. It was reported complete by 1952.

Job 5416, NWO 6584, 04.10.45. Provision of new type piston head fastening

The Stanier locomotives were fitted with flat-faced piston heads screwed on to the end of the piston rod, with no retaining rod or key, in the GWR manner. Fatigue cracks in the roots of the screw threads caused a number of piston failures, and the design was changed. The end of the piston rod was lengthened, and the head was secured by two nuts, one left hand and the other right hand, with a locking washer between. This type of piston was used on the Coronation/Duchess Pacifics, and it was fitted to Class 5 4-6-0s 5052/70, 5190/1, 5230, 5352/98, 5417 under experiment C/LD/11125. Job 5416 then was issued for a further development of this fastening to be applied to 1,040 pre-war Stanier locomotives, including the remaining pre-war Class 5s, at an estimated cost of £52,338.

In addition to the new piston rod and piston head, it also was necessary to replace the front cylinder cover, as the protruding nuts would foul the old cover. The work was to be carried out as pistons required renewal. On 14th February 1947 the CME reported that a revised estimate of £56,325 now had been approved, and he commented that "In many cases this instruction will not be carried out on all the pistons of an engine at the same repair". The job was given a revised number 5416/1.

The LMS financial authority NWO 6584 was closed by an order issued on 11th September 1953, by which time £32,077 had been spent and 1,015 pistons remained unaltered. Job 5416/2 was issued on the same date to cover the 910 pistons on the LMR still requiring treatment, and the M&EE of the Scottish Region dealt with the remainder. This instruction stated also that the 198 pistons outstanding in the Jubilees were to be dealt with when the locomotives passed through the works for any kind of repair, but other classes were to be modified when the piston rod required renewal, as before.

Nearly two years later the M&EE reported that authority now had been obtained for the estimated cost of £27,463 of job 5416/2 under reference NWO/E3698. This note continued: "As this instruction has been open since 1945, it is considered that the majority of the piston rods to be replaced must be about life-expired, and therefore the rate of dealing with engines not completely fitted is to be speeded up. This scheme must be completed by November 1958. Engines may be fitted at any suitable repair provided that no additional expenditure is charged to this scheme, but must be dealt with in any case at General Repairs. Special care must be taken to ensure that no engines are overlooked when in shops". Despite the deadline set in this instruction, Job 5416/2 was not reported as complete until 20th September 1959, by which time it had cost £28,689.

Job 5506, 16.03.48. Intermediate buffing blocks on first 70 Class 5s

A ³/₄" thick steel drag beam was attached to the rear frames by 3¹/₂" x 4¹/₂" x 8³/₈" angle and the intermediate tender buffers bore against 1¹/₄" thick, case-hardened buffing plates riveted to it. 5007-19 and 5070 onwards also had a semi-circular casting or buffing block, above the drawbar, against which the tender rode. Job 5506 was issued in March 1948 to fit these blocks to 5000-06 and 5020-69 and was completed by 29th March 1954.

Job 5676, 14.04.53. Underkeep lubrication and dust shield to trailing axleboxes

In 1945, ten Class 5s were fitted experimentally with dust shields over their axleboxes and the oil feed was transferred to the underkeeps, being carried to the journal by the pad alone. The experiment was successful and new locomotives from 4982 onwards were equipped with the underfed keeps but it was not until April 1953 that Job 5676 was issued for the whole class to be modified. It was closed in December 1958 leaving many engines unaltered.

Job 5796, WO/R7961, 21.02.58. Modifications to exhaust injector auxiliary steam pipe

The job sheet described this modification as follows: "Recently a number of failures has arisen through the fracturing of the exhaust injector control pipe or loosening of the connection, mostly on ex-LMS Class 7 4-6-0, 6P 4-6-0 and Class 5 4-6-0. It is considered that this is due to vibration and relative movement of the foot framing on which the pipe is clipped, and to overcome this trouble it has been decided to strengthen the connection by using a cone joint having a sleeve-type fastening for the pipe, and to clip the pipe to the main frame of the locomotive instead of to the footplating".

The estimated cost was £2,180, and the work was to be done at intermediate or general repairs. The locomotives included 588 Class 5s between 44658 and 45499. On 10.6.53 WO/R 7961 was closed. Works were instructed that if any of the following locomotives were found to require the modification when next in for attention they were to be dealt with and charged to maintenance: 44752/4, 44823/4/34, 44989, 45239/71/94, 45436.

Job 5797, WO/E 4983, 21.02.57. Fitting BR AWS equipment

In July 1935, Derby Order 9174 was issued for fitting Kentish Town-based Class 5s 5052-58 and 5065 with Hudd automatic warning equipment at Bow Works for use on the LT&S section, where the system was being installed. However, it seems unlikely that any of them were actually equipped at that time, 5052-58 being transferred away between February and December 1936. Although 5065 remained at Kentish Town until 1945 there is no evidence to confirm whether or not it actually received the equipment.

The Hudd system was finally brought into use on 1st December 1947 and covered the whole of the LT&S section from Bow to Shoeburyness. It was electro-magnetic, with fixed inductors on the track and a magnetic receiver mounted beneath the locomotive. Passing a distant signal at 'Caution' caused a warning hooter to sound in the cab and unless the driver operated the acknowledging device, the brakes were applied after three seconds, full application being reached smoothly in twenty seconds. When signals were at 'Clear' a short reassuring hoot was given in the cab. 183 locomotives were fitted with the equipment including three Class 5s, 5267 and 5279 based at Kentish Town and 5277 from Cricklewood. It appears that they retained the equipment until the mid-1950s, visiting Bow Works on several occasions for attention. The Hudd system formed the basis of the Automatic Warning System developed by British Railways that was authorised for fitting to several classes by works order E 4983, the work being

45148 from Crewe South, seen on 11th June 1961 at Willesden, was fitted with AWS in November 1959 under works order E 4983 issued in February 1957. Over 400 of the pre-war engines were equipped with the apparatus between January 1959 and June 1963. An extra frame stretcher was fitted at the front of the bogie to which the AWS receiver was fixed. A guard plate attached to the buffer beam protected the receiver from damage by the front coupling. An electrical conduit to the battery box ran inside the platform angle from the receiver, and entered the cab immediately above the footsteps. The smaller timing reservoir can be seen on the running plate immediately in front of the cab.

A. Swain

carried out to Job No. 5797 issued on 21st February 1957. However it was not until January 1959 that the first Class 5s received the equipment, with over 400 of the pre-war engines fitted between then and June 1963, including 45267 and 45277 but not 45279 (Appendix 1).

Installation required an extra frame stretcher at the front of the bogie to which the AWS receiver was fixed. A guard plate attached to the buffer beam protected the receiver from damage by the front coupling. An electrical conduit ran inside the platform angle from the receiver, and entered the cab immediately above the footsteps. The battery box was in the cab on the right hand side at the front and the relay junction box was mounted on the side plate under the driver's seat. The main vacuum reservoir was mounted immediately in front of the cab on the right hand platform with the smaller timing reservoir on the other side. The bell and horn for clear and warning indications were on the inside of the roof, the bell about half way between ventilator and left hand eaves and the horn just to the left of the ventilator.

Job 5810, WO/E 5173, 22.05.59. BR Speed indicators

In 1959 British Railways embarked on a major scheme for fitting speed indicators to steam locomotives, and on 22nd May 1959 Job 5810, WO/E5173, was issued under the title 'Fitting Speed Indicators and Recorders on Steam Locomotives' to cover the 1959 LMR programme. These indicators were electrically operated, speed being calculated from the voltage produced by a generator mounted directly on and driven from a return crank on the rear left-hand crankpin, with an armoured flexible cable leading via a rheostat box into the cab. The Job was cancelled in 1964 after 43 of the pre-war Class 5s had been equipped (Appendix 1).

Other modifications

Other modifications applied to the pre-war Class 5s and their tenders are shown in **Table 8.1**.

8.1 Snowploughs

Many Class 5s had small snowploughs attached to their front buffer beams in winter. Although most were Scottish-based engines, some stationed in England and used on routes prone to heavy snow also were modified. The ploughs were not intended for major snow clearance but to enable train engines to run through small drifts up to two feet deep, and were also used on light engines sent out to prevent build-up of snow during periods of sparse traffic. The first version fitted was the LMS No.5 nose plough which was based on a Caledonian Railway design. It was fixed in place by brackets fitted to the frames and two heavy, upright steel angles attached to the buffer beam by two vertical rows of three bolts approximately one foot inboard of the buffers. It had a drawback because the plough stuck out far enough ahead of the buffer beam to prevent a pilot engine being coupled in front unless it was removed.

The No.5 plough was superseded in 1950 by a BR version known as the No.6 which did not project beyond the buffers, even when they were compressed, thus making the attachment of a pilot engine much easier. Modifying a locomotive to receive a No.6 plough involved fitting brackets to the frames below the buffer beam and drilling bolt holes along the lower edge of the beam itself. In order to adjust the height of the plough and to maintain the correct clearance of 4$^{1}/_{2}$" above the rails, four alternative holes were supposed to be provided in the mounting brackets for each bolt and the lower front footstep also had to be shortened from the front and the support plate leading edge cut back between upper and lower steps. Before a plough could be fitted, the front carriage warming hose and screw coupling had to be removed and a trammel was used to indicate the bolt holes. The plough then was placed in position and bolted to both brackets and buffer

9 ALLOCATION AND DUTIES

With the prevailing motive power situation in Scotland it was not surprising that priority was given to the Northern Division when the first Class 5s were delivered in the summer of 1934, where successfully they began to address its motive power problems. After that the new engines were dispersed to all three English Divisions with the ex-LNWR Western Division receiving the largest share as almost 500 of its pre-grouping 4-6-0s and 4-4-0s were replaced in five years between 1934 and 1938. Wherever they went the result was the same, a complete transformation of the LMS middle order motive power, as the new 4-6-0s took on everything from fast expresses to freight work and everything in between.

9.1 Route availability

The Class 5s had a relatively low axle loading that allowed them to run over at least 70% of the LMS system. The boiler was made from two per cent nickel steel for all plates with the exception of the smokebox tubeplate, and the frames were lightweight, only 1" thick, lightly stayed and made from Chromador alloy steel. The use of only two cylinders also enabled the weight to be minimised. Route availability was helped by keeping the width over cylinders to 8' 7 5/8" and the overthrow on curves was minimised by reducing the width at the drop section of the footplate and buffer beam to 7' 8". The progressive programme of bridge strengthening in both Scotland and England during the mid-1930s opened the system still further, allowing the class to operate over the Oban and the Somerset & Dorset Joint lines by 1938.

9.2 Northern Division

The first engine completed was 5020 which emerged from Vulcan Foundry on 31st July 1934, was delivered to Crewe and entered traffic on 2nd August. By the end of that month, eight had been delivered and the whole of Vulcan's order for 50 engines (5020-69) was in service by the middle of January 1935. They arrived with little fuss and did not seem to cause much excitement among the enthusiasts of the day. This was perhaps because on the LMS most attention at that time was concentrated on the running of the Pacifics, 6200 and 6201, and the recently introduced 5XP Jubilee 4-6-0s, whilst the LNER also was receiving much publicity from its Gresley P2 2-8-2 *Cock o' the North* which been completed at Doncaster in May.

5020-29 were allocated to the Northern Division and 5021-29 went to Scotland on delivery, for service on the Highland Section where there was an acute power shortage in the summer of 1934. Initially they all went to Perth North shed but 5028 and 5029 soon were transferred to Inverness. The first recorded working was by 5021 which hauled a local freight from Perth to Blair Atholl on 15th August returning light engine to Perth. 5023 is believed to have been the first to reach as far north as Aviemore; it arrived there with a freight train from Perth on 27th August and returned the following day with another freight. The engine worked a Perth to Inverness freight on 29th returning south on a similar train next day. On 30th August, 5024 also was noted on a freight train at Aviemore. The first engine to be recorded on a passenger train was 5023 which took the 3.40pm from Perth to Inverness on 31st.

As the other engines arrived they also went to work on the Highland main line, but their introduction did not entirely eliminate double-heading. Indeed, some interesting combinations were noted and observations at Kingussie in September 1934 give a good indication of the sort of work the Class 5s were doing in those early days:

Saturday 1st
5022 – Relief passenger train from Inverness to Perth
5023 – 4.15pm Inverness-Perth, assisted by 14692 *Darnaway Castle* from Aviemore to Dalnaspidal
5024 – 3.40pm (2nd portion) Perth to Inverness
5023 – Freight Aviemore to Perth

Monday 3rd
5022 – Freight Perth to Inverness
5023 – 4.35pm Inverness-Perth
5024 – 8.20am Inverness-Perth, piloted by 2-6-0 13108, then 3.40pm Perth-Inverness

Tuesday 4th
5022 – Freight Inverness to Perth
5023 – Piloting 5024 to Aviemore on 11.55am Perth-Inverness. Piloting 13105 from Aviemore on 3.45pm Inverness-Perth
5024 – 11.55am Perth-Inverness, piloted by 5023 to Aviemore

Wednesday 5th
5022 – 9.30am Perth-Inverness via Forres
5023 – 4.35pm Inverness-Perth, assisted by 14417 *Ben Na Caillach* from Aviemore to Dalnaspidal
5025 – 12.12pm Perth-Inverness via Forres
5026 – Freight Perth to Inverness

Thursday 6th
5022 – 8.20am Inverness-Perth
5023 – 4.35pm Inverness-Perth, assisted by 17920 from Aviemore to Dalnaspidal
5026 – 3.45pm Inverness-Perth

Friday 7th
5022 – 8.20am Inverness-Perth
5023 – 4.15pm Inverness-Perth, assisted by 14419 *Ben Mholach* from Aviemore to Dalnaspidal
5024 – 3.40pm Perth-Inverness

Saturday 8th
5022 – 4.15pm Inverness-Perth, assisted by 14322 *Snaigow* from Aviemore to Dalnaspidal
5023 – 4.35pm Inverness-Perth, assisted by 13100 from Aviemore to Dalnaspidal
5024 – 8.20am Inverness-Perth, then 3.40pm Perth-Inverness
5025 – Piloting 13100 to Aviemore on 11.55am Perth-Inverness, then piloting 13109 from Aviemore on 3.45pm Inverness-Perth

Sunday 9th
5022 – Piloting 14681 *Skibo Castle* on 9.40am Perth-Inverness
5024 – 4.10pm Inverness-Perth
5026 – 4.5pm Inverness-Perth via Forres, piloted by 14768 *Clan Mackenzie*

Monday 10th
5022 – 8.20am Inverness-Perth, assisted by 13102
5023 – 4.10pm Inverness-Perth, assisted by 14322 *Snaigow* from Aviemore to Dalnaspidal
5026 – 9.30am Perth-Inverness, then 4.35pm Inverness-Perth, assisted by 14419 *Ben Mholach* from Aviemore to Dalnaspidal

5021 and 5027 were noted for the first time at Kingussie on 12th, 5028 on 13th and 5029 on Sunday 16th September. The unassisted maximum loads for these engines over the Highland main line were:

Perth to Blair Atholl	370 tons
Blair Atholl to Dalnaspidal	255 tons

The third Class 5 into service, Vulcan Foundry-built 5022 waits to leave Forres with an Inverness to Glasgow express in 1935. It has already had the front footplate step fitted but retains the prominent top feed pipes and tall chimney. It went new to Perth in August 1934 but stayed there only until October 1935 when it was transferred to Edge Hill. In the autumn of 1935 the original ten engines, 5020-29, together with 5000-06, were transferred from Scotland to the Western Division and divided between Crewe and Edge Hill sheds; in return the Northern Division received 30 later build engines with three-row element superheaters, 5081-87 from Crewe North and 5157-79.   *Rail Archive Stephenson*

5010 waits to depart from the southbound island platform at Inverness with the 3.30pm to Forres and Aviemore. It was built at Crewe in April 1935 and after running-in went to St. Rollox for two months before moving to Inverness where it stayed until 1945. It was the first engine to have a 21-element boiler from Crewe fitted, with two washout inspection doors with small domed covers on each shoulder of the firebox.

Locomotive & General Railway Photographs

Aviemore to Slochd Crossing	255 tons
Inverness to Slochd Crossing	255 tons
Aviemore to Dalnaspidal	345 tons
Blair Atholl to Perth	370 tons

The first appearance of a Class 5 at Aberdeen was on Sunday 23rd September when 5024 arrived on the 7.15am from Glasgow; it returned from Aberdeen with the 1.10pm train for the south. The following day it was back on the Highland main line but soon afterwards 5024 and 5025 moved to Perth South shed where they took over some of the important trains between Glasgow and Aberdeen. Their two daily diagrams were:

(a)
    7.00am Perth to Glasgow Buchanan St.
    10.00am Glasgow Buchanan St. to Aberdeen
    5.35pm Aberdeen to Perth
(b)
    7.50am Perth to Gleneagles
    8.30am Gleneagles to Glasgow Buchanan St.
    1.40pm Glasgow Buchanan St. to Aberdeen
    7.50pm Aberdeen to Perth

On both diagrams there was a crew change at Perth and each engine ran 301 miles daily.

The first use of the new engines north of Inverness was during the second week of February 1935 when 5028 worked the 10.20am service from Inverness to Wick on alternate days, returning on Tuesday, Thursday and Saturday with the 3.35pm Wick to Inverness train. The tare loads were made up to 320 tons between Inverness and Bonar Bridge and to 350 tons over the harder grades between Bonar Bridge and Wick. Ordinarily, the ex-Highland Railway Castle class 4-6-0s were responsible for passenger workings over this route.

9.3 5020 early trials

Meanwhile, 5020 had been delivered to Crewe and was retained there for a few weeks to work on the Western Division where it was involved in various platform and crossover tests between Crewe and Euston. The engine was in Crewe Works in the middle of August 1934 but returned to traffic during week ending 24th August. For three days starting on 5th September it was used on dynamometer car tests to obtain details of its running performance and efficiency when working express passenger trains. The trains chosen were the 10.35am Crewe-Euston and 2.40pm Euston-Crewe (a Liverpool express). The booked load for the engine was 370 tons but the actual loadings were:

	05.09.34	06.09.34	07.09.34
10.35am Crewe-Euston	371 tons	373 tons	370 tons
2.40pm Euston-Crewe	410 tons	415 tons	468 tons

Grimethorpe coal was used throughout and all the tests were run under good weather conditions. The engine maintained the booked timings without difficulty and actually gained time with the heaviest load hauled, taking this train out of Euston without banking assistance (468 tons on the 2.40pm on 7th September). With the normal loading the engine operated with the valve gear at 17%-20% cut-off for general running and 25% on the banks, when full regulator was used.

With the heaviest load a 20%-25% cut off was employed for general running and 25%-30% on the banks with full regulator. The steaming of the boiler was uniform and adequate throughout.

The report concluded that the performance of 5020 on these workings was very satisfactory and the work was performed economically. Notable features of the tests were the power development at speed and the apparent low running resistance of the engine, plus its steadiness and freedom in running at high coasting speeds. The results (Crewe-Euston-Crewe) were:

	05.09.34	06.09.34	07.09.34
Total coal burnt	10,780 lbs	11,620 lbs	12,740 lbs
lbs. per mile	34.1	36.8	40.3
lbs. power hour	3.28	3.38	3.48
lbs. per sq.ft. of grate area	71.3	75.4	85.9
Total water from tender (gallons)	9,380	10,220	10,330
Gallons of water per mile	29.7	32.3	32.7
lbs. per drawbar horse power hour	28.3	29.8	28.2
lbs. per lb. of coal	8.7	8.8	8.11

NB. An allowance was made for lighting up of 10cwts of coal when the engine was cold and 7cwts warm. An additional allowance of 1cwt was made in respect of standing between trains.

In the *Railway Magazine* for November 1934 the late Cecil J. Allen described the run of 5020 with the 468-ton train; with its complement of passengers he estimated the full weight of the 15-coach train at 495 tons. It took just under 10 minutes to pass Willesden Junction and speed did not rise above 58½ mph at Wembley. After the long climb, Tring summit was breasted at 54½ mph but then the engine attained 77mph at Sear's Crossing (between Cheddington and Leighton Buzzard) and kept this speed up so well that it covered 58½ miles in the first hour from Euston. The engine was then eased somewhat and, after a signal check outside the station, reached Rugby in 85 mins. 56 secs. (booked time 88 mins.). Onwards to Crewe, 5020 touched 75mph at Nuneaton, was 1½ minutes ahead of time through Lichfield, and had bettered 'even time' by Milford, 46.9 miles from Rugby which was passed in 46½ minutes. After slowing through Stafford, the engine attained 63mph at Standon Bridge, went over Whitmore Summit at 61½ mph, a striking feat with this load,

and touched 78mph on the downhill stretch at Betley Road. Unfortunately adverse signals outside Crewe brought the train to a halt but despite this the time from Rugby to Crewe was 1¾ minutes less than the booked time. Mr. Allen described this run as "an excellent debut indeed for a moderate sized general purpose locomotive".

Whilst the report on the tests did not say so, it was demonstrated that this mixed traffic engine was able to deputise for a Class 6P Royal Scot with the maximum load allowed Special Limit timings.

On 8th September, 5020 was on Longsight shed and for four days in the following week, starting on 10th, it was involved in further tests to obtain particulars of its running performance and efficiency when working fitted freight trains. Dynamometer Car No.1 was used and the trains chosen for the tests were the 8.28pm (FF2) Manchester London Road to Camden and the 7.0pm (FF1) Camden to Manchester. The booked loads were 55 vans on the up train and 50 vans on the down and these were the actual loads on the test days (plus dynamometer car) except on 12th when the 8.28pm from Manchester loaded to 60 vans. The coal used and the

allowances were the same as on the express passenger tests the previous week, except that a 2½ cwt allowance was made for light running and standing instead of 1cwt. Weather conditions were good throughout.

When working on the main rising gradients, with both up and down trains, the valve gear was operated in the 30%–45% cut off range with full regulator. For general running a 15%–20% cut off was used with full regulator. As on the express passenger runs, the steaming of the boiler was uniform and satisfactory throughout and the engine worked these fitted freight trains very economically. Coal consumption per unit of work by the engine at the drawbar when working the freights was less than during the passenger workings. This was partly due to the ratio of the work expended on the engine compared to that on the engine and train being lower on freight workings than on passenger, and partly to the lower rate of combustion when working freight trains. The tabulated results of these tests were:

	10.09.34	11.09.34	12.09.34	13.09.34
Train	8.28pm up	7.00pm down	8.28pm up	7.00pm down
Total Coal burnt	7,181 lbs	7,175 lbs	8,000 lbs	7,518 lbs
lbs. per mile	39.46	39.42	42.6	40.0
lbs. per drawbar horse power hour	2.75	2.68	2.85	2.71
lbs. per sq.ft.of grate area	47.6	44.3	51.6	54.2
Total water from tender (gallons)	6,930	6,540	7,000	6,540
Gallons of water per mile	38.0	35.9	37.2	34.9
lbs. per drawbar power hour	26.6	24.4	25.0	23.6
lbs. per lb. of coal	9.66	9.11	8.75	8.73

From the results of these tests and those with the same engine on passenger working, it was concluded that "the new 2-cylinder 4-6-0 Mixed Traffic engine appeared to be a very efficient and satisfactory mixed traffic power unit".

On 14th September, 5020 hauled a test train from Crewe to Walsall via Rugeley and Hednesford, but no records of this working have come to light. Soon afterwards it went to the Northern Division to join 5021-29.

9.4 Western and Midland Divisions

The next two engines, 5030 and 5031, went to Kentish Town when new but both had moved to Saltley by the end of the year. 5032-54 were all allocated to the Western Division, mostly to Crewe initially, but soon they were distributed between five sheds, Willesden, Northampton, Crewe, Edge Hill and Upperby. Those at Crewe and Edge Hill started to visit north Wales and the Edge Hill engines also took turns on

5083, pictured on 1st July 1937 taking on water at Pitlochry, was one of the Western Division engines transferred to the Northern Division in autumn 1935, moving from Crewe to Perth in October. Except for the addition of tablet changing equipment it is still in original condition as built at Vulcan Foundry in March 1935.
T. G. Hepburn/Rail Archive Stephenson

There is plenty of activity at Dingwall as Armstrong Whitworth-built 5167 waits to depart. It arrived on the Northern Division in June 1936 from Crewe and was allocated to Perth for twenty years.

S. V. Blencowe

the Liverpool (Lime St.) to Leeds (New) expresses. Their use on these trains seemed to result in better timekeeping although Farnley Junction shed, which shared the work, was still using Prince of Wales class 4-6-0s and Hughes 4-6-0s.

5048, originally at Edge Hill, was transferred to Sheffield in w/e 8th December 1934 to work the Sheffield Wicker to Glasgow College fitted freight and the corresponding up train on alternate nights. Carlisle engines worked the trains on the other days.

On the Western Division, further trials were carried out in October to obtain further information on the performance and efficiency of the engines when working fitted freight trains between Camden and Carlisle, this time using 5036 which had been delivered in w/e 22nd September and was allocated to Willesden. The trains chosen for the trials were the 2.53pm Camden-Carlisle (FF1 to Crewe and FF2 Crewe to Carlisle) and the 3.30pm Carlisle-Broad Street (FF1); on the latter, the dynamometer car was detached at Willesden.

5036 worked north on 10th and 15th October and south on 11th and 16th, using Portland coal on the down trains and Kingshill No.1 coal on the up trains. Timekeeping was adversely affected by a derailment at Preston on 10th and another derailment at Stafford on 11th, whilst on 15th and 16th the starts were delayed because the trains had not been marshalled by the scheduled departure time. The down trains loaded to 50 vans plus dynamometer car and were banked between Oxenholme and Grayrigg and between Tebay and Shap summit. The up train loaded to 34 vans plus dynamometer car.

The engine was worked by two sets of men on each run, changes being made at Crewe, but the operation of the engine "did not seem to have been satisfactory in respect of the proper use of the regulator in conjunction with the valve gear" and some time was lost for this reason.

The actual times achieved by the trains were:

Down	Booked Time (mins)	Actual Time 10.10.34	Actual Time 15.10.34
Watford-Tring	21	22m 05s	22m 57s
Bletchley-Roade	19	16m 40s	16m 28s
Stafford-Whitmore	23	23m 00s	29m 24s (1)
Wigan-Standish	8	12m 43s	12m 05s
Carnforth-Oxenholme	22	30m 20s	31m 03s (2)

Up	Booked Time (mins)	Actual Time 11.10.34	Actual Time 16.10.34
Carlisle-Plumpton	18	28m 55s	25m 52s
Penrith-Shap Summit	25	26m 02s	33m 45s (3)
Crewe-Whitmore	15	17m 53s	21m 11s
Rugby-Roade	27	32m 20s (4)	38m 13s (5)
Bletchley-Tring	19	18m 40s	19m 00s

NB

(1) Stopped at Stafford so time was from a standing start
(2) Signal check in addition to stop at Oxenholme for banker
(3) Signal check at Penrith and Shap station
(4) Signal check at Blisworth
(5) Signal checks at Rugby No.1 and Kilsby North

From an analysis of the dynamometer car chart from which calculations of load resistance and power were made, it was indicated that with the loads concerned and assuming an average speed as given by the booked timings, the maximum sustained power development by the engine would be required. The steaming of the engine was reported as good at all times.

9.5 Allocation and work 1935

Of the remaining engines in the first order from Vulcan Foundry, 5055-58 went to Kentish Town, 5059 was allocated to the Western Division at Crewe and 5060-69 were the first of the class to be allocated to the Central Division, 5060-63 at Farnley Junction and 5064-69 at Newton Heath where they

replaced Hughes 4-6-0s. Thus, by January 1935, 23 engines were allocated to the Western Division, ten each to the Central and Northern Divisions and seven to the Midland Division.

Delivery of the 20 engines from Crewe Works in the 1934 building programme started in February 1935 and lasted until May; after running-in from Crewe (in some cases for several weeks) 5000-18 were all working on the Northern Division from Kingmoor, Perth and Inverness by July. In February 1935 also big changes were made to the allocation of the Vulcan-built engines when 17 from the Western Division and three from the Central Division were transferred to the Midland Division, giving it a total of 27 engines allocated as follows:

Saltley	5030/31/38/39	Kentish Town	5036/52-58
Gloucester	5032	Holbeck	5037
Derby	5033	Nottingham	5040/41
Sheffield	5034/48	Bristol	5043/44/66
Trafford Park	5035/42/67-69		

From 12th February 1935 the Class 5s took over from the Class 5XP Jubilees on West of England line expresses and were also used on fast freights. The five at Trafford Park displaced Compounds 1017-19 (which went to Belle Vue) and along with engines from Kentish Town began working the Manchester (Central) to St. Pancras expresses. Their maximum loading between Manchester and Derby was 255 tons; at that time they were the largest engines allowed over this line because of weight restrictions over bridges at Chapel-en-le-Frith. The engines also were used on other services in and out of St. Pancras along with the Class 5XP engines and put up some excellent performances.

On the express trains over the main line to St. Pancras the Class 5 4-6-0s were putting on some stirring performances and in the *Railway Magazine* for May 1935, Cecil J. Allen recorded a thrilling run behind 5052 on the 2.32pm from Leicester to St.Pancras, a train which originated at Manchester Central. With a load of only 227 tons (240 tons full), the train started three minutes late but speed was up to 77$\frac{1}{2}$ mph at East Langton before slowing with exemplary caution to 45mph through Market Harborough. Then followed an acceleration up the 1 in 132 to 48mph before clearing Desborough summit. The acceleration that followed was thrilling to a degree as by Glendon speed had climbed, in three miles, from 45mph to 80$\frac{1}{2}$ mph. Once past Glendon Junction the driver shut off steam so that by Kettering South, where the regulator was re-opened, speed was down to 65mph. Another rapid acceleration to 75mph through Wellingborough and at the top of the 2$\frac{3}{4}$ mile climb at 1 in 120 Sharnbrook summit was passed at a minimum of 55mph. Touching 83$\frac{1}{2}$ mph past Sharnbrook station, the driver then braked to 65mph over Oakley troughs after which there was yet another startling acceleration, for in three miles the engine was worked up from 65mph to 82mph on crossing the Ouse at Bedford. The 19.7 miles from Bedford to Luton were reeled off in 18 min.14 sec. inclusive of a slight signal check at Leagrave and 'CJA', who was travelling in the coach next to the engine, said the exhaust was inaudible on this stretch. Having covered 68.9 miles from Leicester to Luton in the extraordinary time of 66 min 38 sec the driver then seemed somewhat at a loss to know how to fill in another 31 or 32 minutes to St. Pancras and was eventually held up by signal checks. But 'CJA' commented that 5052 comfortably could have completed the 99.1 miles from Leicester to St. Pancras in

96 minutes or less, instead of the 105 minutes allowed. He said also that this run gave a conclusive answer to the question as to whether 6' 0" driving wheels had any perceptible influence on speed capacity.

Delivery of the second order from Vulcan Foundry began in February 1935 and the first engine from Armstrong Whitworth appeared in April; by the end of the year, 225 were in service working from a steadily increasing number of sheds. Of the Vulcan engines, 5075-80 and 5098-5107 were allocated to the Central Division, 5081-94 and 5108-24 went new to the Western Division and 5095-97 to the Midland Division. Most of the first 75 engines from Armstrong Whitworth (5125-99) initially were allocated to Western Division sheds, though a few went to Scotland and 5187-89 started work on the Midland Division.

Stoke received its first engines in April when 5045 and 5046 arrived and in May the first were allocated to North Wales when 5125-28 were sent new to Holyhead, followed in June by 5108-14. 5129 and 5130 were allocated to Llandudno Junction and 5131-42 to Patricroft in June, and these, together with those at Holyhead and Crewe, transformed engine workings on the north Wales main line by replacing many of the LNWR 4-4-0s and 4-6-0s. One of the jobs of the pair at Llandudno Junction was the Llandudno to Manchester 'Club Train' which up to that time had been worked by the shed's Claughtons. Bangor was another shed to receive its first engines when 5093 and 5094 were transferred there from Crewe in July, whilst the first to be allocated to Chester were 5019, 5131 and 5152 in October 1935.

The September 1935 *Railway Observer* summed up the impact of the class in Scotland. "The most noteworthy development on the HR this year is the introduction of standard two-cylinder 4-6-0s of the '5000' series. There are now 20 of these locomotives on the section: thus outnumbering any other single class (even prior to 1923 there were only 19 Castles in service). The new locomotives are to be seen on practically all of the express trains between Perth, Aviemore and Inverness by both the Carr Bridge and Forres routes and are common between Inverness and Wick. Only the Skye line is free from these and there the Jones Goods of 1894 share the work with the Cumming 4-6-0s of 1917-19. Excellent work is also done by Highland engines between Inverness, Forres, Elgin and Keith, where the 'Wee Bennies' handle the through Aberdeen expresses to and from the 'Great North'. On the main line it is a different story. The Clans have all disappeared. The Rivers and the Horwich design of 2-6-0s chiefly are in demand when a Stanier 4-6-0 requires pilot assistance between Perth and Inverness, though this apparently is necessary only when the load exceeds about ten standard corridor coaches, despite the 1,484 feet of Drumochter".

In the autumn of 1935 the original ten engines, 5020-29, together with 5000-06, were transferred from Scotland to the Western Division and divided between Crewe and Edge Hill sheds; in return the Northern Division received 30 later build engines with three-row element superheaters, 5081-87 from Crewe North and 5157-79. These were allocated between Perth (North and South sheds), Inverness, St. Rollox and Kingmoor. Of those allocated to Inverness, two were normally sub-shedded at Wick, two at Helmsdale and two at Aviemore.

The last 25 engines of the 1935 order from Armstrong Whitworth, 5200-24, all went to the Central Division, being divided between Bank Hall, Low Moor, Newton Heath, Wakefield and Farnley Junction. Two other sheds also received

Class 5s for the first time towards the end of 1935; 5145/48-50 went to Warrington for working fitted freight trains and 5199 was transferred to Springs Branch.

By the end of 1935, the 225 engines in service were allocated to 29 sheds and divided between the Divisions as follows:

Central Division	43
Midland Division	51
Northern Division	47
Western Division	84

Crewe had the largest allocation with 34 engines, followed by Perth with 22, Patricroft with 14 and Inverness and Newton Heath each with 13 engines.

9.6 Further testing in 1935

During March 1935 another series of dynamometer car tests was carried out for the Chief Operating Manager to obtain particulars of the loading and running performance of the Class 5P5F 4-6-0s compared with the Class 5P4F 2-6-0s on fitted freight trains between Sheffield and Carlisle. The schedule of the test provided for an engine of each type to run two trips in each direction on the 7.30pm Sheffield Wicker-Carlisle (FF1) with a normal load of 45 vans and the 4.0pm

(FF2) Carlisle-Masboro (FF2) with a normal load of 50 vans, in each case plus dynamometer car and brake. The engines involved were:

5048 (with 2-row 14-element superheater); it had run 22,647 miles since built.

2831 (with 3-row 24-element superheater); it had run 19,384 miles since its last general overhaul.

2751 (with 3-row 24-element superheater); it had run 16,350 miles since its last general overhaul.

All the engines were in good mechanical condition except that some piston gland leakage was experienced with 5048 on its first southbound trip and a hot bearing developed on 2831 on its second northbound trip; consequently 2751 was used to work a single trip. No.2 dynamometer car was attached to each engine and all were supplied with Grimethorpe coal. Weather conditions were generally fine with normal temperatures and dry rails. There was some slipping at Ribblehead with 2851 on its second northbound trip. Wind speed did not exceed 15mph at any time.

The dates when each engine was on test, and the train loads, were:

7.30pm Sheffield Wicker to Carlisle			
11.03	5048	45 vans	517 tons
13.03	5048	45 vans	519 tons
18.03	2831	45 vans	492 tons
20.03	2831	49 vans	560 tons

4.0pm Carlisle to Masboro			
12.03	5048	51 vans	585 tons
14.03	5048	52 vans	596 tons
19.03	2831	48 vans	547 tons
21.03	2751	52 vans	593 tons

AVERAGE RESULTS OF TESTS						
	7.30pm down		4.0pm up		Total	
Engine	5048	2831	5048	2831/2751	5048	2831/2751
Coal						
Total weight (lbs.)	18,340	15,792	21,084	16,800	39,424	32,592
lbs. per mile	61.25	52.75	72.3	57.7	66.7	55.0
lbs. per dbhp	3.85	3.37	3.92	3.49	3.89	3.43
lbs. per sq.ft. of grate area	75.2	64.4	79.9	68.2	77.7	66.3
Water						
Total gallons	14,077	13,435	16,254	13,425	30,331	26,860
gallons per mile	47.0	44.9	55.7	46.1	51.2	45.4
lbs. per dbhp	29.6	28.7	30.3	27.9	29.9	28.3
Evaporation						
lbs. water per lb. coal	7.67	8.52	7.72	8.0		

From this table, it will be seen that on combined workings, the 2-6-0 showed reductions of 17.3% and 11.4% in total coal and water consumption respectively and reductions of 11.8% in coal, and 5.3% in water on the drawbar horse power basis, and an increase of evaporation of 7.1% as compared with the 4-6-0. The decrease in consumption of the 2-6-0 was attributed mainly to the higher degree of superheat and to a somewhat more economical steam distribution in the cylinders.

Following this poor performance by 5048, further tests were carried out over the same route and with the same trains and loads, but this time with two Class 5s. The engines, which worked one trip on each train, were:

(1) 5067 of Trafford Park shed, which had two rows of superheater elements, small tubes of 2" outside diameter, 5¹⁄₈" diameter blast pipe orifice and non-weighted jumper cap. It had run 20,600 miles since built. This engine was attached to dynamometer car No.1 and worked the 7.30pm from Sheffield Wicker to Carlisle (loaded to 514 tons from Masboro) on 16th April 1935 and returned with the 4.0pm

Carlisle to Masboro (loaded to 606 tons) on 17th.

(2) 5079, of Farnley Junction shed, which had three rows of superheater elements, small tubes of 2¹⁄₈" outside diameter, 5¹⁄₄" diameter blast pipe orifice and non-weighted jumper cap. It had run 4,622 miles since built. This engine was attached to dynamometer car No.2 and worked the 4.0pm Carlisle to Masboro (loaded to 610 tons) on 16th April and 7.30pm Sheffield Wicker to Carlisle (loaded to 562 tons from Masboro) on 17th.

The results showed a clear reduction in coal and water consumption (10.98% and 14.6% respectively) by the three-row engine 5079 compared with the two-row engine 5067.

The following week, the same engines with the same dynamometer cars, were tested to compare general performance, coal and water consumption on express passenger trains. 5067 worked the 10.0am St. Pancras-Leeds, with a load of 275 tons, on 24th and returned the following day with the 8.0am Leeds-St. Pancras with a load of 311 tons from Sheffield. 5079 worked the 8.0am from Leeds, with a load of 312 tons from Sheffield, on 24th and 10.0am St.

5048 was transferred from Edge Hill to Sheffield Grimesthorpe, where it was photographed on 15th September 1935, in December 1934 to work the Sheffield Wicker to Glasgow College fitted freight and the corresponding up train on alternate nights. It had been involved in tests during March 1935 when it was tested on Sheffield to Carlisle fitted freight trains against a Horwich Mogul, at the end of which its low two-row 14-element superheating was found to be inferior in coal and water consumption compared to the three-row 24-element 2-6-0. 5048 left Grimesthorpe for Llandudno Junction in November 1936.

Rail Archive Stephenson

Pancras to Leeds with a load of 272 tons on 25th. Again 5079 showed a considerable saving in coal and water consumption compared with 5067 – 12.7% and 14.0% respectively. Indeed, the results were consistent on freight and passenger workings. The steaming of both engines was good throughout. When working the fitted freights, trouble was experienced with 5067 through piston glands blowing but this was rectified and was not considered to have materially affected the results. Both engines were fired with a moderate fire on the grate which was thickened under the firehole door.

Mention was made above of the jumper cap on 5067 and 5079 and in order to investigate the lift of the jumper cap on this class under running conditions, engine 5050 was fitted with a trigger indicator gear which was operated by the cap and which permitted a magnified visual reading of the actual lift of the cap to be obtained. The jumper cap as originally fitted to the engine weighed 33lbs. The trip gear weighed approximately 5oz., a total of 33.3lbs. The blast pipe orifice was $5^{1}/_{8}$". Readings first were obtained when running with a train under these conditions, then the jumper cap was fitted with metal strips, bringing the total weight of the cap up to 43lbs, or 43.3lbs including the trip gear. A further series of readings on a train was then obtained.

With the unweighted cap of 33lbs., the cap was down at a cut off of 20% and began to lift at a cut off of 23%. When working at a cut off of 45% with full regulator opening and full boiler pressure, and at a speed of 20mph, the cap lifted $^{1}/_{4}$". With the weighted cap of 43 lbs, the cap was down at a cut off of 28% and began to lift at a cut off of 30%. The maximum lift observed, under any combination of circumstances, approximately $^{5}/_{16}$". From these results it was concluded that

a jumper cap weighing between 43lbs and 44lbs would be satisfactory in general working conditions for the Class 5s. These jumper cap tests with 5050, which was allocated to Derby, were carried out when the engine was working the 8.15am passenger train from Derby to Bristol and the 2.20pm from Bristol to Birmingham on 27th May, 8th and 12th June 1935.

Further tests were carried out with the engines on the Western Division main line during 1935. On 19th March, 5051, fitted with an indicator shelter, worked the 12.44pm from Crewe to Euston, returning with the 10.30am from Euston the next day. On 22nd the same engine worked the 12.44pm from Crewe again but this time returned the following day on the 5.30pm from Euston.

During June and July 1935, more dynamometer car tests were carried out between Euston and Carlisle to determine the maximum loading for various classes of engine working limited load passenger trains. The engines involved were Class 5 5082 and Jubilee 5646, both of which had three-row element superheaters and had run 13,500 miles and 26,600 miles respectively since new. The tests took place between 17th June and 11th July on the following trains:

11.8am Crewe-Euston   9.31 am Crewe-Carlisle
3.20pm Euston-Crewe   3.57pm Carlisle-Crewe

Four runs were made by each engine on each train. On two of the runs an addition of 30 tons was made to the standard 'Limited Load' and on two of the runs a further 15 tons, or 45 tons above the respective standard 'Limited Load' for each engine, was added. Steaming of 5082 was completely satisfactory throughout and no difficulty was experienced in

January 1937 saw 5305-07 at Carnforth from where they worked round the coast over the Furness line to Workington and Carlisle on trains previously hauled by Compounds. Consequently, 1120/24 were transferred from Carnforth to Chester and 1171 went to Crewe. 5313-16 were the first to be shedded at Rugby, in February 1937, and they began to appear regularly in Birmingham on trains previously handled by Georges or Compounds. Other sheds to receive their first allocation with new engines were Bescot (5387), Bletchley (5390/91), Speke (5414-16), Stockport (5435/36) and Camden (5438-40). The three sent to Camden in week ending 4th December 1937 were some of the very few ever to be shedded there and they stayed only a short time, all moving away by 1st January 1938, 5438 and 5439 to Patricroft and 5440 to Rugby. The pair at Stockport also only stayed a few months and it was many years before any more were on that depot's roster. During 1937, other Western Division sheds received the class for the first time as transfers from elsewhere. These included Preston (5296 in April from Longsight), Walsall (5038 from Bushbury in July) and Mold Junction (5237-39 from Chester in September).

The engines now were appearing on many of the secondary express and semi-fast passenger trains on the Western Division whilst at many sheds their principal duties were hauling fitted freights. In some areas they had become the most common type of motive power, which was well demonstrated in north Wales. On Saturday 11th June 1938 in a period of six hours, 64 different engines were noted and 36 of them (or 56%) were Class 5s which came from 15 different sheds. In the summer of 1939 the daily requirements of Class 5 engines at sheds on the North Wales coast were:

Llandudno Junction	9MO	8MX	4 Sun – allocation 12 engines
Bangor	2SX	3S0	1 Sun – allocation 4 engines
Holyhead		3 daily	- allocation 5 engines

Holyhead had a reputation for turning out very dirty engines; early in 1937 the numbers on some of them were said to be unreadable at close range and on others partly worn off or removed. At one time the number on the cab side of 5111 appeared as '11'.

In 1939 the class began working on to the Southern Railway with transfer freights between Willesden and Norwood Junction in place of LNWR 0-8-0s. Engines from a variety of sheds were used by Willesden on these trains.

9.9 Midland Division

5260-89, which were placed in traffic between October and December 1936, all went to the Midland Division to replace, in the main, the earlier Vulcan Foundry-built engines which moved to the Western Division. The allocation of the new engines and the movement of the earlier engines was:

	New Engines	Transferred away
Kentish Town	5260/77-81 (6)	5052 to Llandudno Junction
		5053/57/58 to Kingmoor
		5054 to Longsight
		5181 to Crewe
Trafford Park	5261-65/87 (6)	5035 to Llandudno Junction
		5055/67 to Tebay
		5068, 5185 to Springs Branch
		5069 to Willesden
Sheffield	5266/67 (2)	5034 to Aston
		5048 to Llandudno Junction
Saltley	5268-72 (5)	5030/38/39, 5183 to Aston
Derby	5273/74/86 (3)	5033/50 to Edge Hill
		5064 to Crewe
		5184 to Willesden
Gloucester	5275/76 (2)	5032 to Shrewsbury
		5066 to Kingmoor
Nottingham	5282 (1)	5189 to Crewe
Bristol	5283/88/89 (3)	5094 to Preston
		5096 to Patricroft
		5097 to Crewe
Holbeck	5284 (1)	5037 to Patricroft
Millhouses	5285 (1)	5090 to Patricroft

Hellifield shed received its first Class 5 in w/e 2nd October 1937 when 5267 was transferred there from Sheffield. It stayed until w/e 26th September 1942 when it moved to Cricklewood.

On the Bristol to Birmingham line the Stanier engines replaced the Midland 4-4-0s and, as one observer at the time put it, "the almost legendary splendour of the old Midland engines gave way to the workaday travel stained exteriors of the 4-6-0s". The northbound road from Bristol was undoubtedly the more difficult. It started with a climb at between 1 in 69 and 1 in 90 for 2¾ miles to Fishponds, after which it undulated for the next 30 miles or so to Gloucester. From here there was another steady climb at between 1 in 304 and 1 in 368 for six miles to Cheltenham, then a gradual rise to Bromsgrove and the start of the Lickey incline.

Class 5s were allowed to take 415 tons on 'Full Load' timings and 370 tons on 'Limited Load' timings without assistance, but up the 2¾ mile bank from Bristol to Fishponds the limit was 345 tons. When the load exceeded this figure the train stopped momentarily by Bristol engine shed for a banking engine to 'buffer up' at the rear. All trains stopped at Bromsgrove for banking help up the Lickey. At a stroke, the loads which could be hauled by a single engine almost had doubled, resulting in a big reduction in piloting. Furthermore, the advance in locomotive engineering practice over the years is well demonstrated by comparing these unassisted loads and the tractive efforts with those of the 4-4-0s which had previously hauled the passenger services.

Locomotive Type	Unassisted Full Load Timings	Nominal Tractive Effort
Stanier 5P5F 4-6-0	415 tons	25,455 lbs
Stanier 5XP 4-6-0	450 tons	26,610 lbs
Midland 2P 4-4-0	200 tons	17,700 lbs
Midland 3P 4-4-0	220 tons	20,065 lbs

The engines based at Saltley and Bristol could be seen on all the main expresses alongside the Jubilees, on many of the secondary passenger trains and also on the express freights.

In April 1937, three experimental runs were made over the Midland Division, two between St. Pancras and Leeds and back, and one return trip between St. Pancras and Manchester Central and back. The Leeds trains were hauled by Jubilees but Class 5s were used on the Manchester runs because, at that time, they were the largest engines allowed over the main line through the Peak District. The official publicity circulated by the LMS said that "the journeys made were purely experimental and no immediate large scale acceleration is necessarily foreshadowed", but clearly, large scale speed-ups were needed, if only to bring the trains back to their pre-1914 levels.

On the Manchester runs, which took place on 22nd April, chief interest obviously centred round the performance between Derby and Manchester. The line climbed to an altitude of nearly 1,000 feet (more than Shap) in the 36 miles from Derby to Peak Forest and the ascent included about nine miles averaging 1 in 110, followed by the final five miles at 1 in 100 and 1 in 90. Southbound, the climb to Peak Forest was even more severe, wholly against the engine with a final nine miles at 1 in 90.

North from Derby on the down run, the engine was 5278 (Kentish Town shed), with Driver W. Smith and Fireman H. Crooks of Trafford Park on the footplate, and they cut the 72-

Armstrong Whitworth 5261, from Trafford Park, on 15th May 1938 with a local train at Chapel-en-le-Frith. It was transferred to Derby in July after the Jubilees took over the London-Manchester workings following the removal of route restrictions at Chapel. *E. R. Morten*

From 12th February 1935 Class 5s took over from Class 5XP Jubilees the Midland Division West of England line expresses and also were used on fast freights. 5043 was photographed in 1935 at Bristol Temple Meads with the northbound "Devonian". It had been transferred from Edge Hill to Bristol in w/e 23rd February 1935 and still had the open front footplate and prominent top feed pipes which identified it as one of the original 25 engines built by Vulcan Foundry.

120

Derby's 5286 passes the limestone 'alps' at Peak Forest on 10th May 1938 with the 12.15pm ex-Manchester shortly before the Jubilees took over the London-Manchester expresses.   *E. R. Morten*

5342 on 29th May 1938 departing from Chinley with a down express; the third coach is a Midland Railway clerestory. The Class 5 had been transferred from Crewe to Sheffield the previous month.   *E. R. Morten*

minute timing for the 61.4 miles to Manchester by almost four minutes, achieving a start to stop average speed of 54mph. By Belper (7.8miles from Derby) the train was travelling at 77mph, an astonishing feat on rising grades. After a permanent speed restriction at Ambergate, speed settled down in the mid-1950s and after Rowsley, where the real climbing started, it varied between 45mph and 57mph. Following a slack to 37mph over Millers Dale Junction, 5278 maintained a steady 38mph up the long 1 in 90 climb to Peak Forest, gaining 14 minutes on schedule from Rowsley. Downhill, speed was not allowed to exceed 68mph to Hazel Grove but then there was some sprightly running through the Manchester suburbs with a maximum speed of 82mph. The overall journey time from St. Pancras to Manchester Central, with stops at Leicester and Derby, was three hours 22 minutes, with an eight-coach train of 260 tons.

On the up journey later in the day the engine was 5264 (of Trafford Park shed) with Driver G. H. Beebe and Fireman R. Foulkes, also Trafford Park men. The load was the same as on the down run but this time they stuck more closely to the test schedule, although they were 2³/₄ minutes ahead of time by Chinley. From Cheadle Heath, passed at 68mph, 14 miles up at 1 in 100 reduced speed to 57¹/₂ mph, then 1¹/₄ miles at 1 in 140 raised it to 59mph at Bramhall Moor Lane but by Hazel Grove it had dropped to 57mph again. After this the line climbed for 34 miles to the south end of Disley tunnel, mostly at 1 in 132 and then the 1 in 90 started. Speed slowly fell to 43mph at Chinley, 38mph at Chapel and 34mph at Peak Forest summit. Downhill speeds were very restrained and so exaggerated was the attention paid to the curves between Rowsley and Ambergate that all the time gained to Chinley was wiped out and the train stopped at Derby in 73 minutes 10 seconds, practically as booked.

Between Derby and London, the main feature of 5264's work was the exceptionally rapid acceleration from checks and the summit of banks. Between Mill Hill and Hendon the engine reached 91mph, the highest speed reached by any of the engines on these test runs. The shorter climbs also were attacked vigorously, with speeds of 65mph at Kibworth North after four miles largely rising at 1 in 200/160, whilst after the service slack at Market Harborough the engine accelerated to 56¹/₂ mph up the 4¹/₂ miles at 1 in 132 to Desborough North. By Kettering, 5264 was nearly two minutes ahead of Jubilee 5614 on one of the Leeds runs, although the latter had an extra coach. The start to stop time of 5264 from Leicester to St. Pancras was 92 mins 36 secs (about 91 minutes net) for the 99.1 miles for which the scheduled time was 96 minutes. The overall journey time from Manchester to London was three hours 24 minutes, the actual running time being three hours 15¹/₂ minutes.

Substantial accelerations of Midland Division passenger trains did, in fact, take place from the start of the winter 1937 timetable, being brought about by the stud of 4-6-0s now available to them. The whole service was recast and some very fast timings were introduced between St. Pancras, Leicester and Nottingham. A determined effort also was made to restore the popularity of the Midland route between London and Manchester over which the Class 5s still were the largest engines allowed north of Derby. Their maximum unassisted load over the Peak was 255 tons and Trafford Park and Kentish Town engines amassed very high mileages on these services. However, following the completion of reconstruction of bridges at Chapel-en-le-Frith, the Jubilees began working through to Manchester from the start of the 1938 summer timetable. Their unassisted maximum load north of Derby was 275 tons, 20 tons more than the Class 5s.

5042, seen here in 1937 at Elstree on the 4.25pm Manchester to St. Pancras, was one of the Class 5s involved in a major re-allocation of the Vulcan Foundry-built engines in February 1935 when 17 from the Western Division and three from the Central Division were transferred to the Midland Division. It moved from Carlisle Upperby to Trafford Park, where it stayed until July 1938. *Real Photographs*

10B Preston (6)	5004, 5054, 5142, 5184, 5424, 5425
10C Patricroft (21)	5019, 5037, 5044, 5055, 5059, 5135, 5137, 5140, 5141, 5143, 5144, 5196, 5250, 5304, 5312, 5329, 5365, 5402, 5420, 5421, 5428
11A Carnforth (11)	5111, 5183, 5293, 5305, 5306, 5307, 5345, 5364, 5372, 5373, 5427
11D Oxenholme (2)	5251, 5426
11E Tebay (3)	5408, 5409, 5410
12B Carlisle (W) (26)	5045, 5057, 5058, 5132, 5133, 5134, 5136, 5138, 5139, 5230, 5231, 5243, 5244, 5363, 5366, 5368, 5414, 5415, 5416, 5435, 5436, 5438, 5439, 5449, 5450, 5451
1A Willesden (14)	5032, 5191, 5323, 5324, 5325, 5326, 5327, 5343, 5344, 5401, 5411, 5413, 5430, 5431
2A Rugby (13)	5022, 5290, 5291, 5313, 5314, 5315, 5330, 5331, 5349, 5350, 5351, 5352, 5441
2B Bletchley (3)	5390, 5391, 5442
3A Bescot (1)	5387
3B Bushbury (4)	5193, 5419, 5429, 5437
3C Walsall (2)	5417, 5418
3D Aston (10)	5030, 5034, 5038, 5039, 5051, 5073, 5308, 5321, 5322, 5388
3E Monument Lane (4)	5245, 5297, 5301, 5395
4A Shrewsbury (8)	5255, 5259, 5397, 5407, 5433, 5434, 5445, 5446
4B Swansea (2)	5091, 5292
5A Crewe (24)	5000, 5001, 5082, 5198, 5299, 5300, 5353, 5354, 5375, 5376, 5378, 5379, 5380, 5381, 5382, 5383, 5384, 5385, 5386, 5393, 5394, 5405, 5406, 5412
5A Crewe North (16)	5002, 5003, 5046, 5097, 5108, 5121, 5125, 5181, 5195, 5197, 5316, 5369, 5374, 5377, 5392, 5404
5B Crewe South (3)	5028, 5131, 5254
5D Stoke (3)	5027, 5146, 5147
6A Chester (8)	5064, 5109, 5190, 5309, 5310, 5311, 5328, 5348
6B Mold Jct (6)	5069, 5240, 5241, 5242, 5422, 5423
7A Llandudno Jct. (11)	5035, 5048, 5052, 5129, 5130, 5235, 5236, 5246, 5253, 5371, 5444
7B Bangor (5)	5070, 5317, 5318, 5346, 5370
7C Holyhead (5)	5110, 5112, 5113, 5247, 5248
8A Edge Hill (17)	5020, 5021, 5026, 5033, 5050, 5072, 5114, 5120, 5122, 5123, 5124, 5128, 5189, 5298, 5303, 5399, 5400
8B Warrington (8)	5095, 5145, 5148, 5149, 5150, 5252, 5332, 5398
9A Longsight (9)	5024, 5025, 5074, 5256, 5257, 5258, 5295, 5296, 5347

One of the final Armstrong Whitworth vertical throatplate Class 5s, 5215, in the 1930s at Tebay on a Glasgow-Birmingham express of decidedly mixed coaching stock. It went new to Bank Hall shed and remained there until reallocated to Aintree in December 1940. It is in 1936 livery applied during a Heavy repair either in late 1937 or mid-1938. *Real Photographs*

9.16 Callander & Oban Line

From the summer of 1934 the ex-Highland Railway Clan class 4-6-0s had worked the principal trains on the Callander & Oban line and whilst a Class 5 had been tried out in October 1937, the Clans continued to reign supreme. However, when the engines 5452-71 were introduced this enabled Perth to release 5358 and 5362 which went to Oban on 5th November 1938. On Monday 7th these two engines began working Oban's principal turns to Glasgow. 5358 worked the 9.10am from Oban to Glasgow, returning from Buchanan St. with the 5.10pm to Oban; this had been the favourite turn of 14766 *Clan Chattan*. 5362 left Oban with the 12.5pm to Glasgow and returned the following day with the 8.0am Glasgow-Oban service, alternating with a St. Rollox engine and taking over from 14764 *Clan Munro* which had been the usual engine on this job. However, the Stanier engines stayed at Oban only for a few months and at the start of the spring 1939 timetable they were transferred to St. Rollox, in week ending 6th May. No other engines of the class ever were shedded at Oban.

From then onwards, St. Rollox shed used Class 5s on the line but turns worked by Oban shed reverted to Clans; Stirling shed also used Clans on its jobs to Oban which included the 12.5am and 5.45am trains from Stirling to Oban. During the summer of 1939, however, the working of the 12.5am was fitted into the roster of a Class 5 from Edinburgh Dairy Road. The 5.10pm Glasgow-Oban continued to be worked by a Clan until May 1940 when Class 5s from St. Rollox took over. Two runs over the Oban line immediately before the war contrast the work of the Clan and Class 5 4-6-0s. The engines were 14764 *Clan Munro* and 5355, both hauling seven-coach trains with tare weights of 231 tons and 234 tons respectively. The details were:

	Distance (miles)	Start to Stop Times 14764	5355
Crianlarich-Tyndrum	5.2	12m 18s	7m 45s
Tyndrum-Dalmally	12.0	19m 35s	20m 0s
Dalmally-Loch Awe	2.7	4m 35s	4m 23s
Loch Awe-Taynuilt	8.8	15m 52s	14m 15s
Taynuilt-Ach-na-Cloich	3.8	7m 30s	6m 25s
Ach-na-Cloich-Connel Ferry	3.4	7m 40s	6m 40s
Connel Ferry-Oban	6.8	17m 08s	15m 07s
Total	**41.7**	**84m 38s**	**74m 35s**

From Crianlarich to Tyndrum, 14764 dropped to 22½ mph on the steep 1 in 44 part of the climb whilst the minimum speed of 5355, which actually started from Crianlarich Junction about ½ mile beyond the station, was 34mph. On the 1 in 50 ascent out of Tyndrum, 5355 was slow off the mark compared with the Clan but after that the Stanier engine had it all its own way. On the climb from Loch Awe to the Pass of Brander, 14764's speed fell from 44mph to 36mph whilst 5355 dropped from 50mph to 42½ mph. Similarly on the climb out of Connel Ferry to Glencruitten summit, mostly at 1 in 50, the speed of the Clan was between 23mph and 20mph and the Stanier 4-6-0 between 31mph and 25mph. This comparison is not intended to decry the efforts of 14764 but it does demonstrate the advantages of the more modern engine.

In the opposite direction, again before the war, 5453 put up a magnificent performance on the short 12-mile run from Dalmally to Tyndrum with a 162ton train. For the first five miles the line climbs at an average of 1 in 63 (two miles being at 1 in 50 or steeper) and for the next 5½ miles the climb averages 1 in 127, a total rise of 625 feet in 10½ miles. 5453 took 16 minutes 42 seconds to the summit with speeds per mile (after the first mile) climbing from 33mph to 46.2mph,

then levelling off. Tyndrum was reached in 19 minutes seven seconds, a start to stop average of 38mph and a gain of six minutes on the 25-minute schedule.

9.17 G&SWR lines

The first of the class to be allocated to the former G&SWR sheds were 5178/79 and 5319/57 which were transferred to Corkerhill in week ending 15th April 1939, the first two from Kingmoor and the others from Perth. These began working on the Stranraer road, amongst others, but they had all moved away by the end of the year.

One interesting working to Stranraer was on 7th July 1939 when 5355, of St. Rollox shed and crewed by R. Cleary and R. Smith of Ayr, worked a six-coach special in connection with the inaugural cruise of the new Stranraer-Larne steamer "Princess Victoria". The engine first worked the special from Glasgow Central to Gourock, then took the empty stock to Stranraer Harbour and returned with the passengers from there to Glasgow Central. On the return journey from Stranraer the engine put up a sprightly performance, cutting six minutes off the booked time over the heavily-graded section from Dunragit to Pinwherry. The uphill work on this run was described as excellent.

One of the early runs over the Stranraer line with a service train was timed by David L. Smith. The train was the 9.17pm from Stranraer Harbour to Glasgow, "The Irishman", with six coaches of 195tons tare and hauled by 5357. With a late start, the Girvan crew cut 7½ minutes off the 63-minute schedule for the 38 miles to Girvan. On another occasion the same engine, with the eight-coach 5.10pm from Glasgow, gained 7½ minutes on the scheduled running time between Girvan and Stranraer Town after making an allowance for a check near New Luce, and stopping at all stations. The start to stop timings were:

	Distance (miles)	Schedule (minutes)	Actual Time
Girvan-Pinmore	4.9	14	11m 15s
Pinmore-Pinwherry	3.2	5½	5m 0s
Pinwherry-Barrhill	4.2	9½	8m 33s
Barrhill-Glenwhilly	8.5	14½	14m 0s
Glenwhilly-New Luce	4.4	7	7m 45s
New Luce-Dunragit	6.7	10	8m 50s
Dunragit-Castle Kennedy	2.8	5	4m 55s
Castle Kennedy-Stranraer	2.7	6	5m 45s
Total	**37.4**	**71½**	**66m 3s**

Over this section, the maximum unpiloted load for Class 5s was 230 tons from Girvan to Pinmore and 260 tons from Pinmore to New Luce. The weight of this train was 239 tons so a banker was provided out of Girvan in the shape of 4-4-0 14333. From the station the line climbs for 2½ miles at 1 in 54, then 1 in 56 for 1¼ miles and the two engines accelerated to 30/31mph up this grade. From Pinwherry, without assistance, 5357 was opened up to 45% cut off with full regulator and was worked like this continuously for the next 15 minutes, except when stopping at Barrhill. No difficulty was experienced in finding steam for this effort which Mr. Smith calculated to have produced a maximum cylinder horsepower of 1,585 at 37mph just before Barrhill. The line climbs steadily from Pinwherry at between 1 in 67 and 1 in 80 through Barrhill to the summit 8.2 miles from Pinwherry.

9.18 Wartime

By the time war broke out in September 1939 the Class 5s had more than proved their capabilities. They could deputise for express engines on heavy trains, they could maintain high speeds, they were good hill climbers and they could work heavy loads on fitted freight trains.

When passenger services were cut back severely in September 1939 more express engines were available so there was less need for mixed traffic engines to work passenger trains. These engines were, however, called on to work the growing number of military specials and much more of their time was spent on the ever-increasing number of freight trains. Between 1st September and 31st December 1939 the LMS operated the highest number of loaded wagon miles since the company came into existence; at 520.6 million miles, this was an increase of 92.6 million miles over the same period in 1938. The LMS then was running an average of 4,000 freight trains (excluding empties) each day. By 1942, LMS engines hauling freight covered 121 million miles, 19 million miles more than in 1938, whilst wagon miles totalled 1,713 million, a 34% increase on 1938.

Passenger traffic involving special trains grew also. In three days during 1943 the LMS reported running 42 specials conveying prisoners of war from ports to inland camps, and in the same three day period they ran 277 specials for military purposes. For these traffics, the Class 5s were invaluable.

Western Division

During the first few weeks of the war, 45 Class 5s were transferred to depots which mainly handled freight traffic, or where freight formed a large part of their work. Twelve moved to Edge Hill, seven went to Mold Junction, Aston and Springs Branch received five each and Shrewsbury and Upperby four each. Patricroft, Rugby, Stockport and Warrington each gained two engines. The engines involved and the depots to which they moved were:

Edge Hill	5024/25/69, 5129/30/95, 5246/48, 5376-78, 5423
Mold Junction	5242, 5382-86, 5422
Aston	5046, 5245, 5301/79/81
Springs Branch	5140/85, 5304, 5424/25
Shrewsbury	5309/30/31, 5405
Upperby	5108/21/25, 5380
Patricroft	5196, 5402
Rugby	5240/41
Stockport	5074, 5148
Warrington	5392/93.

Subsequent transfers of other engines saw the class concentrated at the principal sheds and at the end of 1942 the 252 engines on the Western Division were divided between only 20 sheds. Crewe North and South sheds had 66 between them, Patricroft had 31, Edge Hill 28 and Upperby 20. Next, rather surprisingly, came Mold Junction with 15, followed by Willesden with 12 and Carnforth and Shrewsbury with 11 each. Thirteen sheds which had members of the class in pre-war days had lost their allocation by 31st December 1942.

To demonstrate their haulage capabilities on the Western Division, O. S. Nock reported a run with Edge Hill's 5399 towards the end of the war. The engine was called upon to take over the 7.30pm Bristol to Manchester train from a GWR Castle class 4-6-0 at Shrewsbury. It was an enormous load of 490 tons but the engine maintained 25mph up the $2\frac{1}{2}$ mile climb at 1 in 124/117 out of Shrewsbury. The train then ran fast to Prees, sustaining 65mph on the level beyond Wem. Whitchurch (18.9 miles) was passed in $26\frac{3}{4}$ minutes, speed topped 70mph at Wrenbury and if it had not been for signal checks approaching Crewe, the journey could have been completed in 42 minutes which was very little more than the fastest pre-war booking, and with a much heavier load than in peace time.

Midland Division

Transfers of the class to freight duties on the Midland Division began in March 1940 when seven engines moved to Toton.

More followed and eventually 12 different engines were shedded there for varying periods until they moved away in July 1942, when 2-8-0s became available in numbers. The engines at Toton were 5042/56/67/71/88, 5249/63/64/71/78/83/87. Other sheds to receive Class 5s were Hasland (5264), Staveley which had five at one time or another, Normanton where 5187 was shedded from 20th April 1940 until 18th October 1941 and Cricklewood which had 5281 from 22nd August 1942 to 26th September 1942 when it was replaced by 5267 which stayed until 14th November 1942.

By the end of 1942, however, only 35 of the class remained on the Midland Division and they were concentrated at just six sheds. Kentish Town had ten, Holbeck and Saltley had eight each, Derby had four, Millhouses had three and two were at Gloucester. Bristol and Trafford Park had lost their allocations and received Jubilees for main line passenger work and there were none of the class at Belle Vue, Nottingham or Sheffield.

Central Division

On the Central Division there were some movements of the class for short periods during the early part of the war to depots whose work was mainly on freight. Six were sent to Aintree in November 1940 (5047/90, 5215/16, 5336/38) and several went to Rose Grove and Accrington. Sowerby Bridge had 5060 from 2nd August 1941 to 7th February 1942 and 5079 from 6th June 1942 to 14th November 1942, and Wigan had 5335 from 28th October 1939 until 27th July 1940.

However, at the end of 1942 the position was virtually the same as it was five years earlier. The Division had 62 engines compared with 60 at the end of 1937, and they were divided between the same nine sheds.

Northern Division

There was a large influx of the class to Scotland during 1941 and 1942 when 23 engines were transferred north from English sheds, most of them going to Perth or Inverness. The 20 engines built in 1938, 5452-71, had all gone to Scotland and by the end of 1942, 54 of the class were at Perth, 35 at Inverness, 17 at St. Rollox, 15 at Kingmoor and two at Aviemore, making a total of 123.

The engines transferred from English sheds were:

From	Numbers
Accrington	5047
Agecroft	5049/5090/5098
Bath	5023/5029, 5194, 5389
Bushbury	5429
Crewe	5022, 5241, 5365
Edge Hill	5120/5123/5124, 5309
Holbeck	5266, 5443
Huddersfield	5005/5006
Low Moor	5213
Newton Heath	5192
Nottingham	5036
Patricroft	5251
Rugby	5366
Springs Branch	5121/5122
Upperby	5125

Somerset and Dorset Joint Lines

In March 1940, 5023 and 5194 were moved to Leeds Holbeck and 5029 went to Saltley but they were all back at Bath within a few weeks. However, in September 1941 locomotive working over the S&DJ line was taken over by the Southern Railway and the majority of the 4-6-0s were transferred away. 5023, 5194 and 5389 went to Perth and 5289 (which had been officially allocated to Bath for only a week) and 5432 moved to Holbeck, leaving only 5029 and 5440 still at Bath. These

continued to be seen on the heaviest trains of the day, the 9.45am Bournemouth West to Bath and the 4.25pm Bath to Bournemouth West.

The LMS engines were replaced at Bath by ex-L&SWR 4-4-0s of classes S11 and T9 and one Sunday in November 1941, a Southern S11 piloted 5440 out of Bath on an exceptionally heavy load for the S&D line; the train had 17 vehicles with a tare weight of 440 tons and a gross weight of around 470 tons. The two Class 5s stayed at Bath until the autumn of 1942, 5440 being transferred to Gloucester on 26th September and 5029 to Perth on 31st October.

9.19 The Locomotive Exchanges 1948

Although instituted as a means of obtaining information on which to base plans for locomotive standardisation, the announcement of the proposed exchange of motive power between the various regions of British Railways was received with interest and speculation by locomotive enthusiasts everywhere. It was scheduled to begin on 19th April 1948 and engines were to be worked in normal service over selected routes, with dynamometer cars attached to the trains to record speeds and other essential data. The trains chosen were to be made up to agreed weights to facilitate comparison.

The locomotives chosen were divided into three groups: express passenger, freight and mixed traffic and, in the latter category, the locomotives were the LMS Class 5 4-6-0, LNER Class B1 4-6-0, GWR Modified Hall Class 4-6-0 and Southern Railway West Country 4-6-2. The trains and routes chosen were:

10.15am London (St. Pancras) to Manchester (Central)
1.50pm Manchester (Central) to London (St. Pancras)
10.00am London (Marylebone) to Manchester (London Road)
9.55am Manchester (London Road) to London (Marylebone)
1.45pm Bristol to Plymouth
1.35pm Plymouth to Bristol
4.00pm Perth to Inverness
8.40am Inverness to Perth.

(When the summer timetable came into force, the 'up' train from Manchester (London Road) to Marylebone was changed to a departure from Manchester at 8.25am).

The locomotives all used the same grade of coal when working on the same tests and were manned by enginemen who normally worked them in their home region. The tests were spread over a period of about four months, the mixed traffic tests taking place in the fifth to twelfth weeks.

The tests involving mixed traffic locomotives took place with pre-test runs on Mondays and Wednesdays with the down trains and on Tuesdays and Thursdays with the up trains. The actual test runs with dynamometer cars attached to the trains were on Tuesdays and Thursdays with the down trains and Wednesdays and Fridays with the up trains.

45253 represented the London Midland Region in the mixed traffic category during the 1948 Locomotive Exchanges. Having produced the worst performance of the three engines tested on the Midland main line to Manchester, 45253 continued to disappoint when the tests moved on to the more arduous Great Central London-Manchester route, arriving in London Road station 34 minutes late on one of the runs. 45253 is passing New Basford with a Marylebone to Manchester London Road train on 9th June 1948.   *Rail Archive Stephenson*

Week commencing	Route	Pre-test	Test
31.05.48	St. Pancras-Manchester		LMS Class 5
	Marylebone-Manchester	SR West Country	LNER Class B1
07.04.48	St. Pancras-Manchester	LNER Class B1	
	Marylebone-Manchester	LMS Class 5	SR West Country
14.06.48	St. Pancras-Manchester	SR West Country	LNER Class B1
	Marylebone-Manchester	GWR Modified Hall	LMS Class 5
21.06.48	St. Pancras-Manchester		SR West Country
	Marylebone-Manchester		GWR Modified Hall
28.06.48	Perth-Inverness	SR West Country	LMS Class 5
	Bristol-Plymouth	LNER Class B1	GWR Modified Hall
05.07.48	Perth-Inverness		SR West Country
	Bristol-Plymouth	LMS Class 5	LNER Class B1
12.07.48	Perth-Inverness	LNER Class B1	
	Bristol-Plymouth	SR West Country	LMS Class 5
19.07.48	Perth-Inverness		LNER Class B1

The Locomotive Exchanges were looked upon with great excitement by amateur enthusiasts and many of the LMS supporters had high hopes that the outcome would show the superiority of their engines. However, in the mixed traffic category the tests proved quite a humiliation for the London Midland because it was the Class 5 which let down the side, especially on the metals of the former Great Central between Marylebone and Manchester. The engine selected was 45253 with Driver Smith of Kentish Town which was used on all three routes in England, with a Northern Division classmate taking over for the Scottish tests.

On the Midland main line, the Class 5 was tested against the Eastern Region's B1 61251 *Oliver Bury,* a Kings Cross engine with Driver Howard (also of Kings Cross), whilst the Southern Region was represented by West Country Pacific 34005 *Barnstaple* with Driver James of Nine Elms. The load was light with no more than 325-335 tons (full) and interest centred mainly on the heavily graded Derby to Manchester section through the Peak District with 20-mile climbs in each direction up to the summit at Peak Forest with much at gradients of 1 in 90 or 1 in 100. Between London and Leicester where, in pre-war days, there was some very fast running, the 1948 schedules were slow and running bedevilled by permanent way restriction (PWR) slacks. Nothing of any note was achieved by any of the competing engines though there were a few significant indications of the superior power of the Southern Region Pacific. North of Leicester, the point to point (start to stop) timings achieved by the three engines were as follows:

	Distance (miles)	Schedule (minutes)	01.06.48 45253 min sec	15.06.48 61251 min sec	22.06.48 34005 min sec
Leicester-Loughborough	12.5	16	16 02	14 59	13 58
Loughborough-Derby	16.9	23	22 00	21 16	20 32
Derby-Matlock	17.2	24	28 18	24 29	24 30
Matlock-Millers Dale	14.3	23	24 34	25 44	23 09
Millers Dale-Chinley	10.2	20	20 58	18 46	18 07
Chinley-Manchester (Cen)	19.7	25	24 49	28 22	24 45
Totals	**90.8**	**131**	**136 41**	**133 36**	**125 01**

The Pacific proved much more lively than the B1 or the Class 5, the 4-6-2 reaching 70mph before the Loughborough stop compared with maxima of 66mph (B1) and 62mph (Class 5). On to Derby, 34005 reached 72mph at Kegworth whilst 61251 and 45253 reached 63mph and 62½ mph respectively at the same point. So between Leicester and Derby the West Country gained 4½ minutes on schedule, the B1 gained 2¾ minutes and the Class 5 kept time to Loughborough and gained a minute to Derby.

From Derby to Matlock the best showing was made by the B1, which suffered a PWR near Cromford that did not affect the other two engines. The West Country, without the PWR, registered exactly the same time as the B1 to Matlock, both losing half a minute on schedule. Driver Smith of Kentish Town had some problems with 45253 on leaving Derby and was compelled to run slowly to Ambergate whilst the trouble was rectified and this lost the train 4¼ minutes to Matlock. Each engine had a bad PWR check at Rowsley, just before the start of the long climb to Peak Forest. The Pacific certainly made the best showing, being virtually on schedule to Millers Dale but the B1 lost 2¾ minutes. The Class 5 ran as well as the B1 to Hassop but from there on the upper part of the climb was better than the B1, only losing 1½ minutes to Millers Dale.

From Millers Dale up the steepest part of the climb to Peak Forest (three miles at 1 in 90), 34005 reached the summit in 9¾ minutes attaining 32½mph and keeping time which neither of the others did, the B1 taking eleven minutes and passing Peak Forest at 26½mph whilst 45253 took 12 minutes and achieved 32mph before speed was reduced by brakes to 25mph at the top. Down hill from Peak Forest to Chinley the schedule included a two-minute recovery margin but 45253 was unfortunate in suffering a bad PW check at Chapel-en-le-Frith which was not in force for the other competitors and consequently the Class 5 lost a minute on schedule. The West Country and the B1 cut the schedule by two minutes and 1¾

minutes respectively, 34005 reaching 64½mph and 61251 reaching 63½mph at Chapel-en-le-Frith.

On the final down hill sprint to Manchester Central, the West Country and the Class 5 kept time but the B1 was brought to a dead stand by adverse signals at Throstle Nest and although slightly faster that the Southern engine at Chorlton Junction, was 3½ minutes late on schedule. On arrival in Manchester, 34005 was on time, 61251 was 7½ minutes late and 45253 was nine minutes late.

Great Central Main Line

The work of the competing mixed traffic engines on the Great Central was, size for size, the most difficult task set for any of the engines in the whole series of trials. It involved 5½ hours of continuous steaming with plenty of hard up–hill work but with no opportunities for continuous high speed running down hill or on the level.

The first obstacle northbound was the 6½ mile climb, mainly at 1 in 105, from Rickmansworth to Amersham with a severe service slack at the bottom. Then it was a switchback road with a ruling gradient of 1 in 176 but with no opportunities for rushing the climbs with the impetus gained by the previous descent. There were stops at the foot of many of the 1 in 176 grades and down hill speeds were restricted to levels far below that normally attained every day before the war. The central section between Nottingham and Sheffield included some steep grades (1 in 100 southbound) but it was also plagued with coal mining restrictions. The final section from Sheffield to Manchester took the train over the summit at Dunford Bridge which was just under 1,000ft. above sea level and approached by a 19-mile continuous climb from Sheffield at 1 in 120 and 1 in 132. Eastbound it was an equally difficult up

hill slog for 22 miles from Manchester with grades of 1 in 100 and 1 in 117 from Dinting.

Four engines were involved in the route over Woodhead, 61251 *Oliver Bury* still representing the Eastern Region and Driver Smith with 45253 continuing to represent the London Midland Region. The other engines were Southern West Country 34006 *Bude* with Driver Swain who had come over from Nine Elms and Western Region Hall 6990 *Witherslack Hall* with Driver Russell from Old Oak, which worked only on the GC line and on its own Bristol to Plymouth route.

There were many lineside observers and photographers on the route who drew the obvious conclusion that the Class 5 did not do very well, particularly when 45253 arrived in London Road station 34 minutes late on 15th June 1948. In addition the reputation of the class was not improved when Cecil J. Allen published some logs of runs on the Great Central line. Although some time was lost due to PWR slacks, a considerable amount of time was booked against the engine. There was a general tendency to blame Driver Smith of Kentish Town or the instructions he had been given for the lethargic running, suggesting that he was engaged in the ancient but nefarious practice of 'coal dodging', which meant seeking the minimum coal consumption, regardless of anything else. Driver Smith, however, received some degree of vindication when the official report was published, for it was then revealed that in many cases 45253 had been driven very hard with long cut-offs and full regulator but with very little result. It emerged from the report also that on one of the up runs, a log of which was not published, the engine was coaxed to higher horse powers than on any of the time-losing down runs which had proved so damaging to the reputation of the Class 5s.

POINT TO POINT TIMINGS – NORTHBOUND					
	Distance (miles)	Schedule (minutes)	08.06.48 34006 min sec	15.06.48 45253 min sec	24.06.48 6990 min sec
Marylebone-Harrow	9.2	17	17 38	18 34	16 50
Harrow-Aylesbury	28.7	40	42 45	45 24	45 45
Aylesbury-Woodford	31.2	35	31 24	36 24	37 04
Woodford-Rugby	14.1	17	18 15	21 22	19 52
Rugby-Leicester	19.9	23	20 07	24 44	24 00
Sheffield-Penistone	12.9	25	25 41	34 37	
Penistone-Guide Bridge	23.4	37	41 51	43 37	

POINT TO POINT TIMINGS – SOUTHBOUND					
	Distance (miles)	Schedule (minutes)	09.06.48 34006 min sec	16.06.48 45253 min sec	25.06.48 6990 min sec
Manchester-Guide Bridge	5.0	9	10 38	11 03	10 45
Guide Bridge-Penistone	23.4	42	40 27	41 14	40 53
Penistone-Sheffield	12.9	19	21 07	18 32	20 59
Nottingham-Loughborough	13.5	16	18 25	17 12	17 06
Loughborough-Leicester	9.9	14	13 51	14 13	13 30
Leicester-Rugby	19.9	24	23 35	24 41	25 39
Rugby-Woodford	14.1	18	19 57	21 14	20 26
Woodford-Brackley	9.8	14	12 14	13 41	12 51
Brackley-Aylesbury	21.4	25	24 37	25 55	24 14
Aylesbury-Rickmansworth	20.7	32	27 29	31 23	30 06

NB. No detailed record of timings was made between Sheffield and Guide Bridge. On the southbound runs, the timings of all locomotives between Aylesbury and Rickmansworth are for passing Rickmansworth. All suffered severe PWRs south of Rickmansworth.

The full loads on the down runs were 380 tons with the West Country and the Hall and 390 tons with the Class 5. The route was crowded with PWRs as far north as Rickmansworth. The West Country and the Hall made rousing starts out of Marylebone, both passing Neasden in the

same time, the Pacific travelling at 66mph and the Hall at 58mph, but the Class 5 made a much slower start. The West Country lost 1/2 minute because of a 5mph pw slack before Harrow whilst the Class 5 lost 1 1/2 minutes from the same cause. Only the Hall reached Harrow on time. On to Aylesbury, all the engines lost time, the top speeds attained at Great Missenden being 71 1/2 mph by 34006, 66mph by 45253 and 60mph by 6990, but the overall times differed considerably.

34006 made a sprint from Aylesbury to Woodford which was described by Cecil J. Allan as "one of the most amazing things he had ever timed on the Great Central". Speed leapt to 76 1/2 mph at Quainton Road and 75mph at Finmere and the train almost covered the distance in 'even time', averaging 59.6mph start to stop. The Class 5 took five minutes longer and the Hall nearly six minutes longer. All lost time between Woodford and Rugby, the Class 5 losing 4 1/2 minutes compared with 1 1/4 minutes for 34006 and nearly three minutes for 6990. On to Leicester, only the West Country covered the distance in less than booked time.

West of Sheffield and over Woodhead, the 12.9 miles to Penistone was scheduled for 25 minutes; 34006 took 25 minutes 41 seconds whilst 45253 struggled to arrive there in just over 34 1/2 minutes, losing 9 1/2 minutes. The length of the train made it necessary to 'draw up' at Penistone. From Penistone to Guide Bridge, running was restrained and there was a PWR before Valehouse, the Pacific losing two minutes and the Class 5 losing 6 1/2 minutes, but in the case of the latter there was a further PWR at Mottram. A final comment on the run behind 45253 when it arrived in London Road station 34 minutes late at 4.4pm was that of all the performances that 'C.J.A.' had timed during the exchanges, that of 45253 on this trip on the Great Central line was the most completely unrepresentative of the proven capacity of the locomotive class concerned.

On the southbound journey on 16th June the Class 5 did much better and the loss of time was very much reduced from that on the previous day. From the start at Manchester London Road station all the engines had a very arduous task ahead of them with an almost continuous climb for 22 miles through Woodhead tunnel to the summit at Dunford Bridge and with the additional handicap of a stop at Guide Bridge. The nine-minute schedule for the first five miles to Guide Bridge up hill at 1 in 173-100-132 left nothing to spare and because of the permanent way slack at Fairfield, none of the engines covered this on schedule. When 34006 passed Gorton Works at 41 1/2 mph, a large proportion of the works staff had turned out to inspect the stranger. The Class 5 did not exceed 29 1/2 mph on this section, arriving two minutes late.

The engines had to start from Guide Bridge up the steepest part of the whole ascent at 1 in 97 and then 1 in 183/143 but this slackened to 1 in 462 from Godley to Mottram where it steepened again to 1 in 122 until there was a short level section over Dinting viaduct. From Dinting station the climb was at 1 in 100 for 2 1/2 miles to Valehouse, then 1 in 117 to Woodhead and 1 in 201 through the tunnel to Dunford.

45253 at first took things too easily as it dragged the train up the long ascent and could do no better than 37 1/2 mph at Mottram and 36mph through Dinting. By Valehouse the engine's speed had dropped to 25 1/2 mph but it recovered from here to enter Woodhead tunnel at 36mph, where it was two minutes over schedule. However, faster running down hill brought the train into Penistone 45 seconds early. The Hall made an excellent start from Guide Bridge and was nearly two minutes ahead of time entering the tunnel and was still just

under a minute ahead of schedule at Penistone. The West Country also ran well, being about 1 1/2 minutes under schedule at Woodhead and at Penistone. Maximum speeds on the descent were 66mph with the Class 5 and 55mph with the West Country. Unfortunately speeds reached by the Hall were not recorded.

The schedule for the winding 12.9 miles down hill stretch from Penistone to Sheffield was 19 minutes. This was taken with extreme caution by the Southern 4-6-2 and also by the Hall, each of which lost two minutes, but the Class 5 made the run to Sheffield in 18 1/2 minutes.

From Nottingham, 34006 left on time and as far as Aylesbury the engine was driven quite gently, losing 2 1/2 minutes to Loughborough and two minutes from Rugby to Woodford, both losses of time being accounted for by PW slowings. From Woodford to Brackley it gained 1 3/4 minutes. The Class 5 lost 1 3/4 minutes from Nottingham to Loughborough, a little on to Leicester and 3/4 of a minute from Leicester to Rugby with no pw slowings at all. More time was lost between Rugby and Woodford, Woodford and Brackley and Brackley and Aylesbury. The Hall dropped a minute between Nottingham and Loughborough, and lost a little more on to Leicester. More time was lost on to Woodford, but from there to Brackley and from Brackley to Aylesbury some time was regained.

Top speeds recorded south of Nottingham for the West Country were 74mph between Lutterworth and Rugby, 71 1/2 mph at Braunston and 68mph at Calvert and at Quainton Road. The Class 5 reached 74mph between Lutterworth and Rugby and 72 1/2 mph at Calvert, whilst the maximum recorded by the Hall was 67mph between Lutterworth and Rugby and 75mph at Calvert. Amateur recorders on the Great Central line during the exchanges reported that in the first week Class B1 61163 ran late every day into Sheffield but whether it was in the northbound or southbound direction was not stated. Arrivals in Marylebone were recorded as:

4th June	61163	2 minutes late
9th June	34006	4 minutes late
10th June	45253	18 minutes late
15th June	6990	18 minutes late

Bristol to Plymouth

The third English route on which the mixed traffic locomotives were tested was from Bristol to Plymouth and, from Cogload Junction to Plymouth, the route was the same as that for the express locomotives. Leaving Bristol there is a rising gradient for about five miles to a summit before Flax Bourton, the steepest of which is at 1 in 180, and this is followed by a fall at between 1 in 200 and 1 in 334 for five miles to near Yatton. From here it is virtually level to Taunton. From Norton Fitzwarren there is an unbroken climb of almost nine miles through Wellington to a summit just west of Whitehall tunnel in the Blackdown Hills. It begins gently with 2 3/4 miles at 1 in 369-203, then steepening to 1 in 174 for two miles. Then there is an easier half mile or so, followed by the steepest part of the climb at 1 in 90-86-80 for about 2 1/2 miles and half a mile at 1 in 127 through Whitehall tunnel. From here there is a steady fall to west of Exeter after which the line is almost level through Exminster, Dawlish and Teignmouth to Newton Abbot.

Climbing begins in earnest at Aller Junction where the Paignton line diverges. It starts at 1 in 98 but soon increases to 1 in 36 and 1 in 44 for 2 3/4 miles to the summit at Dainton tunnel. Then there is an extremely winding and severe fall for two miles, the steepest being 1 in 36, followed by an easier fall

Having performed badly on both its home route and on the ex-Great Central line, it was only on the tests over the ex-Great Western line between Bristol and Plymouth that 45253 operated at a level representative of the class. The engine is seen here at Yatton with the 10.40am Wolverhampton-Penzance on 7th July 1948. *Ken Nunn/LCGB*

to Totnes. West of Totnes there is another almost unbroken climb for nine miles up Rattery bank and through Brent to a summit at Wrangaton. For two miles from Totnes the gradient is between 1 in 46 and 1 in 66 after which it eases slightly to 1 in 80-90 to Brent and on to Wrangaton and it is then down hill all the way to Plymouth.

For eastbound trains the climb up Hemerdon bank begins two miles out of Plymouth at Laira Junction with three miles at 1 in 41/42 to Hemerdon sidings, then after a very brief respite the climb begins again for seven miles to Wrangaton. This is less severe, mainly ranging from 1 in 100-150-225-315.

During the trials the line from Plymouth to Newton Abbot was infested with PW slacks and timekeeping was virtually impossible. There was a check at Plym Bridge, just west of Tavistock Junction which was a nasty handicap coming within 1¹/₂ miles of the foot of Hemerdon bank. Although the PW check was followed by half a mile of level track, then a mile up at 1 in 200 and 1 in 100, any attempt to build up speed before the real climb was extremely difficult. From Totnes the line is level for 1¹/₂ miles, then comes the climb to Dainton summit for about three miles with gradients varying between 1 in 125 and 1 in 40 at the summit. From Plymouth to Exeter the mixed traffic engines were loaded to 260tons gross but onwards to Bristol this was increased to 475tons which was almost equal to that of the Royal Scot locomotive on the express passenger trials. This was an onerous proposition on the Exeter-Taunton section where there was a continuous up hill gradient for 20 miles to Whitehall tunnel, culminating with over two miles at 1 in 155 from Cullompton and 1 in 115 for 2¹/₂ miles from Sampford Peverall to Whitehall tunnel.

The 'foreign' engines on test on this line were 45253, still with Driver Smith, 61251 *Oliver Bury* with Driver Ratley, and

34006 *Bude*, and this time the Class 5 performed much better. The indications were that the London Midland authorities had realised that all was not well with 45253 on the Eastern Region and some attempt must have been made to fettle up the engine before its test running on the Western Region in July, although the only recorded works visit was completed on 27th May, before the tests began. The running here was so different from that on the Great Central line that it was difficult to realise that the same engine was involved.

Heading east out of Plymouth, 45253 made the slowest start of the four engines and from Plympton to Hemerdon summit it took 8 minutes 19 seconds compared with 7 minutes 46 seconds with the B1 and 7 minutes 25 seconds for the West Country. However, up the hill from Totnes to Dainton summit there was only ten seconds difference between the times recorded by all four locomotives, the B1 just being in the lead. However, on a later run, 61251 made the fastest climb of all up Hemerdon with the same 260ton load; after slowing down at Plympton, the driver achieved the outstanding feat of passing Hemerdon summit in 6 minutes 4 seconds.

It was between Exeter and Taunton that 45253 really showed its true form. The running here, with a 475ton load, was the finest performance by the Class 5 during the 1948 Exchanges and so different from that on the Eastern Region. On 14th July 1948 the engine was recorded as passing Whitehall summit, 19.9 miles from Exeter, in 24 minutes 9 seconds and speed up the 1 in 155 after Cullompton only dropped from 61¹/₂ mph to 55mph and up the final 1 in 115 from Tiverton Junction to Whitehall, it dropped only from 62mph to 52mph. Even the Royal Scot 46162 with a test load of 485 tons, only ten tons more than 45253, took 25 minutes 30 seconds to pass Whitehall, 1¹/₂ minutes slower than the Class 5. Signal checks

TABLE 9.3 ALLOCATION HISTORY FOR INDIVIDUAL LOCOMOTIVES

Shed	Date	Shed	Date	Shed	Date
5000		**5003**		**5007**	
Bristol	23.02.35	Crewe North	12.09.59	Inverness	19.03.35
Carlisle Kingmoor	30.03.35	Stoke	10.06.61	Crewe	30.03.35 (O/L)
Crewe	05.10.35			Perth	13.07.35
Rugby	05.06.43	**5004**		Inverness	04.04.36 (on)
Speke Junction	26.01.52 (O/L)	Perth	18.03.35	Perth	27.10.45
Rugby	09.02.52	Crewe	02.11.35	Motherwell	15.11.47
Crewe North	17.09.55	Stoke	20.06.36	Perth	31.01.48
Rugby	24.09.55	Tebay	03.10.36	Eastfield	11.02.50 (P/E)
Crewe North	03.03.56	Crewe	03.07.37	Perth	22.07.50
Crewe South	27.10.56	Stoke	14.08.37	St. Rollox	21.07.51
Upperby	09.02.57	Rugby	25.09.37	Carlisle Kingmoor	17.05.52
Crewe South	07.12.57	Llandudno Junction	15.10.38 (O/L)	Dalry Road	20.05.57
Holyhead	20.06.59	Carnforth	05.11.38	Corkerhill	17.07.58
Crewe South	19.09.59	Llandudno Junction	12.11.38 (O/L)	Hurlford	22.09.60 (O/L)
Carnforth	10.06.61	Preston	17.12.38		
Crewe South	16.09.61	Edge Hill	27.03.43	**5008**	
Holyhead	22.06.63	Crewe	13.05.44	Crewe	13.04.35
Chester (Midland)	02.11.63	Rugby	10.06.44	Carlisle Kingmoor	11.05.35
Lostock Hall	27.05.67	Carnforth	04.11.50	Inverness	13.07.35
		Patricroft	13.06.53	Carlisle Kingmoor	22.01.44
5001		Crewe South	15.08.53	Motherwell	04.10.47
Bristol	23.02.35	Springs Branch	21.11.53		
Carlisle Kingmoor	30.03.35	Bletchley	26.02.55	**5009**	
Crewe	19.10.35	Longsight	14.06.58	Inverness	22.03.35
Aston	27.02.43	Crewe North	20.09.58	Crewe	30.03.35 (O/L)
Warrington	10.04.43	Crewe South	06.01.62	Inverness	13.07.35
Holyhead	07.07.51	Llandudno Junction	22.06.63	Perth	31.07.37 (O/L)
Crewe North	15.09.51			Inverness	14.08.37
Speke Junction	26.01.52 (O/L)	**5005**		Perth	11.05.46
Mold Junction	09.02.52	Perth	13.03.35	Carlisle Kingmoor	17.05.47
Crewe South	07.11.59	Crewe	02.11.35	Motherwell	04.02.50
Crewe North	20.06.64	Farnley Junction	04.06.38 (O/L)		
Crewe South	19.09.64	Huddersfield	18.06.38	**5010**	
Rugby	28.11.64	Inverness	06.12.41 (O/L)	Crewe	13.04.35
Nuneaton	12.06.65	Inverness	27.12.41	St. Rollox	11.05.35
Holyhead	04.06.66	Carlisle Kingmoor	11.11.44	Inverness	13.07.35
Carnforth	10.12.66	Perth	27.07.46	Carlisle Kingmoor	08.09.45
		Carlisle Kingmoor	03.05.47	Perth	17.08.46
5002		Edge Hill	09.04.49 (O/L)	Eastfield	11.02.50
Bristol	27.02.35	Edge Hill	30.04.49	Corkerhill	10.03.51
Carlisle Kingmoor	11.05.35	Llandudno Junction	20.12.52	Hurlford	07.04.51
Crewe North	05.10.35	Holyhead	13.06.53		
Rugby	05.06.43	Patricroft	19.09.53	**5011**	
Bletchley	26.08.44 (O/L)	Edge Hill	03.04.54	Crewe	13.04.35
Rugby	28.06.47			Inverness	11.05.35
Crewe North	03.03.56	**5006**		Perth	27.10.45
Crewe South	11.03.56	Perth	15.03.35	Eastfield	11.02.50
Upperby	31.08.57	Crewe	02.11.35	Perth	22.07.50
Crewe South	05.10.57	Farnley Junction	04.06.38 (O/L)	Carlisle Kingmoor	29.12.51
Holyhead	20.06.59	Huddersfield	18.06.38	Grangemouth	16.03.52
Crewe South	19.09.59	Inverness	06.12.41 (O/L)	Eastfield	24.05.54
Carnforth	10.06.61	Inverness	27.12.41	Corkerhill	16.05.55
Preston	15.07.61	Carlisle Kingmoor	04.09.43	Carstairs	03.10.55
Crewe South	09.09.61	Perth	27.07.46		
		Carlisle Kingmoor	03.05.47	**5012**	
5003		Crewe North	28.05.49 (O/L)	Crewe	13.04.35
Perth	05.03.35	Crewe North	25.06.49	Polmadie	11.05.35
Crewe North	02.11.35	Crewe South	01.10.49	Inverness	13.07.35
Monument Lane	04.03.39	Holyhead	05.07.52	Perth	13.05.39
Bangor	01.07.39	Chester	20.09.52	Corkerhill	22.07.39
Llandudno Junction	30.12.39	Holyhead	13.06.53	Inverness	02.12.39
Crewe	06.04.40	Crewe North	26.09.53	Motherwell	08.11.47
Edge Hill	15.02.41	Trafford Park	06.02.54	Inverness	10.06.50
Crewe	25.07.42	Derby	23.11.57	Carlisle Kingmoor	20.09.52
Rugby	05.06.43	Neasden	10.01.59	Carlisle Upperby	10.03.62
Willesden	31.10.53	Derby	18.06.60	Carlisle Kingmoor	22.06.63
Crewe North	14.04.56	Saltley	04.03.61	Barrow	23.04.66
Crewe South	20.10.56	Oxley	10.04.65		
Crewe North	05.01.57	Crewe South	11.03.67	**5013**	
Crewe South	23.11.57			Crewe	13.04.35
Stoke	20.06.59			Inverness	11.05.35

Shed	Date	Shed	Date	Shed	Date
5013		**5015**		**5018**	
Perth	13.05.39	Carlisle Kingmoor	17.08.46	Motherwell	25.10.47
Corkerhill	22.07.39	Crewe North	23.04.49 (O/L)	Inverness	10.12.49
Carlisle Kingmoor	02.12.39	Crewe North	28.05.49	Aviemore	22.04.50
Inverness	11.07.40	Crewe South	01.10.49	Carlisle Kingmoor	18.10.52
Carlisle Kingmoor	28.08.43	Monument Lane	10.06.50	St. Margarets	22.08.53
Crewe North	30.04.49	Bushbury	30.09.50	Carlisle Kingmoor	19.09.53
Crewe South	01.10.49	Edge Hill	18.11.61	Warrington	21.07.62
Carlisle Kingmoor	06.10.51			Bolton	18.05.63
Grangemouth	22.03.52	**5016**		Carlisle Kingmoor	23.11.63
Carlisle Kingmoor	16.08.52	Inverness	25.05.35		
Stockport	06.01.68	Motherwell	15.11.47	**5019**	
		Stirling	01.10.49	Crewe	25.05.35
5014		Ayr	26.08.65	Chester	05.10.35
Crewe	27.04.35			Patricroft	08.02.36
Inverness	13.07.35	**5017**		Shrewsbury	01.06.40 (O/L)
Carlisle Kingmoor	10.05.47 (O/L)	Inverness	25.05.35	Patricroft	29.06.40
Carlisle Kingmoor	31.05.47	Carlisle Kingmoor	28.08.43	Springs Branch	01.11.41
Crewe North	16.04.49 (O/L)	Edge Hill	23.04.49 (O/L)	Preston	16.05.42
Crewe North	30.04.49	Edge Hill	28.05.49	Springs Branch	24.03.45
Crewe South	01.10.49	Rugby	17.02.51	Edge Hill	10.02.51
Carlisle Canal	08.10.49	Edge Hill	24.03.51	Carnforth	07.07.51
Longsight	20.01.51	Carnforth	11.08.51	Springs Branch	02.05.59
Carlisle Upperby	07.07.51	Springs Branch	02.05.59		
Northampton	15.09.51	Southport	20.07.63	**5020**	
Patricroft	09.06.56	Newton Heath	20.06.64	Perth	02.08.34
Carnforth	15.09.56	Trafford Park	14.11.64	Carlisle Kingmoor	20.10.34
Lancaster	02.06.62	Carnforth	21.08.65	Edge Hill	25.11.35
Carnforth	23.04.66			Holyhead	15.02.36
		5018		Edge Hill	07.03.36
5015		Crewe	18.05.35	Crewe South	13.01.40
Crewe	27.04.35 (O/L)	St. Rollox	13.07.35	Crewe North	26.06.43
Inverness	13.07.35	Carlisle Kingmoor	27.07.35	Crewe South	07.08.43
Carlisle Kingmoor	08.09.45	Inverness	17.04.36 (on)	Rugby	26.04.47
Ayr	20.07.46	Perth	08.09.45	Edge Hill	19.09.53

Vulcan Foundry-built 5031, still in pre-war livery, has just passed Elstree & Borehamwood with a St. Pancras to Kettering train in 1946. It was allocated to 13B Belle Vue, a Midland Division shed in Manchester, from November 1943 and remained there until April 1956 when it moved to Newton Heath. 5031 had a domeless boiler from July 1944 and has retained its original riveted tender.

C. R. L. Coles / Rail Archive Stephenson

Shed	Date	Shed	Date	Shed	Date
5062		**5066**		**5070**	
Farnley Junction	19.08.35	Gloucester	18.01.36	Crewe	25.05.35
Huddersfield	06.11.37	Carlisle Kingmoor	28.11.36	Llandudno Junction	17.10.36
Low Moor	16.07.38	Inverness	30.05.42	Bangor	28.05.38
Accrington	12.07.41	Polmadie	16.02.60	Rugby	08.04.39
Huddersfield	11.07.42			Edge Hill	23.08.41
Low Moor	14.11.42	**5067**		Patricroft	06.09.41
Bank Hall	15.05.48	Newton Heath	26.01.35	Crewe South	01.01.44
Farnley Junction	29.04.50	Trafford Park	10.02.35	Aston	08.04.44
Sheffield	11.11.50 (O/L)	Tebay	14.11.36	Bescot	06.05.44
Sheffield	02.02.52	Patricroft	02.07.37	Willesden	28.10.44
Derby	21.09.57	Kentish Town	07.08.37	Springs Branch	24.04.48
Cricklewood	10.01.59	Toton	31.05.41	Chester	08.05.48
Derby	17.02.62	Staveley	07.06.41	Crewe North	21.08.48
Burton	21.09.62	Bescot	18.07.42 (O/L)	Holyhead	28.05.49
Derby	23.11.63	Bescot	15.08.42	Chester	10.02.51
Burton	12.09.64	Aston	29.08.42	Edge Hill	24.03.51
Agecroft	03.07.65 (O/L)	Crewe South	03.10.42	Aston	08.12.51
Agecroft	24.07.65	Crewe North	26.06.43	Bletchley	03.05.52
Trafford Park	22.10.66	Crewe South	07.08.43	Carlisle Upperby	04.07.53
		Walsall	03.08.57 (O/L)	Patricroft	25.06.55
5063		Crewe South	17.08.57	Longsight	09.03.57 (O/L)
Farnley Junction	29.12.34	Crewe North	20.06.64	Patricroft	23.03.57
Newton Heath	23.02.35	Bescot	19.09.64	Carlisle Upperby	21.09.57
Farnley Junction	17.08.35	Saltley	26.03.66	Crewe North	30.01.60
Blackpool	12.07.41	Heaton Mersey	28.05.66	Holyhead	11.06.60
Farnley Junction	12.10.46			Mold Junction	17.09.60
Newton Heath	11.07.53 (O/L)	**5068**		Springs Branch	15.09.62
Farnley Junction	15.08.53	Newton Heath	26.01.35	Warrington	26.06.65
Neville Hill	01.03.64	Trafford Park	10.02.35		
Leeds Holbeck	07.06.64	Springs Branch	29.11.36	**5071**	
		Kentish Town	07.08.37	Crewe	25.05.35
5064		Leeds Holbeck	17.11.45	Northampton	07.03.36
Newton Heath	29.12.34	Bank Hall	22.01.49 (O/L)	Rugby	24.07.37
Wakefield	26.01.35	Bank Hall	05.03.49	Millhouses	02.04.38 (O/L)
Derby	06.04.35	Newton Heath	27.01.51 (O/L)	Millhouses	09.04.38
Crewe North	28.11.36	Bank Hall	17.02.51	Trafford Park	07.01.39
Shrewsbury	25.09.37	Accrington	05.11.55	Toton	09.03.40
Chester	07.05.38	Rose Grove	04.03.61	Rugby	18.07.42 (O/L)
Edge Hill	26.10.40	Aintree	25.01.64	Rugby	15.08.42
Crewe South	14.06.41	Warrington	03.07.65	Crewe South	03.10.42
Crewe North	26.06.43			Willesden	13.11.43
Crewe South	07.08.43	**5069**		Stoke	03.05.47
Willesden	05.06.48	Newton Heath	26.01.35	Willesden	10.05.47
Bescot	07.05.60	Trafford Park	10.02.35	Bletchley	03.05.51
Northampton	03.11.62	Willesden	19.12.36 (O/L)	Crewe North	13.08.53
Bletchley	26.01.63	Preston	02.01.37	Carlisle Upperby	10.09.55
Bescot	14.03.64	Springs Branch	19.06.37	Monument Lane	22.06.57
Stourbridge	26.03.66	Warrington	13.11.37	Bushbury	17.09.60
Llandudno Junction	28.05.66	Chester	02.07.38	Monument Lane	17.06.61
Chester	08.10.66	Mold Junction	24.09.38	Speke Junction	28.10.61
		Chester	04.02.39		
5065		Edge Hill	16.09.39	**5072**	
Newton Heath	29.12.34	Chester	30.12.39	Crewe	01.06.35
Kentish Town	06.04.35	Edge Hill	14.12.40	Edge Hill	07.03.36
Leeds Holbeck	17.11.45	Crewe South	05.09.42	Crewe South	27.06.42
Crewe North	02.10.48 (O/L)	Crewe North	26.06.43	Crewe North	26.06.43
Crewe North	06.11.48	Crewe South	04.03.44	Crewe South	04.03.44
Carlisle Upperby	01.10.49	Walsall	05.06.48	Warrington	01.05.48
Aston	15.09.51	Bushbury	02.10.48	Carnforth	14.10.50
Monument Lane	12.09.59	Monument Lane	28.05.49	Rugby	19.04.58 (O/L)
Aston	07.11.59	Bescot	01.10.49	Carnforth	05.07.58
Rugby	23.02.63	Walsall	10.06.50	Edge Hill	14.05.60
Northampton	30.03.63	Bescot	30.09.50	Holyhead	11.06.60
Willesden	22.06.63	Rugby	09.06.51	Mold Junction	17.09.60
Rugby	17.08.63	Edge Hill	15.03.52 (O/L)	Carlisle Upperby	10.11.62
Crewe South	19.09.64	Northampton	24.05.52 (O/L)	Carnforth	22.06.63
Rugby	28.11.64	Rugby	05.07.52		
Nuneaton	29.05.65	Edge Hill	19.09.53	**5073**	
Heaton Mersey	28.05.66	Crewe South	16.09.61	Crewe	08.06.35
		Edge Hill	09.12.61	Aston	07.03.36
5066		Holyhead	23.06.62	Bescot	19.04.41
Newton Heath	26.01.35	Speke Junction	15.09.62	Crewe North	10.05.41
Bristol	28.09.35 (on)	Trafford Park	16.02.63	Carlisle Upperby	09.02.57
		Springs Branch	22.06.63		
		Edge Hill	06.07.63		

Shed	Date	Shed	Date	Shed	Date
5073		**5079**		**5085**	
Aston	03.08.57	Low Moor	17.08.35	Perth	26.10.35
Carlisle Upperby	17.08.57	Farnley Junction	14.11.36	St.Margarets	11.02.50 (P/E)
Crewe North	19.10.57	Southport	13.02.03 (O/L)	Edinburgh	04.11.50
Lancaster	10.06.61	Southport	27.03.37	Polmadie	17.03.51
Speke Junction	09.09.61	Low Moor	30.10.37	Motherwell	29.09.51
Springs Branch	21.07.62	Wakefield	21.10.39		
Newton Heath	27.07.63	Sowerby Bridge	06.06.42	**5086**	
Trafford Park	28.11.64	Blackpool	14.11.42	Crewe	23.03.35
Stockport	28.10.67	Farnley Junction	12.10.46	Perth	26.10.35
Bolton	13.04.68	Newton Heath	22.11.47	Aberdeen	01.10.49
Lostock Hall	06.07.68	Farnley Junction	18.11.50	Perth	29.10.49
		Huddersfield	11.10.52	Carstairs	04.08.51
5074		Farnley Junction	07.02.53	Dalry Road	29.09.51
Crewe	15.06.35	Leeds Holbeck	05.01.64		
Aston	07.03.36			**5087**	
Longsight	04.06.38	**5080**		Crewe	30.03.35
Chester	02.07.38	Farnley Junction	23.03.35	Perth	05.10.35
Longsight	09.07.38	Low Moor	17.08.35	Inverness	25.06.49
Stockport	30.09.39	Farnley Junction	14.11.36	Carstairs	22.10.49
Stoke	06.01.40	Stourton	02.10.66		
Crewe North	29.03.41	Leeds Holbeck	15.01.67	**5088**	
Crewe South	23.10.41			Crewe	13.04.35
Crewe North	26.06.43	**5081**		Sheffield	19.10.35
Crewe South	04.03.44	Crewe	16.03.35	Millhouses	10.04.37
Bristol	01.07.50 (O/L)	Bushbury	20.04.35	Sheffield	25.09.37
Sheffield	05.08.50 (O/L)	Crewe	04.05.35	Toton	02.03.40
Crewe South	11.11.50	Perth	16.11.35	Derby	04.07.42
Stoke	15.12.62	St. Rollox	22.07.39	Southport	02.09.44 (O/L)
		Perth	30.03.40	Southport	30.09.44
5075		St. Rollox	20.04.40	Derby	09.12.44 (O/L)
Newton Heath	23.02.35	Perth	20.08.41	Derby	18.01.45
Farnley Junction	17.08.35	Carlisle Kingmoor	18.11.44	Longsight	14.02.48 (O/L)
Leeds Holbeck	06.09.64	Carlisle Upperby	10.02.62	Derby	21.02.48
Normanton	25.06.67	Carlisle Kingmoor	22.06.63	Millhouses	29.05.48
		Carlisle Upperby	27.06.64	Sheffield	15.01.49
5076				Leicester Midland	12.11.49
Newton Heath	23.03.35	**5082**		Nottingham	28.11.53
Farnley Junction	17.08.35	Crewe	16.03.35	Saltley	21.11.59
Wakefield	24.06.36 (on)	Bushbury	20.04.35	Leicester Midland	03.08.63
Newton Heath	08.09.56	Crewe	04.05.35	Derby	30.11.63
		Perth	28.10.35 (on)		
5077		St. Rollox	22.07.39	**5089**	
Farnley Junction	23.03.35	Perth	16.12.39	Crewe	13.04.35
Blackpool	02.10.48	St. Rollox	20.04.40	Sheffield	19.10.35
Wakefield	08.12.51	Perth	20.08.41	Millhouses	25.09.37
Farnley Junction	12.04.52 (O/L)	Carlisle Kingmoor	11.11.44	York	26.03.38
Wakefield	24.05.52	Carlisle Upperby	04.08.62	Millhouses	30.09.39
Blackpool	21.06.52	Carlisle Kingmoor	22.06.63	Leeds Holbeck	05.07.41
Rose Grove	23.05.53			Patricroft	26.09.42 (O/L)
Blackpool	13.06.53	**5083**		Patricroft	17.10.42
Southport	25.09.54	Crewe	23.03.35	Crewe North	27.03.43
Blackpool	25.06.55	Stoke	27.04.35	Willesden	28.05.49
Bank Hall	17.11.56	Crewe	04.05.35	Bletchley	27.09.57
Blackpool	05.01.57	Perth	29.10.35	Holyhead	05.07.58
Fleetwood	23.11.63	Edinburgh	29.07.39	Bletchley	04.10.58
Rose Grove	05.12.64	Perth	23.09.39	Bescot	14.03.64
Patricroft	13.02.65	Inverness	28.09.40	Banbury	02.10.65
Newton Heath	19.06.65	Carlisle Kingmoor	17.05.47	Chester	10.09.66
		Carlisle Upperby	04.08.62	Crewe South	29.04.67
5078		Southport	18.05.63		
Farnley Junction	23.03.35	Newton Heath	20.06.64	**5090**	
Wakefield	23.12.35			Crewe	13.04.35
Blackpool	24.07.43	**5084**		Sheffield	19.10.35
Farnley Junction	12.10.46	Crewe	23.03.35	York	08.02.36
Southport	25.10.52	Perth	26.10.35	Millhouses	21.11.36
Huddersfield	23.05.53	Inverness	28.09.40	Patricroft	02.01.37 (O/L)
Southport	04.07.53	Carlisle	31.05.47	Patricroft	16.01.37
Accrington	19.06.54	Stirling	30.03.52	Blackpool	26.06.37
Blackpool	09.01.60	Corkerhill	21.05.66	Aintree	02.11.40
Warrington	05.09.64	Carstairs	11.06.66 (P/E)	Agecroft	22.03.41
				Inverness	30.08.41
5079		**5085**		Perth	27.02.60
Farnley Junction	23.03.35	Crewe	23.03.35		

Shed	Date		Shed	Date		Shed	Date
5166			**5176**			**5182**	
Crewe	10.08.35		Perth	05.10.35		Warrington	19.09.42 (O/L)
Perth	12.10.35		Motherwell	10.10.42		Warrington	17.10.42
Corkerhill	13.10.51		Perth	31.10.42		Patricroft	26.12.42
Carstairs	15.02.56		St. Rollox	13.02.43		Carlisle Upperby	22.09.56
			Motherwell	06.11.48		Patricroft	03.11.56
5167						Trafford Park	14.11.64
Crewe	10.08.35		**5177**			Carlisle Canal	16.01.65
Perth	13.06.36		Crewe	07.09.35			
Ferryhill	16.06.56		Carlisle Kingmoor	05.10.35		**5183**	
Kittybrewster	04.06.60		Perth	28.10.35		Crewe	21.09.35
Ardrossan	15.05.61		Carlisle	10.10.42		Saltley	12.10.35
Ayr	15.02.65		Perth	31.10.42		Aston	29.11.36
Carstairs	08.10.66 (P/E)		St. Rollox	13.02.43		Bushbury	27.02.37
Motherwell	13.11.66		Grangemouth	01.10.60		Llandudno Junction	02.07.38
			Ayr	18.10.65		Patricroft	09.07.38
5168						Carnforth	24.09.38
Perth	17.08.35		**5178**			Patricroft	15.07.39
Corkerhill	29.04.44		Crewe	07.09.35		Crewe South	16.12.44
Perth	23.02.53		Carlisle	16.11.35		Shrewsbury	17.07.48
Polmadie	28.05.60		Corkerhill	15.04.39		Dalry Road	23.09.51
Hamilton	26.09.61		St. Rollox	25.11.39			
Motherwell	29.10.62		Grangemouth	01.10.60		**5184**	
Dalry Road	26.08.63		Motherwell	29.12.62		Crewe	21.09.35
St. Margarets	04.10.65					Leeds Holbeck	05.10.35
			5179			Derby	18.01.36
5169			Crewe	07.09.35		Willesden	19.12.36 (O/L)
Perth	17.08.35		Carlisle Kingmoor	05.10.35		Longsight	02.01.37
Carlisle	28.08.43		Corkerhill	15.04.39		Patricroft	03.07.37
Perth	03.12.49		St.Rollox	28.10.39		Preston	25.09.37
Dumfries	13.10.51		Motherwell	06.11.48		Patricroft	02.07.38
			Inverness	10.12.49		Preston	24.09.38
5170			Perth	01.08.60		Springs Branch	08.02.41
Perth	17.08.35		Hamilton	25.09.61		Longsight	29.03.41
Dalry Road	25.09.61		Motherwell	05.11.62		Carlisle Upperby	05.06.43
						Dalry Road	21.08.48 (O/L)
5171			**5180**			Carlisle Upperby	06.11.48
Carlisle	31.08.35		Crewe	14.09.35		Holyhead	25.06.55
Perth	02.11.35		Derby	05.10.35		Carlisle Upperby	20.08.55
Corkerhill	10.06.61		Saltley	07.11.36		Patricroft	14.06.58
Carstairs	13.06.65		Derby	11.09.37		Bletchley	20.09.58
			Shrewsbury	16.10.43		Rugby	07.11.59
5172			Crewe South	19.05.45		Speke Junction	11.02.61
Carlisle	31.08.35		Shrewsbury	14.07.45		Holyhead	10.06.61
Perth	02.11.35		St. Margarets	07.10.51		Northampton	23.09.61
Polmadie	28.05.60		Chester	19.09.53		Rugby	25.11.61
Carstairs	16.10.61		Holyhead	12.06.54		Chester	22.06.63
			Carlisle Upperby	08.01.55			
5173			Crewe South	14.01.56		**5185**	
Carlisle	31.08.35		Holyhead	14.06.58		Crewe	21.09.35
Perth	02.11.35		Llandudno Junction	04.10.58		Saltley	12.10.35
Polmadie	10.01.53		Monument Lane	21.05.60		Trafford Park	20.06.36
Perth	05.09.53		Bescot	25.06.60		Springs Branch	21.11.36
Polmadie	05.10.53		Saltley	03.04.65		Preston	11.03.39
Corkerhill	28.08.54		Crewe South	19.06.65		Springs Branch	07.10.39
Carstairs	27.02.56					Crewe North	13.04.40
			5181			Springs Branch	15.02.41
5174			Crewe	14.09.35		Preston	05.04.41
Crewe	31.08.35		Kentish Town	12.10.35		Crewe South	20.11.48
Perth	05.10.35		Crewe North	20.12.36		Patricroft	20.11.48 (O/L)
Corkerhill	01.04.50		Crewe South	26.08.44		Crewe South	11.12.48
Carstairs	09.04.56		Edge Hill	04.12.48		Stoke	09.06.56
			Rugby	17.02.51		Crewe South	02.02.57
5175			Edge Hill	24.03.51		Carlisle Upperby	09.02.57
Crewe	31.08.35		Holyhead	23.06.62		Carlisle Kingmoor	22.06.63
Perth	16.11.35		Speke Junction	13.10.62			
Motherwell	10.10.42		Springs Branch	22.06.63		**5186**	
Perth	31.10.42		Carnforth	13.07.63		Crewe	21.09.35
Corkerhill	10.07.54		Speke Junction	14.09.63		Saltley	05.10.35
Carstairs	15.02.56					Leeds Holbeck	05.09.36
			5182			Saltley	25.09.37
5176			Crewe	14.09.35		Derby	14.11.53
Crewe	31.08.35		Derby	05.10.35		Sheffield	23.10.54
						Saltley	27.11.54

Shed	Date	Shed	Date	Shed	Date
5186		**5191**		**5196**	
Leicester Central	07.06.58 (O/L)	Crewe	05.10.35	Patricroft	30.09.39
Saltley	03.01.59	Swansea	25.09.37	Preston	09.03.40
Derby	17.09.60	Willesden	20.08.38	Warrington	08.03.41
Saltley	04.03.61	Northampton	27.01.45	Crewe North	02.04.60 (O/L)
Oxley	03.04.65	Rugby	17.09.60	Warrington	25.06.60
Crewe South	11.03.67	Willesden	11.02.61	Edge Hill	09.07.60
		Stoke	22.02.62	Lancaster	16.03.63
5187				Rose Grove	31.10.64
Nottingham	05.10.35	**5192**			
Leeds Holbeck	10.02.40	Crewe	05.10.35	**5197**	
Normanton	20.04.40	Mold Junction	25.09.37	Crewe North	26.10.35
Leeds Holbeck	18.10.41	Farnley Junction	18.06.38	Crewe South	01.01.38
Rugby	24.07.48 (O/L)	Wakefield	07.10.39	Crewe North	19.03.38
Rugby	06.11.48	Newton Heath	30.11.40	Crewe South	31.01.42
Willesden	15.09.56	Inverness	30.08.41	Crewe North	07.03.42
Edge Hill	14.05.60	Perth	30.07.60 (P/E)	Crewe South	09.09.44
Patricroft	11.05.68	Corkerhill	02.05.61	Carlisle Upperby	17.07.48
		Hurlford	20.07.61	Warrington	10.03.62
5188		Grangemouth	21.10.63	Llandudno Junction	05.05.62
Nottingham	12.10.35			Mold Junction	09.02.63 (O/L)
Kentish Town	25.09.37	**5193**		Llandudno Junction	11.05.63
Warrington	26.09.42 (O/L)	Crewe	12.10.35	Bedford	25.05.63
Warrington	17.10.42	Bushbury	13.11.37	Cricklewood	06.07.63
Patricroft	26.12.42	Aston	20.01.40	Speke Junction	02.05.64 (O/L)
Crewe South	31.12.55	Willesden	10.02.40	Speke Junction	23.05.64
Longsight	29.06.57	Edge Hill	23.08.41	Lostock Hall	11.07.64
Crewe North	31.08.57	Rugby	13.09.41		
Crewe South	23.11.57	Springs Branch	19.09.43	**5198**	
Monument Lane	18.06.60	Edge Hill	11.03.44	Crewe	26.10.35
Preston	27.08.60 (O/L)	Carlisle Upperby	16.03.46	Crewe South	09.09.44
Monument Lane	10.09.60	Carnforth	05.06.48	Bletchley	06.11.48 (O/L)
Willesden	17.09.60	Lancaster	02.06.62	Crewe South	11.12.48
Edge Hill	22.10.60	Carnforth	23.04.66	Stockport	10.06.61
Holyhead	23.06.62			Willesden	07.04.62
Springs Branch	15.09.62	**5194**		Chester	02.11.63
Edge Hill	17.08.63	Crewe	12.10.35	Croes Newydd	02.10.65
Speke Junction	19.10.63	Bath	30.04.38	Springs Branch	11.03.67 (O/L)
		Leeds Holbeck	16.03.40	Springs Branch	01.04.67
5189		Bath	20.04.40		
Nottingham	05.10.35	Perth	14.09.41	**5199**	
Crewe	05.12.36 (O/L)	Corkerhill	29.04.44	Crewe	26.10.35
Crewe	19.12.36	Ayr	09.11.59	Springs Branch	07.12.35
Edge Hill	13.11.37			Llandudno Junction	15.10.38 (O/L)
Crewe North	09.03.46 (O/L)	**5195**		Springs Branch	03.12.38
Crewe North	04.05.46	Crewe North	12.10.35	Preston	04.05.40
Crewe South	26.10.46	Crewe South	25.09.37	Springs Branch	08.06.40
Stoke	20.04.57 (O/L)	Crewe North	19.02.38	Patricroft	14.06.41
Stoke	22.06.57	Edge Hill	23.09.39	Bolton	15.09.62
Crewe North	21.09.57	Warrington	08.06.40	Burton	27.05.63
Crewe South	23.06.62	Carlisle Upperby	30.11.40		
Crewe North	15.09.62	Carnforth	19.07.41	**5200**	
		Willesden	04.10.41	Bank Hall	02.11.35
5190		Crewe South	21.02.42	Trafford Park	21.12.35
Crewe	05.10.35	Crewe North	01.11.52	Bank Hall	01.36 (O/L)
Swansea	25.09.37	Holyhead	06.12.52 (O/L)	Trafford Park	18.01.36
Chester	07.05.38	Crewe North	10.01.53	Southport	14.12.40
Mold Junction	01.11.41	Crewe South	18.04.53	Huddersfield	12.10.46
Chester	28.08.43	Walsall	03.07.54	Southport	18.10.47
Mold Junction	07.07.45	Bletchley	19.02.55	Blackpool	03.03.51 (O/L)
Chester	01.12.45	Carlisle Upperby	31.08.57 (O/L)	Southport	05.05.51
Shrewsbury	27.07.46	Bletchley	05.10.57	Blackpool	09.06.51 (O/L)
Bletchley	01.03.47	Patricroft	04.07.59	Southport	16.06.51
Shrewsbury	19.04.47	Agecroft	17.06.61	Accrington	29.03.52
Annesley	10.10.64	Carlisle Canal	12.01.63	Blackpool	19.09.53
Derby	13.03.65	Carlisle Kingmoor	22.06.63	Stockport	19.02.66
Annesley	14.08.65	Newton Heath	13.07.63	Newton Heath	11.05.68
Kirkby	23.10.65	Carlisle Kingmoor	05.10.63	Carnforth	06.07.68
Colwick	25.12.65 (O/L)				
Colwick	08.01.66	**5196**		**5201**	
Heaton Mersey	28.05.66	Crewe	12.10.35	Bank Hall	09.11.35
		Bushbury	13.11.37	Trafford Park	21.12.35
		Patricroft	17.12.38	Bank Hall	01.36 (O/L)
		Springs Branch	16.09.39	Trafford Park	18.01.36

Shed	Date	Shed	Date	Shed	Date
5238		**5242**		**5249**	
Chester	22.08.36	Chester	22.04.39	Saltley	30.04.38
Mold Junction	25.09.37	Mold Junction	30.09.39	Toton	02.03.40
Newton Heath	04.06.38 (O/L)	Longsight	25.09.43	Mold Junction	18.07.42
Newton Heath	18.06.38	Crewe North	12.10.46	Holyhead	25.07.42 (O/L)
Huddersfield	06.12.41	Crewe South	09.11.46	Holyhead	15.08.42
Sheffield	09.12.50 (O/L)	Edge Hill	04.12.48	Patricroft	20.10.51
Sheffield	02.02.52			Springs Branch	26.01.52
Leeds Holbeck	16.01.54	**5243**		Edge Hill	20.06.53
Sheffield	26.06.54	Carlisle Upperby	05.09.36	Aston	29.07.57 (O/L)
Burton	08.01.55	Edge Hill	03.09.49	Edge Hill	14.08.57
Leeds Holbeck	02.07.55	Crewe North	11.10.58		
Bedford	28.01.56	Crewe South	29.05.65	**5250**	
Kentish Town	16.06.56			Tebay	19.09.36
Cricklewood	31.08.57	**5244**		Patricroft	07.11.36
Bedford	16.09.61	Carlisle Upperby	05.09.36	Springs Branch	19.09.42
Woodford Halse	22.09.62	Kingmoor	17.08.46	Edge Hill	11.03.44
Leicester Central	12.01.63	Upperby	07.09.46	Crewe	13.05.44
Nottingham	13.04.63	Springs Branch	22.06.63	Rugby	10.06.44
Trafford Park	24.03.64 (O/L)	Edge Hill	13.07.63	Shrewsbury	01.03.47
Trafford Park	19.04.64			Rugby	08.03.47
Blackpool	22.07.64	**5245**		Edge Hill	19.09.53
Warrington	05.09.64	Monument Lane	19.09.36	Crewe North	20.09.58
		Walsall	03.07.37	Saltley	12.10.63
5239		Monument Lane	25.09.37	Crewe North	18.04.64
Chester	29.08.36	Aston	30.09.39	Chester	18.07.64
Mold Junction	25.09.37	Monument Lane	30.03.40		
Saltley	30.04.38	Bescot	22.03.41	**5251**	
Crewe	26.09.42 (O/L)	Crewe	10.05.41	Oxenholme	26.09.36
Crewe South	17.10.42	Shrewsbury	07.11.42	Patricroft	01.07.39
Crewe South	09.09.44	Bletchley	08.03.47	Perth	28.11.42
Trafford Park	13.06.53	Shrewsbury	19.04.47	Polmadie	29.04.44
Llandudno Junction	01.09.56	Ferryhill	02.09.51	Corkerhill	21.06.47
Trafford Park	08.09.56	Perth	15.11.54	Ardrossan	19.10.59
Agecroft	04.01.64	St. Margarets	17.05.57		
Bolton	07.11.64	Carstairs	09.06.57	**5252**	
Trafford Park	30.04.66			Warrington	26.09.36
		5246		Preston	28.09.40
5240		Llandudno Junction	19.09.36	Warrington	08.03.41
Chester	29.08.36	Edge Hill	16.09.39	Patricroft	27.06.59
Mold Junction	06.11.37	Carlisle Upperby	16.03.46	Newton Heath	08.08.64
Chester	02.07.38	Newton Heath	22.06.63	Bury	05.12.64
Mold Junction	24.09.38			Bolton	10.04.65
Rugby	29.04.39	**5247**			
Willesden	02.12.39	Holyhead	19.09.36	**5253**	
Crewe	29.05.43	Mold Junction	30.09.44	Crewe	26.09.36
Crewe South	09.09.44	Holyhead	28.10.44 (O/L)	Llandudno Junction	17.10.36
Crewe North	18.04.53	Mold Junction	16.12.44	Kentish Town	17.04.48 (O/L)
Rugby	19.04.58	Chester	29.09.45	Kentish Town	05.06.48
Crewe North	05.07.58	Holyhead	07.07.51	Nottingham	19.10.57
Stoke	22.12.62	Llandudno Junction	15.09.51	Saltley	21.11.59
		Holyhead	05.07.52	Derby	13.10.62 (O/L)
5241		Chester	20.09.52	Saltley	09.03.63
Chester	05.09.36	Mold Junction	18.09.54	Leicester Midland	16.03.63
Mold Junction	06.11.37	Bangor	23.04.60	Derby	21.12.63
Chester	02.07.38	Holyhead	10.04.65	Nottingham	15.02.64
Mold Junction	24.09.38	Chester	10.12.66	Burton	12.09.64
Rugby	29.04.39			Kingmoor	18.07.65
Willesden	02.12.39	**5248**		Heaton Mersey	06.01.68
Crewe	02.11.40	Holyhead	26.09.36		
Perth	31.10.42 (O/L)	Edge Hill	16.09.39	**5254**	
Perth	28.11.42	Crewe	13.06.42	Shrewsbury	03.10.36
Kingmoor	23.09.44	Crewe South	09.09.44	Crewe South	15.10.38
Crewe North	28.04.49	Edge Hill	04.12.48	Crewe North	26.06.43
Llandudno Junction	09.09.50 (O/L)	Upperby	06.12.52	Crewe South	27.01.45
Carnforth	14.10.50	Holyhead	25.06.55	Northampton	19.07.47 (O/L)
Edge Hill	30.06.56	Carlisle	20.08.55	Crewe South	20.12.47
Carnforth	27.10.56	Preston	20.06.59	Holyhead	11.07.53
Crewe North	16.09.61	Llandudno Junction	23.04.60	Crewe North	26.09.53
Stoke	19.01.63	Crewe South	08.10.60	Longsight	14.06.58
Crewe South	12.08.67			Crewe North	20.09.58
		5249		Edge Hill	06.01.62
5242		Tebay	19.09.36	Kingmoor	10.11.62
Chester	05.09.36	Patricroft	07.11.36	Newton Heath	06.01.68
Mold Junction	24.09.38				

Shed	Date	Shed	Date	Shed	Date
5255		**5260**		**5264**	
Shrewsbury	03.10.36	Derby	29.09.51	Staveley	07.06.41
Crewe North	19.05.45	Leeds Holbeck	27.10.51	Edge Hill	18.07.42 (O/L)
Camden	28.07.45	Kentish Town	16.08.52	Crewe	25.07.42 (O/L)
Crewe North	25.08.45	Leeds Holbeck	21.11.53	Crewe	15.08.42
Crewe South	17.11.45	Nottingham	28.11.53	Crewe South	27.01.44
Holyhead	28.05.49	Derby	24.09.55	Bath	06.09.47 (O/L)
Warrington	01.10.49	Millhouses	16.06.56	Bath	27.09.47
Llandudno Junction	08.03.52 (O/L)	Derby	22.09.56	Cricklewood	11.10.47
Bangor	29.03.52 (O/L)	Millhouses	15.06.57	Kentish Town	19.03.49
Warrington	12.07.52	Derby	21.09.57	Millhouses	14.05.49
Holyhead	06.11.54	Neasden	10.01.59	Derby	20.09.52
Warrington	01.01.55	Derby	18.06.60	Millhouses	19.06.54
Patricroft	27.06.59	Saltley	04.03.61	Derby	25.09.54
Newton Heath	14.01.61	Derby	10.08.63	Burton	08.01.55
		Burton	10.09.64	Leicester Midland	10.01.59
5256		Coalville	16.12.64	Saltley	18.05.63
Longsight	03.10.36	Bolton	08.02.65	Oxley	19.06.65
Shrewsbury	24.05.41	Bolton	06.03.65	Tyseley	13.11.65
Mold Junction	17.10.42	Lostock Hall	06.07.68	Oxley	16.04.66
Edge Hill	30.01.43			Crewe South	11.03.67
Holyhead	06.12.52 (O/L)	**5261**			
Edge Hill	10.01.53	Trafford Park	17.10.36	**5265**	
Crewe North	20.09.58	Derby	09.07.38	Trafford Park	24.10.36
Edge Hill	11.10.58	Wakefield	01.05.48 (O/L)	Gloucester	11.09.37
Warrington	07.11.59	Wakefield	05.06.48	Bristol	30.04.38
Chester (Midland)	23.06.62	Huddersfield	13.11.54	Saltley	02.03.40
Longsight	13.10.62	Wakefield	08.01.55		
Stockport	12.10.63	Bank Hall	16.06.56	**5266**	
Trafford Park	27.06.64	Agecroft	09.02.57	Sheffield	31.10.36
Blackpool	11.07.64	Warrington	14.09.63	Belle Vue	02.10.37
Warrington	05.09.64	Edge Hill	08.02.64	Leeds Holbeck	14.03.42
		Stockport	13.11.65	Perth	31.10.42
5257				Carlisle	23.09.44
Longsight	17.10.36	**5262**		Perth	03.12.49
Crewe North	29.07.44	Trafford Park	24.10.36	Hurlford	10.05.52
Willesden	28.10.44	Millhouses	07.01.39		
Stoke	10.05.47	Sheffield	06.09.41	**5267**	
Monument Lane	26.01.57	Millhouses	27.06.42	Sheffield	31.10.36
Edge Hill	14.06.58	Sheffield	26.05.45	Hellifield	02.10.37
Crewe North	20.09.58	Edinburgh	21.08.48 (O/L)	Cricklewood	26.09.42
Crewe South	23.06.62	Sheffield	30.10.48	Kentish Town	14.11.42
Crewe North	15.09.62	Burton	08.01.55	Bedford	16.06.56
Willesden	16.03.63	Brunswick	10.01.59	Kentish Town	30.04.60
Stoke	20.04.63	Leicester Midland	16.09.61	Annesley	15.09.62
Llandudno Junction	22.06.63	Leicester Central	17.03.62	Cricklewood	09.03.63
Stoke	29.06.63	Woodford Halse	29.09.62	Leicester Midland	22.06.63
Chester	20.06.64	Derby	01.12.62	Annesley	19.10.64
Stoke	19.09.64	Cricklewood	09.03.63	Derby	08.03.65
		Derby	16.05.64	Annesley	24.07.65
5258		Burton	27.06.64	Colwick	18.12.65 (O/L)
Longsight	17.10.36	Derby	08.08.65	Colwick	03.01.66
Upperby	11.01.47	Rose Grove	27.02.66	Springs Branch	12.11.66
Barrow	09.07.60				
Lancaster	19.06.65	**5263**		**5268**	
Lostock Hall	14.08.65	Trafford Park	24.10.36	Saltley	31.10.36
Bolton	18.09.65	Millhouses	07.01.39	Stoke	18.04.64
Agecroft	19.02.66	Toton	02.03.40	Springs Branch	20.05.67 (O/L)
Trafford Park	22.10.66	Staveley	18.07.42	Springs Branch	27.05.67
		Millhouses	23.10.42	Newton Heath	04.12.67
5259		Sheffield	02.07.49	Carnforth	06.07.68
Shrewsbury	17.10.36	Leicester Midland	12.11.49		
Patricroft	26.10.40	Derby	24.09.55	**5269**	
Upperby	10.09.55 (O/L)	Leicester Midland	15.06.57	Saltley	07.11.36
Upperby	17.09.55	Nottingham	08.02.58	Bournville	21.02.53
Stoke	05.08.61	Saltley	21.11.59	Saltley	10.05.53
Kingmoor	22.06.63	Oxley	?	Leicester Midland	13.09.58
		Heaton Mersey	06.11.66	Saltley	27.09.58
5260				Brunswick	14.05.60 (O/L)
Kentish Town	17.10.36	**5264**		Saltley	16.07.60
Leeds Holbeck	13.11.43	Trafford Park	24.10.36	Nottingham	18.05.63
Derby	12.06.48	Millhouses	25.09.37	Trafford Park	24.03.64 (O/L)
Leicester Midland	19.06.48	Toton	02.03.40	Trafford Park	19.04.64
Millhouses	18.09.48	Hasland	16.03.40	Stockport	09.03.68
		Toton	15.02.41	Bolton	11.05.68
				Lostock Hall	06.07.68

Shed	Date	Shed	Date	Shed	Date
5323		**5325**		**5328**	
Crewe	27.02.37	Upperby	05.07.52	Patricroft	29.04.39
Willesden	20.03.37	Rugby	07.11.53	Chester	06.05.39
Stoke	03.05.47	Mold Junction	10.04.54	Llandudno Junction	03.05.41
Willesden	10.05.47	Chester	23.04.66	Chester	24.05.41
Upperby	21.06.47			Mold Junction	04.10.41
Kingmoor	22.06.63	**5326**		Chester	26.08.44
Aintree	14.12.63	Crewe	06.03.37	Mold Junction	21.04.45
Warrington	03.07.65	Willesden	20.03.37	Chester	19.06.48
		Stoke	03.05.47	Warrington	11.02.50
5324		Carnforth	22.03.52	Upperby	22.09.56
Crewe North	27.02.37			Warrington	10.11.56
Willesden	20.03.37	**5327**		Walsall	03.08.57
Stoke	07.05.44	Crewe	06.03.37	Warrington	17.08.57
Willesden	20.11.54	Willesden	20.03.37	Carnforth	20.06.64
Rugby	20.06.59	Upperby	21.06.47		
Willesden	19.09.59	Barrow	05.06.48	**5329**	
Rugby	29.09.59 (O/L)	Preston	19.02.49	Crewe	13.03.37
Willesden	05.12.59	Patricroft	28.05.49	Rugby	20.03.37
Rugby	18.06.60	Holyhead	08.12.51 (O/L)	Patricroft	03.07.37
Stoke	05.08.61 (O/L)	Crewe South	22.12.51	Upperby	11.12.54
Rugby	19.08.61	Speke Junction	26.01.52	Patricroft	25.06.55
Crewe North	20.06.64	Crewe South	02.02.52	Upperby	23.07.55
Bescot	19.09.64	Longsight	13.06.53	Kingmoor	20.06.59
Banbury	01.01.66	Carnforth	23.01.54	Lancaster	18.06.60
Colwick	19.02.66 (O/L)	Aston	02.05.59	Speke Junction	24.09.60
Colwick	05.03.66	Edge Hill	21.10.61	Holyhead	23.06.62
Heaton Mersey	20.08.66	Llandudno Junction	02.03.63 (O/L)	Speke Junction	15.09.62
		Llandudno Junction	30.03.63	Springs Branch	22.06.63
5325				Carnforth	13.07.63
Crewe	13.03.57	**5328**		Speke Junction	14.09.63
Willesden	20.03.37	Crewe	13.03.37		
Springs Branch	02.05.42	Rugby	20.03.37	**5330**	
Willesden	30.05.42	Crewe	03.07.37	Crewe	10.03.37
Stoke	10.05.47	Chester	14.08.37	Rugby	20.03.37
Carnforth	22.03.52	Mold Junction	22.04.39	Shrewsbury	28.10.39

Armstrong Whitworth 5317 on a local train in 1948 at Grange-over-Sands. It had been transferred to Barrow from Crewe South in March of that year.

E. R. Morten

Shed	Date
5330	
Dundee	07.10.51
Carlisle	26.07.52
Kingmoor	01.02.58
Aintree	11.05.63
Warrington	?
Newton Heath	02.10.67
Carnforth	01.07.68
5331	
Rugby	20.03.37
Shrewsbury	28.10.39
Carlisle Upperby	18.04.42
Crewe North	30.11.46
Bletchley	08.02.47
Northampton	10.06.50
Llandudno Junction	31.10.53
Bletchley	26.02.55
Willesden	07.03.64
NWL	14.08.66
Springs Branch	20.08.66
5332	
Warrington	20.03.37
Edge Hill	15.02.41
Warrington	04.10.41
Edge Hill	13.12.41
Llandudno Junction	05.06.48
Crewe North	03.07.48
Preston	14.08.48
Chester	17.02.51
Preston	24.03.51
Northampton	11.03.61
Aston	02.12.61
Bushbury	13.01.62
Chester (Midland)	23.06.62
Speke Junction	15.09.62
5333	
Springs Branch	20.03.37
Warrington	06.04.40
Edge Hill	13.12.41
Warrington	02.05.42
Aston	26.12.42
Warrington	09.01.43
Edge Hill	30.04.43
Carnforth	11.05.46
Preston	09.07.49
Carnforth	20.08.49
Edge Hill	30.09.50
Brunswick	27.10.51
Saltley	18.01.58
Nottingham	20.06.59
Leicester Midland	12.12.59
Saltley	18.05.63
Leicester Midland	22.06.63
Annesley	19.10.64
Kirkby	18.10.65
Colwick	25.12.65 (O/L)
Colwick	03.01.66
Trafford Park	02.07.66
5334	
Bank Hall	27.03.37
Carlisle Upperby	24.09.44
Southport	07.01.45
Blackpool	16.06.51
Southport	30.06.51
Blackpool	30.06.51
St. Margarets	08.09.51 (O/L)
St. Margarets	15.09.51
Perth	19.04.52
Kingmoor	17.05.52
Annesley	25.05.63

Shed	Date
5335	
Southport	27.03.37
Wigan	28.10.39
Accrington	27.07.40
Rose Grove	09.11.40
Bank Hall	14.12.40
Accrington	21.10.50
Sheffield	11.11.50 (O/L)
Sheffield	02.02.52
Cricklewood	04.09.54
Derby	24.03.62
Woodford Halse	22.09.62
Leicester Central	12.01.63
Leicester Midland	20.06.64
Annesley	19.09.64
5336	
Blackpool	27.03.37
Newton Heath	19.06.37
Aintree	09.11.40
Bank Hall	14.12.40
Perth	21.08.48 (O/L)
Bank Hall	06.11.48
Newton Heath	21.10.50
5337	
Blackpool	03.04.37
Newton Heath	19.06.37
Blackpool	04.02.39 (O/L)
Newton Heath	25.02.39
Bank Hall	14.12.40
Low Moor	23.10.43
Agecroft	11.10.47
Southport	24.07.63
Kingmoor	14.11.64
5338	
Blackpool	03.04.37
Accrington	27.07.40
Aintree	09.11.40
Bank Hall	14.12.40
Newton Heath	17.10.42
Low Moor	30.10.43
Agecroft	11.10.47
Warrington	14.09.63
Edge Hill	08.02.64
Speke Junction	13.02.65
5339	
Farnley Junction	03.04.37
Wakefield	07.10.39
Sowerby Bridge	07.02.42
Wakefield	06.06.42
Huddersfield	16.06.56
Chester (Midland)	08.11.58
Longsight	07.11.59
Newton Heath	30.04.60 (O/L)
Newton Heath	03.03.62
Rose Grove	06.08.66
Lostock Hall	?
5340	
Farnley Junction	10.04.37
Huddersfield	17.12.49
Preston	08.11.58
Springs Branch	07.11.59
Preston	15.04.61
Llandudno Junction	01.07.61
Edge Hill	21.10.61
Carnforth	23.06.62
Barrow	06.03.65
Upperby	18.09.65
Kingmoor	11.12.66

Shed	Date
5341	
Farnley Junction	10.04.37
Newton Heath	08.09.56
5342	
Shrewsbury	10.04.37
Crewe	12.02.38
Sheffield	02.04.38 (O/L)
Sheffield	09.04.38
Kentish Town	26.09.42
Toton	21.12.46
Leicester Midland	05.07.47
Cricklewood	11.10.47
Leicester Midland	05.06.48
Saltley	04.12.54
Bedford	28.01.56
Kentish Town	30.04.60
Leicester Central	18.06.60
Derby	24.09.60
Woodford Halse	22.09.62
Leicester Central	12.01.63
Annesley	06.07.64
NWL	03.07.65 (O/L)
Carnforth	18.07.65
5343	
Willesden	17.04.37
Edge Hill	23.08.41
Carnforth	11.05.46
Edge Hill	30.09.50
Holyhead	17.02.51
Edge Hill	24.03.51
Warrington	07.11.59
Newton Heath	20.06.64
Rose Grove	06.08.66
5344	
Willesden	17.04.37
Edge Hill	23.08.41
Aston	28.02.48
Longsight	24.04.48
Walsall	30.10.48
Crewe North	04.02.56
Walsall	17.03.56
Llandudno Junction	18.01.58
Walsall	08.02.58
Bescot	14.06.58
Upperby	08.11.58
Carnforth	17.06.61
Crewe North	16.09.61
Speke Junction	14.09.63
Crewe North	20.06.64
Chester	12.12.64
Croes Newydd	02.10.65
5345	
Carnforth	17.04.37
Willesden	04.10.41
Springs Branch	30.05.42
Preston	05.05.45
Patricroft	14.07.45
Preston	06.10.45
Upperby	28.05.49
Holyhead	20.08.55
Mold Junction	04.02.56
Bangor	23.04.60
Holyhead	19.06.65
Llandudno Junction	13.11.65 (O/L)
Llandudno Junction	16.07.66
Chester	08.10.66
Lostock Hall	20.05.67 (O/L)
Lostock Hall	27.05.67

Shed	Date	Shed	Date	Shed	Date
5346		**5351**		**5358**	
Llandudno Junction	24.04.37	Upperby	10.06.50	St.Rollox	07.01.45
Bangor	25.09.37	Preston	18.06.60	Stirling	06.11.48
Llandudno Junction	03.08.40	Upperby	09.07.60	St. Rollox	30.10.56
Holyhead	10.06.50	Kingmoor	22.06.63	Hurlford	16.02.63
Brunswick	24.03.51	Bolton	14.12.63	Dalry Road	30.11.63
Leicester Midland	16.09.61	Lostock Hall	26.06.65		
Derby	14.10.61			**5359**	
Cricklewood	09.03.63	**5352**		Inverness	?
Nottingham	16.05.64	Crewe	08.05.37	St. Rollox	05.06.43
Annesley	18.07.64	Rugby	22.05.37	Stirling	06.11.48
Lostock Hall	03.07.65 (O/L)	Crewe	28.09.40	Motherwell	13.06.66
Lostock Hall	18.07.65	Longsight	02.08.41		
Trafford Park	18.09.65	Crewe North	12.10.46	**5360**	
Stockport	12.03.66	Stoke	18.01.47	Inverness	?
		Edge Hill	24.09.49	Perth	01.08.60
5347		Longsight	27.06.53	Dalry Road	29.09.60
Longsight	24.04.37	Patricroft	19.09.53		
Mold Junction	10.02.40	Trafford Park	14.11.64	**5361**	
Edge Hill	30.01.43			Inverness	?
		5353		Perth	01.08.60
5348		Crewe	08.05.37	Corkerhill	10.06.61
Trafford Park	13.06.53	Longsight	22.09.45 (O/L)	Stirling	25.11.63
Springs Branch	18.06.55	Crewe North	05.01.46	Carlisle Kingmoor	29.05.37
Blackpool	20.07.63	Willesden	02.08.47		
Fleetwood	14.09.63	Bletchley	30.09.50	**5362**	
Lostock Hall	19.02.66	Crewe South	08.08.53	Perth	10.04.37
Chester	24.04.37	Edge Hill	30.06.56 (O/L)	Oban	12.11.38
Rugby	03.05.41	Crewe South	27.10.56	St. Rollox	06.05.39
Upperby	23.08.41	Willesden	09.02.57	Carstairs	22.10.49
Crewe North	04.10.58	Aston	22.11.58	Dalry Road	10.06.50
Preston	15.08.59 (O/L)	Crewe North	09.02.63 (O/L)	Corkerhill	15.04.51
Crewe North	12.09.59	Mold Junction	30.03.63	Grangemouth	21.10.63
Llandudno Junction	05.05.62	Holyhead	22.06.63	Stirling	23.10.65
Mold Junction	09.02.63 (O/L)	Mold Junction	14.09.63		
Llandudno Junction	11.05.63	Chester	07.03.64	**5363**	
Shrewsbury	02.10.65	Crewe South	10.06.67	Crewe	31.05.37
		Lostock Hall	19.08.67	Carlisle Upperby	26.02.38
5349				Carlisle Kingmoor	24.05.41
Crewe	01.05.37	**5354**			
Northampton	08.05.37	Crewe	08.05.37	**5364**	
Rugby	16.07.38	Upperby	03.01.48	Bushbury	31.05.37
Bletchley	28.01.39	Warrington	31.01.48	Llandudno Junction	02.07.38
Willesden	28.03.42	Crewe North	26.09.53	Patricroft	13.08.38
Aston	02.05.42	Warrington	31.10.53	Carnforth	24.09.38
Bescot	02.10.43	Holyhead	23.06.62	Edge Hill	10.02.40
Aston	11.08.45	Warrington	15.09.62	Kingmoor	24.05.41
Northampton	14.09.63	Carnforth	22.06.63	Workington	11.03.61
Willesden	28.11.64	Lancaster	07.12.63	Kingmoor	09.03.63
Northampton	09.01.65				
Tyseley	02.10.65	**5355**		**5365**	
Crewe South	12.11.66	St. Rollox	15.05.37	Patricroft	31.05.37
		Grangemouth	12.02.49	Springs Branch	16.09.39
5350		St. Rollox	22.10.49	Crewe	20.01.40
Crewe	01.05.37	Dalry Road	11.03.61	Perth	05.07.41
Northampton	08.05.37			Corkerhill	15.06.60
Rugby	16.07.38	**5356**		Ardrossan	16.03.64
Edge Hill	10.02.40	Perth	15.05.37	Ayr	15.02.65
Holyhead	17.02.51	St. Rollox	04.02.39	Carstairs	26.11.66
Crewe South	15.09.51	Motherwell	18.08.62		
Crewe North	18.04.53			**5366**	
Southern Region	23.05.53 (O/L)	**5357**		Carlisle Upperby	07.06.37
Crewe North	27.06.53	Perth	15.05.37	Rugby	27.07.40
Willesden	27.06.53 (O/L)	Corkerhill	15.04.39	Perth	05.07.41
Willesden	15.08.53	Carlisle	02.12.39	Corkerhill	12.06.61
Stoke	02.07.60	Perth	11.05.40		
Springs Branch	11.03.67 (O/L)	Stirling	16.07.55	**5367**	
Springs Branch	01.04.67	Corkerhill	09.04.66	Edge Hill	07.06.37
Rose Grove	09.12.67			Barrow	25.09.37
		5358		Newton Heath	18.06.38
5351		Perth	15.05.37	Low Moor	27.07.40
Crewe	01.05.37	Oban	12.11.38 (P/E)	Wakefield	27.02.43
Rugby	22.05.37	St. Rollox	06.05.39	Bank Hall	08.05.43
Edge Hill	10.02.40	Southport	30.09.44	Huddersfield	28.08.43

Shed	Date	Shed	Date	Shed	Date
5367		**5373**		**5379**	
Accrington	11.10.47	Patricroft	28.05.49	Aston	30.09.39
Huddersfield	31.12.49	Edge Hill	30.01.54	Crewe	10.02.40
Accrington	11.03.50	Crewe North	03.03.54	Holyhead	15.06.40 (O/L)
Ferryhill	08.09.51 (O/L)	Springs Branch	20.06.59	Crewe	24.08.40
Ferryhill	15.09.51	Blackpool	20.07.63	Rugby	03.01.48
Fort William	12.06.54	Lancaster	14.09.63	Northampton	20.11.48 (O/L)
Ferryhill	04.09.54	Carnforth	18.04.66	Rugby	19.03.49
Perth	29.09.54	Lostock Hall	01.04.67	Crewe North	09.06.56
Dalry Road	29.09.60			Bletchley	06.05.61
		5374		Derby	14.04.62
5368		Barrow	26.06.37	Willesden	07.03.64
Carlisle Upperby	12.06.37	Crewe North	03.07.37		
Newton Heath	22.06.63	Crewe South	27.11.48	**5380**	
Agecroft	23.11.63	Crewe North	12.02.49	Edge Hill	11.07.37
Springs Branch	08.01.66	Crewe South	26.03.49	Crewe	07.08.37
		Rugby	07.01.50	Carlisle Upperby	20.09.39
5369		Willesden	09.12.50	Edge Hill	27.07.40
Stoke	19.06.37	Rugby	29.10.60	Warrington	07.11.59
Rugby	25.09.37	Willesden	19.11.60	Edge Hill	09.04.60
Crewe North	24.09.38	Bescot	17.03.62	Warrington	31.12.60
Crewe South	27.11.48	Aston	21.07.62	Holyhead	23.06.62
Crewe North	12.02.49	Stafford	16.01.65	Warrington	15.09.62
Crewe South	05.03.49	Carnforth	24.07.65	Springs Branch	30.03.63
Crewe North	05.07.52			Newton Heath	27.07.63
Crewe South	18.04.53	**5375**		Longsight	24.08.63
Crewe North	11.08.56	Bescot	26.06.37	Trafford Park	20.02.65
Llandudno Junction	05.05.62	Crewe	02.07.37		
Mold Junction	09.02.63 (O/L)	Rugby	03.01.48	**5381**	
Llandudno Junction	11.05.63	Willesden	15.09.56	Patricroft	17.07.37
Saltley	05.10.63	Rugby	29.10.60	Crewe	07.08.37
Chester	23.04.66	Willesden	19.11.60	Aston	30.09.39
Mold Junction	19.06.65	Speke Junction	14.01.61	Crewe	10.02.40
		Stoke	05.08.61 (O/L)	Stoke	20.12.47
5370		Speke Junction	19.08.61	Crewe	26.09.53 (O/L)
Llandudno Junction	19.06.37	Springs Branch	22.03.63	Stoke	31.10.53
Holyhead	25.09.37	Southport	06.07.63	Willesden	20.11.54
Bangor	08.10.38	Springs Branch	13.02.65	Edge Hill	15.10.60
Holyhead	14.10.39	Warrington	26.06.65	Warrington	31.12.60
Crewe	28.11.42	Edge Hill	07.10.67	Newton Heath	20.06.64
Longsight	05.12.42			Bury	14.11.64
Llandudno Junction	02.06.45	**5376**		Bolton	10.04.65
Warrington	02.10.48	Aston	26.06.37		
Aston	08.12.51	Crewe	03.07.38	**5382**	
Carnforth	12.09.59	Edge Hill	28.09.39	Patricroft	31.07.37
Crewe South	03.10.59	Preston	24.07.43 (O/L)	Crewe	07.08.37
Llandudno Junction	18.06.60	Edge Hill	13.11.43	Mold Junction	30.09.39
Crewe South	17.09.60	Holyhead	02.09.50 (O/L)	Chester	01.09.45
Speke Junction	15.10.60	Edge Hill	02.09.50	Holyhead	10.06.50
				Crewe North	08.01.55
5371		**5377**		Carlisle	12.03.55
Llandudno Junction	19.06.37	Carlisle Upperby	26.06.37	Holyhead	25.06.55
Holyhead	25.09.37	Crewe North	17.07.37	Upperby	15.12.56
Llandudno Junction	25.12.37	Edge Hill	30.09.39	Holyhead	14.06.58
Crewe	13.12.41	Warrington	11.05.40	Stockport	25.11.61
Willesden	14.07.45	Preston	28.09.40	Newton Heath	?
Upperby	21.06.47	Patricroft	11.04.42	Rose Grove	06.08.66
Rugby	07.11.53	Fleetwood	23.01.60		
Upperby	09.01.54	Blackpool	18.06.60	**5383**	
Kingmoor	11.12.66	Rowsley	14.04.62	Chester	31.07.37
Workington	14.01.67	Bury	19.09.64	Crewe	07.08.37
		Bolton	10.04.65	Mold Junction	30.09.39
5372				Barrow	14.02.48
Carnforth	26.06.37	**5378**		Crewe South	19.06.65
Preston	29.12.45	Crewe	03.07.37	Kingmoor	17.12.66
Rugby	21.12.46	Edge Hill	30.09.39		
Willesden	25.02.56	Crewe	05.09.42	**5384**	
Longsight	20.06.59	Willesden	14.07.45	Chester	20.07.37
Springs Branch	12.09.59	Upperby	21.06.47	Crewe	07.08.37
		Patricroft	05.06.48	Mold Junction	30.09.39
5373		Rugby	14.04.56	Shrewsbury	07.10.39
Carnforth	26.06.37	Patricroft	09.06.56	Mold Junction	17.10.42
Preston	29.12.45	Bolton	15.09.62	Warrington	21.11.42
Llandudno Junction	14.02.48 (O/L)			Crewe South	27.03.43
Preston	06.03.48	**5379**		Crewe North	12.10.46
		Crewe	03.07.37	Shrewsbury	20.12.47

Shed	Date	Shed	Date	Shed	Date
5436		**5440**		**5445**	
Stockport	16.11.37	Patricroft	14.02.59	Crewe	23.04.49
Carlisle Upperby	22.01.38	Birkenhead	28.03.59	Longsight	28.05.49
Crewe North	15.12.45	Edge Hill	14.05.60	Preston	01.10.49
Shrewsbury	06.11.48			Upperby	05.11.49
St.Margarets	07.10.51	**5441**		Barrow	18.06.60
Blackpool	19.09.53	Crewe	04.12.37	Lancaster	26.06.65
Chester (Midland)	15.09.62	Rugby	11.12.37	Carnforth	18.04.66
Warrington	05.09.64	Bletchley	04.02.39		
Birkenhead	20.01.67	Willesden	28.03.42	**5446**	
Lostock Hall	18.08.67	Crewe	20.06.42	Crewe	11.12.37
		Rugby	20.12.47	Shrewsbury	01.01.38
5437		Crewe North	17.09.55	Mold Junction	17.10.42
Bushbury	20.11.37	Longsight	24.09.55	Patricroft	09.01.43
Monument Lane	16.03.40	Chester	06.10.56	Aston	03.05.47
Bescot	22.03.41	Upperby	13.10.56	Crewe South	14.02.53
Aston	10.05.41	Chester	20.10.56	Crewe North	11.04.53
Bescot	02.10.43	Llandudno Junction	26.01.57	Stoke	14.09.63
Bushbury	16.10.43	Holyhead	22.06.57	Crewe South	07.03.64
Bescot	05.07.52	Speke Junction	13.10.62		
Rugby	13.03.54			**5447**	
Willesden	25.02.56	**5442**		Crewe	18.12.37
Rugby	21.04.56	Crewe	04.12.37	Saltley	02.04.38 (O/L)
Llandudno Junction	10.11.56	Rugby	11.12.37	Saltley	09.04.38
Holyhead	22.06.57	Bletchley	28.05.38	Trafford Park	25.12.43 (O/L)
Upperby	05.10.57	Willesden	28.03.42	Saltley	05.02.44
Stoke	04.08.62 (O/L)	Warrington	29.05.43	Leeds Holbeck	16.05.53
Upperby	18.08.62	Edge Hill	25.03.44	Sheffield	26.06.54
Newton Heath	22.06.63	Edge Hill	16.02.46	Kentish Town	12.05.56
Agecroft	23.11.63	Patricroft	21.06.47	Saltley	21.11.59
Carnforth	21.08.65	Fleetwood	23.01.60	Holyhead	19.06.65
Kingmoor	25.09.65	Blackpool	18.06.60	Shrewsbury	17.09.66
		Derby	25.05.63	Kingmoor	11.03.67 (O/L)
5438		Burton	12.09.64	Kingmoor	01.04.67
Crewe	27.11.37	Coalville	19.12.64	Rose Grove	06.01.68
Camden	04.12.37 (O/L)	Kingmoor	13.02.65 (O/L)		
Patricroft	01.01.38	Kingmoor	06.03.65	**5448**	
Carlisle Upperby	22.01.38			Crewe	18.12.37
Longsight	26.10.46	**5443**		Leeds Holbeck	02.04.38 (O/L)
Patricroft	11.01.47	Crewe	30.11.37	Leeds Holbeck	09.04.38
Upperby	15.12.51	Carnforth	11.12.37	Derby	05.11.38
Edge Hill	21.05.60	Crewe	18.12.37	Bristol	06.05.39
Holyhead	11.06.60	Belle Vue	03.04.38	Gloucester	03.02.40
Bangor	17.09.60	Leeds Holbeck	14.03.42	Crewe South	26.09.42 (O/L)
Mold Junction	08.04.61	Perth	31.10.42	Crewe South	17.10.42
Rugby	06.05.61	Carlisle	23.09.44	Llandudno Junction	20.02.43 (O/L)
Mold Junction	10.06.61	St.Rollox	04.03.50	Crewe	10.04.43
Holyhead	22.06.63	Grangemouth	12.05.63	Rugby	20.12.47
Mold Junction	14.09.63			Aston	10.06.50
Chester	07.03.64	**5444**		Rugby	13.10.51
		Carnforth	11.12.37	Aston	27.10.51
5439		Llandudno Junction	18.12.37	Rugby	23.02.63
Crewe	27.11.37	Crewe	13.01.40	Crewe South	19.09.64
Camden	04.12.37 (O/L)	Shrewsbury	24.05.41	Rugby	28.11.64
Patricroft	01.01.38	Patricroft	02.05.42	Nuneaton	29.05.65
Carlisle Upperby	22.01.38	Edge Hill	15.12.45	Heaton Mersey	28.05.66
Willesden	28.10.44	Patricroft	09.03.46 (O/L)		
Upperby	21.06.47	Patricroft	04.05.46	**5449**	
Bescot	17.11.51	Leeds Holbeck	19.11.55	Crewe	18.12.37
Bushbury	13.03.54	Leeds Holbeck	10.12.55	Carlisle Upperby	12.02.38
Aston	13.10.62	Bedford	28.01.56	Preston	07.03.42
Bushbury	15.12.62	Kentish Town	16.06.56	Springs Branch	11.04.42
Aston	17.04.65	Brunswick	14.02.59		
		Annesley	02.07.60	**5450**	
5440		Cricklewood	26.01.63	Crewe	25.12.37
Crewe	27.11.37	Woodford Halse	18.05.63	Carlisle Upperby	12.02.38
Camden	04.12.37 (O/L)	Nottingham	22.06.63	Belle Vue	04.06.49
Rugby	01.01.38	Fleetwood	05.12.64	Blackpool	10.11.51 (O/L)
Bath	30.04.38	Lostock Hall	19.02.66	Blackpool	08.12.51
Gloucester	26.09.42			Belle Vue	26.01.52
Bristol	23.10.43	**5445**		Agecroft	24.09.55
Bath	01.07.44	Carnforth	11.12.37	Leicester Central	24.10.59
Birkenhead	21.05.58 (O/L)	Crewe	18.12.37	Annesley	09.01.60
Birkenhead	21.06.58	Shrewsbury	01.01.38	Lostock Hall	03.07.65 (O/L)
				Lostock Hall	18.07.65

Shed	Date	Shed	Date	Shed	Date
5451		**5457**		**5464**	
Crewe	25.12.37	Perth	10.10.38	Perth	11.05.40
Carlisle Upperby	12.02.38	Ardrossan	09.03.59	Newton Heath	24.02.57
Preston	20.06.59	Ayr	22.06.59	Blackpool	?
Upperby	07.11.59	Ardrossan	14.09.59	Derby	19.05.63
Kingmoor	22.06.63			Burton	10.09.64
Aintree	07.12.63	**5458**		Colwick	25.12.65 (O/L)
Newton Heath	27.06.64	Perth	11.10.38	Colwick	03.01.66
Carnforth	11.07.64	Inverness	30.06.58		
Barrow	18.07.64	Perth	16.10.58	**5465**	
Upperby	18.09.65	St. Rollox	10.11.58	Carlisle Kingmoor	21.11.38
		Polmadie	14.11.58	Perth	26.04.41
5452					
Crewe North	15.09.38 (O/L)	**5459**		**5466**	
Aberdeen	05.11.38	Perth	14.10.38	Carlisle Kingmoor	25.11.38
Crewe North	14.01.39 (O/L)	Crewe	05.11.38 (O/L)	Perth	26.04.41
Aberdeen	04.02.39	Perth	03.12.38	Kingmoor	26.07.52
Edinburgh	22.07.39	Inverness	30.06.58	Speke Junction	14.03.64
Perth	30.03.40	Perth	16.10.58	Edge Hill	20.06.64
Corkerhill	27.06.59	St.Rollox	10.11.58	Speke Junction	13.02.65
Carstairs	07.11.59	Polmadie	14.11.58		
		Hamilton	14.03.60	**5467**	
5453		Polmadie	04.07.60	Carlisle Kingmoor	30.11.38
St. Rollox	19.09.38	Hurlford	26.08.63	Inverness	19.04.41
Motherwell	14.06.47			Perth	26.09.42
Inverness	10.06.50	**5460**		Corkerhill	?
Perth	01.08.60	Perth	18.10.38	Hurlford	13.06.60
Dumfries	28.05.62	Dundee	25.02.50 (P/E)	Corkerhill	19.11.62
		Perth	18.03.50	Dumfries	04.05.64
5454		Inverness	21.10.57	Ayr	12.06.65
St. Rollox	08.10.38	Corkerhill	28.05.60	Motherwell	06.10.66
Kingmoor	04.02.46	Ayr	13.08.62		
Crewe North	23.04.49 (O/L)	Perth	06.05.63	**5468**	
Crewe North	28.05.49			Carlisle Kingmoor	01.12.38
Carlisle Canal	01.10.49	**5461**		St. Rollox	12.04.41
Springs Branch	02.06.51	Perth	19.10.38	Grangemouth	03.07.48
Preston	22.06.57	Carlisle	02.03.46	St. Rollox	22.10.49
Northampton	11.03.61	Motherwell	11.05.46		
Willesden	28.11.64	Inverness	24.06.50	**5469**	
Northampton	09.01.65	Perth	27.07.60	Edinburgh	05.12.38
Banbury	02.10.65			Perth	30.03.40
Colwick	19.02.66 (O/L)	**5462**		Ferryhill	?
Colwick	05.03.66	Carlisle Kingmoor	31.10.38	Kittybrewster	30.05.60
Trafford Park	25.06.66	Perth	11.05.40	Ferryhill	19.06.61
		Motherwell	11.05.46	Dalry Road	27.06.62
5455				St. Margarets	04.10.65
St.Rollox	28.09.38	**5463**			
Kingmoor	02.03.46	Carlisle Kingmoor	07.11.38	**5470**	
		Perth	11.05.40	Edinburgh	12.12.38
5456		Hurlford	22.05.61	Perth	30.03.40
Perth	04.10.38	Ardrossan	23.05.61	Inverness	29.10.61
Ardrossan	09.03.59	Dumfries	11.05.64	Corkerhill	07.04.62
Ayr	22.06.59	Stranraer	21.05.66 (P/E)	Ardrossan	17.04.62
Ardrossan	02.09.59			Stranraer	01.10.62
Dumfries	04.05.64	**5464**			
		Carlisle Kingmoor	08.11.38	**5471**	
		Crewe	03.12.38 (O/L)	St. Rollox	12.12.38
		Carlisle Kingmoor	31.12.38	Dumfries	18.01.65

Table 9.4 Engines covering more than 70,000 miles in one year

No.	Mileage	Year	Allocation
5281	82,254	1938	Kentish Town
5260	77,202	1937	Kentish Town
5454	76,839	1942	St. Rollox
5176	75,453	1936	Perth
5165	75,086	1936	Perth
5288	74,842	1937	Bristol
5166	74,039	1936	Perth
5277	73,520	1937	Kentish Town
5116	73,212	1936	Kingmoor and Perth
5469	72,524	1939	Edinburgh Dalry Road
5469	72,286	1945	Perth
5173	70,917	1936	Perth
5162	70,729	1936	Perth and Inverness
5175	70,579	1936	Perth
5456	70,574	1940	Perth
5059	70,509	1935	Crewe, Upperby and Patricroft
5177	70,470	1936	Perth
5055	70,372	1935	Kentish Town
5283	70,249	1937	Bristol
5155	70,119	1936	Kingmoor and St. Rollox

One Central Division engine recorded over 65,000 miles, Bank Hall's 5217 running 65,990 miles in 1938. Surprisingly, only one Western Division engine topped 65,000 miles in a year; that was 5059 which ran 70,509 miles in 1935 when it was shedded at Upperby for about eight months, Crewe for ten weeks and Patricroft for about seven weeks.

Allocated to Bristol (22A) from February 1935, 5066 pictured at Derby in that year, was transferred to Gloucester in January 1936. It has the tall chimney and prominent top feed pipes characteristic of the first 50 engines built by Vulcan Foundry, but not the open front footplate which was only on the first 25. 5066 ran over a quarter of a million miles in its first five years and its final mileage was 1,131,886, one of over 100 pre-war engines to record over a million miles.

www.rail-online.co.uk

Substantial accelerations of Midland Division passenger trains were made from the start of the winter 1937 timetable and, since Jubilees were not allowed over the Peak District line until mid-1938, Class 5s held the fort on the Manchester trains. Trafford Park and Kentish Town engines amassing very high mileages on these services including Kentish Town's 5281, which was the only pre-war Class 5 to run more than 80,000 miles in any one year, recording 82,254 miles in 1938. It was photographed on a Western Division express at Bushey during that year.

Real Photographs

TABLE 9.5 INDIVIDUAL MILEAGES 1934-39, 1950 and to 1960

No.	1934	1935	1936	1937	1938	1939	CUMULATIVES 1939	1950	Total to 1960
5000	-	56,390	35,304	34,202	37,768	33,984	197,648	616,452	960,239
5001	-	52,303	40,268	33,798	34,953	36,766	198,088	542,410	897,685
5002	-	52,742	39,952	32,209	39,160	36,909	200,972	608,515	949,991
5003	-	52,753	35,333	36,299	28,605	41,302	194,292	625,473	999,598
5004	-	58,188	49,400	47,160	48,022	41,946	244,716	651,482	1,058,823
5005	-	60,613	54,210	29,944	42,541	41,326	228,634	689,425	1,107,520
5006	-	59,223	58,502	35,893	35,732	29,360	218,710	693,724	1,084,523
5007	-	59,386	61,646	58,408	54,464	46,018	279,922	783,870	1,239,781
5008	-	46,559	60,980	54,251	55,251	51,267	268,308	791,129	1,246,480
5009	-	47,395	63,693	60,630	52,312	41,835	265,865	773,348	773,348
5010	-	49,764	63,180	50,219	51,169	54,386	268,718	815,208	1,251,725
5011	-	43,985	66,644	49,740	53,639	43,880	257,888	763,137	763,137
5012	-	35,521	60,906	56,462	61,906	44,759	259,554	764,458	1,224,390
5013	-	48,204	65,482	54,331	46,917	46,566	261,500	745,165	1,220,345
5014	-	44,517	54,554	62,378	42,703	50,653	254,805	774,891	1,164,559
5015	-	41,389	54,162	59,439	54,453	43,065	252,508	748,664	1,072,840
5016	-	37,701	67,731	55,480	45,565	47,355	253,832	782,676	782,676
5017	-	42,385	60,630	52,231	52,068	52,511	259,825	760,284	1,180,345
5018		42,154	63,703	57,630	51,971	45,652	261,110	764,816	1,148,615
5019	-	37,710	50,053	41,039	43,094	38,031	209,927	537,547	949,047
5020	26,663	46,661	48,584	44,150	48,426	38,930	253,414	629,675	1,017,990
5021	16,343	65,404	44,868	37,693	45,154	49,080	258,542	626,868	1,049,070
5022	22,944	53,234	38,691	42,958	46,464	37,280	241,571	667,402	1,159,693
5023	24,637	66,021	57,426	43,708	50,437	42,683	284,912	749,426	1,171,401
5024	31,013	54,770	55,782	41,523	49,038	34,995	267,121	628,846	1,014,705
5025	27,121	58,918	51,090	37,049	44,961	35,732	254,871	635,300	1,007,920
5026	24,589	66,715	44,568	46,051	49,215	44,056	275,194	617,365	908,992
5027	17,422	66,788	58,417	37,198	43,987	48,306	272,118	588,948	966,966
5028	18,825	54,512	62,141	37,496	35,675	33,783	242,432	609,381	977,527
5029	21,054	60,138	59,470	35,691	43,940	51,394	271,687	792,106	792,106
5030	18,565	50,924	46,270	40,868	35,787	36,393	228,807	578,507	1,033,843
5031	16,241	56,275	41,046	50,812	48,164	39,660	252,198	598,891	951,916
5032	18,522	49,993	53,524	44,814	42,264	42,350	251,467	630,111	1,001,461
5033	17,876	46,873	43,510	44,950	46,480	42,408	242,097	604,983	1,022,642
5034	16,288	51,924	55,647	39,645	32,938	38,715	235,157	587,698	944,337
5035	13,943	62,966	52,340	40,291	41,185	38,185	248,910	569,840	947,694
5036	14,198	51,757	56,735	42,874	48,474	43,848	257,886	799,591	1,192,043
5037	14,874	58,485	61,824	41,594	50,726	30,278	257,781	618,666	991,845
5038	17,392	50,433	43,562	32,489	38,926	33,385	216,187	549,770	931,898
5039	17,559	48,690	45,471	33,292	31,931	36,576	213,519	622,703	1,039,131
5040	15,042	48,710	43,720	47,629	38,036	30,149	223,286	732,881	1,106,637
5041	16,703	55,347	40,679	43,548	32,941	50,922	240,140	710,443	1,070,161
5042	14,323	60,328	47,729	47,897	50,911	48,013	269,201	689,180	1,051,497
5043	10,792	50,373	36,688	57,113	61,367	42,371	258,704	705,466	1,072,679
5044	12,087	50,442	48,133	52,391	44,659	40,702	248,414	615,604	996,483
5045	14,450	42,892	44,875	44,184	38,107	51,776	236,284	612,435	1,001,436
5046	12,737	46,559	50,911	39,416	52,062	41,527	243,212	651,543	1,052,545
5047	9,215	65,234	52,589	51,834	46,445	35,100	260,417	702,539	702,539
5048	9,958	52,612	50,398	42,095	43,374	49,646	248,083	584,400	963,830
5049	12,286	56,442	55,875	45,627	36,449	36,315	242,994	701,309	1,152,723
5050	4,423	57,682	49,865	45,130	49,283	48,775	255,158	674,335	1,055,022
5051	5,574	35,002	56,931	48,130	45,243	39,377	230,257	606,599	961,650
5052	5,169	63,721	53,889	42,524	41,004	42,808	249,115	675,718	1,062,209
5053	4,883	46,160	60,574	46,503	53,658	58,021	269,799	786,233	786,233
5054	5,832	57,424	61,425	46,015	51,573	38,901	261,170	656,251	1,103,900
5055	4,625	70,372	57,729	37,190	49,845	40,694	260,455	669,202	1,023,430
5056	4,537	66,225	44,242	36,923	67,033	57,922	276,882	701,947	1,101,529
5057	4,449	58,515	59,307	41,013	51,007	45,010	259,301	672,404	1,012,180
5058	3,453	59,224	63,253	43,131	65,890	47,637	282,588	664,952	1,046,040

Goods, 27,813 for the Precursor and 37,055 for the Prince of Wales, see **Table 9.7.**

Another important factor in assessing performance was the use of coal; consumption per engine mile for the Class 5s was 53.76lbs, which was between 7lb and 10lb per mile lower than either of the standard Moguls and much better than the 71.36lb per mile for the 19" Goods. It was, however, similar to that of the ex-LNWR engines – the Prince of Wales used 51.23, the Precursor 52.52 and the George the Fifth 55.84lbs per mile.

These figures are not entirely unexpected given that brand new engines were being compared with locomotives which had been in service for around 20 years, and the Class 5s were generally used on much heavier duties and more intensive diagrams than the ex-LNWR engines. Comparing the days under repair against the mileage run, the Class 5s showed a significant improvement; the figures also indicate that the 4-4-0s and the 19" Goods had already been displaced by newer engines from their previous duties and were mostly reduced to pottering around on local work. The Class 5s were putting in high mileages at good average daily availability and with reasonable economy thus meeting the original requirement when they were ordered to replace the older locomotives.

TABLE 9.7 INDIVIDUAL COSTS OF LOCOMOTIVES FOR THE THREE YEARS 1933-35

Operating Class	Wheel Type	Type	No. of Locos. in service at Dec. 1935	Average annual mileage	Average mileage between General Repairs	Weekdays not in service	
						Under repair	Not required
5MT	4-6-0	Mixed Traffic (Standard)	225	55,310	-	77	4
Passenger Classes							
5	4-6-0	L&Y Old Class 8	40	32,265	88,472	82	33
4	4-6-0	Prince of Wales	131	37,055	117,174	64	18
4	4-6-0	Caledonian	32	33,482	103,114	52	28
4	4-6-0	Highland	8	33,052	121,179	89	27
4	4-4-0	Standard Compound	240	47,589	125,396	73	17
3	4-4-0	LNW Precursor	55	27,813	109,865	52	72
3	4-4-0	LNW George V	76	20,754	102,021	43	117
Freight Classes							
4	4-6-0	LNW 19"	75	21,241	92,881	43	55
4	4-6-0	Highland - Superheated	8	26,243	115,349	75	23
4	4-6-0	Highland - Non-Superheated	7	25,021	-	55	24
4	2-6-0	Standard (Tapered)	40	39,652	-	63	4
4	2-6-0	Standard (Parallel)	240	38,022	138,356	56	7
4	0-6-0	Standard	727	27,590	111,372	49	9

The Railway Gazette in 1939, no doubt with help from the LMS public relations department, confirmed the superiority of the new engines. "While it is not possible to quote actual cost figures, these engines, owing to the simplicity and robustness of their design, have proved very free from casualties and inexpensive in maintenance. The average mileage obtained up to service repairs is 58,000 and 145,000 between general repairs. As an indication of their freedom from trouble on the road it can be stated that in this class of nearly 500 engines there have, in the last two years, been only 54 cases of heated axleboxes, which represents a probability of a hot axlebox on any given engine occurring only once in 15 years. Hot big ends also, which in days gone by used to be such a troublesome operating feature, may be said, in a modern design of this nature, to have practically disappeared, there having been only 18 cases on these engines in the last two years".

In November 1953 all of the Southern Region's Merchant Navy class Pacifics were taken out of service following an accident at Crewkerne on 24th April when the crank axle of 35020 *Bibby Line* fractured at speed. Examination showed a flaw due to metal fatigue and prompt steps were taken to examine all the Southern Region Pacifics. As replacements for the Merchant Navy engines, six ex-LNER Class V2 2-6-2s were sent from the Eastern Region and seven Britannia 4-6-2s from the Western and London Midland Regions. When the Merchant Navy engines returned to service, the lightweight Pacifics were all checked. Some of the replacements for these were Class 5s, seven of which were transferred to Nine Elms shed, including 45051 from Monument Lane. The engines were allowed to work on the Waterloo to Bournemouth West and Exeter Central lines and between Eastleigh and Portsmouth Harbour, provided the cab footsteps were cut back to an overall width of 8' 3" and the cab windscreens were either removed or closed and securely fastened back. The Class 5s also had smoke box brackets welded on to carry the Southern headcode discs as shown on 45051 as it waits to depart from Waterloo with the 12.54pm to Salisbury on 22nd May 1953.

R. C. Riley

Armstrong Whitworth-built 5378 from Willesden shed with an up goods near Apsley near Hemel Hempstead in 1946. It moved north to Carlisle Upperby in June 1947.

C. R. L. Coles/Rail Archive Stephenson

10 REPAIRS AND MAINTENANCE

Under the LMS organisation most sheds carried out minor running repairs and adjustments, including boiler wash-outs etc. Jobs which required the engine to return to works or one of the larger sheds, such as Rugby, were usually designated under one of the 'Classified Repair' codes. These were either 'Heavy' (H), or 'Light' (L), further sub-divided into 'Casual' (C), 'Intermediate' (I), 'Overhaul' (O), 'Service' (S) or 'General' (G), although no cases of 'LG' have been noted in the surviving documentation. Occasionally engines were sent to a main works for other reasons such as modifications and in these cases the code 'NC' (Non-Classified) was used. The other code which appears from time to time on the Engine History cards is 'TRO', which stands for 'Tender Repair Only'. Sometimes the codes have the suffix '(EO)', which indicates 'Engine Only'. A suffix, usually after 'NC' was 'Rect.', or 'Rect. (EO)' used when an engine had to be returned to works for attention soon after a works visit.

According to the Board of Trade classification a Heavy repair was one during which an engine was reboilered or had its boiler removed from the frames. It was also when any two of the following were carried out:

Fitting new tyres to four or more wheels.
Fitting new cylinders.
Fitting new axles.
Re-tubing or otherwise repairing the boiler whilst still in the frames with not less than fifty firebox stays renewed.
Turning the wheels and refitting axleboxes.
Stripping and renewing both motion and brake gear.

Light repairs often involved major work such as fitting new axles, replacing cylinders, partially retubing or patching the boiler in situ, or refurbishing the motion, axleboxes, frames, etc. As long as only one of these items was involved, however, the repair was still regarded as Light. Most Heavy repairs were Generals whilst most Light repairs were Intermediates. General repairs were carried out either at set time intervals or at predetermined mileages, beyond which it was deemed that an engine could not safely remain in service, and were designed to return it virtually to 'as new' condition. Intermediate repairs were normally undertaken when a major component reached the stage where it had to be attended to before the engine was due for General repair, but the aim was to carry out as few Intermediate repairs as possible. Therefore Heavy General repairs were usually done at approximately three to four-yearly intervals, with, typically two Intermediate repairs (either Light or Heavy) between. The opportunity was often taken to carry out modifications at the Heavy works visits.

For the Class 5s the proposal period, the time after a scheduled repair when an engine would be inspected and assessed for its next works visit, was originally 14 months. By the time of the last LMS review of proposal periods in January 1947, the time interval for Northern Division engines had been reduced to 12 months, except for those on the ex-Callander & Oban and Highland sections where it was further lowered to eight months. This is another indication of the higher mileages and more intensive work of the Class 5s in Scotland.

Crewe Works was responsible for Heavy repairs to Class 5s on the Central, Midland and Western Divisions, and St. Rollox for those allocated to the Northern Division. The LMS Engine History Cards did not record which particular workshop carried out the repairs, although the British Railways cards do usually have this information from around 1946/47 for English-based engines and 1950/51 for Scottish Region

engines. One regional variation is that the Scottish records show significantly more minor works visits for rectification than their English counterparts, reflecting that this type of work was more likely to be done at the large running sheds south of the border.

Under British Railways auspices the two works continued to share the bulk of Class 5 repairs with Crewe maintaining the London Midland Region engines and those allocated at various times to the Southern Region (S&DJR), Western Region (mainly Shrewsbury) and the North Eastern Region (after transfer of the Yorkshire sheds), with St. Rollox maintaining the Scottish Region engines, including those at Carlisle Kingmoor up to August 1962 even though the shed had been transferred to the London Midland Region for operational purposes in February 1958.

After St. Rollox stopped repairing steam locomotives in 1964, its last General being 45213 which was returned to traffic on 7th December 1963, responsibility for the Scottish Region Class 5s passed to the ex-North British and LNER Cowlairs Works. The last recorded Crewe repair on a pre-war engine was a Non-Classified on 45273 completed on 25th November 1966; its last Heavy overhaul was 45269 which left the works on 2nd December 1966.

The two main works were supplemented by Horwich and Rugby for the London Midland Region Class 5s and Inverness and Cowlairs, initially for those based in Scotland but later for engines from English sheds too. Derby and Bow also played a minor role as did Inverurie and three workshops outside the two regions are known to have carried out repairs to the class. All of these are dealt with in detail later in this chapter.

10.1 Boilers

The early boiler changes (mostly to release domeless 14-element boilers for rebuilding and later to create the float of straight throatplate boilers) were done at Crewe, inter-divisional transfers being made as necessary. A HG repair at Crewe during the LMS period usually took between 25 and 40 weekdays: this was insufficient time to do the necessary work on the boiler, so engines undergoing HG repairs invariably left works with a different boiler from that with which they had entered. This meant that it was necessary to create a pool of spare boilers.

All 61 of the spare boilers built at Crewe between 1936 and 1956 were of the sloping throatplate, long-firebox type. Between October 1936 and December 1937 13 of the first 225 engines which had been built with straight throatplate boilers had their frames adapted to take the later type of boiler, thus creating a pool of spare straight throatplate boilers without having to build any new ones to a design which was by then obsolete.

At the end of 1939 after the 13 former straight throatplate engines had been adapted to take sloping throatplate boilers, the Divisional allocation of engines and boilers was:

Division	Straight throatplate	Sloping throatplate	Total
Central	49	21	70
Midland	23	41	64
Western	85	168	253
Total (Crewe Responsibility)	157	230	387
Northern	55	30	85
Grand Total of Engines	212	260	472
Spare boilers in pool	13	15	28
	225	275	500

The spare ratios were thus about 6%.

It is difficult to be sure when St. Rollox started repairs involving boiler changes, since the surviving Engine Record Cards do not identify the works at which repairs were carried out until after the war. There is however evidence to suggest St. Rollox started changing boilers at Heavy repairs from around mid-1940, and to facilitate this, spare boilers were sent north from the Crewe pool.

More than 50 boilers of both types were moved from the Crewe pool to St. Rollox when the Northern Division engine allocation increased during the war and by the end of 1944 the Divisional allocations were:

Division	Straight throatplate	Sloping throatplate	Total
Central	39	21	60
Midland	11	73	84
Western	86	190	276
Total (Crewe Responsibility)	136	284	420
Northern	76	65	141
Grand Total of Engines	212	349	561
Spare boilers in pool	★ 13	† 17	30
	225	366	591

★ Approx. 5 at St. Rollox   † Approx. 6 at St. Rollox

Further adjustments were made to the numbers in the Crewe and St. Rollox boiler pools over the years. Although the last 110 Class 5s built had a four-inch longer coupled wheelbase this did not affect the spare boiler position because the extra length was taken up in the smokebox which did not stay with the rest of the boiler during the repair cycle. In 1951, shortly after the last two engines went into service, two new spare boilers were built, bringing the total number of spare boilers up to 57, and the total for all Class 5 or 3B boilers up to 899. Four more spare boilers were subsequently built in 1956, and sent to St. Rollox. At the beginning of 1954 the Scottish Region had 280 3B boilers on its Register, (82 straight throatplate, of which 18 were domed, and 198 sloping throatplate, of which 56 had forward top feeds). At that time there were some 260 engines under Scottish Region maintenance.

When maintenance responsibility for the Carlisle Kingmoor allocation was transferred to the London Midland Region from the Scottish Region on 12th August 1962, its engines then went to LMR works for attention. 52 Class 5s were involved, 12 straight throatplate and 40 sloping throatplate. There was a corresponding adjustment in the spare boiler pool, and a further four sloping throatplate boilers (including one with forward top feed) were sent to Crewe before the end of August, and two straight throatplate boilers (one domed) followed in November 1962.

Crewe usually sent sloping throatplate engines out with a boiler of the same type as that with which they came in. St. Rollox with a smaller pool of spare boilers of each type at its disposal, appears to have run short of certain types of boiler from time to time. In 1951 for example, and again in 1955, some of the straight throatplate boilers needed extensive firebox repairs, which resulted in the boilers concerned taking several months longer than usual to repair. Boiler overhauls typically took three or four times as long as the engines anyway, but these situations exacerbated the problem. The solution was to fit a sloping throatplate boiler which would result in a corresponding surplus of these some four years or so later. It also meant that the total of straight throatplate engines and the spares ratio of sloping throatplate boilers were both reduced, which in turn sometimes meant that straight throatplate boilers were available when there was a shortage of sloping throatplate ones, hence the three 'reverse conversions' of 45433, 45443 and 45461 in 1955.

St. Rollox, and later Cowlairs, often fitted engines with whichever type of top-feed casing was available, leading to domeless engines with the later pattern narrow top feed cover, and domed engines with the earlier domed style of top feed cover, giving rise to a 'double domed' effect.

10.2 Frame changes

As described in Chapter 4, a major weakness of the Class 5 design was the frames which were prone to cracking, particularly at the top corners of the horn gaps, and various stiffening stay arrangements were tried. Repair was usually achieved by welding, but in extreme cases patches were welded on.

R. C. Bond, then Works Manager at Crewe, in his book **A Lifetime with Locomotives** (Goose & Son, Cambridge 1975) described an important measure to improve the process of frame repairs introduced there. "We were at this time (1943) running into a cycle of heavy frame repairs. Crewe locomotives had never really had adequate main frames, and the situation was now aggravated by increasing trouble with cracks in the high tensile frames of the standard Class 5 4-6-0s. A stock of spare boilers had long been regarded as indispensable for reducing the time out of traffic as locomotives undergoing repairs. If, as was now the case, heavy frame repairs were taking up to a fortnight for engines which were due out of the erecting shop in six to eight days, why not spare frames? It seemed to me entirely logical to apply to frames the same argument as for boilers. We obtained authority to build three sets of frames complete with cylinders, dragboxes and all other fittings, one for Class 5 4-6-0s, one for LNW G1 0-8-0s and one for the standard Class 4 0-6-0s, these being the most numerous classes in which interchangeability could be fully exploited".

It was usual for frame and cylinder records to be kept by railway administrations and on the LMS these took the form of a card with a frame diagram on it. On this card all defects found during overhaul were noted, as were the repairs carried out, the class of overhaul and the date. Cylinder changes and dates were also recorded. The cards were held at the works at which the engine was normally repaired and, if the engine was repaired elsewhere, the card would be sent to the works concerned.

Frames had no identity number, other than the running number of the complete locomotive of which the frames formed part, and this was the number on the record card. So in the early part of 1943 there was a new frame at Crewe with no apparent identity. In June 1943, engine 5226 entered Crewe Works and the new frames were placed under that engine and the record card was then endorsed '5226'. Later that month, engine 5027 came on the works and received the repaired frame which was previously under 5226. That particular card then had its number altered from 5226 to 5027, and this went on continually with one frame at a time hovering in limbo between two identities.

The frame changes were confined to the pre-war engines and did not involve any of the later Class 5s. Almost 300 exchanges were recorded at Crewe between June 1943 and the last one on 45114 released to traffic in February 1958. It is extremely unlikely that works plates on the engine frames were deliberately or even accidentally changed from one frame to another. Consequently from 1943, the works plate seen on the frame of an engine could bear no relationship to the running number carried by the engine at that time or when it was built. Therefore engines which had nominally been built at Crewe or Vulcan Foundry, appeared with

Armstrong Whitworth plates and vice versa. The full list of frame changes in Table 10.2 was published in the December 1959 *Railway Observer*; it is likely that the exchanges continued until the early 1960s but no details have been published to confirm this.

TABLE 10.1 RECORDED FRAME CHANGES

1943	7
1944	9
1945	18
1946	13
1947	20
1948	28
1949	28
1950	26
1951	21
1952	13
1953	15
1954	19
1955	15
1956	26
1957	21
1958	2
	281

5000–5224	144
5225–5451	136
5452–5471	1
	281

218 different locomotives were involved, with 53 having their frames changed twice and five (45063, 45203, 45217, 45294 and 45316) undergoing three changes.

TABLE 10.2 FRAME CHANGES

Date	From	To	Date	From	To	Date	From	To
Jun 43		5226	Jul 46	5362	5025	May 48	45181	45219
Jun 43	5226	5027	Aug 46	5025	5010	May 48	45219	45395
Aug 43	5027	5017	Sep 46	5010	5113	Jun 48	45395	45252
Sep 43	5017	5081	Sep 46	5113	5331	Jun 48	45252	45234
Oct 43	5081	5044	Oct 46	5331	5316	Jun 48	45234	45263
Nov 43	5044	5026	Oct 46	5316	5290	Aug 48	45263	45073
Nov 43	5026	5140	Nov 46	5290	5116	Aug 48	45073	45373
Jan 44	5140	5232	Nov 46	5116	5149	Sep 48	45373	45196
Jan 44	5232	5086	Jan 47	5149	5137	Sep 48	45196	45208
Feb 44	5086	5235	Jan 47	5137	5216	Oct 48	45208	45321
Mar 44	5235	5234	Feb 47	5216	5060	Oct 48	45321	45270
Apr 44	5234	5249	Mar 47	5060	5182	Nov 48	45270	45057
Apr 44	5249	5203	Mar 47	5182	5223	Nov 48	45057	45280
Jun 44	5203	5063	Mar 47	5223	5199	Nov 48	45280	45011
Aug 44	5063	5201	Apr 47	5199	5207	Dec 48	45011	45092
Aug 44	5201	5004	Apr 47	5207	5314	Dec 48	45092	45387
Jan 45	5004	5080	May 47	5314	5368	Dec 48	45387	45274
Feb 45	5080	5185	Jun 47	5368	5279	Jan 49	45274	45294
Apr 45	5185	5042	Jun 47	5279	5190	Jan 49	45294	45318
May 45	5042	5210	Jul 47	5190	5228	Feb 49	45318	45353
Jul 45	5210	5024	Aug 47	5228	5341	Feb 49	45353	45247
Jul 45	5024	5265	Aug 47	5341	5044	Mar 49	45247	45233
Aug 45	5265	5428	Sep 47	5044	5131	Mar 49	45233	45229
Aug 45	5428	5294	Nov 47	5131	5217	Mar 49	45229	45408
Aug 45	5294	5338	Nov 47	5217	5203	Apr 49	45408	45132
Aug 45	5338	5386	Nov 47	5203	5104	Apr 49	45132	45255
Sep 45	5386	5384	Dec 47	5104	5105	Apr 49	45255	45391
Oct 45	5384	5335	Dec 47	5105	5106	May 49	45391	45322
Oct 45	5335	5418	Jan 48	5106	5283	May 49	45322	45014
Oct 45	5418	5327	Jan 48	5283	5048	Jun 49	45014	45065
Nov 45	5327	5319	Feb 48	5048	5352	Jun 49	45065	45072
Dec 45	5319	5442	Feb 48	5352	5099	Jul 49	45072	45338
Dec 45	5442	5287	Feb 48	5099	5289	Aug 49	45338	45378
Dec 45	5287	5165	Mar 48	5289	5064	Aug 49	45378	45397
Feb 46	5165	5111	Mar 48	5064	5236	Aug 49	45397	45400
Feb 46	5111	5355	Mar 48	45236	45261	Sep 49	45400	45074
Mar 46	5355	5087	Apr 48	45261	45249	Sep 49	45074	45250
Apr 46	5087	5160	Apr 48	45249	45004	Sep 49	45250	45107
Jun 46	5160	5362	Apr 48	45004	45181	Oct 49	45107	45349

Date	From	To	Date	From	To	Date	From	To
Oct 49	45349	45448	Mar 52	45199	45134	Nov 55	45203	45230
Oct 49	45448	45282	Apr 52	45134	45143	Nov 55	45230	45131
Nov 49	45282	45218	May 52	45143	45197	Dec 55	45131	45182
Nov 49	45218	45308	Jun 52	45197	45267	Jan 56	45182	45415
Dec 49	45308	45210	Aug 52	45267	45445	Jan 56	45415	45285
Dec 49	45210	45063	Sep 52	45445	45232	Feb 56	45285	45278
Jan 50	45063	45428	Sep 52	45232	45260	Feb 56	45278	45240
Jan 50	45428	45079	Oct 52	45260	45019	Feb 56	45240	45193
Jan 50	45079	45025	Nov 52	45019	45305	Mar 56	45193	45052
Feb 50	45025	45325	Dec 52	45305	45268	Mar 56	45052	45062
Feb 50	45325	45013	Jan 53	45268	45371	Apr 56	45062	45388
Mar 50	45013	45224	Feb 53	45371	45071	Apr 56	45388	45382
Mar 50	45224	45006	Mar 53	45071	45022	May 56	45382	45420
Mar 50	45006	45133	Mar 53	45022	45164	May 56	45420	45411
Mar 50	45133	45003	Apr 53	45164	45029	May 56	45411	45220
Apr 50	45003	45312	Jun 53	45029	45253	Jun 56	45220	45048
Apr 50	45312	45139	Jun 53	45253	45034	Jun 56	45048	45290
Apr 50	45139	45190	Jul 53	45034	45247	Jul 56	45290	45283
May 50	45190	45316	Aug 53	45247	45257	Aug 56	45283	45450
May 50	45316	45327	Sep 53	45257	45263	Aug 56	45450	45201
Jun 50	45327	45245	Sep 53	45263	45370	Sep 56	45201	45039
Jun 50	45245	45375	Oct 53	45370	45312	Sep 56	45039	45325
Jul 50	45375	45110	Nov 53	45312	45187	Oct 56	45325	45292
Aug 50	45110	45421	Nov 53	45187	45054	Oct 56	45292	45106
Aug 50	45421	45021	Dec 53	45054	45248	Nov 56	45106	45406
Oct 50	45021	45058	Jan 54	45248	45180	Nov 56	45406	45316
Oct 50	45058	45217	Feb 54	45180	45315	Dec 56	45316	45075
Oct 50	45217	45238	Feb 54	45315	45065	Dec 56	45075	45297
Oct 50	45238	45130	Mar 54	45065	45241	Dec 56	45297	45110
Nov 50	45130	45020	Apr 54	45241	45126	Jan 57	45110	45076
Nov 50	45020	45220	May 54	45126	45294	Jan 57	45076	45370
Dec 50	45220	45206	May 54	45294	45017	Feb 57	45370	45042
Jan 51	45206	45284	May 54	45017	45212	Feb 57	45042	45217
Jan 51	45284	45039	Jun 54	45212	45460	Feb 57	45217	45323
Jan 51	45039	45088	Jun 54	45460	45082	Mar 57	45323	45054
Feb 51	45088	45253	Jun 54	45082	45280	Apr 57	45054	45015
Feb 51	45253	45447	Aug 54	45280	45337	May 57	45015	45288
Mar 51	45447	45381	Aug 54	45337	45006	May 57	45288	45014
Mar 51	45381	45272	Sep 54	45006	45040	Jun 57	45014	45350
Apr 51	45272	45137	Oct 54	45040	45418	Jun 57	45350	45284
May 51	45137	45188	Oct 54	45418	45215	Jul 57	45284	45408
May 51	45188	45105	Nov 54	45215	45129	Jul 57	45408	45308
May 51	45105	45214	Nov 54	45129	45061	Aug 57	45308	45187
Jun 51	45214	45262	Dec 54	45061	45005	Aug 57	45187	45349
Jul 51	45262	45181	Jan 55	45005	45069	Sep 57	45349	45296
Aug 51	45202	45202	Feb 55	45069	45223	Sep 57	45296	45393
Aug 51	45202	45041	Feb 55	45223	45097	Oct 57	45393	45394
Sep 51	45041	45216	Mar 55	45274	45274	Oct 57	45394	45270
Sep 51	45216	45246	May 55	45274	45063	Oct 57	45270	45440
Oct 51	45246	45431	Jun 55	45348	45348	Nov 57	45440	45027
Oct 51	45431	45416	Jun 55	45348	45430	Jan 58	45027	45055
Nov 51	45416	45207	Aug 55	45430	45202	Jan 58	45055	45114
Dec 51	45207	45097	Aug 55	45202	45043	Jan 58	45114	
Jan 52	45097	45092	Sep 55	45043	45427			
Feb 52	45092	45227	Oct 55	45427	45449			
Feb 52	45227	45199	Oct 55	45449	45203			

10.3 Northern Division engines repaired at Crewe

It was noted in the August 1942 *Journal* of the Stephenson Locomotive Society that, in most weeks, two of the Northern Division allocation of Class 5s and Jubilees were being sent to Crewe for repair. On completion, they ran trials to Birmingham, Manchester or Shrewsbury before returning to Scotland on the 6.20pm from Crewe.

Twenty such repairs at Crewe were recorded on the Class 5 Engine History Cards between February 1942 and March 1947, of which nine also included frame changes. Next, there was one in 1948/9 which had both a change of frames and a brand-new forward top feed boiler. There was a break of several years before the visits resumed with 22 repairs recorded between February 1953 and July 1954, five involving frame changes.

No.	Type	Dates out of traffic	Allocated to	Comments
TABLE 10.3 NORTHERN DIVISION ENGINES REPAIRED AT CREWE WORKS				
5466	HG	17.02.42-25.04.42	Perth	
5458	HG	19.03.42-23.05.42	Perth	
5083	HG	14.04.42-16.05.42	Inverness	
5016	HS	24.04.42-30.05.42	Inverness	
5320	LS	08.05.42-20.06.42	Inverness	
5452	HG	08.07.42-05.09.42	Perth	
5364	HG	21.05.43-19.06.43	Kingmoor	Frame changed
5086	HG	05.01.44-02.02.44	Perth	Frame changed
5081	HG	31.07.44-24.08.44	Perth	Frame changed
5463	HG	14.02.45-17.03.45	Perth	
5458	LS	23.04.45-16.06.45	Perth	
5319	HG	04.10.45-26.11.45	Inverness	Frame changed
5165	HG	04.12.45-12.01.46	Perth	Frame changed
5355	HG	28.01.46-01.03.46	St. Rollox	Frame changed
5087	HG	05.03.46-06.04.46	Perth	Frame changed
5160	HG	30.03.46-02.05.46	Inverness	Frame changed
5458	HG	22.04.46-18.05.46	Perth	
5362	HG	15.05.46-18.06.46	St. Rollox	
5116	HG	12.09.46-15.11.46	St. Rollox	Frame changed
5241	HS	05.02.47-25.03.47	Kingmoor	
45011	G	10.11.48-03.01.49	Perth	Frame changed, fitted with new forward top feed boiler
45118	G	02.02.53-20.03.53	Kingmoor	
45022	G	13.02.53-19.03.53	Dalry Road	Frame changed
45099	HI	13.02.53-26.03.53	Motherwell	
45164	HI	03.53-11.04.53	Perth	Frame changed
45455	G	06.03.53-02.04.53	Inverness	
45159	HI	06.03.53-27.04.53	St. Rollox	
45163	LI	13.03.53-11.04.53	Kingmoor	
45125	LI	13.03.53-18.04.53	Perth	
45029	LI	19.03.53-30.04.53	Motherwell	Frame changed
45330	HI	24.03.53-22.04.53	Kingmoor	
45160	HI	06.04.53-27.04.53	Corkerhill	
45012	HI	07.04.53-02.05.53	Kingmoor	
45432	HG	08.06.53-06.08.53	Dumfries	
45013	HI	29.06.53-10.08.53	Kingmoor	
45318	G	28.09.53-11.12.53	St. Margarets	
45176	HI	10.12.53-20.01.54	Motherwell	
45266	G	06.03.54-15.04.54	Hurlford	
45126	LI	23.03.54-21.04.54	Kingmoor	Frame changed
45120	HI	04.05.54-03.06.54	Kingmoor	
45166	HI	24.05.54-23.06.54	Corkerhill	
45460	HG	27.05.54-25.06.54	Perth	
45082	HI	01.06.54-03.07.54	Kingmoor	Frame changed

10.4 Cowlairs

After nationalisation on 1st January 1948 ex-LMS engines began to visit Cowlairs Works, the former LNER facility about a mile away from St. Rollox. The first Class 5s noted in *The Railway Observer* were 44702 and 45470 both of which were slightly damaged when the former, whilst working the 9.45pm Buchanan St.-Holytown, collided with the latter at Germiston Junction, during November. The former LMS and LNER motive power departments were combined into a new Scottish Region organisation from 1st January, 1949 and at least two Class 5s, 45086 from Kingmoor and Dalry Road's 45022, were recorded as receiving Light Intermediate repairs at Cowlairs during that year. Others may have been dealt with there but the surviving Scottish Region Engine Record Cards do not identify at which works repairs were carried out prior to 1950. The only other recorded visit by a pre-war engine up to 1959 was 45214 for a Non-Classified repair in November 1953.

No.	Type	Dates out of traffic
45086	LI	30.05.49-16.07.49
45022	LI	06.08.49-17.09.49
45022	NC(R)	05.10.49-14.10.49
45214	NC(EO)	21.11.53

From mid-1959 onwards the works carried out regular Light and Non-classified repairs on Scottish Region Class 5s. There is a slight doubt about first engine to receive a Heavy overhaul there; the late 1959 repair to 45030 is shown as taking place at Crewe on its Engine History Card and Cowlairs on the Record Card, although the latter is more likely given its allocation to Dalry Road at the time. Following this, there are recorded details of almost 30 more pre-war Class 5s visiting Cowlairs for Heavy repairs up to early 1966.

After St. Rollox completed its last Class 5 repair, a Light Casual (EO) on 45461 which was outshopped on 11th January 1964, maintenance responsibility for the Scottish Region Class 5s passed to Cowlairs. A little later, as Crewe wound down its steam engine repairs, the LMR engines also began to be sent to Cowlairs, with some undergoing a boiler change whilst there. In most cases spare boilers from the Crewe pool seem to have been sent specially and when Cowlairs itself closed at least one boiler was sent back to Crewe, evidently unused.

Altogether at least 300 Light and Unclassified repairs were carried out to Class 5s at Cowlairs between January 1964 and July 1966, and almost 200 of these were on pre-war engines.

No.	Shed	Division	Class of Repair	Out of traffic
45030	Dalry Road	ScR	HI	26.10.59-28.11.59
45087	Carstairs	ScR	HG*	29.10.60-10.12.60
45433	Motherwell	ScR	HG*	05.12.60-04.02.61
45361	Corkerhill	ScR	HI*	03.08.61-30.09.61
45432	Dumfries	ScR	HC(EO)	12.03.62-11.05.62
45470	Stranraer	ScR	HG	05.11.63-11.01.64
45389	Stirling	ScR	HG	02.12.63-18.01.64
45037	Stoke	W	HG	09.01.64-01.02.64
45312	Edge Hill	W	HG	20.02.64-21.03.64
45143	Shrewsbury	W	HG	18.03.64-18.04.64
45471	St. Rollox	ScR	HI	06.04.64-02.05.64
45341	Newton Heath	C	HI +	29.04.64-27.06.64
45242	Edge Hill	W	HI	15.05.64-22.08.64
45254	Kingmoor	W	HI	09.06.64-04.07.64
45184	Chester (M)	W	HI	18.06.64-18.07.64
45065	Rugby	W	HI +	19.06.64-04.07.64
45281	Springs Branch	W	HI (CB)	30.06.64-14.11.64
45321	Crewe South	W	HI	27.10.64-21.11.64
45222	Bescot	W	HI(CB)	17.12.64-30.01.65
45394	Lancaster	W	HI	24.12.64-23.01.65
45377	Bury	C	HI	24.12.64-30.01.65
45424	Agecroft	C	HI	26.01.65-27.02.65
45390	Carnforth	W	HI	08.04.65-08.05.65
45403	Chester (M)	W	HI	04.05.65-22.06.65
45202	Newton Heath	C	HI	22.06.65-10.07.65
45421	Fleetwood	C	HI	03.08.65-18.09.65
45013	Kingmoor	W	HI	29.09.65-13.11.65
45253	Kingmoor	W	HI	29.11.65-08.01.66
45423	Ayr	ScR	HI	11.02.66-02.04.66
45176	Motherwell	ScR	H (EO)	18.02.66-15.03.66

TABLE 10.4 HEAVY REPAIRS AT COWLAIRS

* fitted with AWS during overhaul   + fitted with speed indicator during overhaul

TABLE 10.11 RECORD OF WORKS VISITS OF EACH LOCOMOTIVE

The key to this table is as follows:

BW	Bow
CS	Cowlairs
CW	Crewe
DN	Darlington
DY	Derby
EH	Eastleigh
GN	Gorton
HW	Horwich
IE	Inverurie
IS	Inverness
RY	Rugby
SR	St. Rollox
S	Shed
C.D	Collision Damage
Cas	Casual
CBC	Cost borne by contractors
G	General
H	Heavy
HC	Heavy Casual
HG	Heavy General
HI	Heavy Intermediate
HO	Heavy Overhaul
HS	Heavy Service
Int	Intermediate
LC	Light Casual
LC-E	Light Casual - Engine only
LC-T	Light Casual - Tender only
LI	Light Intermediate
LI-E only	Light Intermediate - Engine
LO	Light Overhaul
LS	Light Service
N.R	No repairs
NC	Non-classified
NC-E only	Non-classified - Engine
NC-R	Non-classified - rectification
NC-T only	Non-classified - Tender
P.O	Painting only
S.E	Special examination
TO	Tender Repair only
Uns	Unscheduled
W.O	Weighing only

Engine no 5000

/type.	Date of repair	Works
LS	12.02.36-28.02.36	
LO	05.09.36-01.10.36	
HS	22.05.37-08.06.37	
LO	20.10.37-29.11.37	
HG	20.02.39-15.03.39	
LS	23.10.40-06.11.40	
TO	20.07.42-15.08.42	
HG	28.12.42-16.01.43	
HS	18.05.44-02.06.44	
LS	08.11.45-14.12.45	
LS	06.07.47-27.08.47	RY
HG	21.12.48-22.01.49	CW
HI	25.01.50-21.02.50	CW
LI	30.08.51-27.10.51	CW
HG	09.03.53-24.04.53	CW
NC-R	09.05.53-23.05.53	CW
LC-E	21.12.53-18.01.54	RY
LC-E	21.04.54-10.05.54	RY
LI	18.11.54-05.01.55	RY
LC	31.10.55-16.11.55	RY
HI	21.07.56-14.08.56	CW
HG	26.08.57-21.09.57	CW
NC-R	21.10.57-08.11.57	CW
LI	02.03.59-04.04.59	CW
LC-E	19.09.59-27.11.59	GN
HI	31.01.61-10.03.61	CW
HI	07.01.63-29.01.63	CW
LI	10.04.64-05.06.64	CW
LC	03.11.64-19.11.64	CW
LI	20.09.65-25.10.65	CW

5001

/type.	Date of repair	Works
LS	08.04.36-27.04.36	
HS	01.04.37-01.05.37	
HG	04.02.38-14.03.38	
HS	09.03.40-21.03.40	
HG	24.07.41-08.08.41	
LS	12.12.42-02.01.43	
HS	08.08.44-22.08.44	
LS	10.05.46-30.05.46	
HG	20.06.47-01.08.47	CW
LI	16.02.49-14.03.49	CW
LC	10.02.50-02.03.50	CW
HG	03.10.50-07.11.50	CW
LI	17.11.51-15.12.51	CW
HI	19.10.53-07.11.53	CW
LC-E	16.07.54-14.08.54	CW
HG	23.09.55-09.10.55	CW
LI	14.10.56-21.11.56	CW
HC	30.07.57-24.08.57	CW
LI	27.08.58-03.10.58	CW
NC-E	16.02.59-21.02.59	CW
LI	24.02.60-08.04.60	CW
HG	07.08.61-14.09.61	CW
LI	01.01.63-01.11.63	CW
LI	10.05.66-21.06.66	CW

5002

/type.	Date of repair	Works
LS	03.04.36-21.04.36	
HS	16.04.37-10.05.37	
HG	19.11.37-28.12.37	
LS	23.11.39-21.12.39	
HG	16.05.41-07.06.41	
LS	09.11.42-25.11.42	
HG	09.06.44-23.06.44	
LS	26.06.45-31.07.45	
LO	25.11.45-15.12.45	
LS	16.06.46-18.07.46	
HS	12.09.47-17.10.47	CW
LO	08.10.48-26.10.48	CW
LO	08.11.48-16.11.48	RY
HG	13.06.49-29.07.49	CW
LI	12.06.50-24.07.50	CW
HI	10.03.52-29.03.52	CW
HG	17.10.53-12.11.53	CW
NC-R	19.11.53-23.11.53	CW
HI	29.05.55-22.07.55	RY
LC-E	15.02.56-02.03.56	RY
LI	23.02.57-22.03.57	CW
HG	18.11.58-20.12.58	CW
NC-E	29.01.59-05.02.59	CW
LI	31.01.61-08.03.61	CW

5003

/type.	Date of repair	Works
LS	19.02.36-06.03.36	
HS	08.03.37-25.03.37	
LO	03.04.38-09.04.38	
HG	30.12.38-30.01.39	
LS	22.07.40-05.08.40	
HG	16.05.42-30.06.42	
LO	06.05.43-29.05.43	
LS	24.06.44-15.07.44	
LO	14.04.45-03.05.45	
HG	07.11.45-22.11.45	
LS	18.04.47-26.05.47	CW
LS	28.09.48-15.10.48	CW
HC	23.03.49-29.04.49	CW
HG	09.03.50-04.05.50	CW
HI	09.07.51-02.08.51	CW
LI	22.03.53-17.04.53	RY
LC	01.07.53-22.08.53	CW
HG	23.06.55-05.08.55	CW
HI	23.05.57-14.06.57	CW
LC-E	23.06.58-12.08.58	CW
NC-E	17.02.59-24.02.59	CW
HI	11.04.59-13.05.59	CW
HG	21.08.60-11.10.60	CW
LC-E	05.09.61-20.10.61	CW
LI	19.11.63-24.12.63	CW
LC	20.07.64-21.08.64	CW

5004

/type.	Date of repair	Works
LS	19.02.36-04.03.36	
HS	01.06.37-14.06.37	
LS	28.06.38-01.08.38	
HG	20.09.39-11.10.39	
HS	04.09.41-27.09.41	
LS	03.03.43-18.03.43	
LO	16.10.43-02.11.43	
HG	13.10.44-28.10.44	
LS	21.06.46-23.07.46	CW
LO	17.12.46-16.01.47	CW
HG	08.04.48-17.05.48	CW
HI	16.04.49-02.07.49	CW
LI	30.08.50-19.09.50	CW
HG	05.04.52-07.06.52	CW
LI	14.02.53-18.03.53	CW
NC	15.09.53-09.10.53	CW
LI	30.12.53-26.01.54	CW
HI	31.08.55-27.09.55	DY
LC-E	18.06.56-25.07.56	CW
HG	05.04.57-16.05.57	CW
LC-E	12.05.58-27.05.58	CW
HI	10.12.58-10.01.59	CW
HI	22.04.61-26.05.61	CW
HG	25.02.63-23.03.63	CW
LI	24.06.65-31.07.65	CW

5005

/type.	Date of repair	Works
LS	04.03.36-20.03.36	
HO	21.04.36-27.05.36	
HS	17.05.37-31.05.37	
HG	15.11.37-22.12.37	
TO	13.07.39-15.07.39	
HS	23.08.39-06.09.39	
HG	13.09.40-11.10.40	
LS	20.05.41-27.06.41	
HS	02.11.42-31.12.42	
LS	18.10.43-11.11.43	
LS	21.08.44-16.09.44	
HG	03.10.45-07.11.45	
LS	20.12.46-01.02.47	SR
HS	04.08.48-11.09.48	SR
LC	01.12.48-20.01.49	SR
LC	07.06.49-26.06.49	CW
HG	01.10.49-29.10.49	CW
LI	10.05.51-01.06.51	CW
LI	16.09.52-16.10.52	CW
LI	26.10.53-21.11.53	CW
HG	06.11.54-05.01.55	CW
LC	02.05.56-26.05.56	CW
HG	23.04.57-17.05.57	CW
LI	09.02.59-14.03.59	CW
HI	09.06.61-26.07.61	CW
HC	13.02.63-07.03.63	CW
HI	05.06.64-10.10.64	CW

5006

/type.	Date of repair	Works
LS	30.03.36-14.04.36	
HG	17.02.37-19.03.37	
HS	30.12.38-11.02.39	
HG	18.06.40-10.07.40	
LS	22.09.41-18.10.41	
LS	24.08.42-26.09.42	
HG	31.07.43-01.09.43	
LS	24.07.44-17.08.44	
HG	03.10.45-08.11.45	
LS	04.09.46-08.10.46	IS
LO	28.01.47-22.02.47	SR
LO	13.05.47-26.05.47	SR
LS	02.12.47-08.01.48	SR
LO	20.02.48-13.03.48	SR
NC	02.07.48-06.07.48	SR
LI	13.04.49-20.05.49	SR
LC	09.08.49-03.09.49	CW
NC-R	08.09.49-16.09.49	CW
HG	04.03.50-05.04.50	CW
HI	27.02.52-17.03.52	CW
LI	12.09.53-02.10.53	CW
NC-R	29.10.53-13.11.53	CW
HG	20.08.54-16.09.54	CW
LI	12.04.56-09.05.56	CW
HG	19.09.57-28.10.57	CW
LC-E	17.11.58-05.12.58	RY
LI	18.08.60-24.09.60	CW

5007

/type.	Date of repair	Works
LS	24.03.36-04.04.36	
LS	19.05.37-05.06.37	
LS	02.05.38-11.05.38	
HG	03.02.39-24.03.39	
LS	20.03.40-12.04.40	
LS	14.11.40-12.12.40	
LO	17.03.41-31.03.41	
HG	09.08.41-13.09.41	
HS	30.06.42-18.08.42	
LS	27.11.42-08.01.43	
HG	18.11.43-17.12.43	
LS	19.10.44-21.11.44	
LS	04.09.45-06.10.45	
LO	30.11.45-21.12.45	
LO	08.02.46-04.03.46	
LS	26.09.46-30.10.46	
LO	29.04.47-16.05.47	
HS	04.10.47-07.11.47	
LS	01.11.48-11.12.48	
NC	05.02.49-12.02.49	
G	17.10.49-26.11.49	SR
LC	13.11.50-25.11.50	SR
HI	19.03.51-19.04.51	SR
LC	12.09.51-28.09.51	SR
LI	17.06.52-18.07.52	SR
HI	25.05.53-27.06.53	SR
LC	18.11.53-28.11.53	SR
G	20.12.54-12.02.55	SR
HI	09.08.56-01.09.56	SR
LC-E	01.03.57-08.03.57	SR
LI	29.01.58-22.02.58	SR
LC-E	09.04.58-17.04.58	SR
LC-E	29.07.58-06.08.58	SR
LC-E	25.08.58-06.09.58	SR
LC-E	20.06.59-01.07.59	SR
G	12.12.59-30.01.60	SR
NC	02.03.60-05.03.60	SR
LC	26.05.61-17.06.61	SR

Engine no /type.	Date of repair	Works
5007		
NC	26.02.62-09.03.62	SR
LI	10.08.62-31.08.62	SR
LC	03.07.63-08.07.63	SR
5008		
LS	14.04.36-23.04.36	
TO	15.12.36-11.01.37	
LS	27.05.37-15.06.37	
LS	05.03.38-22.03.38	
HG	01.04.39-10.05.39	
LS	24.04.40-25.04.40	
TO	03.02.41-28.02.41	
LS	02.10.41-30.10.41	
HG	24.04.42-30.05.42	
HS	26.01.43-23.02.43	
LS	14.12.43-12.01.44	
LS	20.11.44-27.12.44	
HG	20.06.45-02.08.45	
LO	27.03.46-27.04.46	
HS	28.09.46-31.10.46	
LS	30.04.47-19.06.47	
HS	12.06.48-16.07.48	
NC	27.10.48-28.10.48	
LC	10.06.49-01.07.49	
G	17.09.49-05.11.49	SR
HI	01.12.50-16.02.51	SR
HI	26.08.52-11.11.52	SR
NC	01.12.52-04.12.52	SR
LC	29.01.53-27.02.53	SR
LC	04.07.53-16.07.53	SR
LC	20.08.53-29.08.53	SR
LC-E	22.09.53-10.10.53	SR
G	20.09.54-20.11.54	SR
NC-E	06.12.54-11.12.54	SR
5008		
LC-E	04.10.55-21.10.55	SR
HI	26.04.56-02.06.56	SR
NC-E	30.11.56-15.12.56	SR
NC-E	28.02.57-11.03.57	SR
HI	04.02.58-07.03.58	SR
LC-E	13.04.59-24.04.59	SR
G	04.12.59-16.01.60	SR
LI	22.01.62-24.02.62	SR
5009		
LS	04.05.36-16.05.36	
LS	14.06.37-07.07.37	
LS	08.10.37-27.10.38	
HG	27.11.39-11.01.40	
LO	17.05.40-25.05.40	
LS	04.11.40-16.12.40	
LS	11.08.41-03.10.41	
LO	03.03.42-30.04.42	
LS	19.10.42-21.11.42	
HG	13.09.43-09.10.43	
HS	12.09.44-05.10.44	
LS	01.10.45-19.11.45	
LO	22.03.46-01.05.46	
HG	26.10.46-27.12.46	
LS	06.04.48-11.05.48	
HI	12.10.49-05.11.49	
LC	03.04.50-08.04.50	
LC	01.06.50-19.06.50	
NC	21.07.50-15.08.50	
HG	05.02.51-28.04.51	SR
HI	22.03.52-26.04.52	SR
HI	08.10.53-28.11.53	SR
LC-E	14.06.54-15.06.54	SR
G	19.10.54-20.11.54	SR
5009		
LI	24.08.56-15.09.56	SR
LC-E	12.11.56-29.11.56	SR
LC-E	10.12.56-15.12.56	SR
LC-E	18.02.57-23.02.57	SR
LI	18.08.58-06.09.58	SR
G	01.02.60-19.03.60	SR
HC	08.08.60-20.08.60	SR
NC-E	15.09.60-17.09.60	SR
LI	11.05.62-29.05.62	IE
LC-E	02.09.63-10.09.63	SR
LI	25.11.63-18.01.64	CS
NC	15.07.65-17.07.65	CS
5010		
LS	31.03.36-10.04.36	
LS	07.04.37-24.06.37	
LS	17.05.38-26.05.38	
HS	19.01.39-15.02.39	
HG	29.05.40-05.07.40	
LO	28.12.40-18.01.41	
LS	27.06.41-01.08.41	
HG	23.01.42-28.02.42	
LS	10.11.42-12.12.42	
HS	18.09.43-16.10.43	
LS	26.06.44-04.08.44	
LO	02.02.45-01.03.45	
HS	24.07.45-08.09.45	
HG	17.06.46-03.09.46	
LS	24.11.47-13.12.47	
HI	08.12.48-22.01.49	
LC	22.08.49-21.09.49	
G	09.02.50-01.04.50	SR
NC-R	24.04.50-25.04.50	SR
HI	11.03.52-02.05.52	IS
5010		
LI	09.11.53-12.12.53	SR
LC-E	06.05.54-22.05.54	SR
LC-E	22.12.54-29.12.54	SR
G	18.01.55-11.02.55	SR
LC-E	06.05.55-21.05.55	SR
LC-E	28.05.55-15.07.55	SR
HI	08.12.56-23.01.57	IS
HI	23.04.58-17.05.58	IS
G	25.05.59-06.06.59	SR
HI	03.10.60-03.11.60	SR
LI	06.06.52-29.06.62	SR
5011		
LS	04.06.36-30.06.36	
LO	01.06.37-15.06.37	
LS	15.02.38-10.03.38	
HG	16.05.39-05.07.39	
LS	08.10.40-30.12.40	
LS	22.09.41-24.10.41	
LO	24.03.42-03.04.42	
HG	21.11.42-23.12.42	
HS	27.10.43-20.11.43	
LO	15.05.44-08.06.44	
LS	28.06.45-01.09.45	
LS	21.06.46-15.08.46	
LS	27.08.47-18.10.47	
G	10.11.48-03.01.49	CW
LC	23.08.49-07.09.49	SR
HI	20.07.50-24.08.50	SR
HI	03.09.51-02.11.51	IS
HI	16.02.53-06.03.53	SR
G	20.09.54-23.10.54	SR
LC-E	03.11.54-06.11.54	SR
HI	01.11.55-18.11.55	SR

5010 pictured at Perth on 20th May 1935, was built at Crewe Works and entered traffic on 27th March 1935. It had one of the new 21–element boilers introduced because of concerns about the efficiency of the original 14–element boilers. They had the same firebox washout arrangement as the older type, but beginning with 5010 had two washout inspection doors with small domed covers on each shoulder of the firebox. After 'running–in' from Crewe North, 5010 was allocated to St. Rollox in w/e 11th May, but stayed only until w/e 13th July when it moved to Inverness.

Fred A.Plant/Caledonian Railway Association

45001 departing eastwards from Colwyn Bay in the early 1950s. It was allocated to Mold Junction from February 1952 until transferred to Crewe South in November 1959. Crewe-built 45001 was always domeless and kept its original riveted tender until withdrawn.

J. A. G. H. Coltas

Engine no /type.	Date of repair	Works
5011		
LC-T	30.11.55-01.12.55	SR
LC-E	12.11.56-22.11.56	SR
HI	02.05.57-18.05.57	SR
LC-E	02.07.57-11.07.57	SR
LC-E	05.08.57-10.08.57	SR
LC-E	16.09.57-04.10.57	SR
LC-E	27.03.58-03.04.58	SR
HI	19.06.58-05.07.58	SR
LC-E	11.07.58-16.07.58	SR
G	18.02.59-27.02.59	SR
LC-E	16.10.61-26.10.61	SR
LC-E	17.11.61-18.11.61	SR
LC-E	25.09.62-11.10.62	SR
LI	10.03.64-01.05.64	CS
LC	08.06.65-26.06.65	CS
5012		
LS	19.06.36-03.07.36	
LS	24.04.37-22.05.37	
LS	20.05.38-18.06.38	
HS	23.12.38-17.01.39	
HO	18.05.39-29.06.39	
LO	18.09.39-20.10.39	
LS	17.06.40-07.07.40	
LS	04.04.41-05.05.41	
HS	18.06.42-21.07.42	
LO	04.09.42-10.10.42	
HG	19.01.43-23.02.43	
HS	17.11.43-07.01.44	
LS	09.11.44-09.12.44	
LO	26.02.45-31.03.45	
LS	25.10.45-30.11.45	
HG	03.07.46-31.08.46	
LO	26.04.47-10.06.47	
HS	30.12.47-18.02.48	
LI	11.08.49-16.09.49	
G	25.11.50-13.01.51	SR

Engine no /type.	Date of repair	Works
5012		
LI	23.02.52-27.03.52	IS
HI	07.04.53-02.05.53	CW
G	02.11.54-25.12.54	SR
LC-E	08.12.55-29.12.55	SR
LI-E	22.01.57-14.02.57	SR
LC-E	27.02.57-27.02.57	SR
LC-E	16.08.57-30.08.57	SR
LC-E	04.11.57-13.11.57	SR
HI	?-14.08.58	SR
LC-E	07.11.58-13.11.58	SR
G	22.03.60-14.05.60	SR
LC	04.09.61-21.09.61	SR
HI	04.12.61-13.01.62	SR
5013		
LS	20.04.36-01.05.36	
LS	09.06.37-01.07.37	
LS	28.04.38-24.05.38	
HS	17.09.38-11.10.38	
HG	17.05.39-23.06.39	
LS	24.03.40-03.07.40	
LS	06.02.41-28.02.41	
HO	12.06.41-12.08.41	
LS	22.08.42-26.09.42	
HS	27.07.43-21.08.43	
LS	11.12.44-29.12.44	
HO	08.06.45-13.07.45	
HG	29.10.45-26.11.45	CW
LO	22.01.46-16.02.46	CW
LS	06.06.47-17.07.47	
LO	31.03.48-17.04.48	
HI	05.02.49-16.03.49	
HG	02.02.50-16.03.50	CW
TO	22.03.50-24.03.50	CW
HI	24.05.52-14.06.52	SR
HI	29.06.53-10.08.53	CW
NC	12.08.53-19.08.53	SR

Engine no /type.	Date of repair	Works
5013		
G	05.03.55-23.04.55	SR
HI	20.12.56-12.01.57	SR
HI	10.02.58-08.03.58	SR
G	22.06.59-15.07.59	SR
LC-E	22.01.60-11.02.60	SR
HI	07.09.61-04.11.61	SR
HG	23.10.63-27.11.63	CW
HI	29.09.65-13.11.65	CS
5014		
LS	15.05.36-29.05.36	
TO	10.11.36-27.11.36	
LS	23.06.37-09.07.37	
LS	21.02.38-21.03.38	
LO	05.05.38-26.05.38	
HS	07.09.38-06.10.38	
HG	03.03.39-24.04.39	
HS	17.04.40-24.05.40	
HO	19.09.40-10.10.40	
LO	18.04.41-25.06.41	
LO	16.12.41-21.01.42	
LS	26.06.42-08.08.42	
HG	17.05.43-22.06.43	
LS	24.04.44-19.05.44	
LS	26.02.45-30.03.45	
LS	17.12.45-19.01.46	
HG	29.08.46-12.10.46	
LO	15.09.47-04.10.47	SR
LS	02.04.48-07.05.48	SR
NC	29.06.48-02.07.48	SR
HG	30.04.49-14.06.49	CW
LI	21.12.50-19.01.51	CW
LI	30.06.52-02.08.52	CW
HC	03.01.53-21.01.53	CW
HG	30.12.53-19.01.54	CW
LC-E	06.08.54-18.09.54	CW
LI	01.11.55-19.11.55	CW

Engine no /type.	Date of repair	Works
5014		
HG	10.05.57-13.06.57	CW
HI	04.08.59-29.08.59	CW
HI	05.04.61-17.05.61	CW
LC	03.01.63-26.01.63	CW
Int	07.07.64-14.08.64	CS
5015		
LS	27.04.36-09.05.36	
LS	29.06.37-15.07.37	
LO	16.06.38-08.07.38	
LS	25.01.39-11.02.39	
HG	11.11.39-29.12.39	
LO	06.03.40-12.04.40	
LS	21.10.40-15.11.40	
LS	28.05.41-28.06.41	
HG	05.05.42-12.06.42	
HS	06.07.43-30.07.43	
HS	09.06.44-01.07.44	
LO	22.12.44-19.01.45	
LS	25.07.45-15.09.45	
HG	30.08.46-07.11.46	SR
HS	27.08.48-01.10.48	SR
HI	30.11.49-24.12.49	CW
LC	03.02.50-27.02.50	CW
HG	02.09.50-09.10.50	CW
HG	05.09.52-11.10.52	CW
LI	08.06.54-30.06.54	CW
HI	05.05.56-07.06.56	CW
HG	12.03.57-03.05.57	CW
LI	05.11.59-03.12.59	CW
LC-E	20.06.60-30.07.60	CW
HC	30.01.61-08.03.61	CW
HG	18.03.63-17.04.63	CW
NC	09.07.63-10.07.63	HW
5016		
LS	26.06.36-09.07.36	

Engine no /type. | Date of repair | Works

5016

Type	Date of repair	Works
TO	21.01.37-08.02.37	
LO	25.05.37-04.06.37	
LS	17.02.38-09.03.38	
LO	01.04.38-19.04.38	
HO	27.05.38-15.06.38	
HG	07.09.39-01.11.39	
LO	03.07.40-20.07.40	
LS	13.03.41-12.04.41	
HO	21.07.41-29.08.41	
TO	14.10.41-13.11.41	
HS	24.04.42-30.05.42	CW
LS	19.02.43-25.03.43	
LS	27.12.43-29.01.44	
HS	08.01.45-17.02.45	
LS	08.02.46-16.03.46	
LS	24.02.47-20.03.47	
LO	28.08.47-30.10.47	
LO	08.02.48-26.02.48	
LS	01.11.48-02.12.48	
G	28.01.50-10.03.50	SR
LI	28.07.51-23.08.51	SR
LI	28.01.53-28.02.53	SR
LC	16.10.53-30.10.53	SR
NC-E	10.11.53-14.11.53	SR
LC	22.01.54-06.02.54	SR
G	04.08.54-17.09.54	SR
LC	01.05.56-22.05.56	S
HI	12.04.57-10.05.57	SR
LC-E	24.10.57-09.11.57	SR
HI	03.02.58-28.02.58	SR
NC-E	07.10.58-16.10.58	SR
NC-E	13.04.59-28.04.59	SR
LC-E	01.06.59-04.06.59	SR
G	29.10.59-30.12.59	SR
HI	27.06.62-17.08.62	SR
LC-E	17.04.63-25.05.63	SR
LC-E	24.08.64-23.09.64	IE

5017

Type	Date of repair	Works
LS	29.05.36-12.06.36	
LO	27.05.37-05.06.37	
LS	29.10.37-18.11.37	
LO	12.04.38-11.05.38	
HG	25.04.39-02.06.39	
LS	10.09.40-02.10.40	
LO	18.01.41-07.03.41	
HG	10.11.41-20.12.41	
LS	24.08.42-03.10.42	
HS	14.07.43-26.08.43	
HS	30.12.44-03.02.45	
LS	14.05.46-07.06.46	
LO	17.03.47-16.05.47	SR
HG	18.09.48-12.10.48	SR
HI	21.03.50-11.04.50	CW
NC	02.09.50-28.09.50	CW
LC	02.12.50-30.12.50	CW
LI	29.06.51-30.07.51	CW
HG	07.03.52-26.04.52	CW
HI	19.10.52-06.11.53	CW
LI	07.05.54-18.06.54	CW
HG	11.08.56-08.09.56	CW
HG	31.01.59-13.03.59	CW
HI	27.06.62-03.08.62	CW
LC-E	20.02.64-07.03.64	CS
HI	15.09.65-16.10.65	CW

5018

Type	Date of repair	Works
LS	06.04.36-17.04.36	
LS	13.05.37-02.06.37	
LS	09.05.38-17.05.38	
LO	20.08.38-01.09.38	
LO	22.02.39-02.03.39	
HG	16.05.39-27.07.39	
LO	27.02.40-26.04.40	
LO	01.05.40-11.05.40	
LS	07.12.40-02.01.41	
LS	17.09.41-25.10.41	
HS	18.05.42-13.07.42	
HG	10.06.43-20.07.43	
LS	11.04.44-12.05.44	
LO	22.07.44-09.09.44	
LS	14.05.45-30.06.45	
LS	16.05.46-21.06.46	
HS	26.03.47-09.05.47	
HG	15.01.48-25.02.48	
LI	04.02.49-05.03.49	
LI	07.02.50-17.03.50	
HC	21.10.50-25.11.50	
LI	22.01.52-16.02.52	SR
NC-T	06.03.52-07.03.52	SR
G	04.11.53-26.12.53	SR
NC	05.01.54-09.01.54	SR
HI	25.05.55-18.06.55	SR
NC-E	11.07.55-14.07.55	SR
LI-E	15.05.56-16.06.56	SR
NC-E	23.06.56-30.06.56	SR
HI	17.06.57-01.08.57	SR
HG	06.11.58-29.11.58	SR
LC-E	07.01.59-21.01.59	SR
LC-E	27.03.59-08.04.59	SR
LC-E	11.05.59-28.05.59	SR
LC	11.07.59-22.08.59	SR
LC	20.10.59-21.11.59	SR
HI	03.07.61-25.08.61	SR
LI	07.12.61-19.01.62	SR

5019

Type	Date of repair	Works
LS	21.09.36-08.10.36	
LO	21.01.37-27.01.37	
HO	08.04.37-02.06.37	
LS	19.02.38-28.03.38	
LO	27.12.38-10.01.39	
HG	01.09.39-23.09.39	
LO	18.10.40-06.11.40	
HS	02.08.41-23.08.41	
LO	18.01.43-26.02.43	
HG	03.07.43-31.07.43	
LS	11.01.46-06.02.46	
LO	07.12.46-03.01.47	CW
LO	10.10.47-22.10.47	S
HG	05.04.48-12.05.48	CW
HI	23.10.50-17.11.50	CW
HG	04.10.52-08.11.52	CW
LI	16.10.54-16.11.54	CW
HG	18.10.56-13.11.56	CW
NC-R	27.11.56-05.12.56	CW
LI	22.08.58-26.09.58	CW
NC-E	19.02.59-27.02.59	CW
LI	20.03.61-25.04.61	CW
HG	02.12.63-01.02.64	CW

5020

Type	Date of repair	Works
LS	14.05.35-17.06.35	
LS	29.10.35-25.11.35	
LO	19.10.36-24.10.36	
HG	25.01.37-25.03.37	
LO	18.10.37-30.10.37	
HS	19.08.38-03.06.38	
HG	17.08.39-15.09.39	
HS	18.03.41-29.03.41	
LS	21.08.43-11.09.43	
HG	15.09.45-13.10.45	CW
LS	05.10.46-28.10.46	CW
HS	29.05.48-15.06.48	CW
LI	30.08.49-30.09.49	CW
HG	13.10.50-07.12.50	CW
LI	28.05.52-24.06.52	HW
LI	10.04.53-18.05.53	RY
HI	08.08.54-27.08.54	CW
NC-R	30.08.54-09.09.54	CW
HG	17.08.55-19.09.55	CW
LI	19.11.56-13.12.56	CW
LC-E	13.12.57-31.12.57	CW
LI	10.05.58-12.06.58	CW
NC-R	05.06.58-12.06.58	CW
LC-E	02.02.59-28.02.59	CW
HG	06.06.50-21.07.60	CW
LC-E	02.09.60-24.09.60	CW
Int	13.04.62-08.05.62	CW
LC	16.01.63-04.02.63	CW
LC	08.04.64-10.04.64	CS

5021

Type	Date of repair	Works
LS	24.06.35-08.07.35	
LS	04.11.35-27.11.35	
LS	11.09.36-30.09.36	
NC	20.05.37-29.06.37	
HS	17.10.38-11.11.38	
HG	09.05.40-29.05.40	
LS	15.09.41-04.10.41	
LS	18.06.42-11.07.42	
LS	22.03.43-15.04.43	
HG	16.05.44-30.05.44	
LS	08.12.45-12.01.46	
LO	23.12.46-24.01.47	CW
LS	16.06.47-11.08.47	CW
HO	03.02.48-11.03.48	CW
LI	23.02.49-10.03.49	CW
HG	22.08.50-27.09.50	CW
NC-R	13.11.50-28.11.50	CW
HI	01.04.52-06.05.52	CW
LC-E	28.11.52-19.12.52	CW
HI	30.12.53-19.01.54	CW
HG	28.04.55-25.05.55	CW
LC-E	13.04.56-08.05.56	CW
LI	15.04.57-16.05.57	CW
LI	16.05.58-13.06.58	CW
NC-E	27.04.59-09.05.59	CW
LC	22.05.59-02.06.59	DY
HI	14.12.59-16.01.60	CW
NC-R	20/1/6/0-29.01.60	CW
HG	25.04.61-20.07.61	CW

5022

Type	Date of repair	Works
LS	14.10.35-14.11.35	
HG	23.09.36-03.11.36	
LO	23.07.37-16.08.37	
LS	17.10.38-14.11.38	
HG	22.11.39-14.12.39	
LO	27.09.40-12.10.40	
HS	16.06.41-02.07.41	
LS	28.09.42-17.10.42	
LS	06.08.43-24.09.43	
HG	29.04.44-16.09.44	
LS	10.09.45-13.10.45	
LS	11.02.47-20.03.47	
LO	30.04.47-07.05.47	
HG	08.06.48-07.07.48	SR
LI	06.08.49-17.09.49	CS
NC-R	05.10.49-14.10.49	CS
LC	14.04.50-18.05.50	SR
HI	13.11.50-13.12.50	SR
LI	07.01.52-02.02.52	SR
NC	14.02.52-15.02.52	SR
G	13.02.53-19.03.53	CW
LI	07.06.54-25.06.54	SR
HI	04.04.55-30.04.55	SR
NC-E	01.06.55-22.06.55	SR
NC-E	26.10.55-02.11.55	SR
LC-E	23.01.56-21.01.56	SR
NC-E	13.07.56-19.07.56	S
LI	05.12.56-22.12.56	SR
LC-E	29.05.57-05.06.57	SR
LC	11.11.57-21.11.57	SR
LC	14.05.58-22.05.58	SR
G	04.10.58-25.10.58	SR
NC-E	18.05.59-23.05.59	SR
LC-E	10.08.59-10.09.59	SR
HI	30.11.59-09.01.60	SR
LC-E	16.01.61-26.01.61	SR
HI	11.09.61-10.11.61	SR

5023

Type	Date of repair	Works
LS	29.10.35-28.11.35	
HS	18.01.37-22.02.37	
LO	10.11.37-01.12.37	
HO	23.12.37-11.01.38	
LS	14.02.39-29/2/39	
HS	31.10.39-29.11.39	
LO	16.09.40-28.09.40	
HG	16.04.41-14.05.41	
LS	27.07.42-05.09.42	
HG	23.07.43-04.09.43	
HS	23.06.44-08.08.44	
LS	07.07.45-08.09.45	
LO	27.03.46-19.04.46	
LS	13.05.46-22.06.46	
HG	08.12.47-26.01.48	SR
LO	04.10.48-18.10.48	SR
HI	18.05.49-25.06.49	SR
LC	05.04.50-22.04.50	SR
LC	15.05.50-16.06.50	SR
LI	28.07.50-09.09.50	SR
HI	12.11.51-15.12.51	SR
LC	17.04.52-01.05.52	SR
LC	01.09.52-04.10.52	SR
G	07.01.53-07.03.53	SR
LC	18.08.53-17.09.53	SR
HI	15.05.54-22.06.54	IS
HC	01.07.54-14.08.54	SR
LC-E	23.08.54-02.09.54	SR
LC-E	24.12.54-31.12.54	SR
LC-E	11.04.55-27.04.55	SR
LI	16.07.55-20.08.55	SR
NC-E	14.12.55-20.12.55	SR
NC-E	03.02.56-09.02.56	SR
HC	17.02.56-24.03.56	SR
HI	30.07.56-25.08.56	SR
LC-E	12.11.56-23.11.56	SR
LC-E	11.06.57-18.06.57	SR
G	02.04.58-05.06.58	SR
HI	11.08.59-28.08.59	SR
LC	17.06.60-09.07.60	SR
LI	28.07.61-09.09.61	SR
LC-E	09.04.63-03.05.63	SR

5024

Type	Date of repair	Works
LS	29.10.35-29.11.35	
HS	15.02.37-09.03.37	
HG	30.12.37-21.02.38	
LS	18.03.39-27.04.39	
HS	26.03.40-10.04.40	
HG	19.05.41-05.06.41	
LS	11.03.43-26.03.43	
LS	12.04.44-28.04.44	
HG	26.06.45-26.07.45	
LO	02.11.45-22.11.45	
LS	24.09.47-30.10.47	CW
LI	17.12.48-13.01.49	CW
HG	23.05.50-29.06.50	CW
HG	15.10.51-17.11.51	CW
LC-E	19.04.52-30.04.52	HW
HI	29.04.53-06.06.53	CW
HI	06.11.54-27.11.54	CW
LC-E	01.08.55-20.08.55	CW
LC-E	21.09.56-10.10.56	RY

Engine no /type.	Date of repair	Works
5024		
HG	25.02.57-06.04.57	CW
LC-E	01.05.58-15.05.58	RY
HI	02.06.59-20.06.59	CW
LC-E	26.04.60-16.06.60	CW
LC-E	02.09.60-27.09.60	CW
LI	29.07.61-31.08.61	CW
HG	19.09.63-29.10.63	CW
5025		
LS	29.10.35-10.12.35	
HS	09.10.36-01.12.36	
LO	13.04.37-26.04.37	
HG	14.09.37-05.10.37	
LO	21.10.37-09.11.37	
LO	19.07.38-17.08.38	
HS	17.04.39-11.05.39	
HS	13.10.39-16.12.39	
LS	27.01.41-08.02.41	
LO	06.09.41-24.09.41	
LO	02.01.42-27.01.42	
HG	24.09.42-24.10.42	
LS	04.03.44-20.03.44	
HS	19.04.45-23.05.45	
HG	05.07.46-09.08.46	
HO	10.02.47-29.03.47	CW
LS	21.02.48-19.03.48	CW
HG	16.01.50-09.02.50	CW
LI	10.10.51-21.11.51	RY
LC	04.02.52-13.03.52	CW
HI	26.06.53-03.08.53	CW
HG	29.12.54-29.01.55	CW
LC-E	13.08.55-02.09.55	CW
LI	06.09.56-12.10.56	CW
LC-E	04.01.57-08.02.57	CW
LC-E	21.01.58-30.01.58	CW
LI	21.04.58-23.05.58	CW
LC-E	13.03.59-23.05.59	CW
HG	10.12.59-22.01.60	CW
HI	13.07.61-29.08.61	CW
LC	26.02.62-23.03.62	CW
HI	29.10.63-06.12.63	CW
HI	15.04.66-21.05.66	CW
5026		
LS	27.08.35-18.09.35	
LS	22.06.36-04.07.36	
HG	18.01.37-24.02.37	
HS	19.03.38-06.04.38	
HS	03.07.39-02.08.39	
LS	03.07.40-18.07.40	
HG	11.06.41-17.07.41	
LO	22.12.41-26.01.42	
LS	14.08.42-11.09.42	
LO	09.12.42-08.01.43	
LS	02.11.43-19.11.43	
HS	28.05.45-20.06.45	
HG	30.08.46-25.09.46	CW
NC	19.12.47-27.01.48	CW
LS	17.03.48-28.04.48	CW
LI	20.12.49-17.01.50	CW
HG	02.12.51-16.01.52	CW
LI	25.03.54-14.04.54	RY
HG	16.02.56-29.03.56	CW
HG	27.11.58-03.01.59	CW
LI	24.11.61-19.12.61	CW
5027		
LS	20.11.35-12.12.35	
HG	07.11.36-19.12.36	
HS	03.01.38-19.01.38	
LS	26.07.39-10.08.39	
LO	03.02.40-09.02.40	
HG	18.07.40-03.08.40	
LS	17.06.42-11.07.42	

Engine no /type.	Date of repair	Works
5027		
LS	25.06.43-17.07.43	
HG	06.04.45-21.04.45	
LO	22.06.46-27.07.46	
HS	04.07.47-20.08.47	RY
LS	01.10.48-04.11.48	CW
NC	29.12.48-29.01.49	CW
HG	03.05.50-05.06.50	CW
HI	27.08.51-14.09.51	CW
LI	22.04.52-15.05.52	CW
HG	18.02.54-16.03.54	CW
LI	26.04.56-18.05.56	RY
LC-E	15.10.56-02.11.56	CW
HG	19.11.57-01.01.58	CW
NC-E	26.04.60-07.05.60	CW
LI	03.11.60-02.12.60	CW
HG	07.05.63-05.06.63	CW
5028		
LS	28.06.35-10.07.35	
LS	25.11.35-14.12.35	
LS	01.02.37-22.02.37	
LO	12.04.37-26.04.37	
HG	21.02.38-06.04.38	
LS	05.10.39-31.10.39	
HG	17.11.41-19.12.41	
LS	09.06.43-23.06.43	
LS	21.09.44-07.10.44	
HG	11.12.45-29.12.45	
LS	30.01.48-21.02.48	CW
HI	13.04.49-18.05.49	CW
HG	25.03.50-08.05.50	CW
LI	10.12.51-07.01.52	CW
HC	13.11.52-13.12.52	CW
LI	10.06.53-29.06.53	CW
HC	12.07.53-17.08.53	CW
HG	09.09.54-14.10.54	CW
HC	28.12.55-04.02.56	CW
HI	19.03.57-13.04.57	CW
LI	22.12.58-15.01.59	CW
HG	29.07.60-02.09.60	CW
HI	20.10.62-10.11.62	CW
LI	24.11.64-16.01.65	CS
LC	08.04.65-22.05.65	CS
5029		
LS	09.12.35-01.01.36	
LS	21.11.36-03.12.36	
LS	18.08.37-15.09.37	
LO	02.10.37-26.10.37	
HG	28.02.38-19.04.38	
HS	29.06.39-24.07.39	
HG	17.07.40-03.08.40	
LS	03.01.42-28.01.42	
HG	27.01.43-27.02.43	
HS	05.11.43-24.11.43	
LS	04.09.44-21.09.44	
LO	17.02.45-03.03.45	
LO	07.05.45-30.05.45	
LS	10.07.45-09.08.45	
LO	17.12.45-26.12.45	
LS	02.05.46-25.05.46	
HG	03.06.47-11.07.47	
HS	18.11.48-24.12.48	
LC	09.04.49-28.05.49	
LI	28.10.49-02.12.49	
G	22.01.52-06.03.52	SR
LC-E	23.09.52-03.11.52	S
LC-E	17.11.52-12.12.52	SR
LI	19.03.53-30.04.53	CW
LC-E	08.03.54-01.04.54	SR
LI	19.02.55-10.03.55	SR
NC-E	10.05.55-19.05.55	SR
LC-E	26.10.55-12.11.55	SR
G	13.06.56-09.08.56	SR

Engine no /type.	Date of repair	Works
5029		
LC-E	01.04.57-06.04.57	SR
LC-E	15.04.57-25.04.57	SR
NC-E	21.01.58-28.01.58	SR
LI	11.09.58-26.09.58	SR
HI	28.03.60-30.04.60	SR
LC	01.08.61-22.08.61	SR
G	14.11.62-11.12.62	SR
LC	04.12.64-05.12.64	CS
LC-E	10.05.65-05.06.65	CS
NC-E	19.11.65-01.12.65	CS
LC-E	16.05.66-18.06.66	CS
5030		
LS	10.01.36-27.01.36	
LS	07.09.36-25.09.36	
HG	03.01.38-26.01.38	
LO	29.04.38-20.06.38	
LS	14.11.39-09.12.39	
HS	07.12.40-09.01.41	
HG	16.11.42-19.12.42	
LS	08.01.44-27.01.44	
HS	13.08.45-15.09.45	
HS	11.10.47-08.11.47	
HG	17.11.49-16.12.49	CW
LI	01.06.51-23.06.51	CW
HI	30.04.52-12.06.52	IS
HC	07.10.52-14.11.52	SR
LC	17.12.52-17.01.53	SR
LC-E	08.05.53-23.05.53	SR
G	24.08.53-10.10.53	SR
NC-E	12.10.53-14.10.53	SR
HI	18.11.54-11.12.54	SR
LC-E	12.04.55-27.04.55	SR
LI	01.08.56-26.08.56	SR
NC-E	19.12.56-25.12.56	SR
LC	01.05.57-09.05.57	SR
G	26.02.58-17.05.58	SR
NC-E	04.06.59-06.06.59	SR
HI	26.10.59-28.11.59	CS
LI	31.08.60-30.09.60	SR
NC-E	20.10.60	SR
LC	04.10.61-24.10.61	SR
5031		
LS	07.02.36-20.03.36	
LO	17.10.36-18.11.36	
LO	03.04.37-21.04.37	
HG	22.06.37-29.07.37	
LS	03.03.38-29.03.38	
LS	22.03.39-19.04.39	
LO	09.11.39-06.12.39	
LO	28.12.39-12.01.40	
HG	17.07.40-06.08.40	
LS	20.12.41-14.01.42	
LS	17.12.42-22.01.43	
HG	26.06.44-29.07.44	
LS	03.05.45-01.06.45	
LS	08.02.47-31.03.47	CW
HG	01.11.48-25.11.48	CW
HI	05.10.50-28.10.50	CW
HI	06.10.52-31.10.52	CW
HG	20.02.54-19.03.54	CW
LI	20.12.55-14.01.56	CW
LI	15.03.57-16.04.57	CW
HG	27.02.58-01.04.58	CW
HI	12.09.59-22.10.59	CW
NC-E	24.07.61-08.08.61	CW
LI	26.09.62-27.10.62	CW
LC	17.01.63-07.02.63	CW
LC	24.08.64-07.01.65	CW
5032		
LS	06.12.35-30.12.35	
LO	04.12.36-19.12.36	

Engine no /type.	Date of repair	Works
5032		
HS	24.03.37-03.05.37	
HG	07.06.38-18.07.38	
LS	27.11.39-13.12.39	
HG	19.08.41-04.09.41	
LS	19.12.42-07.01.43	
LS	07.02.44-19.02.44	
LO	17.10.44-28.10.44	
HG	23.10.45-10.11.45	
LO	19.07.46-10.08.46	
LO	07.03.47-22.04.47	CW
HS	23.02.48-24.03.48	CW
HG	22.07.49-17.08.49	CW
LI	03.05.51-28.05.51	CW
LC	01.12.51-18.01.52	CW
LI	21.02.53-16.03.53	RY
HG	15.01.54-15.02.54	CW
HI	07.04.56-08.05.56	CW
LI	02.11.57-30.11.57	CW
HG	30.03.59-01.05.59	CW
LC	11.05.59-20.05.59	DY
HI	05.01.61-03.02.61	CW
5033		
LO	11.01.36-24.01.36	
LS	05.03.36-26.03.36	
HS	23.02.37-15.03.37	
HG	19.03.38-12.04.38	
HS	07.06.39-24.07.39	
LS	22.08.40-12.09.40	
HG	10.04.42-16.05.42	
LS	04.11.43-20.11.43	
LS	02.02.45-03.03.45	
LO	20.02.46-29.03.46	
HG	07.01.47-25.01.47	CW
HS	02.11.48-24.11.48	CW
NC	13.12.48-21.12.48	RY
HI	31.05.50-19.06.50	CW
LC	04.01.51-05.02.51	CW
HG	21.08.52-27.09.52	CW
LI	27.03.54-23.04.54	CW
LC-E	03.02.55-26.02.55	CW
HG	14.02.56-24.03.56	CW
LC-E	04.03.57-26.03.57	CW
LI	18.03.58-12.04.58	CW
NC-E	21.04.60-29.04.60	CW
HG	02.08.60-23.09.60	CW
LC	25.10.61-17.11.61	CW
HI	27.12.62-09.02.63	CW
NC	03.06.63-14.06.63	CW
5034		
LS	14.04.36-06.05.36	
HS	29.03.37-14.04.37	
HG	25.02.38-19.05.38	
LS	12.01.40-09.02.40	
HG	28.08.41-18.09.41	
LO	20.05.42-20.06.42	
LS	26.11.43-16.12.43	
HS	06.10.44-11.11.44	
LS	13.07.46-30.07.46	
HG	22.03.48-24.04.48	CW
HI	14.07.49-05.08.49	CW
HI	11.09.50-29.09.50	CW
HI	17.03.52-09.04.52	CW
HG	18.06.53-25.07.53	CW
LI	24.10.54-17.11.54	CW
LI	29.08.56-12.10.56	RY
LC-E	14.03.57-12.04.57	CW
LC-E	17.09.57-12.10.57	CW
HG	25.10.58-27.11.58	CW
NC-E	10.02.59-16.02.59	CW
HI	29.06.60-10.08.60	CW
Int	07.12.61-11.01.62	CW
NC	16.01.62-25.01.62	CW

5034

type	Date of repair	Works
LC	25.04.62-10.05.62	CW
LI	13.04.65-08.05.65	CW

5035

type	Date of repair	Works
LS	16.10.35-06.11.35	
LS	14.05.36-04.07.36	
HS	18.03.37-09.04.37	
HG	14.03.38-23.05.38	
HS	27.11.39-19.12.39	
HG	22.08.41-04.10.41	
LS	04.02.43-02.03.43	
LO	29.10.43-03.12.43	
LS	13.03.45-13.04.45	
HG	28.07.46-21.08.46	
LS	19.06.48-30.07.48	CW
LC	21.01.49-21.02.49	CW
HI	05.03.50-27.03.50	CW
LC	25.08.50-19.09.50	CW
HG	13.07.51-22.08.51	CW
LC-E	27.10.51-12.11.51	HW
LI	11.06.53-03.07.53	CW
HG	03.12.54-24.12.54	CW
HI	02.08.56-07.09.56	CW
LI	02.08.57-24.08.57	CW
HI	20.04.59-22.05.59	CW
HG	01.07.60-25.08.60	CW

5036

type	Date of repair	Works
LO	10.06.35-16.07.35	
LS	09.12.35-16.01.36	
LS	27.10.36-20.11.36	
LS	15.09.37-05.10.37	
HG	18.02.38-28.03.38	
LO	13.10.38-02.11.38	
LS	11.03.39-28.04.39	
HG	10.07.40-09.08.40	
HS	16.05.41-11.06.41	
HS	14.08.42-19.09.42	
LS	15.05.43-16.06.43	
LO	28.08.43-07.12.43	
LS	03.07.44-27.07.44	
HG	08.03.45-14.04.45	
LS	03.04.46-27.04.46	
LS	22.01.47-06.03.47	
HG	08.11.47-26.12.47	
HI	29.11.48-12.01.49	
LI	14.12.49-25.01.50	
LI	08.05.51-23.06.51	IS
LC	19.05.52-28.05.52	S
G	21.10.52-27.12.52	SR
NC-E	23.01.53-20.02.53	SR
LC	15.04.53-02.05.53	SR
HI	13.01.54-05.02.54	SR
LC-E	11.10.54-06.11.54	SR
LI	25.04.55-08.06.55	IS
LC-E	26.01.56-08.02.56	SR
NC-E	09.07.56-11.07.56	SR
G	04.12.56-19.01.57	SR
LC-E	08.01.58-18.01.58	SR
LI	30.04.58-11.06.58	IS
NC	28.05.59-03.06.59	SR
HI	18.04.60-20.05.60	SR
NC-E	02.09.60-15.09.60	SR
LC-E	15.03.61-22.03.61	SR
LC-E	28.04.61-02.05.61	SR
NC	26.09.61-05.10.61	SR

5037

type	Date of repair	Works
LS	12.03.36-24.04.36	
HS	01.03.37-19.03.37	
HG	06.10.37-15.11.37	
HS	05.05.39-21.06.39	
LS	26.12.40-11.01.41	
HG	26.06.42-01.08.42	
LO	05.11.42-28.11.42	
LS	30.03.44-15.04.44	
HS	06.04.45-02.05.45	
HG	09.09.46-28.10.46	CW
LS	06.04.48-04.05.48	CW
HI	25.01.50-08.02.50	CW
HG	10.02.52-04.04.52	CW
LI	23.11.53-22.12.53	RY
LI	03.10.55-26.10.55	CW
HG	15.08.57-20.09.57	CW
HI	26.06.59-08.08.59	CW
HI	01.06.60-29.07.60	CW
LC-E	03.01.61-04.02.61	CW
HI	11.05.62-05.06.62	CW
G	09.01.64-01.02.64	CS
NC	10.02.64-15.02.64	CS
NC-R	21.12.64-31.12.64	CS

5038

type	Date of repair	Works
LS	17.12.35-17.01.36	
LS	11.01.37-26.01.37	
LO	14.04.37-29.04.37	
HG	20.08.37-22.09.37	
LS	22.11.38-28.01.39	
HS	23.11.39-30.12.39	
LS	06.05.41-23.05.41	
LS	01.12.42-26.12.42	
HG	23.08.44-08.09.44	
LS	09.07.46-10.08.46	
HG	06.11.48-06.12.48	CW
LI	01.09.50-06.10.50	RY
HI	31.03.52-25.04.52	CW
NC-R	01.05.52-10.05.52	CW
HG	18.12.53-26.01.54	CW
LI	01.04.55-12.05.55	CW
LI	03.12.56-01.01.57	CW
LC-E	07.02.57-06.03.57	CW
HG	28.01.58-20.02.58	CW
NC-E	05.10.59-23.10.59	CW
HI	01.02.60-03.03.60	CW
HI	29.09.61-07.11.61	CW
HI	02.06.64-24.10.64	CW

5039

type	Date of repair	Works
LO	31.01.35-25.02.35	
LS	28.01.36-10.02.36	
LO	06.10.36-17.10.36	
LS	28.12.36-11.01.37	
LO	16.04.37-30.04.37	
HG	24.02.38-19.05.38	
LS	02.01.40-30.01.40	
LS	13.02.41-01.03.41	
HG	24.08.42-26.09.42	
LS	27.03.44-13.04.44	
LS	13.08.45-19.09.45	
HG	07.06.46-29.06.46	CW
LS	17.01.48-10.02.48	CW
HI	30.07.49-18.08.49	CW
HG	11.01.51-29.01.51	CW
LI	07.06.52-23.07.52	CW

Patricroft's 45055 gained its BR number during a Heavy General repair at Crewe from 25th November 1948 to 12th January 1949. This picture was probably taken as it returned to traffic in lined black livery, albeit still with BRITISH RAILWAYS on the tender. Having been at Patricroft since August 1937, 45055 was transferred to Springs Branch in September 1952. It has a domeless boiler and the welded tender, No.9515, was attached in July 1944.

5039

/type.	Date of repair	Works
LC-E	27.12.52-16.01.53	CW
LI	18.06.53-07.07.53	CW
LC-E	01.08.53-26.08.53	CW
LC-E	18.02.54-13.03.54	CW
HI	29.04.55-28.05.55	CW
NC-R	15.06.55-27.06.55	CW
LC-E	26.03.56-28.04.56	CW
HG	11.09.56-13.10.56	CW
LI	05.12.58-10.01.59	CW
HG	27.02.61-15.04.61	CW
HI	07.09.64-31.10.64	DN
NC-R	11.01.65-29.01.65	DN
HC	27.04.66-15.05.66	CW

5040

/type.	Date of repair	Works
LS	06.11.35-10.12.35	
LO	30.06.36-13.07.36	
HG	08.10.36-04.12.36	
HO	15.12.36-18.01.37	
LO	05.06.37-01.07.37	
LS	28.10.37-15.11.37	
LO	04.04.38-04.05.38	
LO	03.08.38-23.08.38	
LS	02.03.39-30.03.39	
LO	29.05.39-12.07.39	
LO	08.11.39-16.11.39	
HG	05.03.40-30.03.40	
LS	12.05.41-31.05.41	
LO	29.12.41-31.01.42	
HG	16.11.42-02.01.43	
HS	23.06.43-27.07.43	
LO	15.11.43-04.12.43	
HS	26.12.44-03.02.45	
HG	04.03.46-05.04.46	
LS	27.09.47-08.11.47	CW
LS	28.09.48-01.11.48	CW
HG	16.10.49-29.11.49	CW
HI	21.03.51-18.04.51	CW
LI	12.08.52-08.09.52	CW
LI	19.10.53-14.11.53	CW
HG	15.09.54-22.10.54	CW
HI	03.08.56-28.08.56	CW
LC-E	23.05.57-06.06.57	RY
LI	07.06.58-15.07.58	CW
HG	01.08.60-09.09.60	CW
NC-R	16.09.60-26.09.60	CW
HI	06.03.63-24.03.63	CW

5041

/type.	Date of repair	Works
LS	11.09.35-11.10.35	
LO	09.06.36-30.06.36	
LS	04.09.36-15.10.36	
HG	08.03.37-28.04.37	
HS	02.11.37-06.12.37	
LO	04.06.38-13.06.38	
HS	17.10.38-04.01.39	
LO	17.07.39-09.08.39	
HG	20.12.39-03.02.40	
HS	27.12.40-25.01.41	
LS	01.12.41-03.01.42	
LO	30.03.42-18.04.42	
LS	15.02.43-05.03.43	
HG	05.05.44-27.05.44	
HS	09.11.45-08.12.45	
HG	16.04.47-13.06.47	CW
LI	22.12.48-14.01.49	CW
LI	14.01.50-06.02.50	CW
HG	16.08.51-15.09.51	CW
HI	20.07.53-18.08.53	CW
HG	24.08.54-01.10.54	CW
HI	10.10.56-09.11.56	CW
LC-E	08.06.57-28.06.57	CW
HI	27.01.58-27.02.58	CW
HG	12.10.59-19.11.59	CW

5041

/type.	Date of repair	Works
HI	09.10.61-08.11.61	CW
LI	07.05.63-30.05.63	CW
HI	10.05.65-15.06.65	CW
LC	09.07.66-30.07.66	CW

5042

/type.	Date of repair	Works
LS	29.08.35-15.10.35	
LO	21.10.35-04.11.35	
LS	26.10.36-07.12.36	
HS	12.03.37-02.04.37	
LO	10.08.37-30.08.37	
HG	09.02.38-02.03.38	
HS	15.03.39-21.04.39	
HS	09.04.40-25.04.40	
LS	20.12.41-24.01.42	
LO	14.04.42-07.05.42	
LS	14.12.42-05.01.43	
LO	05.11.43-20.11.43	
HG	27.03.44-11.04.44	
HS	27.04.45-16.05.45	
LS	16.12.46-08.01.47	CW
HO	09.09.47-10.10.47	CW
LO	03.12.47-24.12.47	CW
HG	16.02.49-31.03.49	CW
LI	16.05.50-02.06.50	CW
HI	15.10.51-09.11.51	CW
HG	30.06.53-12.08.53	CW
LI	22.01.55-12.02.55	CW
HG	25.01.57-02.03.57	CW
LI	16.01.59-06.02.59	CW

5043

/type.	Date of repair	Works
LS	30.10.35-04.12.35	
LO	02.09.36-14.12.36	
HG	30.11.37-03.01.38	
LO	04.07.38-29.07.38	
LS	15.02.39-07.03.39	
LO	18.04.39-09.05.39	
LO	15.05.39-02.06.39	
HS	06.12.39-03.01.40	
LO	24.12.40-23.01.41	
LS	14.01.42-14.02.42	
HG	26.09.42-24.10.42	
LI	08.06.43-30.06.43	
LS	08.02.44-03.03.44	
HG	21.05.45-19.07.45	
HS	11.09.46-18.10.46	
HS	27.02.48-10.04.48	
HG	02.08.49-23.09.49	CW
LI	22.02.51-04.04.51	HW
NC-R	14.04.51-17.04.51	HW
NC	04.06.51-25.06.51	
LC	23.07.51-17.08.51	
NC	26.10.51-31.10.51	SR
HI	03.02.53-07.03.53	SR
HI	01.02.54-05.03.54	CW
G	25.08.55-24.09.55	CW
LI	11.03.58-02.04.58	CW
?	13.10.59-31.10.59	CW
LI	31.10.60-17.12.60	CW
HC	16.02.62-13.03.62	CW
Int	08.03.65-27.03.65	CW

5044

/type.	Date of repair	Works
LS	07.11.35-16.12.35	
LS	18.11.36-07.12.36	
LO	05.04.37-16.04.37	
HG	08.05.37-11.06.37	
LS	30.06.38-21.07.38	
HG	28.12.39-18.01.40	
HS	30.01.41-15.02.41	
LS	31.08.42-16.09.42	
HG	12.10.43-30.10.43	
LO	29.02.44-06.03.44	

5044

/type.	Date of repair	Works
LS	27.04.45-26.05.45	
LO	04.06.46-17.07.46	
HG	24.07.47-08.09.47	CW
LO	25.05.48-15.06.48	CW
LI	04.10.49-04.11.49	RY
HG	06.11.50-09.12.50	CW
LI	04.11.51-28.11.51	CW
LC	01.12.52-24.12.52	CW
HI	04.01.54-23.01.54	CW
HG	04.12.55-31.12.55	CW
LI	31.10.57-30.11.57	CW
LI	22.03.59-21.04.59	CW
LC-E	18.08.59-01.09.59	CW
LC-E	12.04.60-13.05.60	CW
HG	25.01.61-25.02.61	CW
Int	12.04.62-09.05.62	CW
NC-R	11.02.65-27.02.65	CS
LC	20.05.65-31.05.65	CW
C.D	07.02.66-11.03.66	CW

5045

/type.	Date of repair	Works
LS	06.09.35-25.09.35	
LO	16.08.36-03.09.36	
LS	09.11.36-23.11.36	
LO	14.04.37-29.04.37	
HG	16.04.38-10.06.38	
LS	05.01.40-02.02.40	
HS	13.05.41-29.05.41	
LO	07.02.42-28.02.42	
LS	14.08.42-12.09.42	
HG	04.10.43-16.10.43	
LO	21.08.44-02.09.44	
LO	05.02.45-15.02.45	
LS	27.08.45-22.09.45	
LS	07.02.47-13.03.47	CW
LO	17.03.48-09.04.48	CW
HG	15.08.48-09.09.48	CW
HI	15.08.50-02.09.50	CW
LI	23.11.51-11.01.52	RY
HG	17.02.53-18.03.53	CW
LC-E	21.11.53-18.12.53	CW
LC-E	24.02.54-13.03.54	CW
HG	09.10.54-08.11.54	CW
HI	10.02.56-08.03.56	CW
LI	09.05.57-01.06.57	CW
HI	04.05.59-13.06.59	CW
NC-R	22.06.59-25.06.59	CW
HC	07.11.59-12.12.59	CW
LI	13.05.61-10.08.61	CW
LC	18.10.62-10.11.62	CW
HI	20.01.64-15.02.64	CW

5046

/type.	Date of repair	Works
LO	01.08.35-15.08.35	
LS	05.05.36-22.05.36	
HO	15.03.37-12.04.37	
HG	28.12.37-17.01.38	
HS	12.06.39-17.07.39	
HG	06.02.41-28.02.41	
LS	05.08.42-03.09.42	
LS	11.06.43-24.06.43	
HG	10.08.45-29.08.45	
HS	29.07.47-06.09.47	CW
HG	28.03.49-20.04.49	CW
LC	31.10.49-16.11.49	CW
HI	20.07.50-28.08.50	CW
HI	08.09.51-26.10.51	CW
HG	22.04.53-22.05.53	CW
LI	06.04.55-05.05.55	CW
LC-E	05.12.55-07.01.56	CW
HG	21.06.57-03.08.57	CW
HI	16.05.59-11.06.59	CW
HI	21.05.60-25.06.60	CW
LI	14.11.61-16.12.61	CW

5046

/type.	Date of repair	Works
HC	31.07.62-23.08.62	CW
LI	05.04.65-06.05.65	CW

5047

/type.	Date of repair	Works
LS	06.11.35-25.11.35	
HG	28.11.36-13.01.37	
HS	13.05.38-15.06.38	
LS	26.01.39-27.02.39	
LO	08.09.39-17.10.39	
HG	15.07.40-07.08.40	
HS	13.08.41-20.09.41	
LS	17.04.42-22.05.42	
LS	14.01.43-03.02.43	
LS	26.11.43-20.12.43	
HS	17.07.44-14.08.44	
HG	29.09.45-02.11.45	
LO	25.05.46-22.06.46	
LO	18.10.46-30.11.46	
LS	24.05.47-07.07.47	
HS	23.06.48-12.08.48	
LC	30.11.48-05.01.49	
HI	24.03.49-27.04.49	
LC	26.12.49-29.12.49	
LC	13.01.50-26.01.50	
TO	23.05.50-24.05.50	
G	14.08.50-07.10.50	SR
LC	21.11.50-18.01.51	SR
HI	07.11.51-01.12.51	SR
NC-E	24.03.52-11.04.52	SR
HI	21.08.52-04.10.52	SR
LI-E	05.10.53-07.11.53	SR
HC	27.11.53-27.11.53	SR
G	01.08.55-24.09.55	SR
LC-E	16.12.55-28.12.55	SR
HI	09.04.57-27.05.57	IS
LC-E	27.09.58-23.10.58	SR
G	01.09.59-16.10.59	SR
LC-E	24.03.60-08.04.60	SR
HI	17.05.61-22.06.61	SR
HI	30.05.63-04.07.63	SR
NC	09.07.63-10.07.63	SR
LC	01.03.65-06.03.65	IE

5048

/type.	Date of repair	Works
LS	28.10.35-10.12.35	
LO	08.01.36-17.02.36	
LO	25.07.36-22.08.36	
HS	15.06.37-30.06.37	
HG	23.08.38-22.09.38	
HS	14.02.40-16.03.40	
LS	18.03.42-11.04.42	
LS	22.10.42-20.11.42	
HG	11.01.44-08.02.44	
TO	13.09.44-06.10.44	
HS	10.04.46-03.05.46	
HG	13.01.48-19.02.48	CW
HI	02.01.50-20.01.50	CW
HG	11.12.51-19.01.52	CW
HI	12.10.53-05.11.53	CW
LI	24.03.55-22.04.55	CW
HG	31.05.56-20.07.56	CW
HI	03.04.58-23.05.58	CW
NC-E	07.05.59-16.05.59	CW
LC	25.05.59-12.06.59	GN
HC	02.08.59-12.09.59	CW
HG	14.12.60-20.01.61	CW
HI	23.09.63-28.10.63	CW

5049

/type.	Date of repair	Works
LS	25.11.35-16.12.35	
LS	01.10.36-22.10.36	
HG	06.05.38-22.06.38	
HS	03.01.40-20.01.40	
HS	31.01.41-14.02.41	

Engine no /type.	Date of repair	Works
5049		
LS	15.05.42-05.06.42	
LS	06.05.43-29.05.43	
LS	11.01.44-10.02.44	
LO	10.07.44-05.08.44	
LS	15.05.45-14.06.45	
HS	08.02.46-09.03.46	
HG	18.12.46-14.02.47	
LO	30.10.47-12.11.47	
LS	20.03.48-01.05.48	
LO	19.07.48-29.07.48	
LO	25.10.48-06.11.48	
LC	09.12.48-14.01.49	
HI	07.03.49-07.04.49	
NC-R	11.04.49-13.04.49	
LC	24.08.49-02.09.49	
LC	27.10.49-24.11.49	
NC-R	30.11.49-03.12.49	
HI	13.02.50-18.03.50	
NC-R	03.04.50-08.04.50	
LC	25.08.50-10.10.50	
G	04.01.51-21.04.51	SR
HI	22.02.52-20.03.52	SR
HI	10.02.53-14.03.53	SR
G	07.05.54-16.07.54	SR
LC-E	24.02.55-09.03.55	SR
LC-E	14.03.55-19.03.55	IS
LC	01.08.55-12.08.55	SR
HI	01.02.56-25.02.56	SR
LC-E	27.08.56-31.08.56	SR
LC-E	13.02.57-02.03.57	SR
HI	03.08.57-22.08.57	SR
G	23.06.59-07.08.59	SR
LC	05.04.60-14.04.60	SR
LI	31.07.61-16.09.61	SR
5050		
LS	11.03.36-01.04.36	
LO	20.10.36-12.11.36	
HG	20.04.37-02.06.37	
LS	09.01.39-02.02.39	
HG	29.07.40-21.08.40	
HO	24.02.41-14.03.41	
LS	23.10.41-08.11.41	
HS	23.04.43-08.05.43	
LS	02.08.44-16.08.44	
LO	18.11.44-16.12.44	
LS	10.12.45-12.01.46	
LO	12.10.46-01.11.46	
HG	25.10.47-13.12.47	CW
HI	03.09.49-29.09.49	CW
LI	14.06.50-30.06.50	CW
HG	02.01.52-02.02.52	CW
LC	05.06.52-28.06.52	CW
HI	26.01.53-21.02.53	CW
NC-R	10.03.53-20.03.53	RY
HI	12.05.54-03.06.54	CW
HG	17.11.55-16.12.55	CW
LI	07.01.57-31.01.57	CW
LC-E	07.12.57-20.12.57	RY
LI	08.08.58-04.09.58	CW
LC-E	31.01.59-20.03.59	CW
HG	16.05.60-24.06.60	CW
NC-R	12.08.60-19.08.60	CW
LC-E	18.04.61-01.06.61	CW
HI	27.07.62-18.08.62	CW
Int	30.04.65-25.05.65	CW
5051		
LO	05.04.35-07.05.35	
LO	17.08.35-09.09.35	
LO	28.10.35-14.11.35	
LO	05.02.36-17.02.36	
LS	20.04.36-05.05.36	
HG	03.03.37-08.04.37	

Engine no /type.	Date of repair	Works
5051		
LS	22.08.38-07.09.38	
HG	21.11.39-16.12.39	
LS	12.08.41-06.09.41	
LS	11.12.42-07.01.43	
HG	08.04.44-26.04.44	
HS	10.12.45-05.01.46	
LO	08.01.47-01.03.47	CW
LS	24.02.48-23.03.48	CW
HG	02.05.49-31.05.49	CW
LI	14.10.50-09.11.50	CW
HI	10.11.51-12.12.51	CW
HG	13.03.53-17.04.53	CW
HI	23.08.54-22.09.54	CW
LC-E	21.02.55-17.03.55	CW
LC-E	13.08.55-03.09.55	CW
LC-E	26.03.56-06.04.56	RY
HI	15.09.56-18.10.56	CW
LC-E	03.06.57-21.06.57	CW
LC-E	27.08.57-26.09.57	CW
HG	16.06.58-04.07.58	CW
NC-E	21.04.59-02.05.59	CW
LI	04.09.59-23.10.59	CW
5052		
LS	24.10.35-14.12.35	
LS	18.07.36-18.08.36	
LO	20.04.37-06.05.37	
LO	11.08.37-25.08.37	
HG	02.05.38-24.06.38	
LS	04.04.40-18.04.40	
HG	13.01.42-31.01.42	
LS	16.04.43-06.05.43	
LS	20.07.44-05.08.44	
HG	10.09.45-06.10.45	
LS	04.06.47-21.07.47	RY
LO	06.04.48-12.05.48	CW
HI	07.04.49-09.05.49	CW
HG	08.09.50-05.10.50	CW
LI	12.11.51-15.12.51	CW
LI	21.05.53-16.06.53	RY
LC-E	19.03.54-31.03.54	S
LI	21.06.54-29.07.54	CW
LC-E	02.02.55-11.02.55	CW
HC	13.04.55-17.05.55	CW
HG	03.03.56-05.04.56	CW
LI	01.02.58-21.02.58	CW
LC-E	02.04.59-02.05.59	CW
LC	08.05.59-21.05.59	GN
HI	04.03.61-12.04.61	CW
5053		
LS	20.11.35-20.12.35	
LS	26.07.37-26.08.37	
HO	03.03.38-28.03.38	
HS	02.12.38-29.12.38	
LS	13.10.39-03.11.39	
LO	08.04.40-02.05.40	
LS	01.11.40-23.11.40	
LO	24.02.41-08.03.41	
HG	01.09.41-08.10.41	
HS	24.09.42-07.11.42	
HS	16.06.43-26.07.43	
LO	29.03.44-01.04.44	
HS	24.04.44-24.05.44	
LO	06.12.44-27.01.45	
LS	23.06.45-11.08.45	
LS	24.12.45-09.02.46	
LO	01.06.46-29.06.46	
HG	15.02.47-09.04.47	
LO	08.11.47-22.11.47	
LS	22.05.48-12.06.48	
LI	25.06.49-29.08.49	
NC	11.10.49-12.10.49	
LC	19.12.49-25.01.50	

Engine no /type.	Date of repair	Works
5053		
HI	24.06.50-19.08.50	
LC	02.12.50-29.12.50	
G	28.02.52-07.06.52	SR
LI	27.05.53-24.07.53	IS
NC-E	14.01.54-16.01.54	SR
HI	25.03.54-14.04.54	SR
LI	17.01.55-12.02.55	SR
LC-E	17.03.55-23.03.55	SR
NC-E	16.05.55-19.05.55	SR
NC-E	28.07.55-06.08.55	SR
LC-E	28.09.55-15.10.55	SR
LI	27.02.56-23.03.56	SR
NC-E	06.04.56-21.04.56	SR
NC-E	04.05.56-19.05.56	SR
NC-E	01.06.56-23.06.56	SR
NC-E	08.10.56-11.10.56	SR
G	24.01.57-22.02.57	SR
LC	10.04.57-18.04.57	SR
HI	11.01.58-19.02.58	IS
LC-E	12.05.58-22.05.58	SR
HI	20.12.58-17.01.59	SR
HI	13.11.59-18.12.59	SR
LC-E	29.01.60-12.02.60	SR
LC-E	04.04.60-14.04.60	SR
NC-E	26.04.60-30.04.60	SR
LC-E	14.09.60-29.09.60	SR
LC-E	16.02.61-01.03.61	SR
G	20.03.61-13.05.61	SR
LC	15.05.61-01.06.61	SR
HI	27.05.63-28.06.63	SR
NC	09.07.63-10.07.63	SR
NC	30.10.64-07.11.64	CS
LC	03.03.65-20.03.65	CS
5054		
HS	23.10.35-10.01.36	
LO	29.01.36-17.02.36	
HG	06.01.37-11.02.37	
HS	21.03.38-20.04.38	
LS	21.06.39-08.08.39	
HG	26.10.40-15.11.40	
LS	02.01.43-23.01.43	
LS	21.06.44-13.07.44	
LO	27.11.44-16.12.44	
HG	13.03.46-04.04.46	
HS	19.07.47-01.09.47	CW
LO	01.05.48-31.05.48	CW
LI	23.02.49-28.03.49	CW
HG	25.09.50-18.10.50	CW
LI	06.05.52-29.05.52	CW
LC-E	05.06.52-01.07.52	CW
HG	09.11.53-15.12.53	CW
HI	14.03.55-14.04.55	CW
LC-E	20.09.55-14.10.55	CW
HG	16.03.57-12.04.57	CW
HI	04.07.59-13.08.59	CW
HG	24.07.61-21.09.61	CW
LC	08.05.62-26.05.62	CW
Int	01.04.65-17.04.65	CS
5055		
LS	30.09.35-29.10.35	
LS	17.11.36-01.12.36	
LO	21.04.37-10.05.37	
HG	18.10.37-18.11.37	
LS	27.04.39-12.05.39	
HG	14.12.40-10.01.41	
LO	09.02.42-07.03.42	
LS	18.01.43-13.02.43	
LS	02.05.44-16.05.44	
LO	17.06.44-21.07.44	
HG	10.10.45-21.11.45	
HS	17.04.47-22.05.47	CW
HG	25.11.48-12.01.49	CW

Engine no /type.	Date of repair	Works
5055		
LI	11.08.50-01.09.50	CW
LI	05.12.51-18.01.52	CW
NC-R	23.01.52-01.02.52	CW
HG	16.12.53-16.01.54	CW
HI	27.01.56-25.02.56	CW
HG	30.12.57-01.02.58	CW
NC-E	26.04.60-07.05.60	CW
LI	17.08.60-24.09.60	CW
HG	04.02.63-07.03.63	CW
LI	27.04.66-03.06.66	CS
5056		
LS	08.10.35-13.11.35	
LS	29.10.36-04.12.36	
LO	08.04.37-26.04.37	
HG	21.10.37-24.11.37	
LO	28.03.38-17.05.38	
HS	04.10.38-17.11.38	
LS	24.04.39-23.05.39	
HG	28.05.40-14.06.40	
LS	20.12.41-23.01.42	
LO	17.07.42-06.08.42	
HS	06.01.43-27.01.43	
HG	01.02.44-19.02.44	
LO	10.04.44-02.05.44	
LO	02.03.45-23.03.45	
LS	11.12.45-14.01.46	
HS	24.03.47-14.05.47	CW
HS	07.11.47-04.12.47	CW
HG	21.09.48-20.10.48	CW
LI	14.12.49-10.01.50	CW
LI	27.08.51-28.09.51	CW
LC-E	05.05.52-28.05.52	CW
HG	04.06.53-06.07.53	CW
LC-E	21.01.54-20.02.54	CW
HI	17.02.55-16.03.55	CW
LC-E	15.08.55-17.09.55	CW
HG	11.02.57-20.03.57	CW
LC-E	18.09.57-09.10.57	CW
LI	01.10.58-30.10.58	CW
NC-E	19.02.59-27.02.59	CW
LI	18.12.59-04.02.60	CW
HI	24.05.61-19.06.61	CW
HG	11.06.63-26.07.63	CW
NC	26.09.66-15.11.66	CW
5057		
LS	21.10.35-27.11.35	
LS	23.07.36-18.08.36	
LO	10.10.36-16.11.36	
LO	03.03.37-01.04.37	
LO	28.05.37-14.06.37	
HG	27.11.37-23.12.37	
LS	12.05.39-20.06.39	
LS	15.05.40-04.06.40	
LS	29.10.41-15.11.41	
LO	23.01.42-13.02.43	
LS	22.07.43-09.08.43	
LO	21.02.44-11.03.44	
HG	14.09.44-04.11.44	
HS	11.01.46-09.02.46	
HS	24.05.47-26.06.47	CW
LO	06.04.48-05.05.48	CW
HG	18.10.48-17.11.48	CW
HI	22.09.50-28.10.50	CW
HI	29.11.51-02.01.52	CW
HG	30.06.53-17.08.53	CW
HI	28.04.56-09.06.56	CW
LC	28.04.56-30.05.56	CW
HG	01.03.58-30.05.58	CW
NC-E	29.04.59-14.05.59	CW
LC	25.05.59-12.06.59	DY
HI	15.11.60-16.12.60	CW
HI	18.10.62-10.11.62	CW

The clean lines of the front of Armstrong Whitworth 5240 are apparent in this 1930s view as is the carriage warming pipe fitted to the sloping throatplate Class 5s, but which were only on the earlier Crewe–built engines and not those built by contractors. 5240 has a 6B, Mold Junction, shedplate and spent several years in the area starting with Chester in August 1936, Mold Junction in November 1937, back to Chester from July 1938 and Mold Junction again in September 1938 before moving to Rugby in April 1939.

Engine no /type.	Date of repair	Works
5057		
LI	11.09.64-10.10.64	CS
LC	24.05.66-01.07.66	CS
5058		
LS	19.10.35-18.11.35	
LS	11.09.36-14.10.36	
LO	01.03.37-12.04.37	
HG	03.11.37-30.11.37	
LS	13.03.39-03.05.39	
HG	17.01.41-04.02.41	
LS	11.02.43-01.03.43	
LS	21.04.44-05.05.44	
LO	25.07.44-05.08.44	
HG	13.06.45-18.07.45	
HS	12.01.47-06.02.47	CW
LS	17.02.48-10.03.48	CW
LI	14.05.49-09.06.49	CW
HG	05.09.50-27.09.50	CW
LI	23.02.52-28.03.52	CW
HI	22.08.53-10.09.53	CW
HG	13.04.55-27.05.55	CW
LI	22.09.56-18.10.56	CW
LC-E	18.12.57-02.01.58	CW
LI	08.08.58-29.08.58	CW
NC-E	12.01.59-20.01.59	CW
HG	09.02.60-11.03.60	CW
LI	29.01.62-28.02.62	CW
LI	29.04.64-23.05.64	CS
NC	10.06.64-10.06.64	CS
LC	18.06.64-19.06.64	CS
LC	18.02.65-20.02.65	CS
5059		
LS	24.03.36-07.04.36	
LO	11.01.37-23.01.37	

Engine no /type.	Date of repair	Works
5059		
HG	11.03.37-15.04.37	
LS	25.03.39-17.05.39	
LO	01.06.40-15.06.40	
LO	15.09.41-22.09.41	
HG	04.12.41-20.12.41	
HS	06.11.42-03.12.42	
LS	29.08.44-16.09.44	
HG	26.05.45-14.07.45	
LS	21.08.47-23.09.47	CW
LO	27.01.48-05.03.48	CW
HI	16.12.48-22.01.49	CW
HG	09.03.50-06.04.50	CW
LI	18.08.51-26.09.51	CW
LI	15.01.53-19.02.53	CW
LC-E	27.10.53-26.11.53	S
HG	05.05.54-04.06.54	CW
HI	21.01.56-18.02.56	CW
LI	22.02.57-22.03.57	CW
HG	12.02.58-09.05.58	HW
LI	15.02.60-18.03.60	CW
HG	08.10.63-14.11.63	CW
5060		
LS	20.01.36-04.02.36	
LO	12.11.36-19.12.36	
HS	23.03.37-08.04.37	
HG	20.08.38-16.09.38	
LO	12.06.40-29.06.40	
HS	14.01.41-29.01.41	
LO	16.09.41-18.10.41	
HG	25.01.43-19.02.43	
LS	25.05.44-09.06.44	
LO	07.07.45-04.08.45	
LS	24.11.45-27.12.45	
HG	30.01.47-08.03.47	CW

Engine no /type.	Date of repair	Works
5060		
HS	06.08.48-28.08.48	CW
LI	23.10.50-17.11.50	CW
LC	25.04.51-31.05.51	CW
HG	13.08.52-18.09.52	CW
HI	28.09.53-16.10.53	CW
LI	03.04.55-28.04.55	CW
HG	26.09.56-17.11.56	CW
LI	10.03.59-10.04.59	CW
HI	23.01.61-24.02.61	CW
5061		
LS	24.02.36-09.03.36	
LO	09.06.36-11.06.36	
LO	24.06.36-27.06.36	
HS	06.07.37-29.07.37	
LO	04.10.37-03.11.37	
HG	09.11.38-05.12.38	
LS	26.10.40-13.11.40	
HS	23.03.42-21.04.42	
HG	22.02.43-15.03.43	
LS	05.01.44-12.02.44	
LS	24.04.45-12.05.45	
HS	05.11.46-18.12.46	CW
HG	25.03.48-28.04.48	CW
NC	13.09.48-03.11.48	CW
HG	25.01.50-14.02.50	CW
NC-R	24.02.50-02.03.50	CW
P.O	14.03.50-17.03.50	HW
LI	18.12.51-12.01.52	HW
NC-R	19.01.52-23.01.52	HW
HI	05.12.52-07.01.53	CW
LC-E	28.07.53-08.08.53	HW
HG	01.11.54-23.12.54	CW
HI	15.04.57-10.05.57	CW
LC-E	15.01.58-15.02.58	CW

Engine no /type. | Date of repair | Works

5061

/type.	Date of repair	Works
NC-E	18.02.58-11.03.58	CW
HG	14.09.59-16.10.59	CW
NC	05.12.61-15.12.61	CW
HI	18.09.62-12.10.62	CW
LI	15.03.65-10.04.65	CS

5062

/type.	Date of repair	Works
LS	15.01.36-03.02.36	
LO	13.10.36-19.10.36	
HS	09.03.37-02.04.37	
LO	14.07.37-16.07.37	
LO	06.09.37-16.09.37	
HG	24.08.38-10.10.38	
TO	01.10.39-03.10.39	
HS	12.12.39-28.12.39	
LS	28.01.41-13.03.41	
HG	10.01.42-31.01.42	
LS	02.03.43-30.03.43	
LS	26.09.44-07.10.44	
HG	22.03.46-12.04.46	
LS	18.12.47-24.01.48	HW
LI	13.05.49-02.06.49	CW
HG	28.08.50-13.10.50	CW
LI	28.04.52-19.05.52	CW
HI	18.04.54-11.05.54	CW
LC	18.12.54-12.01.55	CW
HG	16.03.56-17.04.56	CW
HI	28.01.58-13.03.58	CW
LC-E	25.08.58-26.09.58	CW
LC-E	01.06.59-16.06.59	RY
HI	02.01.61-14.03.61	CW
HG	01.02.63-01.03.63	CW

5063

/type.	Date of repair	Works
LS	27.01.36-10.02.36	
LO	07.07.36-10.07.36	
HS	09.03.37-01.04.37	
LO	07.09.37-10.09.37	
LS	04.05.38-03.06.38	
HG	25.08.39-21.09.39	
LS	02.12.40-19.12.40	
LS	16.11.42-24.12.42	
LO	23.07.43-07.08.43	
HG	15.06.44-30.06.44	
LS	26.11.45-29.12.45	
HS	18.10.46-26.11.46	CW
LS	20.05.48-17.06.48	CW
HG	13.12.49-20.01.50	CW
LI	01.10.51-01.11.51	CW
LI	22.09.53-21.10.53	CW
HG	25.04.55-26.05.55	CW
HI	24.10.56-10.11.56	CW
NC-R	12.11.56-22.11.56	CW
LI	25.11.57-01.01.58	CW
HG	07.08.59-18.09.59	CW
NC-E	06.01.61-17.01.61	CW
HI	28.11.62-01.01.63	CW
Int	16.09.65-21.10.65	CW

5064

/type.	Date of repair	Works
LS	07.12.35-03.01.36	
LO	21.05.36-17.07.36	
LS	14.10.36-12.11.36	
LO	03.03.37-30.03.37	
HG	14.04.38-17.06.38	
LS	01.11.39-23.11.39	
TO	25.05.40-05.07.40	
LS	25.02.41-19.03.41	
LO	24.12.41-09.01.42	
HG	22.02.43-23.03.43	
LS	21.09.44-07.10.44	
LS	17.09.46-10.10.46	
HG	21.02.48-25.03.48	CW
TO	06.01.50-25.01.50	S

5064 (continued)

/type.	Date of repair	Works
HI	07.03.50-27.03.50	CW
HG	12.01.52-23.02.52	CW
LC-E	10.12.53-13.12.53	S
HI	19.03.54-12.04.54	CW
NC-E	24.05.54-09.06.54	CW
HI	29.08.55-12.10.55	CW
LC-E	26.10.56-06.11.56	RY
HG	25.05.57-26.06.57	CW
LI	24.11.58-20.12.58	CW
NC-E	05.02.59-12.02.59	CW
LC-E	25.08.59-02.10.59	HW
LI	10.04.61-09.05.61	CW
LC	05.09.62-22.09.62	CW
HI	10.04.64-06.06.64	CW
NC-R	03.07.64	CW

5065

/type.	Date of repair	Works
LS	15.01.36-24.02.36	
LO	05.10.36-26.10.36	
HG	10.02.37-01.04.37	
LO	19.04.37-03.05.37	
HS	19.01.38-28.02.38	
LO	22.06.38-10.08.38	
HG	06.03.39-12.04.39	
LS	15.03.40-26.04.40	
HS	29.04.41-31.05.41	
LO	04.08.41-22.08.41	
LS	27.03.42-05.05.42	
LS	15.03.43-06.04.43	
HS	18.01.44-18.02.44	
HG	08.02.45-28.02.45	
LO	02.10.45-01.11.45	
LS	21.08.46-19.09.46	
LO	06.12.46-19.12.46	DY
LS	08.10.47-12.11.47	CW
LO	10.06.48-15.07.48	S
LO	18.08.48-27.09.48	CW
HG	08.06.49-23.06.49	CW
HI	03.01.51-26.01.51	CW
LI	29.05.52-21.06.52	CW
HG	01.02.54-03.03.54	CW
HI	17.12.55-11.01.56	CW
LI	22.12.56-18.01.57	CW
LC-E	23.12.57-15.01.58	RY
HG	20.09.58-21.10.58	CW
NC-E	17.02.59-24.02.59	CW
LI	09.05.60-10.06.60	CW
LC-E	29.06.60-19.08.60	CW
HI	16.07.62-09.08.62	CW
HI	19.06.64-04.07.64	CS
NC	23.07.65-28.08.65	CW

5066

/type.	Date of repair	Works
LS	13.11.35-18.12.35	
LO	14.07.36-05.08.36	
LS	24.02.37-17.04.37	
LO	16.03.38-31.03.38	
HS	06.10.38-24.10.38	
HS	08.04.39-04.05.39	
HG	09.01.40-21.02.40	
LS	27.01.41-20.02.41	
LS	14.11.41-13.12.41	
LO	18.12.41-02.01.42	
LS	03.11.42-11.12.42	
HG	20.09.43-13.10.43	
LO	30.11.43-25.12.43	
LS	12.08.44-06.09.44	
LS	24.08.45-18.10.45	
HG	28.10.46-11.01.47	
LO	04.09.47-18.09.47	
LS	08.05.48-19.06.48	
LO	25.10.48-09.11.48	
LI	10.09.49-28.11.49	
LC	21.07.50-20.09.50	

5066 (continued)

/type.	Date of repair	Works
G	16.06.51-20.10.51	SR
LI	13.12.52-23.01.53	IS
LC	05.02.53-13.02.53	IS
LC	30.03.53-11.04.53	IS
LC-E	19.10.53-30.10.53	IS
LI	07.04.54-21.05.54	IS
LC-E	20.11.54-17.12.54	IS
G	17.09.55-14.10.55	SR
HI	29.12.56-31.01.57	SR
NC	10.04.57-12.04.57	IS
LI	01.02.58-10.03.58	IS
NC-E	06.05.58-09.05.58	IS
LI	27.01.59-03.03.59	IS
G	13.04.60-04.06.60	SR
HI	02.10.61-25.11.61	SR
LI	06.08.63-13.09.63	IE
LC	23.09.63-26.09.63	IE

5067

/type.	Date of repair	Works
LS	20.11.35-16.12.35	
LO	04.05.36-27.05.36	
LO	29.06.36-18.07.36	
HG	11.06.37-21.07.37	
LO	03.01.38-31.01.38	
LS	31.05.38-23.06.38	
HG	06.05.39-12.06.39	
HS	14.05.40-27.05.40	
LS	25.11.41-18.12.41	
HG	16.11.42-04.12.42	
LS	22.08.44-09.09.44	
LS	15.09.45-17.10.45	
HG	28.11.46-28.12.46	CW
HS	13.10.48-12.11.48	CW
HI	21.11.49-07.12.49	CW
HG	24.04.51-30.05.51	CW
LI	09.04.53-09.05.53	CW
HI	22.01.55-11.02.55	CW
HG	03.12.56-10.01.57	CW
HI	11.04.59-07.05.59	CW
NC-R	18.06.59-27.06.59	CW
LC-E	13.07.60-14.09.60	CW
LI	02.10.61-28.10.61	CW
HG	16.04.63-11.05.63	CW

5068

/type.	Date of repair	Works
CBC	18.01.35-05.02.35	
LS	12.11.35-20.12.35	
HO	23.06.36-10.08.36	
HG	23.04.37-15.05.37	
LS	18.03.38-28.04.38	
LO	01.06.38-02.08.38	
LS	05.01.39-25.05.39	
HG	05.02.40-28.03.40	
LS	03.07.41-01.08.41	
LO	19.10.41-27.11.41	
LO	20.04.42-13.05.42	
LS	19.10.42-13.11.42	
HG	28.10.43-23.11.43	
LS	25.09.44-12.10.44	
HS	10.09.45-17.10.45	
LS	06.11.46-14.12.46	CW
HG	08.07.47-28.08.47	CW
LI	14.12.48-18.01.49	CW
HI	23.06.50-26.07.50	CW
HG	21.11.51-01.01.52	CW
LI	10.08.53-09.09.53	CW
LC-E	21.04.54-08.05.54	CW
HI	30.11.55-10.01.56	CW
HG	01.10.57-07.11.57	CW
LI	02.05.60-07.06.60	CW
LC-E	21.12.60-17.01.61	HW

5069

/type.	Date of repair	Works
LS	14.01.36-11.02.36	

5069 (continued)

/type.	Date of repair	Works
LO	24.06.36-17.07.36	
TO	12.10.36	
HS	27.05.37-11.06.37	
HG	21.12.38-23.01.39	
LS	15.05.40-29.05.40	
LS	26.05.42-13.06.42	
HG	13.03.44-27.03.44	
HS	12.02.46-02.03.46	
HG	26.02.48-07.04.48	CW
HI	23.08.49-20.09.49	CW
HG	25.06.51-08.08.51	CW
LC	19.02.52-12.03.52	RY
HI	02.02.53-27.02.53	CW
LC-E	02.02.54-06.03.54	CW
HG	14.01.55-10.02.55	CW
LC	14.02.56-16.03.56	CW
LI	23.05.57-14.06.57	CW
HC	29.04.58-29.05.58	CW
LI	27.09.59-07.11.59	CW
HG	02.08.60-01.11.60	CW
LI	10.01.64-07.02.64	CW

5070

/type.	Date of repair	Works
LS	15.06.36-29.06.36	
HS	23.04.37-10.05.37	
HG	19.10.38-28.11.38	
HS	12.04.40-25.04.40	
LS	10.04.42-08.05.42	
HG	17.11.43-11.12.43	
HS	03.09.45-09.10.45	
HS	25.09.47-03.11.47	CW
HG	16.02.49-02.03.49	CW
LI	08.06.50-27.06.50	CW
LI	12.10.51-01.11.51	CW
LC	06.02.52-29.02.52	HW
HG	27.06.53-10.08.53	CW
HC	24.04.54-15.05.54	CW
LI	18.01.55-07.02.55	CW
HI	25.11.56-24.12.56	CW
HG	14.08.58-18.09.58	CW
NC-E	12.01.59-20.01.59	CW
HI	15.10.59-27.11.59	CW
HI	24.05.61-21.06.61	CW
HG	30.07.63-30.08.63	CW
LI	23.09.65-23.10.65	CS

5071

/type.	Date of repair	Works
LS	02.10.36-22.10.36	
LO	19.04.37-03.05.37	
LS	25.11.37-15.12.37	
LO	05.07.38-09.07.38	
HG	09.08.38-03.11.38	
LS	30.01.40-28.02.40	
LO	16.10.41-19.10.41	
LS	19.01.42-07.02.42	
LO	09.05.42-25.05.42	
HG	29.06.43-21.07.43	
HS	01.09.44-23.09.44	
HO	22.06.45-26.07.45	
LS	02.01.47-01.02.47	CW
HG	19.06.48-05.08.48	CW
LI	01.06.50-19.06.50	CW
LI	11.12.51-22.01.52	CW
NC-R	04.02.52-08.02.52	CW
HG	03.02.53-28.02.53	CW
HC	01.05.54-15.05.54	CW
HI	24.05.55-15.06.55	CW
LC	27.02.56-20.03.56	CW
HG	08.03.57-30.04.57	CW
LC-E	19.09.58-15.10.58	CW
NC-E	24.02.59-05.03.59	CW
HI	08.12.59-22.01.60	CW
HG	15.11.62-22.12.62	CW

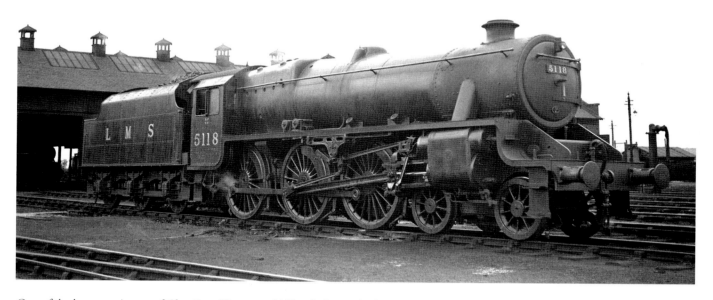

One of the large contingent of Class 5s at Kingmoor, 5118 at its home shed on 27th June 1936. It was delivered from Vulcan Foundry in June 1935 and after two months based at Edge Hill was transferred to Carlisle. It stayed there until July 1936 when it went to Perth for three months, returning to Kingmoor for a much longer spell before going back to Perth in 1950. *Fred A.Plant/Caledonian Railway Association*

Engine no /type.	Date of repair	Works	Engine no /type.	Date of repair	Works	Engine no /type.	Date of repair	Works	Engine no /type.	Date of repair	Works
5072			**5073**			**5074**			**5076**		
LS	11.05.36-25.05.36		LS	21.07.43-13.08.43		HG	31.03.59-25.04.59	CW	HS	22.07.40-03.08.40	
HS	19.04.37-04.05.37		HG	23.09.44-12.10.44		NC-R	29.05.59-01.06.59	CW	HS	08.08.42-22.08.42	
HG	15.07.38-19.08.38		LS	24.09.46-12.10.46		LC-E	12.05.59-21.05.59	HW	HG	25.10.43-09.11.43	CW
TO	01.10.39-23.10.39		HG	20.07.48-21.08.48	CW	LC-E	25.02.60-14.04.60	CW	LS	03.08.45-25.08.45	HW
HS	13.02.40-17.02.40		HI	05.01.50-06.02.50	RY	LI	19.09.62-13.10.62	CW	HS	11.01.47-31.01.47	CW
LS	11.12.41-10.01.42		HI	05.11.51-06.12.51	CW				HO	15.03.47-02.05.47	CW
HG	22.12.42-06.02.43		HG	02.10.53-28.10.53	CW	**5075**			NC	17.03.48-21.04.48	CW
LO	10.02.44-16.03.44		LI	04.09.55-01.10.55	CW	LS	19.03.36-03.04.36		LI	14.01.49-08.02.49	CW
LO	23.05.44-03.06.44		LI	17.11.56-14.12.56	CW	HS	03.03.37-24.03.37		LI	02.09.50-03.10.50	CW
HS	13.02.45-10.03.45		LO	05.08.57-14.09.57	CW	HG	11.05.38-29.06.38		LC	19.06.51-13.07.51	HW
HS	02.12.47-31.12.47	CW	HG	26.07.58-23.09.58	CW	HS	15.12.39-04.01.40		HG	20.03.52-14.05.52	CW
HG	02.06.49-28.06.49	CW	NC-E	02.02.59-21.02.59	CW	LS	18.06.41-07.07.41		NC-R	26.05.52-16.06.52	CW
LC	29.11.49-16.12.49	CW	LC-E	08.08.59-20.11.59	GN	HG	05.12.42-24.12.42		LI	18.03.54-06.04.54	RY
NC	15.02.50-28.02.50	CW	HI	05.07.60-15.09.60	CW	LS	13.05.44-27.05.44		HI	19.01.55-16.02.55	CW
LC	08.05.50-26.05.50	CW				LS	01.02.46-20.02.46		NC-R	18.02.55-22.02.55	CW
LI	19.05.51-07.06.51	CW	**5074**			HG	14.07.47-19.09.47	CW	HG	08.01.57-02.02.57	CW
HG	28.03.53-05.05.53	CW	HS	28.10.36-16.11.36		LI	19.05.49-09.06.49	CW	LC	06.11.57-21.12.57	CW
LC-E	14.12.53-07.01.54	CW	HS	11.01.38-26.01.38		LI	04.09.50-02.10.50	CW	HI	21.09.59-30.10.59	CW
HI	05.03.55-01.04.55	CW	HG	12.08.38-16.09.38		LC	12.03.51-04.01.51	CW	HG	18.01.62-02.03.62	CW
LC-E	09.09.55-05.10.55	CW	LS	16.04.40-30.04.40		HG	08.03.52-15.05.52	CW	NC-R	09.04.62-19.04.62	CW
LC-E	29.10.55-19.11.55	CW	HG	25.07.41-14.08.41		HI	26.07.54-20.08.54	CW	LI	30.12.64-23.01.65	CW
HG	30.07.57-05.09.57	CW	LO	03.04.42-18.04.42		LC	30.08.55-30.09.55	CW			
HI	14.10.59-13.11.59	CW	HS	19.04.43-05.05.43		HG	12.11.56-20.12.56	CW	**5077**		
LI	28.03.61-03.05.61	CW	LS	05.09.44-20.09.44		LC-E	22.02.57-19.03.57	CW	LO	04.04.35-29.04.35	
HG	07.11.63-16.12.63	CW	HG	25.06.45-20.08.45		LI	12.12.58-08.01.59	CW	LS	17.04.36-12.05.36	
			LS	16.10.47-29.11.47	CW	LC-E	08.08.59-06.10.59	CW	LO	29.05.37-04.06.37	
5073			LO	02.06.48-03.07.48	CW	NC-E	23.11.60-15.12.60	CW	HS	16.06.37-14.07.37	
LS	29.09.36-16.10.36		HO	13.09.48-19.10.48	CW	HI	07.06.61-29.07.61	CW	HG	26.09.38-04.11.38	
LO	04.06.37-17.06.37		HG	10.08.49-12.10.49	CW	G	07.02.64-28.03.64	CW	HG	09.08.40-24.08.40	
HG	15.02.38-19.04.38		LI	31.07.51-25.08.51	CW				HG	26.10.42-14.11.42	
LS	27.10.39-18.11.39		HG	02.10.52-05.11.52	CW	**5076**			LS	14.08.44-02.09.44	
LO	05.03.41-12.03.41		LI	27.08.54-22.09.54		LS	08.06.36-24.06.36		LO	08.12.45-12.01.46	
HG	28.07.41-23.08.41		HG	07.08.56-17.09.56		HS	13.07.37-09.08.37		LS	11.07.46-17.08.46	
LO	17.09.42-30.09.42		NC-R	26.09.56-10.10.56	CW	HG	05.12.38-10.01.39		HG	23.01.48-06.03.48	CW

Engine no /type.	Date of repair	Works
5077		
LI	31.03.50-25.04.50	CW
LI	13.02.52-13.03.52	HW
HG	21.10.53-21.11.53	CW
LC-E	17.01.55-15.02.55	CW
HI	11.04.56-14.05.56	CW
LC-E	11.03.57-06.04.57	CW
HG	14.10.58-13.11.58	CW
LC-E	17.08.59-23.10.59	GN
LI	07.11.60-09.12.60	CW
NC-E	20.09.61-11.10.61	CW
HI	22.01.63-15.02.63	CW
5078		
LS	28.11.35-23.12.35	
HS	23.03.37-13.04.37	
HG	27.07.38-25.08.38	
HS	15.07.40-31.07.40	
LS	07.10.41-25.10.41	
HG	05.06.43-19.06.43	
LO	18.10.43-05.11.43	
LS	19.08.44-01.09.44	
HS	07.12.45-05.01.46	
HG	02.07.47-26.08.47	CW
HG	28.01.49-09.04.49	HW
N.R	07.05.49-13.05.49	HW
LI	30.11.50-05.01.51	RY
HI	27.03.52-25.04.52	CW
HG	18.11.53-19.12.53	CW
LC-E	10.08.54-25.08.54	CW
LI	28.05.56-23.06.56	CW
HG	01.09.58-03.10.58	CW
HI	04.07.60-23.08.60	CW
LC-E	10.04.61-13.05.61	CW
5079		
LS	23.04.36-14.05.36	
LO	25.01.37-01.02.37	
HS	03.04.37-11.05.37	
HG	26.05.38-13.07.38	
HS	26.03.40-12.04.40	
HS	01.04.41-22.04.41	
LS	18.03.42-25.04.42	
LS	23.03.43-10.04.43	
LO	19.10.43-11.11.43	
LS	26.06.44-15.07.44	
LO	20.02.45-03.03.45	
LO	25.04.45-12.05.45	
HG	25.08.45-15.09.45	
LS	25.11.47-17.01.48	HW
NC	17.03.48-06.05.48	HW
LO	26.08.48-25.09.48	CW
HG	12.01.50-16.02.50	CW
TO	17.02.50-03.03.50	CW
HI	01.01.52-26.01.52	HW
HI	29.07.53-29.08.53	CW
LC-E	10.08.54-03.09.54	CW
HG	10.03.55-07.05.55	CW
LI	25.05.57-21.06.57	CW
LI	27.12.58-24.01.59	CW
HI	27.02.61-08.04.61	CW
HC	08.05.62-26.05.62	CW
Int	18.11.64-12.12.64	CS
5080		
LS	02.03.36-17.03.36	
LO	04.08.36-07.08.36	
HS	17.03.37-16.04.37	
LO	28.09.37-02.10.37	
HO	26.11.37-22.12.37	
HG	10.06.38-04.08.38	
LS	05.04.40-22.04.40	
HS	01.02.41-22.02.41	
LS	23.09.42-14.10.42	
LS	25.11.43-18.12.43	

Engine no /type.	Date of repair	Works
5080		
HG	10.01.45-27.01.45	
HS	09.04.47-26.05.47	RY
LO	08.04.48-21.05.48	CW
LS	08.12.48-31.12.48	CW
HG	03.05.50-08.06.50	CW
LI	30.01.52-20.02.52	HW
HI	28.04.53-01.06.53	CW
HC	02.04.54-10.05.54	CW
HG	16.07.55-20.08.55	CW
LI	29.01.57-22.02.57	CW
LI	10.09.58-13.10.58	CW
HC	10.08.59-26.09.59	CW
NC-E	05.12.60-17.01.61	CW
HG	30.05.61-26.06.61	CW
Int	01.04.64-07.05.64	CW
NC	01.02.65-09.03.66	CW
5081		
LO	13.11.35-21.11.35	
LS	18.03.36-28.03.36	
LS	04.03.37-26.03.37	
LS	23.02.38-07.03.38	
HO	12.09.38-04.10.38	
LS	15.09.39-23.10.39	
HS	23.07.40-10.08.40	
HO	05.02.41-15.03.41	
LO	09.10.41-14.10.41	
LS	21.01.42-28.02.42	
LS	15.12.42-22.01.43	
LS	23.08.43-25.09.43	
LO	07.02.44-14.02.44	
HG	31.07.44-24.08.44	
LO	24.01.45-15.02.45	
LS	21.04.45-29.08.45	
LS	03.06.46-05.04.46	
LS	07.01.48-05.02.48	
LO	11.03.48-10.04.48	
G	01.08.49-17.09.49	
LI	24.01.51-17.02.51	SR
NC-R	07.03.51-09.03.51	SR
NC-R	22.03.51-23.03.51	SR
HI	09.09.52-11.10.52	SR
LC	12.11.52-07.12.52	S
LC	09.02.53-06.03.53	SR
G	28.08.53-31.10.53	SR
LC	19.11.53-20.11.53	SR
LC-E	08.03.54-20.03.54	SR
LI	31.03.55-23.04.55	SR
NC-E	06.05.55-11.05.55	SR
LI	10.07.56-24.08.56	SR
LC-E	15.04.57-24.04.57	SR
NC-E	20.05.57-30.05.57	SR
HI	15.07.57-17.08.57	SR
NC-E	03.10.57	SR
LC-E	13.03.58-26.03.58	SR
LC-E	11.06.58-12.06.58	SR
HG	29.01.59-21.02.59	SR
NC-E	25.02.59-26.02.59	SR
LC-E	04.05.60-14.05.60	SR
LI	27.07.60-26.08.60	SR
5082		
LO	14.10.35-28.10.35	
LS	18.12.36-12.01.37	
LS	26.04.37-20.05.37	
LS	03.05.38-12.05.38	
HG	21.04.39-26.05.39	
LS	03.06.40-03.07.40	
LS	29.03.41-19.04.41	
HG	25.02.42-24.04.52	
LS	18.12.42-09.01.43	
HG	31.12.43-05.02.44	
LO	21.02.44-07.03.44	
HS	24.04.44-26.05.44	

Engine no /type.	Date of repair	Works
5082		
LS	11.01.45-22.02.45	
LO	31.03.45-12.05.45	
LS	08.10.46-09.11.46	
HG	13.01.48-07.02.48	
HI	25.02.49-26.03.49	
HI	24.07.50-01.09.50	
LC	19.03.51-18.04.51	SR
G	31.01.52-02.04.52	SR
HI	30.11.52-26.12.52	SR
LC	11.08.53-29.09.53	SR
HI	01.06.54-03.07.54	CW
LC-E	19.07.54-25.08.54	SR
G	06.12.56-28.12.56	SR
LI	19.12.58-10.01.59	SR
HI	12.12.60-21.01.61	SR
G	13.03.62-12.04.62	SR
LC	22.04.63-17.05.63	CW
LC-E	05.08.64-14.08.64	CS
5083		
LO	14.10.35-29.10.35	
LS	27.11.36-19.12.36	
LO	24.04.37-03.05.39	
LO	30.11.37-24.12.37	
LS	10.10.38-02.11.38	
LO	11.11.38-02.12.38	
HG	26.10.39-01.12.39	
LS	01.07.40-13.07.40	
LS	03.05.41-04.06.41	
HG	14.04.42-16.05.42	CW
LS	27.11.42-30.12.42	
HS	11.10.43-06.11.43	
LO	28.11.43-30.11.43	
HS	28.08.44-06.10.44	
LS	30.08.45-27.09.45	
LS	11.09.46-16.10.46	
HG	23.02.48-20.03.48	SR
NC-R	06.04.48-07.04.48	SR
HI	15.02.49-19.03.49	SR
HI	28.09.50-28.10.50	SR
HI	23.04.52-14.08.52	SR
HI	18.05.53-20.06.53	SR
LI-E	27.07.54-26.08.54	SR
LC-T	16.11.54	SR
HI	14.12.55-12.01.56	SR
LC	19.09.56-13.10.56	SR
LI	24.12.56-19.01.57	SR
LC-E	26.02.57-16.03.57	SR
G	22.02.58-18.04.58	SR
LC-E	08.09.58-25.09.58	SR
LI	04.07.59-08.08.59	SR
NC-E	20.08.59	SR
LI	06.06.61-01.07.61	SR
HG	31.12.62-29.01.63	CW
LC	29.05.64-12.06.64	CS
LC	22.07.66-19.08.66	CW
5084		
LS	23.09.36-14.10.36	
LO	05.05.37-13.05.37	
LS	26.10.37-17.11.37	
HS	10.10.38-28.10.38	
LO	14.11.38-28.11.38	
HG	25.03.39-26.04.39	
LS	12.01.40-03.02.40	
HS	05.03.41-02.04.41	
LS	13.01.42-18.02.42	
HG	20.03.42-20.05.42	
LS	11.01.43-06.02.43	
LS	02.12.43-15.01.44	
LO	22.02.44-01.04.44	
HS	17.02.45-17.03.45	
HG	06.05.46-05.06.46	
HS	06.06.47-16.07.47	

Engine no /type.	Date of repair	Works
5084		
LO	21.06.48-10.07.48	
LI	04.05.49-11.06.49	
HG	19.06.50-12.08.50	SR
NC	26.08.50-31.08.50	SR
LI	11.09.51-06.10.51	SR
HI	17.12.52-17.01.53	SR
LC	02.05.53-16.05.53	SR
NC-E	03.08.53-06.08.53	SR
LC-E	12.08.53-22.08.53	SR
LC-E	08.09.53-23.09.53	SR
LC-E	12.10.53-24.10.53	SR
LC-E	15.02.54-06.04.54	SR
G	04.09.54-10.11.54	SR
LC	17.03.55-24.03.55	SR
LC-E	12.04.55-20.04.55	SR
LC-E	07.09.55-16.09.55	SR
LC-E	30.01.56-18.02.56	SR
LC	21.05.56-04.07.56	SR
HI	15.01.57-07.02.57	SR
LC	26.03.58-03.04.58	SR
LC-E	16.04.58-26.04.58	SR
HI	20.08.58-12.09.58	SR
LC-E	23.10.58-30.10.58	SR'
LC-E	30.04.59-09.05.59	SR
NC-E	23.06.59-26.06.59	SR
NC-E	25.09.59-03.10.59	SR
NC-E	28.12.59-08.01.60	SR
LC-E	08.03.60-17.03.60	SR
LC-E	29.03.60-07.04.60	SR
LC-E	19.04.60-13.05.60	SR
LC-E	13.06.60-24.06.60	SR
G	04.07.60-26.08.60	SR
LC-E	28.08.61-05.09.61	SR
LC-E	19.10.61-27.10.61	SR
LC-E	02.05.62-10.05.62	SR
LI	23.08.62-22.09.62	SR
LC	19.06.63-04.07.63	SR
LC-E	09.10.63-09.11.63	SR
LI	11.11.64-25.12.64	IE
NC-T	18.02.65	CS
LC-E	19.01.66-05.02.66	CS
5085		
LS	18.08.36-09.09.36	
LO	19.05.37-26.05.37	
LS	15.10.37-04.11.37	
LS	21.12.38-12.01.39	
HG	08.03.39-14.09.39	
HS	20.05.40-05.06.40	
LS	16.06.41-22.07.41	
HG	01.06.42-14.07.42	
HG	19.05.43-01.07.43	
LS	07.02.44-21.03.44	
LS	07.12.44-06.01.45	
HG	08.02.46-07.03.46	
LS	07.02.47-13.03.47	
LO	16.10.47-28.11.47	
HS	31.05.48-12.07.48	
NC-R	16.08.48-18.08.48	
LI	03.05.49-11.06.49	
G	09.02.50-22.04.50	SR
LC	02.08.50-08.08.50	SR
LC-E	23.12.50-03.02.51	SR
LI	28.12.51-19.01.52	SR
LC-E	01.02.52-13.02.52	SR
LC-E	11.10.52-12.11.52	SR
HI	25.04.53-23.05.53	SR
LC-E	30.06.53-11.07.53	SR
G	16.08.54-02.10.54	SR
LC-E	26.12.55-07.01.56	SR
HI	15.09.56-13.10.56	SR
NC	31.10.56-02.11.56	SR
LC-E	05.09.57-10.09.57	SR
HI	14.10.57-29.11.57	IS

Engine no 5180

/type.	Date of repair	Works
5180		
LO	29.04.42-20.05.42	
LS	18.10.42-14.11.42	
LS	12.12.43-20.01.44	
HG	28.04.45-19.05.45	
LS	17.12.46-18.01.47	
HS	06.10.47-02.12.47	
HG	25.03.49-13.04.49	CW
LI	08.09.50-29.09.50	CW
HI	23.07.52-30.08.52	SR
G	06.01.54-05.02.54	CW
HI	04.11.55-23.11.55	CW
LC-E	30.08.56-28.09.56	CW
LI	26.01.58-15.02.58	CW
HG	11.08.59-16.09.59	CW
LI	26.08.61-30.09.61	CW
NC	30.09.61-06.10.61	CW
LI	31.10.62-28.11.62	CW
5181		
LS	01.06.36-15.07.36	
LO	01.07.37-22.07.37	
HG	01.04.38-31.05.38	
LS	13.10.39-03.11.39	
LS	05.10.40-09.11.40	
LS	08.01.42-27.01.42	
HG	11.05.43-27.05.43	
LO	10.05.44-24.05.44	
LS	07.05.46-28.05.46	
HG	22.04.48-20.05.48	CW
HI	04.02.50-25.02.50	CW
LC	30.10.50-24.11.50	CW
HG	10.07.51-11.08.51	CW
HI	31.01.53-26.02.53	CW
LC-E	14.08.53-04.09.53	CW

Engine no 5181

/type.	Date of repair	Works
5181		
HG	25.11.54-23.12.54	CW
LC	18.06.55-23.07.55	CW
HI	04.08.56-30.08.56	CW
LI	18.12.57-11.01.58	CW
LI	20.12.58-23.01.59	CW
HC	29.11.59-22.01.60	CW
LC-E	19.07.60-19.08.60	CW
HG	23.08.61-29.09.61	CW
5182		
LO	15.04.36-08.05.36	
LS	05.11.36-20.11.36	
HS	29.09.37-28.10.37	
HG	24.02.38-04.04.38	
LO	27.09.38-25.10.38	
HS	31.01.39-06.03.39	
LO	17.08.39-02.09.39	
HS	03.08.40-04.09.40	
LO	09.12.40-06.01.41	
HG	07.01.42-20.02.42	
LS	19.06.43-03.07.43	
LS	23.07.45-25.08.45	
LO	26.04.46-23.05.46	
HG	21.02.47-15.03.47	CW
LS	02.10.48-21.10.48	CW
LI	25.07.50-15.08.50	CW
LC	01.03.51-20.03.51	CW
HG	23.06.52-29.08.52	CW
HI	14.06.54-05.08.54	RY
HG	12.12.55-11.01.56	CW
HI	13.02.58-07.03.58	CW
HG	21.10.59-12.12.59	CW
HI	17.04.61-27.05.61	CW

Engine no 5183

/type.	Date of repair	Works
5183		
LO	15.06.36-05.07.36	
LS	05.01.37-18.01.37	
LO	06.11.37-22.11.37	
HG	18.08.38-12.10.38	
LS	29.12.39-10.01.40	
LS	21.08.41-06.09.41	
HG	19.12.42-23.01.43	
LO	09.02.43-06.03.43	
LS	29.11.44-14.12.44	
LS	09.08.46-07.09.46	
HG	06.11.47-22.12.47	
HI	13.06.49-22.07.49	
LC	03.06.50-30.06.50	
HI	01.03.51-29.03.51	CW
LC	19.06.51-17.07.51	CW
LC	05.12.51-20.12.51	SR
G	10.04.52-18.07.52	SR
LC	13.01.53-04.03.53	SR
HI	07.09.53-09.10.53	SR
HI	15.01.55-25.02.55	IS
G	10.10.56-03.11.56	SR
HI	18.06.58-12.07.58	SR
NC-E	29.01.59-04.02.59	SR
NC-E	29.06.59-02.07.59	SR
G	01.03.61-06.05.61	SR
LC-E	08.05.61-19.05.61	SR
LC	15.03.63-20.03.63	SR
NC	26.03.63-28.03.63	SR
LI	29.06.64-06.08.64	CS
NC	14.08.64	CS
5184		
LS	18.01.37-04.02.37	
HS	27.11.37-13.12.37	
HO	23.02.38-19.04.38	

Engine no 5184

/type.	Date of repair	Works
5184		
LO	10.08.38-09.09.38	
LS	30.10.39-14.11.39	
HG	26.05.41-11.06.41	
LO	14.10.41-24.10.41	
LS	03.10.42-27.10.42	
LO	03.03.43-20.03.43	
LO	17.08.43-03.09.43	
HS	14.03.44-29.03.44	
HG	26.10.45-30.11.45	
LS	05.06.47-05.07.47	HW
LS	15.06.48-22.07.48	CW
LO	02.09.48-12.10.48	SR
LC	13.04.49-29.04.49	CW
HG	13.06.50-25.07.50	CW
HI	13.08.51-01.09.51	CW
HG	03.03.53-26.03.53	CW
LI	12.05.54-31.05.54	CW
LI	28.11.55-28.12.55	CW
HG	15.10.57-26.11.57	CW
LC-E	21.11.58-04.12.58	RY
HI	18.05.59-12.06.59	CW
HI	21.01.61-17.02.61	CW
LI	07.08.62-01.09.62	CW
HI	18.06.64-18.07.64	CS
5185		
LO	01.04.36-07.05.36	
LS	03.12.36-17.12.36	
LO	28.05.37-07.06.37	
HG	17.10.38-02.12.38	
LS	29.04.40-11.05.40	
LS	23.02.42-11.03.42	
LO	06.06.42-17.07.42	
HG	14.08.43-28.08.43	
LS	29.01.45-08.03.45	

5188 at its home shed, Patricroft, on 3rd May 1949 had only riveted tenders and domed boilers since 1938, replacing its original welded tender and domeless boiler. It was one of a small number of Class 5s to be repainted in 1936 livery but had lost this, possibly during the war, replaced with plain black with high 12" cab numbers. 5188 was renumbered as 45188 in July 1949 during a Heavy Intermediate overhaul at Crewe.

Cooper's Railway Photographs

Engine no /type.	Date of repair	Works
5185		
LS	12.02.47-19.03.47	CW
HG	21.07.48-21.08.48	CW
LI	12.05.50-06.06.50	CW
LI	05.06.51-27.06.51	CW
HC	30.10.51-24.11.51	CW
HG	26.08.53-26.09.53	CW
HI	20.08.55-10.09.55	CW
LC-E	28.02.56-28.03.56	CW
HC	25.10.56-24.11.56	CW
HG	25.07.57-13.09.57	CW
NC-E	24.03.58-17.04.58	CW
LC-E	19.08.58-30.09.58	CW
NC-E	03.03.59-12.03.59	CW
HI	16.03.60-29.04.60	CW
LC-E	20.07.60-27.08.60	CW
LC-E	07.02.61-10.03.61	CW
LC-E	19.06.61-29.07.61	CW
5186		
LS	31.10.36-11.12.36	
LO	24.06.37-16.07.37	
HG	16.02.38-21.03.38	
HS	23.06.39-29.07.39	
HG	22.04.41-13.05.41	
LS	16.07.42-08.08.42	
HS	08.03.43-13.04.43	
LO	21.01.44-15.02.44	
LS	24.10.44-10.11.44	
HG	31.12.45-23.01.46	
LS	02.06.47-28.07.47	CW
HS	12.09.48-02.10.48	CW
LC	15.09.49-24.10.49	CW
HG	08.05.50-25.05.50	CW

Engine no /type.	Date of repair	Works
5186		
LI	14.02.52-13.03.52	CW
LI	17.04.53-16.05.53	CW
HG	25.06.54-19.08.54	CW
HI	21.05.56-13.06.56	CW
LC-E	08.11.56-21.11.56	RY
HG	11.03.58-08.05.58	CW
LC-E	23.03.59-15.04.39	RY
LI	15.04.60-10.06.60	CW
5187		
LS	17.10.36-04.11.36	
LO	20.04.37-01.05.37	
LS	03.07.37-18.08.37	
LO	12.11.37-06.12.37	
HG	12.04.38-13.06.38	
HS	10.05.39-06.06.39	
HS	24.05.40-13.06.40	
HG	30.10.41-11.12.41	
LS	07.10.42-24.10.42	
LS	22.04.44-11.05.44	
HG	28.05.45-13.06.45	
HS	06.08.46-28.08.46	
LO	27.06.47-04.07.47	S
LS	04.02.48-02.03.48	CW
LO	18.10.48-11.11.48	CW
HG	26.07.49-10.09.49	CW
LI	13.04.51-04.05.51	CW
LI	18.06.52-26.07.52	CW
HG	02.11.53-04.12.53	CW
LC-E	28.07.54-13.08.54	RY
HI	27.08.55-23.09.55	CW
LC	31.07.56-18.08.56	CW
HG	03.08.57-31.08.57	CW

Engine no /type.	Date of repair	Works
5187		
LC-E	03.10.58-24.10.58	CW
NC-E	10.02.59-16.02.59	CW
LI	09.11.59-01.01.60	CW
HG	07.08.62-07.09.62	CW
5188		
HO	16.03.36-14.04.36	
LS	28.09.36-26.10.36	
LO	24.05.37-25.06.37	
HG	29.11.37-11.02.38	
LO	10.08.38-27.08.38	
LS	22.11.38-14.12.38	
LO	17.02.39-24.03.39	
LS	17.07.39-15.08.39	
HG	10.06.40-27.07.40	
LS	17.04.41-10.05.41	
LO	16.12.41-14.01.42	
LS	02.08.42-02.09.42	
HG	10.01.44-24.01.44	
LS	09.02.46-23.02.46	
HG	17.07.47-30.08.47	CW
HI	28.06.49-28.07.49	CW
HG	19.04.51-26.05.51	CW
LI	20.05.53-19.06.53	RY
HG	07.02.55-12.03.55	CW
HI	09.02.57-02.03.57	CW
LI	01.04.59-24.04.59	CW
LC	11.05.59-19.05.59	HW
LC-E	08.01.60-19.02.60	CW
HG	23.10.61-22.11.61	CW
Int	11.02.64-07.03.64	CS

Engine no /type.	Date of repair	Works
5189		
LS	09.01.37-25.01.37	
HS	29.08.37-12.10.37	
HG	15.02.39-28.03.39	
LS	22.05.40-01.06.40	
LO	14.07.41-09.08.41	
LS	11.03.42-22.04.42	
LO	02.05.42-16.05.42	
HG	14.05.43-28.05.43	
LO	16.10.43-06.11.43	
LS	07.07.45-18.08.45	
HG	26.07.47-12.09.47	CW
HI	28.07.49-27.08.49	CW
HI	28.08.50-06.10.50	CW
HG	20.06.52-12.08.52	CW
LI	17.11.53-12.12.53	CW
HI	29.04.55-26.05.55	CW
HG	16.10.56-06.12.56	CW
HI	31.07.58-05.09.58	CW
HNC-E	10.03.59-18.03.59	CW
LC-E	07.05.59-19.06.59	CW
LI	12.04.60-27.05.60	CW
HI	30.05.61-31.07.61	CW
HG	08.12.62-16.01.63	CW
5190		
LS	07.11.36-19.11.36	
LO	28.04.37-13.05.37	
HG	21.04.38-22.06.38	
LS	03.02.40-15.02.40	
HG	12.02.42-06.03.42	
HS	14.01.44-29.01.44	
HO	09.05.44-23.05.44	
LS	27.09.45-20.10.45	

Armstrong Whitworth-built 45192 in front of the distinctive water tower covered with dressed stone at Inverness in July 1955. It had moved up to 60A during the war from Newton Heath and remained there until transferred to Perth in July 1960. As with other engines working from the Highland shed, it has holes for the attachment of a snowplough and fixing brackets below the bufferbeam. It was paired with several riveted tenders between 1943 and 1957 before reverting to a welded type. The cab has the large 10" cab numbers used by St. Rollox for several years following nationalisation.

Real Photographs

Engine no 5190

/type.	Date of repair	Works
HG	09.06.47-01.08.47	CW
LS	13.11.48-06.12.48	CW
HG	21.04.50-25.05.50	CW
LI	28.10.51-09.11.51	RY
LC	28.01.52-20.02.52	CW
HC	23.08.52-26.09.52	CW
HG	19.03.54-21.04.54	CW
LI	28.09.55-22.10.55	CW
HI	20.05.57-13.06.57	CW
HG	01.01.59-21.02.59	CW
HI	17.01.61-03.03.61	CW
LC	18.10.61-30.11.61	CW
LI	10.06.63-27.06.63	CW
Int	21.06.65-09.08.65	CW

5191

/type.	Date of repair	Works
LS	13.12.36-04.01.37	
LO	04.06.37-17.06.37	
HG	13.01.38-10.02.38	
LS	11.03.40-28.03.40	
HG	14.01.42-02.02.42	
HS	04.05.44-19.05.44	
LO	12.07.44-21.07.44	
HG	18.06.45-21.07.45	CW
LS	03.10.46-19.11.46	CW
HS	05.01.48-19.02.48	CW
LI	15.03.49-28.04.49	RY
LI	17.06.50-20.07.50	CW
HG	15.11.51-22.12.51	CW
LI	21.03.53-29.04.53	RY
HI	06.03.54-01.04.54	CW
HG	26.08.55-28.09.55	CW
LC-E	18.09.56-05.10.56	RY
LC	26.10.56-01.12.56	CW
HI	21.09.57-17.10.57	CW
LI	28.10.58-28.11.58	CW
NC-E	12.02.59-18.02.59	CW
LC-E	18.08.59-03.09.59	DY
HC	15.02.60-13.04.60	CW
HG	31.07.61-12.09.61	CW
LI	28.08.64-10.10.64	CW

5192

/type.	Date of repair	Works
LO	05.05.36-18.05.36	
HG	02.02.38-14.03.38	
HS	28.03.40-20.04.40	
LS	13.05.42-30.06.42	
HS	01.03.43-02.04.43	
HG	03.02.44-14.03.44	
LS	25.01.45-03.03.45	
LS	23.02.46-18.04.46	
HS	31.05.47-08.07.47	
LS	12.05.48-03.07.48	
NC-R	06.07.48	
NC	17.07.48-02.08.48	
HI	02.06.49-12.07.49	
LC	11.03.50-07.04.50	
HI	07.09.50-13.10.50	
G	15.01.52-16.02.52	SR
HNC-T	21.02.52	SR
NC-T	27.02.52-29.02.52	SR
LI	28.02.53-28.03.53	IS
HI	05.03.54-17.04.54	IS
LI	22.04.55-27.05.55	IS
NC-E	06.08.55-09.08.55	IS
NC-E	17.03.56-27.03.56	IS
G	08.09.56-06.10.56	SR
NC-E	17.10.56-18.10.56	SR
LC-E	15.01.57-08.02.57	SR
HI	09.11.57-30.11.57	SR
NC-E	12.05.58-19.05.58	IS
LI	06.12.58-29.01.59	IS
NC-E	07.07.59-17.07.59	IE
HI	04.06.60-09.07.60	SR

5192

/type.	Date of repair	Works
LC	12.05.61-09.06.61	SR
G	23.05.62-23.06.62	SR
LC-E	30.01.63-12.02.63	SR
NC	04.03.65-10.03.65	CS

5193

/type.	Date of repair	Works
LS	27.11.36-17.12.36	
LO	03.05.37-20.05.37	
LO	18.08.37-01.10.37	
LO	21.04.38-29.04.38	
HG	13.08.38-16.09.38	
LS	06.03.40-11.04.40	
LS	11.02.41-27.02.41	
HG	21.10.42-26.11.42	
LO	28.12.42-23.01.43	
HS	11.04.44-26.04.44	
HS	19.06.45-28.07.45	
HS	06.07.46-20.08.46	
HG	15.11.47-10.01.48	CW
HI	25.06.49-28.07.49	CW
HI	30.12.50-19.01.51	CW
HG	07.07.52-29.08.52	CW
HC	11.12.52-17.01.53	CW
LI	20.02.54-12.03.54	CW
HG	18.02.56-17.03.56	CW
HI	12.02.58-08.03.58	CW
NC-E	28.04.60-10.05.60	CW
HG	25.07.60-27.08.60	CW
LI	20.06.62-25.07.62	CW
LI	30.12.64-21.01.65	CW

5194

/type.	Date of repair	Works
LS	14.10.36-31.10.36	
LS	27.10.37-11.11.37	
LO	19.09.38-30.09.38	
HG	03.02.39-16.03.39	
LS	21.03.40-18.04.40	
LS	24.02.41-15.03.41	
HO	22.04.41-08.05.41	
LS	22.05.42-18.07.42	
LO	16.01.43-13.02.43	
HG	21.12.43-22.01.44	
LS	18.12.44-27.01.45	
LO	15.10.45-23.11.45	
HS	01.08.46-11.09.46	
LO	06.06.47-17.07.47	
HG	16.02.48-18.03.48	SR
HI	19.04.49-18.05.49	SR
HI	06.01.50-11.02.50	SR
LC	13.04.50-17.05.50	SR
HI	02.07.51-11.08.51	SR
LC-E	01.01.52-22.01.52	SR
NC-E	11.07.52-08.08.52	SR
G	05.02.53-28.03.53	SR
LI	04.08.54-28.08.54	SR
NC-E	05.05.55-21.05.55	SR
HI	20.07.56-18.08.56	SR
LC-E	03.06.57-14.06.57	SR
G	22.02.58-21.03.58	SR
LI	06.06.59-27.06.59	CS
NC-E	03.08.59-12.08.59	CS
LI	23.03.61-21.04.61	SR
G	24.04.62-25.05.62	SR
LC	05.11.63-15.11.63	SR
NC-T	27.11.63-28.11.63	SR
LI	19.03.64-17.04.64	IE
LC	03.03.65-26.03.65	CS

5195

/type.	Date of repair	Works
LS	02.10.36-16.10.36	
LO	19.02.37-25.03.37	
HG	18.05.38-02.07.38	
LS	20.10.39-18.11.39	
LO	27.02.40-09.03.40	

5195

/type.	Date of repair	Works
LO	14.08.40-14.09.40	
HG	25.02.41-24.03.41	
LS	04.11.42-01.12.42	
HS	10.07.44-29.07.44	
HG	15.09.45-15.10.45	
LS	13.08.47-09.10.47	RY
LO	12.06.48-03.07.48	CW
LI	30.03.49-20.04.49	CW
HG	13.04.50-05.06.50	CW
NC-R	06.06.50-17.06.50	CW
HI	03.01.52-23.02.52	CW
LC-E	02.10.52-24.10.52	CW
LC-E	23.05.53-13.06.53	CW
LI	05.01.54-04.02.54	CW
HG	20.06.55-30.07.55	CW
HI	30.07.57-17.08.57	CW
LC-E	06.09.58-08.10.58	RY
HI	11.03.59-14.04.59	CW
HG	29.03.60-28.05.60	CW
LC-E	17.11.60-17.12.60	CW
HI	25.05.62-15.06.62	CW
LI	12.05.64-06.06.64	CS

5196

/type.	Date of repair	Works
LS	19.11.36-12.12.36	
LO	24.05.37-03.06.37	
HG	15.09.38-20.10.38	
LS	16.05.40-20.05.40	
LS	18.04.41-10.05.41	
HG	15.02.42-07.03.42	
HS	22.05.43-05.06.43	
LO	25.09.44-07.10.44	
HS	13.02.45-02.03.45	
HS	28.09.46-15.10.46	
LS	29.10.47-24.11.47	CW
HG	20.08.48-08.10.48	CW
LC	14.06.49-02.07.49	CW
LI	11.12.50-26.01.51	RY
HC	14.09.51-19.10.51	CW
LI	31.12.51-30.01.52	CW
NC-R	04.02.52-09.02.52	CW
LC	14.01.53-14.02.53	CW
HG	12.01.54-13.02.54	CW
HI	05.03.56-06.04.56	CW
HI	18.05.57-11.06.57	CW
LC-E	10.02.58-14.03.58	CW
LC-E	07.05.58-10.06.58	CW
HG	04.03.59-09.05.59	CW
LC-E	18.05.59-29.05.59	HW
LI	17.03.61-24.04.61	CW
LI	27.11.62-29.12.62	CW
HC	23.05.63-14.06.63	CW
LI	11.03.65-03.04.65	CS

5197

/type.	Date of repair	Works
HS	27.10.36-10.11.36	
LO	16.07.37-30.07.37	
HG	25.04.38-13.06.38	
LS	16.09.39-30.09.39	
HG	21.07.41-07.08.41	
LO	05.10.41-01.11.41	
HO	07.05.42-06.06.42	
HS	28.05.43-12.06.43	
LS	27.05.44-13.06.44	
LO	17.06.44-20.07.44	
LO	14.08.45-19.09.45	
HG	10.10.46-11.11.46	CW
HS	20.12.47-31.01.48	CW
HI	31.10.49-17.11.49	CW
HI	17.03.51-16.04.51	CW
HG	14.04.52-17.06.52	CW
LI-E	20.12.52-15.01.53	CW
LI	14.08.54-14.09.54	CW
HG	14.09.55-15.10.55	CW

5197

/type.	Date of repair	Works
LC-E	10.09.56-11.10.56	CW
LI	18.04.57-24.05.57	CW
LI	16.05.58-13.06.58	CW
NC-E	29.09.59-13.10.59	CW
HI	15.10.59-13.11.59	CW
HG	28.03.60-14.05.60	CW
HI	23.10.61-01.12.61	CW
LI	11.02.64-11.03.64	CW

5198

/type.	Date of repair	Works
LS	12.11.36-26.11.36	
LO	06.05.37-30.05.37	
HG	28.02.38-05.05.38	
LS	24.02.40-08.03.40	
HG	23.07.42-15.08.42	
HS	08.06.44-21.06.44	
HS	12.10.45-10.11.45	
HG	04.09.47-12.11.47	CW
LI	09.11.49-24.12.49	CW
HC	05.01.50-20.01.50	CW
LC	02.10.50-19.10.50	CW
LC	02.12.50-30.12.50	CW
HG	06.08.51-06.09.51	CW
HI	04.09.52-01.10.52	CW
NC-R	02.10.52-11.10.52	CW
LC-E	23.05.53-11.06.53	CW
HG	07.04.54-11.05.54	CW
LC-E	02.06.55-22.06.55	CW
HI	24.02.57-03.04.57	CW
HI	27.04.58-12.06.58	CW
NC-E	23.04.59-06.05.59	CW
LC	08.05.59-25.05.59	GN
HG	01.02.61-15.03.61	CW

5199

/type.	Date of repair	Works
HS	22.02.37-07.04.37	
HG	26.08.38-11.10.38	
LS	03.04.40-18.04.40	
HG	21.05.42-04.07.42	
HS	06.01.44-22.01.44	
HS	09.12.44-06.01.45	
LS	19.06.46-20.07.46	
HG	13.03.47-14.04.47	CW
HS	17.11.48-10.12.48	RY
LI	11.08.50-30.08.50	CW
HG	22.02.52-04.04.52	CW
LI	03.02.54-25.02.54	CW
NC-R	01.03.54-09.03.54	CW
HG	20.05.56-23.06.56	CW
LI	11.03.59-10.04.59	CW
HG	26.06.61-18.08.61	CW

5200

/type.	Date of repair	Works
LS	02.02.37-16.02.37	
HO	11.08.37-17.09.37	
HG	18.01.38-22.08.38	
LS	26.12.39-08.01.40	
HG	21.09.41-17.10.41	
HS	27.10.42-28.11.42	
LS	09.09.43-09.10.43	
LO	04.04.44-22.04.44	
LS	12.08.44-26.08.44	
LO	05.12.44-09.12.44	
LO	17.05.45-07.06.45	
HG	19.11.45-06.12.45	
LS	31.03.47-12.05.47	CW
LO	01.08.47-29.08.47	CW
HI	28.01.49-22.02.49	CW
HG	20.12.50-22.01.51	CW
LI	22.09.52-24.10.52	HW
LC-E	28.03.53-07.05.53	CW
LI	13.12.54-11.01.55	CW
HG	19.09.56-10.11.56	CW
LI	25.10.58-27.11.58	CW

Engine no /type.	Date of repair	Works
5200		
LC-E	29.06.59-10.07.59	HW
LI	23.01.61-02.03.61	CW
HG	23.12.63-04.03.64	CW
5201		
LS	28.10.36-01.12.36	
LO	20.08.37-17.09.37	
LO	30.09.37-13.10.37	
HG	08.02.38-08.03.38	
HS	20.04.39-01.06.39	
HG	26.03.41-19.04.41	
LS	19.08.42-18.09.42	
LS	26.10.43-08.11.43	
HG	05.08.44-24.08.44	
LS	26.09.45-13.10.45	
HG	29.08.47-28.10.47	CW
LI	31.01.49-02.03.49	CW
HI	16.05.50-14.06.50	CW
HG	31.12.51-09.02.52	CW
HI	31.12.53-26.01.54	CW
HG	21.08.56-27.09.56	CW
HI	28.08.58-02.10.58	CW
HI	28.11.60-07.01.61	CW
NC	29.11.61-15.12.61	CW
LC	02.02.62-03.03.62	CW
HG	10.09.63-16.10.63	CW
5202		
LS	04.01.37-03.02.37	
LO	20.09.37-21.10.37	
LS	05.02.38-11.04.38	
HG	08.03.39-25.04.39	
LS	27.09.40-19.10.40	
HS	21.03.42-11.04.42	
HG	28.02.43-19.03.43	
LO	28.08.43-24.09.43	
LS	28.03.44-27.04.44	
LS	25.01.45-17.02.45	
LS	06.12.45-05.01.46	
LO	08.05.46-17.05.46	
HG	05.09.47-07.11.47	CW
HO	18.11.48-11.12.48	CW
LI	22.11.49-20.12.49	CW
HG	16.07.51-25.08.51	CW
HI	21.09.53-15.10.53	CW
HG	04.08.55-31.08.55	CW
HI	10.05.57-11.06.57	CW
HG	20.08.59-06.10.59	CW
NC-E	03.03.60-11.04.60	CW
LI	05.04.62-28.04.62	CW
HI	22.06.65-10.07.65	CS
NC	27.09.65-16.10.65	CW
5203		
HS	02.03.37-19.03.37	
LO	13.12.37-02.02.38	
LS	30.08.38-19.09.38	
TO	12.07.39	
HG	28.03.40-19.04.40	
HS	04.12.41-27.12.41	
LS	15.04.43-08.05.43	
HG	12.04.44-02.05.44	
LS	01.03.46-23.03.46	
HG	16.10.47-06.12.47	CW
LI	29.06.49-03.08.49	CW
HG	12.09.51-18.10.51	CW
LI	27.10.53-14.11.53	CW
NC	05.01.54-28.01.54	CW
HG	06.10.55-15.11.55	CW
LC-E	07.03.56-21.03.56	CW
HI	03.02.58-25.02.58	CW
LC-E	29.05.58-14.06.58	CW
HG	30.05.61-01.07.61	CW
NC	20.02.62-06.03.62	CW

Engine no /type.	Date of repair	Works
5203		
HI	08.06.64-23.07.64	CW
LC	27.06.66-31.08.66	CW
5204		
HS	07.04.37-07.05.37	
HS	17.01.38-26.02.38	
HG	17.04.39-11.05.39	
HS	26.05.41-19.06.41	
HS	01.09.42-19.09.42	
LS	08.05.44-23.05.44	
HG	17.09.45-29.09.45	CW
LS	20.02.48-31.03.48	CW
NC	12.04.48-13.04.48	CW
LI	15.07.49-19.08.49	CW
HG	08.06.50-28.06.50	CW
LI	28.07.52-30.08.52	CW
HG	11.10.54-13.11.54	CW
HI	27.11.56-29.12.56	CW
LC-E	16.09.57-05.10.57	CW
LI	03.11.58-11.12.58	CW
HG	07.12.60-25.01.61	CW
LC	23.09.61-20.10.61	CW
LI	19.08.63-13.09.63	CW
Uns	15.11.65-04.12.65	CS
5205		
HS	06.04.37-05.05.37	
HO	11.10.37-19.11.37	
HG	19.12.38-19.01.39	
LS	25.06.40-09.07.40	
HS	01.09.41-25.09.41	
HS	03.03.43-23.03.43	
HG	28.11.44-09.12.44	
LS	27.09.46-07.11.46	CW
LS	21.05.48-18.06.48	CW
HG	19.07.49-31.08.49	CW
HI	11.04.51-07.05.51	HW
HI	22.09.52-25.10.52	CW
HG	12.02.54-09.03.54	CW
LI	08.10.56-31.10.56	CW
HG	18.08.58-18.09.58	CW
LC-E	27.05.59-25.07.59	CW
HI	20.02.61-08.04.61	CW
LC	06.12.62-05.01.63	CW
LI	26.09.63-05.11.63	CW
5206		
LO	21.11.36-14.12.36	
HS	24.05.37-10.06.37	
HG	20.04.38-02.06.38	
HS	20.07.39-08.08.39	
HG	19.09.40-18.10.40	
HS	20.11.42-09.01.43	
LS	15.07.44-29.07.44	
HG	11.06.45-28.06.45	CW
HS	12.08.47-04.10.47	HW
LI	08.07.49-12.08.49	CW
LC	11.05.50-01.06.50	S
HG	23.11.50-06.01.51	CW
LI	11.11.52-02.12.52	RY
HI	21.05.54-24.06.54	CW
HG	19.05.56-22.06.56	CW
LI	15.09.58-15.10.58	CW
LI	18.01.61-11.02.61	CW
NC	07.11.61-17.11.61	CW
HG	18.02.63-15.03.63	CW
LI	30.09.65-06.11.65	CW
5207		
HS	16.02.37-11.03.37	
HS	02.02.38-12.03.38	
LC	17.08.38-13.09.38	
LO	07.03.39-08.03.39	
HG	26.06.39-14.08.39	

Engine no /type.	Date of repair	Works
5207		
LS	25.02.41-18.03.41	
HG	27.11.42-02.01.43	
LS	14.02.44-10.03.44	
LO	12.09.44-16.09.44	
LS	08.08.45-31.08.45	
HG	19.03.47-28.04.47	CW
HS	01.11.48-30.11.48	CW
LI	25.04.50-11.05.50	CW
W.O	31.10.50-01.11.50	HW
W.O	24.11.50-28.11.50	HW
HG	05.11.51-13.12.51	CW
HI	15.10.53-05.11.53	CW
HG	19.01.56-01.03.56	CW
LI	21.04.58-15.05.58	CW
NC-E	04.11.60-12.11.60	CW
G	07.10.61-09.11.61	CW
Int	07.10.65-06.11.65	CS
5208		
HS	23.02.37-12.03.37	
LS	29.11.37-23.12.37	
HG	06.12.38-13.01.39	
LS	01.06.40-18.06.40	
TO	05.10.41-07.10.41	
HG	27.12.41-16.01.42	
LS	16.08.43-31.08.43	
HG	24.05.45-07.06.45	
HS	06.03.47-29.03.47	HW
LO	28.11.47-13.12.47	HW
HG	18.09.48-01.11.48	CW
LI	25.04.50-16.05.50	CW
LI	18.06.51-09.07.51	HW
HG	02.12.52-24.12.52	CW
LI	23.10.54-19.11.54	CW
HG	19.09.56-31.10.56	CW
LI	22.10.59-05.12.59	CW
NC-E	19.01.61-07.02.61	CW
G	06.01.62-15.02.62	CW
NC	29.01.66	CS
5209		
LO	13.01.36-13.02.36	
LS	27.01.37-12.02.37	
HS	28.09.37-29.10.37	
HG	24.04.39-18.05.39	
LS	20.08.40-07.09.40	
HS	26.09.41-18.10.41	
HG	01.07.43-14.08.43	
LS	04.11.44-18.11.44	
LS	04.06.46-22.06.46	
HG	16.08.47-23.10.47	CW
LI	30.04.49-31.05.49	HW
LI	08.05.51-01.06.51	HW
LC-T	30.08.51-30.08.51	S
HG	12.05.52-05.07.52	CW
HI	07.07.54-17.08.54	CW
HG	06.09.56-11.10.56	CW
LI	04.02.59-12.03.59	CW
LC-E	31.07.59-24.08.59	GN
LC	19.01.60-24.03.60	CW
NC-E	17.02.61-03.03.61	CW
HG	18.01.62-17.02.62	CW
LI	01.06.65-28.06.65	CW
5210		
LS	01.12.36-23.12.36	
LO	01.09.37-12.10.37	
HG	11.02.38-12.04.38	
LS	28.08.39-21.09.39	
HG	03.01.41-21.02.41	
LO	12.08.41-30.08.41	
HS	11.03.42-04.04.42	
LS	06.03.43-27.03.43	

Engine no /type.	Date of repair	Works
5210		
LS	06.09.44-20.09.44	
HG	03.05.45-16.06.45	
HS	16.07.47-22.08.47	CW
HO	18.10.48-19.11.48	CW
LO	24.08.49-21.09.49	CW
HG	02.12.49-24.12.49	CW
NC	28.02.50-09.03.50	CW
LI	08.06.51-04.07.51	HW
WO	27.08.51-30.08.51	HW
HI	07.05.53-06.06.53	CW
HG	16.06.55-23.07.55	CW
LI	26.10.56-14.11.56	CW
HI	14.04.58-10.05.58	CW
HG	16.07.59-27.08.59	CW
LI	15.07.60-02.09.60	CW
NC-E	03.10.61-20.10.61	CW
5211		
LS	20.01.37-08.02.37	
LO	02.09.37-16.09.37	
HG	04.03.38-21.04.38	
LS	11.03.39-12.04.39	
HG	20.02.40-20.03.40	
HS	30.08.41-20.09.41	
LS	29.10.42-28.11.42	
HG	06.03.44-29.03.44	
HS	08.10.45-26.10.45	
LS	12.06.47-28.07.47	HW
HG	19.04.49-03.06.49	CW
LI	19.06.50-25.07.50	CW
HI	07.04.52-03.06.52	HW
HC	07.01.53-04.02.53	CW
HG	12.05.54-21.06.54	CW
LC-E	20.04.55-18.05.55	CW
LI	05.06.56-02.07.56	CW
LI	02.05.58-28.05.58	CW
HG	02.05.60-10.06.60	CW
NC-E	17.11.60-26.11.60	CW
LC	06.01.62-07.02.62	CW
Int	06.12.64-09.01.65	CS
5212		
LS	08.01.37-28.01.37	
LO	23.08.37-15.09.37	
LS	16.12.37-07.01.38	
LO	12.04.38-27.04.38	
HG	06.02.39-10.03.39	
LS	24.07.40-13.08.40	
HS	06.06.42-26.06.42	
HG	22.11.43-08.12.43	
LS	07.07.45-11.08.45	
HS	12.06.47-02.08.47	HW
LO	20.09.48-10.11.48	HW
HG	10.06.49-30.07.49	CW
LI	19.12.51-15.01.52	HW
HG	17.05.54-16.06.54	CW
LI	24.01.56-18.02.56	CW
HI	18.08.58-18.09.58	CW
HC	09.09.59-30.10.59	HW
LC-E	01.05.61-23.05.61	HW
NC	04.01.62-19.01.62	CW
HI	02.11.62-30.11.62	CW
LC	07.01.63-26.01.63	CW
HI	20.12.65-29.01.66	CW
5213		
LO	13.01.36-27.02.36	
LO	22.06.36-05.08.36	
HG	05.01.38-07.02.38	
LS	15.05.39-27.05.39	
HG	10.09.40-03.10.40	
HS	15.05.42-06.06.42	
LS	25.04.43-15.05.43	

The class worked all over the country and were frequent visitors on excursion trains to resorts such as Scarborough where 45201 was being turned on 25th May 1955. It was always on the Central Division and was shedded at Wakefield from November 1951 until June 1956. It has a welded tender and a 21-element domeless boiler with missing domed covers on the firebox. *Brian Webb Collections/IRS*

Engine no /type.	Date of repair	Works
5213		
LS	22.03.44-15.04.44	
LO	28.10.44-15.11.44	
HG	10.12.45-19.01.46	
LS	03.02.47-11.03.47	
LS	25.02.48-03.04.48	
LO	22.07.48-18.09.48	
G	24.08.49-08.10.49	SR
LI	11.01.51-21.02.51	IS
NC	01.05.51-03.05.51	IS
LC	14.08.51-06.09.51	SR
LC-E	28.11.51-08.12.51	SR
LC-T	19.12.51	SR
LI	07.08.52-26.09.52	IS
G	20.04.53-30.05.53	SR
NC-E	15.06.53-20.06.53	SR
HI	21.07.54-01.09.54	IS
HI	25.01.56-17.02.56	SR
LC-E	05.07.56-10.08.56	SR
LC-E	31.12.56-12.01.57	SR
G	15.06.57-11.07.57	SR
LC	20.09.58-04.10.58	SR
HI	14.07.59-20.08.59	SR
LI	29.07.61-09.09.61	CS
LC-E	06.04.62-16.04.62	SR
G	31.08.63-07.12.63	SR
LC	13.03.64-10.04.64	CS
NC	14.08.64-11.09.64	IE
NC	18.12.64-23.12.64	IE
5214		
HO	12.08.37-23.09.37	
HG	20.06.38-27.07.38	
LS	01.02.40-16.02.40	
HG	21.02.41-25.03.41	
LO	04.11.41-15.11.41	

Engine no /type.	Date of repair	Works
5214		
HS	11.01.43-06.02.43	
LS	19.08.44-08.09.44	
LO	24.05.45-06.06.45	
LO	17.07.45-04.08.45	
HG	13.04.46-07.05.46	
LO	21.04.47-17.03.47	
LS	03.09.48-29.09.48	
HI	29.03.50-21.04.50	
HG	21.05.51-19.06.51	SR
NC-E	11.09.52-19.09.52	SR
HI	06.10.52-08.11.52	SR
NC-E	21.11.53	CS
HI	04.02.54-26.02.54	SR
LC-E	07.06.54-22.06.54	SR
LC-E	14.09.54-23.09.54	SR
G	21.01.56-03.03.56	SR
HI	31.08.57-21.09.57	SR
LC-E	25.11.58-03.12.58	SR
LI	09.05.59-28.05.59	SR
LC	19.05.60-04.06.60	SR
G	29.04.61-02.06.61	SR
HI	06.04.63-25.05.63	SR
LI	05.02.65-09.03.65	IE
NC	28.10.65-13.11.65	CS
5215		
LS	21.10.36-24.11.36	
HS	02.09.37-01.10.37	
LO	03.01.38-21.01.38	
HG	23.03.38-24.05.38	
LS	21.11.39-05.12.39	
HG	19.01.41-08.02.41	
HS	09.05.42-12.06.42	
LO	15.07.43-07.08.43	
LS	01.01.44-20.01.44	

Engine no /type.	Date of repair	Works
5215		
HG	22.06.45-17.07.45	
LS	25.06.47-15.08.47	RY
HO	24.02.48-05.04.48	CW
LS	05.10.48-29.10.48	CW
HG	03.10.49-18.11.49	CW
LI	20.06.51-27.07.51	CW
LI	18.02.53-11.03.53	CW
HG	15.10.54-23.11.54	CW
LI	05.01.57-30.01.57	CW
HI	01.06.59-27.06.59	CW
LC-E	24.06.60-20.08.60	CW
HG	25.11.61-29.12.61	CW
LC	25.04.63-22.05.63	CW
LI	13.10.64-28.11.64	CW
5216		
LS	21.01.37-08.02.37	
LO	12.04.37-24.05.37	
HG	29.08.38-04.10.38	
LS	01.04.40-17.04.40	
HG	27.09.41-22.10.41	
LS	28.06.43-20.07.43	
LS	24.02.45-24.03.45	
LO	16.10.45-24.11.45	
HG	06.01.47-21.01.47	CW
HS	31.08.48-25.09.48	CW
HI	20.01.50-09.02.50	CW
HG	27.08.51-06.10.51	CW
HI	11.12.52-02.01.53	CW
LI	25.05.54-15.06.54	CW
HG	21.11.55-17.12.55	CW
LC-E	30.10.56-07.12.56	CW
HI	10.12.57-04.01.58	CW
LI-E	23.12.58-23.01.59	CW
LC-E	29.08.59-30.10.59	CW
LI	09.01.61-15.02.61	CW

Engine no /type.	Date of repair	Works
5217		
LS	21.11.36-15.12.36	
LO	31.05.37-28.06.37	
LS	30.11.37-22.12.37	
HG	22.02.39-21.03.39	
LS	17.06.40-02.07.40	
HG	16.09.42-01.10.42	
HG	07.02.44-26.02.44	
LS	01.01.46-26.01.46	
LO	14.06.46-02.07.46	
HG	07.10.47-25.11.47	
HI	12.03.49-02.04.49	HW
HG	06.09.50-24.10.50	CW
HI	09.04.52-03.05.52	CW
HG	21.01.53-12.03.53	CW
LC-E	06.08.53-04.09.53	CW
LI	20.09.54-22.10.54	CW
LI	28.01.56-21.02.56	CW
HG	18.02.57-15.03.57	CW
LC-E	18.05.58-24.06.58	CW
HI	29.06.59-12.08.59	CW
HG	31.01.61-30.03.61	CW
LC	20.12.62-18.01.63	CW
Int	23.03.64-04.08.64	CW
5218		
HS	22.02.37-16.03.37	
HG	14.02.38-09.04.38	
LO	28.03.39-07.04.39	
LS	30.06.39-08.09.39	
HG	19.12.40-31.01.41	
HS	27.06.42-18.07.42	
LS	18.12.43-08.01.44	
HG	12.02.45-06.03.45	
LS	07.12.46-11.01.47	CW
HS	07.06.48-03.07.48	CW

Engine no /type.	Date of repair	Works
5218		
HG	31.10.49-17.12.49	CW
LI	26.09.51-27.10.51	HW
NC-R	03.11.51-08.11.51	CW
LI	27.07.53-26.08.53	CW
NC-R	31.08.53-05.09.53	CW
HG	24.09.55-22.10.55	CW
HI	13.09.57-09.10.57	CW
LC-E	13.06.58-01.07.58	CW
LC-E	06.04.59-28.05.59	CW
LI	29.04.60-09.06.60	CW
HG	12.06.61-07.08.61	CW
LI	17.07.63-09.08.63	CW
5219		
HS	16.11.37-08.12.37	
HO	24.02.38-25.02.38	
LO	20.02.39-28.02.39	
HG	09.11.39-30.11.39	
LS	10.02.41-01.03.41	
HS	26.11.42-02.01.43	
HG	25.04.44-10.05.44	
LS	19.06.45-12.07.45	
HS	26.11.46-18.12.46	CW
LO	02.01.48-31.01.48	HW
HG	28.04.48-04.06.48	CW
LI	10.01.50-27.01.50	CW
LI	06.11.51-28.11.51	HW
G	05.08.53-16.09.53	CW
HI	30.08.54-01.10.54	CW
LI	15.10.56-15.11.56	CW
HG	10.06.58-03.07.58	CW
HI	04.12.59-18.01.60	CW
HI	21.12.60-27.01.61	CW
HI	01.06.62-29.06.62	CW
Int	30.07.65-11.09.65	CW

Engine no /type.	Date of repair	Works
5220		
LS	25.01.37-10.02.37	
HO	11.10.37-09.11.37	
HO	18.02.38-23.03.38	
LS	06.09.38-23.09.38	
HG	01.06.40-22.06.40	
HS	05.12.41-10.01.42	
LO	04.04.42-09.05.42	
LS	23.10.43-17.11.43	
HG	10.05.45-09.06.45	
LS	06.11.46-04.12.46	CW
HS	22.11.47-24.12.47	HW
NC	10.03.48-21.04.48	HW
LI	23.03.49-28.04.49	CW
HG	21.11.50-21.12.50	CW
LI	17.11.52-06.12.52	CW
LI	09.06.54-29.06.54	CW
HG	29.05.56-28.06.56	CW
HI	26.03.58-29.04.58	CW
LC-E	05.08.59-16.09.59	GN
HG	19.09.60-05.11.60	CW
NC-E	25.10.61-03.11.61	CW
5221		
LS	08.02.37-21.02.37	
LO	27.10.37-25.11.37	
HS	12.05.38-30.05.38	
HG	14.08.39-06.09.39	
HS	27.03.41-16.04.41	
HS	12.03.42-11.04.42	
LS	11.02.43-09.03.43	
LS	04.07.44-29.07.44	
LO	26.06.45-13.07.45	
HG	31.12.45-23.01.46	
HS	28.08.47-11.10.47	HW

Engine no /type.	Date of repair	Works
5221		
NC-R	29.10.47-11.11.47	HW
LI	30.04.49-26.05.49	HW
HG	11.09.50-10.10.50	CW
LI	13.11.52-09.12.52	RY
HI	05.10.53-27.10.53	CW
HG	12.04.55-07.05.55	CW
LI	27.12.56-19.01.57	CW
LI	24.01.58-27.02.58	CW
LC-E	16.02.59-18.03.59	CW
LC-E	19.05.59-29.05.59	RY
HI	02.10.59-06.11.59	CW
HG	28.10.60-06.01.61	CW
5222		
LS	03.02.37-23.02.37	
LO	29.10.37-03.12.37	
HG	17.06.38-29.07.38	
LS	23.07.40-08.08.40	
LS	30.01.42-21.02.42	
HG	21.05.43-12.06.43	
LS	27.11.44-21.12.44	
HS	16.01.46-09.02.46	
HG	30.10.47-24.12.47	CW
HI	18.01.49-15.02.49	CW
NC	08.06.50-04.07.50	HW
HI	24.10.50-21.11.50	CW
HG	04.12.52-01.01.53	CW
HI	12.04.54-12.05.54	CW
HI	08.11.55-26.11.55	CW
LC-E	21.11.56-07.12.56	HW
HG	15.03.58-23.04.58	CW
HI	20.05.59-13.06.59	CW
LI	24.05.61-20.06.61	CW
LI	17.12.62-11.01.63	CW

Engine no /type.	Date of repair	Works
5222		
HI	17.12.64-30.01.65	CS
NC	09.12.66-19.12.66	EH
5223		
LS	26.01.37-12.02.37	
LO	08.11.37-08.12.37	
HG	15.06.38-22.07.38	
HS	17.06.40-01.07.40	
HG	04.09.42-02.10.42	
HS	20.01.44-08.02.44	
LO	20.12.44-13.01.45	
LS	26.09.45-20.10.45	
HG	24.02.47-22.03.47	CW
HS	16.06.48-31.07.48	CW
HG	08.04.50-24.05.50	CW
LI	16.10.51-10.11.51	HW
HI	02.02.53-06.03.53	CW
HG	20.01.55-23.02.55	CW
HI	29.11.56-10.01.57	HW
HI	08.10.58-01.11.58	CW
HG	02.01.61-07.03.61	CW
LI	08.10.63-06.11.63	CW
5224		
HS	17.02.37-22.03.37	
LS	26.05.38-07.06.38	
HG	01.04.40-25.04.40	
LS	02.10.41-23.10.41	
LO	07.05.42-15.05.42	
HS	05.10.42-24.10.52	
LO	26.02.43-19.03.43	
LS	06.11.43-27.11.43	
HG	06.11.44-02.12.44	
LS	25.05.46-15.06.46	

45222 on 28th May 1963 with a mixed freight on the ex-LNWR Cambridge-Bedford line is about to cross over the East Coast Main Line at Sandy. It was allocated to Bletchley from July 1962 until it moved to Bescot in March 1964. 45222 has a domed boiler fitted during a Heavy General repair at Crewe from 15th March 1958 to 23rd April 1958; its AWS was fitted in June 1959.

K. C. H. Fairey

11 ACCIDENTS AND WARTIME DAMAGE

11.1 Pre-war accidents

Three Class 5s were involved in serious accidents before the war.

5188 at Leicester (Midland) – 20th December 1935

On the Friday night before Christmas, 5188 of Nottingham shed was working the Rowsley to Somers Town goods train when it collided with the last coach of an empty passenger train which was being drawn out of sidings at the south end of Leicester station. This accident completely wrecked the signal box which controlled the entrance to the station. Happening at such an inopportune moment, it had a serious effect on the timekeeping of trains on the Saturday immediately before Christmas. However, a new box was brought from Crewe, erected on the site of the old one, and was fully connected and working by 11.00pm on the Saturday night.

5282 at Sandal & Walton – 30th May 1937

At about 11.43am, the 9.50am excursion from Todmorden to Birmingham, consisting of ten bogie coaches hauled by 5282 of Nottingham shed was traversing facing points on the up passenger line about 1/4 mile north of Sandal & Walton station, south of Wakefield on the former Midland Railway Leeds to Derby line, when the trailing bogie of the last vehicle became derailed, then the leading bogie. The coach was dragged along askew and demolished the post of a signal gantry. The coach remained upright and coupled and the vacuum connection did not part but the impact with the post tore off the trailing bogie, then the leading one. The coach was thrown on its side and dragged 250 yards until the driver, feeling something was amiss, looked back and stopped the train. One passenger, Mrs Phyllis Robinson, was killed and another, Mr. J. Wilson, died in hospital; four passengers were detained. An inquest recorded death by misadventure. The driver of 5282 was G. T. Dett and the train was travelling under clear signals at between 30 and 40mph.

5025 at Bletchley – 13th October 1939

The 7.37pm Euston-Inverness express, consisting of 12 coaches, was standing at the down fast platform of Bletchley station and a shunting engine, ex-L&NWR G1 0-8-0 9169, was attaching a van to the rear. At this moment, the 7.50pm Euston-Stranraer express, also due to stop at Bletchley, ran into the shunting engine. Four people died – a RAF man, the driver of 9169, a porter and a postman who was working at the rear of the Inverness train. Five other passengers and one company servant were seriously injured whilst 27 other passengers and seven railwaymen received minor injuries. The Stranraer train consisted of eleven coaches hauled by 5025 piloting Royal Scot 6130. The collision took place at considerable speed, chimney to chimney, the impact causing the 0-8-0 shunting engine (which was stationary at the time with its brakes on) to destroy the van and the two rear coaches of the Inverness train (brake vans). In doing so, this engine mounted the down fast platform, demolished the refreshment room and waiting room, where some of the casualties occurred, and also brought down a large portion of the station roof. More of the roof had to be taken down to clear the wreckage. The two engines hauling the Stranraer train were derailed and 5025 mounted the wreckage.

Weather conditions were bad. There was driving rain and a strong east wind, it was very dark and no landmarks could be seen on account of the blackout and the absence of moonlight. The accident was attributable to the failure on the part of the two drivers of the Stranraer express to observe the last six signal indications, covering a distance of over two miles before this train reached the obstruction.

5025 was in charge of Passed Fireman C. W. E. Haynes. He was tried at Buckinghamshire Assizes on 12th January 1940 on a charge of Manslaughter but in the absence of any conclusive evidence he was found 'Not Guilty' and discharged.

5025 went into works immediately for a Heavy repair and did not return to traffic until 16th December.

(From the official Accident Report).

11.2 Engines damaged by enemy action

Throughout the war, only eight engines of the class were recorded as damaged by enemy action, a surprisingly small number in view of the fact that, at that time, 472 were in service. The engines involved were:

5386 at Kentish Town – 10th October 1940

On Saturday, 7th September 1940, a week before 'Battle of Britain' day, the German Luftwaffe switched its attacks from RAF bases in southern England to London and on that first night of the 'Blitz', which lasted about eight hours, nearly 2,000 people were killed or wounded. The Luftwaffe lost 63 aircraft and the RAF lost 42 planes. After that, London was bombed on 57 consecutive nights but during that period only one Class 5 was damaged, 5386 at Kentish Town on 10th October.

This was the first of the class to suffer damage by enemy action. The engine was shedded at Mold Junction at the time. No details of damage have survived but the engine entered works on 15th October and received replacement boiler 9467 in place of 9560 which it had only carried since 25th September. 5386 returned to traffic on 16th November, still at Mold Junction.

5265 at Birmingham – 19th November 1940

In November the enemy turned their attention to provincial cities, starting with Coventry on the night of 14th November 1940. The following week Birmingham arms factories were the target and 5265, a Saltley engine at the time, was a casualty on 19th November. There is no record available of the damage caused, or of the engine going into works.

5225 Ordsall Lane – 22nd December 1940

At 6.39pm on 22nd December 1940 the air raid sirens sounded in Manchester and heralded a night of bombing by over 250 aircraft. 5225 from Newton Heath was damaged at Ordsall Lane, Salford. No details of damage were recorded and there is no record of the engine going into shops until 28th April 1941 for a 'light repair'.

5336 Manchester (Victoria) – 23rd December 1940

The bombers were back again the following evening and kept up the attack for over six hours. Much of the city centre was destroyed, Exchange and Victoria stations were badly damaged by fire and explosion and a second Class 5 was a victim. This engine was a recent transfer from Aintree to Bank Hall in w/e 14th December at the time of the raid. No details of damage are available and no record of the engine going into works. No boiler or tender changes are recorded.

5050 Swansea – 19th February 1941

South Wales was another area to suffer and during an attack on port installations at Swansea on 19th February 1941, 5050 sustained damage. It was allocated to Patricroft at the time and was out of traffic (in works) from 24th February to 14th March, during which it had a heavy repair and boiler change. No details were recorded of the damage caused to the engine.

5425 was badly damaged by a German air raid on Crewe during 7th April 1941. As the picture shows, the boiler was pierced causing steam to enter the cab and resulting in the death of both crewmen. It was in Crewe Works for extensive repairs which took over four months to complete. *LMS Official*

5425 Crewe – 7th April 1941

On Saturday, 12th April 1941, the *Crewe Chronicle* reported that low flying raiders damaged property in a 'north west town' on Monday, 7th April. After detailing damage to houses, churches etc, the report goes on to say "Four members of the LMS Home Guard succeeded in freeing two enginemen who had been trapped in their locomotive by an enemy bomb. Dashing from the guard room, the lights of which had been extinguished by the explosion, Platoon Commander E. E. M. Clarke, Section Commander C. E. Cornwall and Post Commanders D. Horne and Donovan found the locomotive had been hit. With the boiler pierced, steam was entering the cab and both driver and fireman were prisoners. Despite the steam, Cornwall climbed into the cab and was instrumental in freeing the imprisoned men. Unfortunately, the fireman was found to be dead whilst the driver passed away whilst having his wounds dressed".

The same newspaper reported that General Sir Robert Gordon Finlayson, G.O.C. Western Command, had expressed his appreciation of the courage and devotion to duty during an air raid on a north west town by two members of a Home Guard battalion of a railway company. They were Section Commander R. Lavin and Volunteer F. Atkinson. Exposed to considerable danger, they climbed along a roof in darkness and extinguished incendiary bombs. On descending they dealt with more incendiaries whilst bomb splinters and shrapnel fell around them.

The 'north west town' could only have been Crewe and it seems fairly certain that the engine on which the footplatemen were killed must have been 5425. It was shedded at Springs Branch at the time of damage. 5425 was recorded as in works for 'heavy general' from 8th April to 23rd

August (119 working days). When returned to traffic, it had replacement boiler 9565. No other details were recorded of the damage sustained.

5248 Basford Hall – 2nd June 1941

The *Crewe Chronicle* on Saturday 7th June 1941 referred to a minor incident on Monday 2nd June 1941, again on a 'north west town' when there was a small amount of damage but no casualties. This was the date when 5248 from Edge Hill is recorded as being damaged by enemy action at Basford Hall. There are no surviving details of the damage and no record of shopping.

5270 Bath – 27th April 1942

A raid on London on 10th May 1941 was the last of the night time 'Blitz' though bombing raids continued sporadically almost to the end of the war. However, in March and April 1942 the so called 'Baedeker Raids' on historic cities took place in retaliation for the RAF bombing of Lubeck and Rostock and during such a raid at Bath on 27th April, 5270 from Saltley was damaged; it was the last of the class to suffer from air attacks. No details are available of the damage but the engine was in Crewe Works from 19th May to 4th July for heavy overhaul. When released to traffic, 5270 was transferred to Crewe North.

11.3 Wartime Accidents

5015 between Aviemore and Carrbridge – 5th March 1940

The 1.30pm mineral train from Perth to Inverness arrived at Aviemore behind 5160 (Inverness) where 5017 (also of Inverness) was attached as pilot. About 11 miles after leaving Aviemore on the steep climb to Slochd summit, the train parted due to the failure of a drawbar hook, just as it was entering the Slochd crossing loop at the summit. The rear portion, consisting of 21 wagons and brake van, after running

downhill and travelling out of control for some 9¼ miles, came into violent collision with the following double-headed freight about two miles north of Aviemore. The second train was the 2.45pm from Perth to Inverness hauled by Highland Loch class 4-4-0 14381 *Loch Ericht* piloting 5015 (Inverness shed).

The brake and 14 rear vehicles of the runaway train were wrecked and three others derailed and extensively damaged. 14381 was thrown on to its side and lay at right angles to the track beneath the wreckage whilst the train engine 5015 remained on the rails and sustained slight damage. Owing to the sudden stopping of the 2.45pm ex-Perth train when travelling at about 35mph, telescoping occurred near the front and five vehicles were either totally wrecked or extensively damaged, whilst four others were derailed. The permanent way was torn up for about six rail lengths and damage occurred to signal and telegraph equipment alongside the track.

William Pirie and William Malcolm, the driver and fireman of 14381, were killed instantly and Duncan Macintosh, the guard of the same train, was badly bruised. George Moyes, the guard on the 1.30pm train was in the rear van which was in the runaway section but when he found he was unable to control it, he jumped from the brake and escaped with a severe shaking and subsequent shock.

5210 at Kirkby – 19th April 1945

At 9.37am on 19th April 1945 the 6.15am Bradford to Liverpool Exchange express passenger train, consisting of six all-timber bogie coaches on steel frames and hauled by 5210 from Low Moor shed, ran into an engine and brake standing on the main line near Dale Lane No.1 signal box at Kirkby. This engine was an ex-L&Y 0-6-0 12117. The express was running at about 60mph under clear signals but there was a thick morning mist and visibility was estimated at between 20 and 30 yards. Fogmen were not out as the fog was expected to clear shortly but double block was being worked. The drivers of both engines were killed, together with two drivers on 5210 who were learning the road, and a shunter in the goods brake also died. Both fireman and 19 passengers were taken to hospital.

The impact reduced the goods brake to matchwood and 12117, which was ahead of it, was driven forward 80 yards, turned end for end and came to rest on its side and leaning against the side of the cutting. 5210 also finished on its side to the right of 12117, its bogie was torn off and left under the tender, and the tender's trailing corner penetrated and crushed the front compartment of the leading coach. This vehicle suffered considerable damage. The second coach and six leading wheels of the third coach derailed and there was considerable damage to the permanent way over a length of about 120 yards. 5210 was out of traffic for two months until 16th June and it left works with tender 9233 in place of 9314 which it had had since new.

11.4 Post-war Accidents

The pre-war engines were involved in only a small number of accidents during the two post-war decades.

5358 in Pass of Brander – 8th August 1946

The 6.05am train from Oban to Glasgow, hauled by 5358 from St. Rollox, narrowly escaped disaster when a large boulder fell from the hillside on to the track. The train hit the boulder and was derailed, but the engine and coaches remained upright and came to rest on the edge of a steep bank 100ft. above the River Awe.

At this point the line ran along the lower slopes of Ben Cruachan beside the swift flowing river, and to minimise the danger from falls of rock an elaborate system of special signals, officially termed 'automatic stone signals', was installed. These signals, 14 in number, were entirely different from the normal signalling system and were placed at points commanding a good view in both directions. The signals were connected by a number of wires which formed a screen running along the hillside and above the railway. As long as the wires were intact the signals remained in the 'off' position, but if one wire was broken by the rock fall, all signals in both directions went to danger. The breaking of a wire also alerted the nearest signal box and caused a bell to ring in the houses of local permanent way men. The speed of trains was also severely restricted through the pass, especially at night.

On this occasion a falling boulder failed to break the protective wire although the reason was not ascertained. It was thought that the boulder might have bounced over the wire fence but the fact was that the driver of the Class 5 received no warning and was unable to stop in time to avoid a collision. It is unlikely that the boulder passed through the screen without breaking any of the wires although the lower wire was bent but showed no sign of having been struck. The highest wire was more than seven feet above the ground.

The locomotive went into St. Rollox works on 12th August and was back in traffic on 17th September.

5143 on Stockport Viaduct – 30th November 1948

An accident in which 5143 of Shrewsbury shed was involved but was undamaged occurred at about 7.39pm on Tuesday 30th November 1948 between Heaton Norris and Stockport Edgeley stations, on Stockport viaduct. In darkness and dense fog, the combined 5.40pm and 5.50pm trains from Manchester London Road to Buxton, composed of nine coaches and hauled by two Fowler 2-6-4Ts 2370 and 2367, started against signals from Heaton Norris station and, after travelling about 230 yards, ran into the rear of the combined 5.11pm train from Manchester London Road to Crewe and the 5.17pm from Manchester London Road to Disley which had been standing on the viaduct at Stockport No.2 signal box for nearly eight minutes. The latter train had twelve coaches and was double-headed with 2-6-4T 2354 piloting Class 5 5143.

Five passengers in the Crewe/Disley train died, five were seriously injured and a further 21 passengers plus the guard were detained in hospital. Damage to the Buxton train was negligible.

45274 at Sutton Coldfield – 23rd January 1955

At 4.13pm on Sunday 23rd January 1955, the 12.15pm express train from York to Bristol, consisting of ten bogie coaches hauled by 45274 of Bristol shed, derailed at Sutton Coldfield station. About 300 passengers were on the train and 12 passengers plus the conductor driver and the fireman were killed outright; two other passengers and a driver travelling on duty died later in hospital. In addition, 40 passengers together with the regular driver of the train and a goods guard travelling on duty were taken to hospital, 17 passengers being discharged the same afternoon after treatment but the rest were detained, some with very serious injuries.

Because of permanent way work on the main line, the train was diverted via Sutton Coldfield. Driver Martin, a Gloucester man who was in charge of the train, was not familiar with this route so Driver Allen joined at Burton-on-Trent to act as conductor to Birmingham. At Lichfield Driver Martin left the engine and took a seat in an empty compartment in the leading coach because he considered Driver Allen (the conductor) competent to handle the train throughout.

The wreckage of 45274 on the day after the derailment at Sutton Coldfield on 23rd January 1955 which resulted in 17 fatalities and many serious injuries. The accident report attributed the cause solely to excessive speed over the sharp curves through the station, with speed estimated at double the 30mph restriction. 45274 was taken to Crewe Works for investigation and repair and it was eventually returned to traffic on 19th April.
J. A. G. H. Coltas

Although the maximum line speed was 60mph a permanent restriction of 30mph was in force through Sutton Coldfield station because of a severe left hand curve of 15 chains radius. The train entered this curve at an estimated 55-60mph with the result that the engine and all coaches except the last were derailed to the outside of the curve between the platforms. The engine and tender overturned and there was heavy damage to the rolling stock which included the destruction of the first, fourth and fifth coaches. There was also considerable damage to both platforms and to the tracks between them, and part of the down platform awning was carried away.

The derailment blocked both lines. The signal box was switched out and the station closed as there were no local passenger trains on Sunday. The 1.20pm express from Bristol to York was already in the section on the down line but was stopped at the down home signal well clear of the wreckage by the very commendable action of the train ticket collector and Fireman D. H. Smith who were on the derailed train and who ran to the unoccupied signal box. Two lineside residents, on seeing the wreck, also ran along the line to warn opposing traffic. The train from Bristol was eventually drawn back to Birmingham with the uninjured passengers from the derailed train, some of whom continued their journey in a special train which left Birmingham at 7.30pm after refreshments had been provided.

All traffic through Sutton Coldfield was suspended for the next two days, the up and down lines being re-opened at 6.5am and 6.55am respectively on 26th January. Use of the station was restricted pending final clearance of debris and platform repairs being completed.

45274 had run 747,517 miles since it was built in 1936, 102,283 miles since its last general repair in October 1952 and 24,928 miles in the five months since its last Heavy Intermediate repair in August 1954. The ten corridor coaches weighed 304 tons. The body of the leading coach, a corridor built in 1923 (3rd class), was all timber but the remaining nine coaches were framed in hardwood with sheet steel panels and built between 1931 and 1950.

In reaching its final position the engine travelled about 25 yards from where it was probably derailed. It turned over through more than 90 degrees to the right and lay at an angle of about 45 degrees to the tracks with its front end on the down line and its rear end raised on to the severely damaged platform. The engine received severe damage to platework, including cab sides and roof, and to external fittings; the chimney was broken off and the smokebox crushed. There was also much damage to the boiler clothing on both sides and the right hand top feed casting was broken away. The main frames, however, were not severely buckled and damage to the cylinder castings was confined to broken flanges. The bogie remained in position and there was only a slight twist in its frame, though the bolster carrier steel casting was bent on the right hand side. The coupled wheels and axles were virtually undamaged. The boiler shell withstood the shock well but the water was lost when the firebox corner inspection door was torn off, and also through the broken top feed casting. There were signs of slight overheating of the copper crown plate but the two fusible plugs were intact. The brick arch had partially collapsed, probably as the engine overturned. The regulator was found to be slightly open to steam in the 'drifting' position with the reversing screw in forward gear at 45% cut-off. The brake handle was off but with the vacuum destroyed it would have been loose and may well have been thrown to this position by the overturning of the engine.

45274 was towed to Aston shed on 25th January where a new bogie was fitted and it left there for Crewe Works in the early

Engine no.	To traffic	Renum-bered	With-drawn	Original boiler	Original tender	Works/motion no.	Steam sanding	Removal of vacuum pump	BTH speed indicator	Modern-isation	BR AWS equipment	Smith-Stone speed indicators
5435	16.11.37	19.02.49	29.06.68	9555	9671	1490	–	11.06.38	10.12.40	08.02.57	04.04.62	–
5436	16.11.37	12.06.48	13.04.68	9556	9843	1491	–	22.04.39	–	25.10.57	27.02.62	–
5437	16.11.37	02.07.49	14.10.67	9557	9673	1492	–	22.04.39	10.12.40		07.05.59	–
5438	23.11.37	02.10.48	03.09.66	9558	9674	1493	–	22.04.39	09.10.39	16.03.57	28.07.59	–
5439	23.11.37	21.08.48	16.10.65	9559	9675	1494	–	22.04.39	–		17.02.59	–
5440	23.11.37	14.08.48	16.09.67	9560	9676	1495	–	05.08.38	20.06.39	28.11.57	04.11.61	–
5441	30.11.37	25.03.50	04.02.67	9561	9677	1496	–	22.04.39	09.10.40		18.05.60	–
5442	30.11.37	24.04.48	27.08.66	9562	9678	1497	–	20.02.39	–		15.08.59	–
5443	30.11.37	11.09.48	28.08.65	9563	9679	1498	–	?	–		07.05.59	–
5444	07.12.37	31.12.48	03.08.68	9564	9680	1499	–	22.04.39	11.12.40	05.06.58	–	21.10.60
5445	07.12.37	20.05.50	29.06.68	9565	9681	1500	–	11.10.39	–	27.12.57	19.11.59	–
5446	07.12.37	01.10.49	11.02.67	9566	9682	1501	–	22.04.39	13.12.40		09.04.59	–
5447	14.12.37	20.11.48	03.08.68	9567	9683	1502	–	?	16.09.39	05.12.56	–	09.12.60
5448	14.12.37	26.06.48	26.08.67	9568	9684	1503	–	?	–		19.01.59	–
5449	14.12.37	05.02.49	02.12.67	9569	9685	1504	–	22.04.39	–	28.10.55	18.03.59	–
5450	21.12.37	06.08.49	18.11.67	9570	9686	1505	–	22.04.39	17.09.40	08.09.56	–	30.09.60
5451	21.12.37	27.11.48	12.11.66	9571	9687	1506	–	?	–		11.04.59	–
5452	15.09.38	20.11.48	13.05.63	10339	9708		–	–	–		19.02.60	–
5453	19.09.38	02.04.49	29.12.62	10340	9709		–	–	–		25.03.61	–
5454	27.09.38	26.02.49	02.09.67	10341	9710		–	–	–		24.09.59	–
5455	28.09.38	21.08.48	02.09.67	10342	9711		–	–	–	30.05.57	?	–
5456	04.10.38	17.04.48	07.12.64	10343	9712		–	–	–		04.12.59	–
5457	10.10.38	28.08.48	16.09.63	10344	9713		–	–	–		30.12.61	–
5458	11.10.38	20.11.48	29.12.62	10345	9714		–	–	–		29.05.59	–
5459	14.10.38	15.05.48	14.05.64	10346	9715		–	–	–		06.06.59	–
5460	18.10.38	13.11.48	26.06.65	10347	9716		–	–	–		?	–
5461	19.10.38	11.09.48	22.08.66	10348	9717		–	–	–		–	–
5462	31.10.38	12.03.49	29.09.64	10366	9718		–	–	–		14.07.60	–
5463	07.11.38	23.10.48	29.11.66	10367	9719		–	–	–		?	–
5464	08.11.38	29.05.48	01.10.66	10368	9720		–	–	–	30.09.55	?	–
5465	21.11.38	07.05.49	13.02.64	10369	9721		–	–	–		10.06.61	–
5466	25.11.38	05.03.49	25.02.67	10370	9722		–	–	–		26.11.60	–
5467	30.11.38	05.06.48	31.12.66	10371	9723		–	–	–		?	–
5468	01.12.38	05.03.49	18.06.64	10372	9724		–	–	–	31.01.58	13.05.59	–
5469	05.12.38	24.04.48	19.11.66	10373	9725		–	–	–		–	–
5470	12.12.38	20.11.48	10.09.64	10374	9726		–	–	–	06.06.57	19.11.60	–
5471	12.12.38	24.04.48	03.07.65	10375	9727		–	–	–		?	–

APPENDIX 2 – LMS AND BRITISH RAILWAYS ENGINE DIAGRAMS

The pre-war Class 5s were allocated to a number of different Engine Diagrams. These diagrams were produced to show the basic dimensions, weights, braking power and tractive effort of locomotives for the information of the Mechanical and Civil Engineer's Departments and for the Motive Power and Accountant's Departments. There were four diagrams for the vertical throatplate engines as built and two with 3,500 gallon tenders which were not representative of any pairing in service.

ED 177   Estimated weights and mild steel boiler with 'old standard' Fowler type straight-sided 3,500 gallon tender (not applicable to any locomotive as built)

ED 178   With 14-element, 160-tube boiler and 4,000 gallon Mk.1 riveted tender (actual weights).

ED 178A   As ED 178 but with 3,500 gallon, 7 tons coal capacity Stanier tender (estimated weights - not applicable to any locomotive as built).

ED I78B   With 21-element, $1^1/4$in diameter, 13 swg superheater and 136 tubes.

ED 178C   As ED 178B but $1^1/8$in diameter, 11 swg superheater elements (weight of welded tender included).

ED I78D   As ED 178 with original boiler rebuilt to have 21 elements (not applicable to any locomotive).

The first sloping-throatplate engines were allocated to ED 178E. Subsequent alterations to the boilers resulted in various additional diagrams.

ED 178E   As ED 178 with original boiler rebuilt to have 24 elements, 159 tubes and dome.

ED 178F   As ED 178E with 1" thick firebox tubeplate in place of $^7/8$in. tubeplate.

ED I78G   As ED I78F with Mk.2 welded tender.

ED 178J   As ED 178G (note and weights for fabricated tender deleted).

ED 178H   As ED 178G with altered locomotive and Mk.1 tender weights (issued a year after ED 178J).

ED I78K   As ED I78J with Mk.2 welded tender.

ED I78L   As ED I78F with standard superheater elements.

ED I78M   As ED I78L with top feed on first ring and Mk.2 tender.

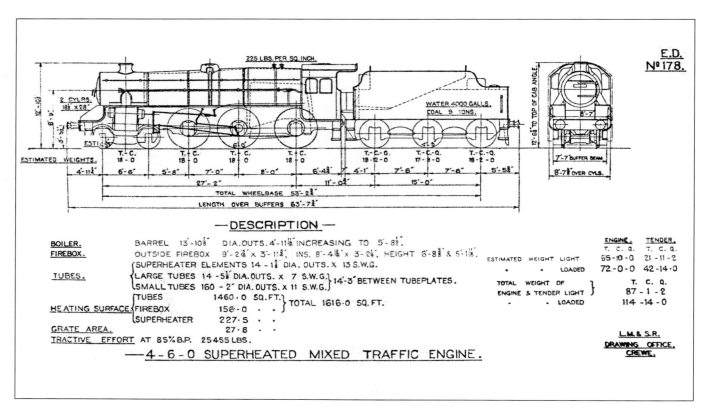

Diagram ED 178

TANK

All riveted joints shall, before being put together, receive one coat of Mixture No.1., and brown paper with red lead, or tarred paper, may be used in making the joint.

All rivet heads on the outside of the tank are to be shallow snap.

The tank is to be tested before being placed on the frames, by filling with cold water, when all joints and rivets must be perfectly tight. When emptied the tank must be thoroughly cleaned before being painted.

The Railway Company will allocate to each tender a distinctive number, and number plates (to drawing) bearing this number must be affixed, to the rear of the tank.

The tank is fixed to the frames by means of bolts, and wood packings fitted as shewn on drawings.

FRAMES

The frames are to be carefully straightened without hammering, and finished with a good smooth surface, free from cross windings.

All holes must be from one template, and drilled and rearnered to the sizes given when the fittings are in position.

Bolts for frame mountings must be a good driving fit, and the rivets securing stretchers, spring link brackets, etc, are to be cold turned.

The sharp edges on the frames and platforms must be removed.

When the frames are assembled with drag boxes and cross stays, and the tank is bolted down in position the accuracy of the work must be carefully checked by square and suitable gauges, and by means of lines stretched along the whole length of the frame. The axlebox guides must be square with the vertical and horizontal centre lines.

WHEELS

All wheel centres must be passed by the Company's representative before being pressed on to the axles. Wheels to be pressed on to the axles at a pressure of not less than 10tons or more than 12tons per inch diameter of axle, and to be carried out in the presence of the Railway Company's representative. The wheel centres are to be turned to the dimensions on the drawing, shrinkage allowance being left on the tyres. No keys to be fitted.

Tyres to be put on after the wheels are pressed on to the axles. When completed, all wheels are to be submitted to the Railway Company's representative for his approval.

TYRES

The surface of the centre and the inside of the tyre must be a good smooth finish, the tyre being bored .0425" less in diameter than the wheel centre. The tyres to be fitted to the wheel centres with the Gibson type retaining rings.

The outside face of the tyres to be finished bright.

AXLES

All axles to be machined all over, and the journals finished by wet scrape and scoured with felt pad and emery. The approval, in writing, for any other method of finishing must be obtained from the Chief Mechanical Engineer, Euston.

Centre holes for turning must be left in the ends of each axle, the angle to be 75 degrees as shewn on Drawing F.151.

AXLEBOXES

The axleboxes are to be steel castings, and the axlebox brasses are to be well fitted into the tops of the boxes. Bottom lubricating only is required and the oil pads are to be of the Railway Company's standard pattern.

The boxes are to have .010" to .018" clearance in their guides. The brasses must be carefully bedded on their respective journals, a total side play of $1/_{32}$" must be allowed for between the axlebox and brass, to permit the brass being readily withdrawn when required. The axleboxes to have $1^1/_4$" total end play in the journals and $1/_2$" total end play in the guides.

SPRING GEAR

The spring plates to be Silico Manganese Steel as quoted in the engine specification.

Each spring to be tested, and must conform to the deflection shown on the drawings, and after being repeatedly scragged to a deflection of three inches it must resume its original form, without loss of camber.

The plates are to be well brushed and free from scale, and the ends dressed square by grinding. All sharp edges to be removed.

Each spring plate to be machined from the solid and the spring plates to be placed in the buckle while cold, and the wedge fixing driven home tight, with a 7lb. fitting hammer. Maker to be approved.

BRAKE GEAR

The holes in the brake hangers are to be bushed with steel bushes, and the holes in the brake shaft levers with bronze bushes, as shown. The bushes to be pressed in.

DRAW GEAR

A draw hook and screw coupling to be provided at the back of the tender. The drawbar to be fitted with two of the Railway Company's standard draw pads, No. 232, as supplied by Messrs. Spencer, Moulton & Co.

WATER PICK-UP GEAR

Water pick up, with deflector plate and gear is to be fitted as shown on drawings, and care should be taken to ensure that when the scoop mouthpiece is dropped to its lowest position the lip should be one inch below rail level when the tender is fully loaded with coal and water.

GANGWAY DOORS

Gangway doors to be fitted between engine and tender.

An Armstrong Whitworth-built engine, 45254 breasts the summit at Shap with a northbound Class H freight on 26th July 1963. It was shedded at Carlisle Kingmoor from November 1962 until the end of 1967. Its AWS was fitted in April 1959. *Rodney Lissenden*

ACKNOWLEDGEMENTS AND BIBLIOGRAPHY

ACKNOWLEDGEMENTS

National Railway Museum, York
The National Archives, Kew
Scottish Record Office, Edinburgh

BIBLIOGRAPHY

LMS Locomotive Profiles No.5 The Mixed Traffic Class 5s - Nos. 5000-5224	D. Hunt, F. James, R. J. Essery (Wild Swan Publications)
LMS Locomotive Profiles No.6 The Mixed Traffic Class 5s - Nos. 5225-5499 and 4658-4999	D. Hunt, F. James, R. J. Essery (Wild Swan Publications)
LMS Locomotive Design and Construction	A. F. Cook (RCTS)
Raising Steam on the LMS	A. F. Cook (RCTS)
LMS Locomotive Names	J. Goodman (RCTS)
Stanier 4-6-0s at Work	A. J. Powell (Ian Allan)